THE Directory OF
Wooden Boat
Builders & Designers

THE Directory OF
Wooden Boat
Builders & Designers

A Guide to
Building and Repair Shops
and Designers
in North America

Compiled by Anne Bray
and Cynthia Curtis

WoodenBoat Publications

Copyright © 1994
by WoodenBoat Publications, Inc.
ISBN 0-937822-30-2

Text design by Blythe Heepe; cover design by Nina Kennedy;
cover photography by Tom Stewart

Library of Congress Catalog Number 86-50329

Published by WoodenBoat Publications
P.O. Box 78, Naskeag Road
Brooklin, ME 04616-0078

INTRODUCTION

In the 20 years since **WoodenBoat** magazine began publication, the business of wooden boat and yacht building and repair in North America has enjoyed a great resurgence. Owners, builders, and designers have worked together in increasingly more interesting and inventive ways, developing new designs, dusting off old designs, and adapting as necessary to the requirements of both traditional and modern wood construction. Considering what has evolved in the fields of wood technology, adhesives, fastenings, and coatings, the opportunities for building boats and yachts of integrity and durability have multiplied greatly. And considering our need to express individuality in our boats, we owners have found reliable ways of saluting craftsmanship and classic beauty in their creation. Wooden boats and yachts of all sizes and types have been designed, built, or restored to their former glory, and the art and industry of the wooden boat builder has come into its own once again.

It is in support of this great industry that we have revised and expanded this *Directory*, the first edition of which we published in 1986. The individual designers, builders, and shops listed in these pages represent our best efforts to discover the artists and artisans who remain committed to the present and future of wooden boats. We know there are probably some builders and designers out there whom we have missed, but we will continue to be on the lookout for new and additional information. In that regard, if you have any suggestions or additions (or corrections), we would be most grateful to hear from you.

The Directory of Wooden Boat Builders and Designers is an information resource of which we are very proud. The builders listings are grouped by states, and the information is indexed by designer's name, builder's name, or company name to make the information accessible to the widest possible range of users. It is gratifying to be able to offer this revised and expanded edition, and we hope that the *Directory* serves its users well.

—Jon Wilson, Editor
WoodenBoat Magazine

CONTENTS

■

UNITED STATES (BOATBUILDERS)

ALABAMA ——————————— 1

ALASKA ——————————— 1

ARIZONA ——————————— 2

CALIFORNIA ——————————— 2

COLORADO ——————————— 8

CONNECTICUT ——————————— 9

FLORIDA ——————————— 14

GEORGIA ——————————— 20

HAWAII ——————————— 21

IDAHO ——————————— 21

ILLINOIS ——————————— 22

IOWA ——————————— 22

LOUISIANA ——————————— 23

MAINE ——————————— 24

MARYLAND ——————————— 49

MASSACHUSETTS ——————————— 57

MICHIGAN ——————————— 69

MINNESOTA ——————————— 77

MONTANA ——————————— 80

NEW HAMPSHIRE ——————————— 81

NEW JERSEY ——————————— 86

NEW MEXICO ——————————— 88

NEW YORK ——————————— 89

NORTH CAROLINA ——————————— 102

OHIO ——————————— 106

OREGON ——————————— 109

PENNSYLVANIA ——————————— 112

RHODE ISLAND ——————————— 114

SOUTH CAROLINA ——————————— 116

TENNESSEE ——————————— 117

TEXAS ——————————— 118

U.S. VIRGIN ISLANDS ——————————— 119

VERMONT ——————————— 120

VIRGINIA ——————————— 122

WASHINGTON ——————————— 124

WISCONSIN ——————————— 137

CANADA (BOATBUILDERS)

ALBERTA ——————————— 141

BRITISH COLUMBIA ——————————— 142

MANITOBA ——————————— 146

NEW BRUNSWICK ——————————— 147

NOVA SCOTIA ——————————— 148

ONTARIO ——————————— 153

QUEBEC ——————————— 163

DESIGNERS

DESIGNERS ——————————— 165

INDEX ——————————— 179

BOATBUILDERS

■ RESMONDO BOAT WORKS

L.W. Resmondo
30662 Faires Rd.
Perdido Beach, AL 36530
205-962-7737

Builder Information
Years in business: 36
Carpenters employed: 4
Shop capacity: 78'

Recent New Construction
Though recent new construction has been fiberglass, company does have facilities to build large commercial wooden fishing boats. In-house designs include 55' and 57' charter/sportfishing boats, 62' and 78' shrimp boats, and a 75' longliner.

Recent Repair Projects
35'–75' sportfishing boats, shrimp boats, and longliners. Numerous types of repairs. Several boats worked on each year.

Yard Information
Services
Marina facilities
Maintenance
Number of boats maintained per year: 30
Percentage of wooden boats: 50
Owner maintenance allowed.
Retail supplies:
Paint, fastenings, and other materials used for boat repair.

■ BREIBY'S BOATBUILDING

John Breiby
HC 33, Box 3205-A
Wasilla, AK 99654
907-376-8818

Builder Information
Years in business: 19
Carpenters employed: 1
Shop capacity: 32'
Willing to travel for on-the-site building projects.

Recent New Construction
22' lapstrake outboard skiff. John Breiby design. Current project.
15' plywood/composite sprit-rigged catboat. Phil Bolger design. 2 built 1990–'91.
13' lapstrake plywood Butternut canoe. R.D. Culler design. Built 1990.

Recent Repair Projects
16' wood/canvas canoe. Replaced several ribs and some planking. Recanvased hull. 1993.
18' Old Town guide canoe. Replaced 25% of ribs and 50% of planking, inwales, seats, and stem. Recanvased hull. 1992–'93.
32' whaleboat (1920s). Restored shape. Replaced forefoot, 30% of planking, and 50% of frames. 1988.

■ DAVID McFADDEN, SHIPWRIGHT

David McFadden
P.O. Box 668
Petersburg, AK 99833
907-772-9382

Builder Information
Years in business: 25
Carpenters employed: 1
Shop capacity: 60'
Willing to travel for on-the-site building projects.

Recent Repair Projects
48' seiner. Repairing pilothouse. Current project.
40' troller. Rebuilt horseshoe stern. Renewed aft deckbeams and deck, and guardrail. 1993.
40' troller. Rebuilt aft deckbeams and deck, carlins, aft bulwarks, and cockpit. 1993.
36' troller. Rebuilt cockpit and net well timbers. 1993.
27' troller. Replaced deckbeams and deck, carlins, toerail, guardrail, tabernacle, and mast. 1992.
54' seiner. Built false deck. 1990.
42' troller. Replaced break timber, repaired clamps. 1990.

TOLMAN SKIFFS

Renn Tolman
Box 1343
Homer, AK 99603

Builder Information
Years in business: 14
Carpenters employed: 1
Shop capacity: 22'

Recent New Construction
20' and 22' plywood skiffs. Renn Tolman designs. 18 built 1990–'93.

Recent Repair Projects
Specializes in the repair and restoration of Tolman-built skiffs

OLD TYME SAIL AND OAR

John W. Lumsden
4129 E. Bluefield Ave.
Phoenix, AZ 85032
602-971-4944

Builder Information
Years in business: 6
Carpenters employed: 1
Shop capacity: 40'
Willing to travel for on-the-site building projects.

Recent New Construction
18' strip-planked, ketch-rigged Carpenter whaleboat. Modified L.F. Herreshoff design. 1 under construction, 2 built 1993.
16' and 18' double-paddle canoes. Modified L.F. Herreshoff designs. 18-footer built 1991; six 16-footers built 1990–'92.

Recent Repair Projects
32' Trojan Express cruiser (1959). Completely rebuilding. Renewing power plants and steering. Current project.
42' Chris-Craft power cruiser (1972). Designed and built off-bow boarding ramp. 1993.
22' Chris-Craft day cruiser. Built new engine cover and teak swim platform. 1992.
26' Chris-Craft cabin cruiser (1972). Replaced cabintop and beams. 1991.

Yard Information
Services
  Rigging
Maintenance
  Number of boats maintained per year: 4-6
  Percentage of wooden boats: 100
  Owner maintenance allowed on limited basis.

ARK WORKS

Lance Alldrin
11088 Midway
Chico, CA 95928
916-893-2171 Fax: 916-899-1835

Builder Information
Years in business: 4
Carpenters employed: 2
Shop capacity: 45'

Recent New Construction
45' strip/DuraKore bridge-deck catamaran. Kurt Hughes design. Current project.
31' strip/DuraKore F-9A aft-cockpit folding trimaran. Ian Farrier design. Built 1993.
31' strip-planked F-9A folding trimaran. Ian Farrier design. Built 1992.
15'6" plywood Windmill-class sloop. Clark Mills design. Built 1990.

Recent Repair Projects
17' Thistle-class sloop. Replaced rails, renewed rigging. Refinished. 1993.
25' Piver trimaran. Renewed hull planking. 1993.
20' Flying Dutchman-class sloop. Faired hull and sheathed in fiberglass. 1992.

Yard Information
Maintenance
  Number of boats maintained per year: 5
  Percentage of wooden boats: 50
  Owner maintenance allowed above and below rail.
Retail supplies:
  Glass reinforcements, epoxy, fillers, deck gear.

BAY SHIP AND YACHT CO.

Helmut Tutass
310 W. Cutting Blvd.
Point Richmond, CA 94804
510-237-0140 Fax: 510-237-2253

Builder Information
Years in business: 16
Carpenters employed: 8

Shop capacity: 400'
Willing to travel for on-the-site building projects.

Recent Repair Projects
60' scow-schooner ALMA. Extensively rebuilt. 1992.
170' 3-masted schooner C.A. THAYER. Replaced planking.
1991.

Yard Information
Services
Marina facilities
Launching facilities
Moorage
Engine repair
Rigging
Maintenance
Number of boats maintained per year: 480
Percentage of wooden boats: 20
Owner maintenance allowed above and below rail.
Retail supplies:
Complete inventory of supplies.

■ BRIGHTCRAFT BOATS

Erik Wahlman
9395 Mountain Meadow Rd.
Shingletown, CA 96088
916-474-1175

Builder Information
Years in business: 14
Carpenters employed: 1
Shop capacity: 22'
Willing to travel for on-the-site building projects.

Recent Repair Projects
16' Old Town Otca canoe. Recanvased hull and refinished
interior. 1992-'93.
17' Trojan runabout (1963). Repaired hull and deck.
Refinished. 1992-'93.
17' Old Town Otca canoe. Renewed ribs, deck, and gunwales. Recanvased and refinished. 1992.

■ BRISTOL SERVICES CO.

Gary Croan
16081 Melody
Huntington Beach, CA 92649
714-846-2039 Fax: 714-840-8113

Builder Information
Years in business: 16
Carpenters employed: 1-7
Shop capacity: Any size
Willing to travel for on-the-site building projects.

Recent New Construction
85' cold-molded cruising luxury yacht. Ron Holland
design. Completed 1993.

Recent Repair Projects
75' Egg Harbor motoryacht. Replaced fuel tanks and after
deck, made general repairs. 1990.

16'–30' utilities, runabouts, and cabin cruisers. Chris-Craft,
Century, Tollycraft, Mercury, and Lyman models.
Bottom, hull, deck, and superstructure repairs and
replacements. Fastening and hardware renewal.
Company also specializes in engine repair, rebuilding, and
repowering with Graymarine 4-, 6-, and 8-cylinder
engines.

Yard Information
Services
Marina facilities
Launching facilities
Overland transport
Moorage
Engine repair
Rigging
Storage
Inside storage facilities
Maximum size for hauling and storing: Inquire.
Maintenance
Number of boats maintained per year: 20
Percentage of wooden boats: 90
Owner maintenance allowed above and below rail.
Retail supplies:
Complete inventory of supplies. Company is Western
distributor for Graymarine engines, and representa-
tive for Century boat parts. Also carry parts for Chris-
Craft, Tollycraft, Mercury, and Lyman boats.

■ CLARK CUSTOM BOATS

Bill Clark
3665 Hancock St.
San Diego, CA 92110
619-542-1229 Fax: 619-542-0488

Builder Information
Years in business: 24
Carpenters employed: 2-5
Shop capacity: 70'
Willing to travel for on-the-site building projects.

Recent Repair Projects
54' Warner ketch (1930). Rebuilt cockpit, chain locker, and
ceiling. Replaced rudder, bulwarks, railcaps, skylight,
and hatches. Installed new masts, booms, bowsprit,
boomkin, and rigging.
46'6" Potter Cal 32 sloop. Renewed 80% of planking and
sistered 25 frames. Replaced transom and framing,
decks, cockpit, coaming, bulwarks, railcaps, and
covering boards. Installed new mast and boom, and
hardware.
47' yawl. Replaced 8 'midship frames and 6 planks.
Completely refastened bottom. 1993.
60' Rhodes yawl. Renewed hull planking and transom. 1993.
47' Sparkman & Stephens yawl. Renewed frames and
planking. 1993.

Yard Information
Services
Rigging

◼ CLYDE CRAFT

Clyde Kirkpatrick
6409-B Camino Vista
Goleta, CA 93117
805-685-2705 Fax: 805-685-2233

Builder Information

Years in business: 4
Carpenters employed: 1
Shop capacity: 18'
Willing to travel for on-the-site building projects.

Recent New Construction

11'9" lapstrake plywood Acorn skiff. Iain Oughtred design. Current project.
11'8" strip-planked Wee Lassie canoe. Mac McCarthy/J.H. Rushton design. Current project.
12'8" Catspaw dinghy. Herreshoff/White design. Current project.
14'10" plywood/epoxy sea kayak. Chris Kulczycki design. Built 1993.
12' plywood Fisherman's Skiff. H.H. Payson design. Built 1993.
11'6" plywood Cartopper. Phil Bolger design. Built 1993.

Recent Repair Projects

29' sloop. Modified motor mounts and installed new diesel engine. 1992.

◼ JIM CROCKET BOATBUILDER

Jim Crocket
1442 N. Fruit Ave.
Fresno, CA 93728
209-233-0131 Fax: 209-233-9840

Builder Information

Years in business: 5
Carpenters employed: 1
Shop capacity: 20'
Willing to travel for on-the-site building projects.

Recent New Construction

15' Lincolnville salmon wherry. Walt Simmons design. Current project.
7'6" Acorn dinghy. Iain Oughtred design. Current project.
12'6" Yankee Tender skiff. WoodenBoat design. Built 1992.
15' double-paddle canoe. Walt Simmons design. Built 1991.

◼ CURTIS MARINE

Don Curtis
670 Bld. D East H St.
Benicia, CA 94510
707-745-6246

Builder Information

Years in business: 23
Carpenters employed: 1-2
Shop capacity: 40'

Recent New Construction

10' lapstrake rowing boat. Don Curtis design. Built 1993.
18' batten-seamed runabout. John Hacker design. Built 1993.
17' runabout. Don Curtis design. Built 1993.

Recent Repair Projects

Complete rebuilding of the following classic powercraft (including engines):
40' launch (1904). Current project.
27' Hacker-Craft runabout (1929). Current project.
17' Chris-Craft runabout. 1993.
26' Gar Wood runabout. 1992.
27' Hacker-Craft runabout. 1992.
21' Chris-Craft runabout (1955). 1991.

Yard Information

Services
    Engine repair
    Rigging
Storage
    Number of boats stored per year: 25
    Percentage of wooden boats: 100
    Inside storage facilities
    Maximum size for hauling and storing: 40' LOA
Maintenance
    Number of boats maintained per year: 12
    Percentage of wooden boats: 100

◼ DAWE CRAFT BOATS

Ernie Dawe
82-138 Tahquitz
Indio, CA 92201
619-347-3287

Builder Information

Years in business: 27
Carpenters employed: 1
Shop capacity: 18'
Willing to travel for on-the-site building projects.

Recent New Construction

9'–13' stock outboard racing hydroplanes and runabouts. Plywood construction. Ernie Dawe designs. 20 boats built 1990–'93.

Recent Repair Projects

9'–13' hydroplanes and runabouts. Deck and sponson replacement, and various other repairs. 1990–'93.

Yard Information

Services
    Overland transport
    Engine repair
    Rigging
Retail supplies:
    Safety equipment, boat hardware, and Yamaha outboard engines.

DOWNUNDER BOAT WORKS

Malcolm Davy
P.O. Box 1287, 3590 Big Valley Rd.
Kelseyville, CA 95451
707-279-2628 Fax: 707-279-4248

Builder Information
Years in business: 25
Carpenters employed: 1
Shop capacity: 60'
Willing to travel for on-the-site building projects.

Recent New Construction
21' cold-molded runabout. Davy design. Built 1992.

Recent Repair Projects
16'–22' mahogany runabouts. Minor repairs to total reconstruction and refinishing.

WILLIAM KRASE, BOATWRIGHT

William Krase
Box 1454
Mendocino, CA 95460
707-937-0830

Builder Information
Years in business: 15
Carpenters employed: 1
Shop capacity: 24

Recent New Construction
Boats designed by William Krase for lapstrake construction:
24' 4-oared rowing gig. Current project.
16' kayak. Built 1993.
16' cat-yawl. Built 1991.
16' Whitehall. 3 built 1990.
Other new construction:
16' plywood kayak. W. Krase design. Built 1993.

Recent Repair Projects
16' Whitehall. Repaired damage from trailer crash. 1991.

Yard Information
Maintenance
    Number of boats maintained per year: 3
    Percentage of wooden boats: 100

THE MARINE EXCHANGE

John Skoriak
30 Libertyship Way
Sausalito, CA 94965
415-332-9231 Fax: same

Builder Information
Years in business: 13
Carpenters employed: 2-3
Shop capacity: 120'
Willing to travel for on-the-site building projects.

Recent Repair Projects
36' Controversy yawl. Renewed engine and rig. Refinished. 1992–'93.
27' Atkin gaff sloop. Renewed rudder shaft and decks. 1990–'93.
37' Colonial cruiser. Refastened bottom planking, refinished. 1992.
60' Fife sloop. Refitted interior, renewed decks, refinished. 1991–'92.
103' schooner FAIR SARAE. Renewed decks and rig. 1991.
18' Mercury-class sloop. Renewed keel, rudder, and deck. 1991.

Yard Information
Services
    Overland transport
    Engine repair
Storage
    Number of boats stored per year: 20
    Percentage of wooden boats: 60-70
    Maximum size for hauling and storing: Inquire
Maintenance
    Number of boats maintained per year: 20-30
    Percentage of wooden boats: 50

MENDOCINO BAY BOATS

John Myers
41001 Little River Airport Rd.
Little River, CA 95456
707-937-5696

Builder Information
Years in business: 35
Carpenters employed: 1
Shop capacity: 32'
Willing to travel for on-the-site building projects.

Recent New Construction
12' lapstrake Chamberlain dory. Plans by Simon Watts. 2 built through 1991.
14' plywood drift boat. John Myers design. 2 built 1991–'92.

Recent Repair Projects
Complete restoration of the following boats:
27' Elco power cruiser (1947). Current project.
16' Mercury runabout (1957). 1991–'92.

Yard Information
Services
    Overland transport
    Engine repair
Storage
    Number of boats stored per year: 3
    Percentage of wooden boats: 100
    Inside storage facilities
    Maximum size for hauling and storing: 22' LOA; storage for runabouts
Maintenance
    Number of boats maintained per year: 4-5
(continues)

(Mendocino Bay Boats, continued)
> Percentage of wooden boats: 100
> Owner maintenance allowed.

Retail supplies:
> Available on order basis.

 ARTHUR F. MULVEY CONSTRUCTION

Art Mulvey
3440 James Dr.
Carlsbad, CA 92008
619-434-4791

Builder Information
Years in business: 14
Carpenters employed: 1
Shop capacity: 27'
Willing to travel for on-the-site building projects.

Recent New Construction
12' lapstrake sailing skiff. Atkin design. Built 1993.
8' plywood skiff. Art Mulvey design. Built 1993.
16' lapstrake dory. Art Mulvey design. Built 1993.
24' plywood/foam dory. Spaulding design. Built 1992.
16' and 21' plywood/epoxy dory-skiffs. O'Brien designs.
> Built 1991 and '92.

21' lapstrake dory-skiff. Art Mulvey design. Built 1990.

 STEVE NAJJAR, BOATBUILDER

Steve Najjar
639 Bair Island Rd. #108
Redwood City, CA 94063
415-366-3263

Builder Information
Years in business: 6
Carpenters employed: 1
Shop capacity: 25'
Willing to travel for on-the-site building projects.

Recent New Construction
8' lapstrake plywood Sea Horse dinghy. Fesenmeyer
> design. Built 1993.

21' cold-molded transoceanic rowing boat. Phil Bolger
> design. Built 1992–'93.

10'6" lapstrake plywood dory. George Chaisson design.
> Built 1991.

8'6" lapstrake plywood Fiddler's Green yawlboat. R.D.
> Culler design. Built 1990.

11' Ethyl canoe yawl. George Holmes design. Completed
> interior and trim. 1992.

 NORTH BOATS

Emmet Jones
12074 Lilac Hill
Valley Center, CA 92082
619-749-0517

Builder Information
Years in business: 23
Carpenters employed: 3
Shop capacity: 60'
Willing to travel for on-the-site building projects.

Recent New Construction
Although no wooden boats have been built recently, the
> shop does have complete facilities to restore, repair, or
> build wooden boats. Foundry and machine shop on
> premises.

Prior to 1990, company built the Friendship sloop
> GENEVIEVE — winner of the San Francisco Master
> Mariner's Race.

Recent Repair Projects
18' Chris-Craft. Repair and restoration work. Current
> project.

Yard Information
Services
> Engine repair
> Rigging

Maintenance
> Number of boats maintained per year: 5
> Percentage of wooden boats: 50

 RUTHERFORD'S BOAT SHOP

Jeffrey Rutherford
320 W. Cutting Blvd.
Richmond, CA 94804
510-233-5441

Builder Information
Years in business: 18
Carpenters employed: 3
Shop capacity: 70'

Recent New Construction
24' strip-planked launch. R.D. Culler design. Current
> project.

24' plywood catamaran. Robert Beebe design. Built 1992.

Recent Repair Projects
50' Stone sloop. Reframing, renewing some planking.
> Current project.

38' Matthews cruiser. Reframing, replanking, renewing
> deck. Current project.

39' Farallone Clipper sloop. Replaced bulwarks, sheer
> plank, and mast. 1992.

23' Nunes Bros. Bear-class sloop. Replaced transom.
> Sistered frames. 1992.

59' Edson Schock cutter. Completely rebuilt. Renewed
> floors, frames, planking, deck, house, and rig. 1990–'91.

Yard Information
Services
> Marina facilities
> Rigging

■ SAUSALITO BOAT BUILDERS CO-OP

Mike Davis, Manager
2350 Marinship Way
Sausalito, CA 94965
415-332-9832

Builder Information
Years in business: 20
Carpenters employed: 12
Shop capacity: 60'

Recent New Construction
14' plywood Ace daysailer. Arch Davis design. Built 1994.
39' cold-molded catamaran. Ginisty design. 2 built 1993.

Recent Repair Projects
56' Lester Stone sloop PRONTO II (1914). Renewing frames, planking, rails, and railcaps. Current project.

Yard Information
Storage
    Number of boats stored per year: 5
    Percentage of wooden boats: 100
    Inside storage facilities
    Maximum size for hauling and storing: Inquire
Maintenance
    Number of boats maintained per year: Varies
    Percentage of wooden boats: 100
    Owner maintenance allowed above and below rail.

■ DOUGLAS SMITH-GINTER & ASSOCIATES

Douglas Smith-Ginter
177F Riverside Dr.
Newport Beach, CA 92663
714-650-5107

Builder Information
Years in business: 42
Carpenters employed: 1-7
Shop capacity: 150'
Willing to travel for on-the-site building projects.

Recent New Construction
Boats designed by Douglas Smith-Ginter:
20' plywood/Dynel English Boom dory prototype. Built 1993.
12' work barge. Built 1992.
16' plywood/epoxy dory prototype. Built 1991.
8' plywood/epoxy dory-skiff prototype. Built 1991.

Recent Repair Projects
47' Alden ketch. Replaced deck, house, and cockpit. Gutted and rebuilt interior. Refinished. 1990–'93.
42' Hinckleys. 2 boats refinished. 1990–'93.
18' Chris-Craft runabouts (1952 and 1956 models). Repaired as needed, refinished. 1992–'93.
30' Viennese water taxi. Replaced 3 bulkheads, repowered, and refinished. Routine maintenance. 1979–'93.

62' Geary motoryacht SILVER KING. Completely restored from keel to truck. Completed 1990.

Yard Information
Services
    Marina facilities
    Overland transport
    Engine repair
    Sail repair
    Rigging
Storage
    Number of boats stored per year: 4
    Percentage of wooden boats: 100
    Inside storage facilities
    Maximum size for hauling and storing: 30' LOA, 4' draft, 4 tons
Maintenance
    Number of boats maintained per year: 12
    Percentage of wooden boats: 65
    Owner maintenance allowed above rail.

■ SORENSEN WOODCRAFT

Darrell Sorensen
13307 Ave. 22-1/2
Chowchilla, CA 93610
209-665-5236 Fax: same

Builder Information
Years in business: 22
Carpenters employed: 1
Shop capacity: 17'

Recent New Construction
9'–17' racing hydroplanes, raceboats, and runabouts. Plywood construction. Designs by Darrell Sorensen. Available as kit boats.

Yard Information
Retail supplies:
    Kit boat supplies. Yamato racing engines.

■ THOMAS FABRICATION & BOATWORKS

Steven Thomas
4839 Caterpillar Rd.
Redding, CA 96003
916-246-0305

Builder Information
Years in business: 12
Carpenters employed: 3
Shop capacity: 75'

Recent New Construction
17' strip-planked canoe. Traditional design. Built 1991.
15'6" and 18'6" strip-planked racing canoes. Alan Adler designs. 1 of each size built 1990.

(continues)

(Thomas Fabrication & Boatworks, continued)

Recent Repair Projects

26' Hacker Gold Cup runabout (1923). Renewing frames and refinishing. Repowering. Current project.

27' Fay & Bowen launch (1924). Replacing convertible top, refinishing. Current project.

26' Fry launch (1913). Renewing floor and upholstery. Refinishing brightwork. Current project.

34' Astoria commuter (1929). Completely restoring. Current project.

32' Albany triple-cockpit runabout (1923). Completely restored. 1993.

20' Chris-Craft Custom Runabout (1947). Restored hull and engine. 1993.

18'6" Old Town sailing canoe (1946 and 1959 models). Completely restored both canoes. 1991–'92.

Yard Information

Services
Overland transport
Engine repair

Storage
Number of boats stored per year: 10
Percentage of wooden boats: 100
Inside storage facilities
Maximum size for hauling and storing: 75' LOA, 6' draft

Maintenance
Number of boats maintained per year: 20-30
Percentage of wooden boats: 95

Retail supplies:
Wood, fastenings, paint.

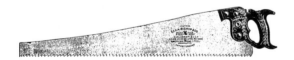

■ BATES DESIGNS LTD.

Charles W. Bates
Box 6165
Steamboat Springs, CO 80477

Builder Information

Years in business: 24
Carpenters employed: 1
Shop capacity: Any size
Willing to travel for on-the-site building projects.

Recent New Construction

Boats designed by Alex Vetter, and available as kits or completed boats:
16' cold-molded Aspen Leaf sloop.
16' lapstrake plywood Grey Jay sloop.

Yard Information

Services
Rigging

■ CANONITA DORIES

Derald Stewart
1375 Florida Rd.
Durango, CO 81301
303-259-0809

Builder Information

Years in business: 14
Carpenters employed: 2
Shop capacity: 20'

Recent New Construction

Boats designed by Derald Stewart for taped-seam plywood construction:
14'6", 16', and 17'6" river dories. 13 boats built 1989–'94.
14'6" fly fishing skiff. 6 built 1989–'94.
Other new construction:
15'6" Gloucester rowing dory. Taped-seam plywood construction. Built 1992.

Recent Repair Projects

14'6", 16', and 17'6" river dories. Repair work has involved gunwale and transom replacements, repairs to damaged hulls, and installation of self-bailing decks. 4 boats worked on 1991–'93.

Yard Information

Maintenance
Number of boats maintained per year: 6-8
Percentage of wooden boats: 90

Retail supplies:
Wood, fastenings, paint.

■ GRAND MESA BOATWORKS

Jim Thayer
Rte. 1, Box 75
Collbran, CO 81624
303-487-3088

Builder Information

Years in business: 20
Carpenters employed: 1
Shop capacity: 25'
Willing to travel for on-the-site building projects.

Recent New Construction

Boats designed by Jim Thayer:
8' Wee Punkin pram. Cold-molded bottom with lapstrake topsides. 3 built 1990–'93, 1 under construction.
16' daysailer ZINGBAT. Plywood/foam sandwich construction. 1 built 1992–'93, 1 under construction.
10' cold-molded catboat LIMPET. 1 built 1993, 1 under construction.

Recent Repair Projects

24' double-ended Dutch-built sloop. Renewing mast, deck and cabin joinery. Refinishing varnished topsides. Current project.

20' Atalanta-class sloop. Completely rebuilding. Applied cold-molded overlay to deck and hull, 1992–'93. Interior under construction.

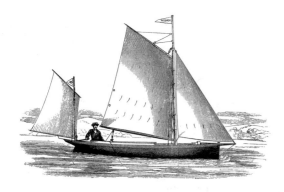

■ BAYBERRY CREEK BOATSHOP, INC.

Elliot J. Wilcox
311 Chaffinch Island Rd.
Guilford, CT 06437
203-453-2720

Builder Information
Years in business: 6
Carpenters employed: 1
Shop capacity: 17'

Recent New Construction
10'6" plywood duckboat. E.I. Shock design. Built 1993.
10'6" plywood skiff. Phil Bolger design. 2 built 1992.
10'10" plywood Mirror-class dinghy. Holt/Bucknell design. 2 built 1990 and 1991.
13' Geodesic rowing shell. Platt Monfort design. Built 1991.
14' lapstrake plywood canoe. Tom Hill design. Built 1991.
15'9" plywood center-console skiff. Glen-L Marine design. Built 1991.
16' lapstrake plywood Shearwater pulling boat. Joel White design. Built 1990.

Recent Repair Projects
9' plywood skiff. Repaired chines and transom. 1993.
91' Biloxi freight schooner. Renewed hatch covers, cavil boards, crew berths, and gang planks. 1991–'93.
14' Medway River salmon wherry. Replaced gunwales. 1993.
19' Lightning-class sloop. Repaired transom, rudder, and hull. 1992.
13'6" Blue Jay-class sloop. Replaced transom and decks. 1992.
16' strip-planked canoe. Added keel, replaced seats, and refinished. 1991.
19' Lightning-class sloop. Replaced transom frame, after-deck, and rubrails. Recanvased deck. 1990.

■ BLACK DUCK BOAT SHOP

Don Metz Sr.
53 Blackberry Rd.
Danbury, CT 06811
203-797-8047

Builder Information
Years in business: 5

Carpenters employed: 1
Shop capacity: 20'
Willing to travel for on-the-site building projects.

Recent New Construction
17' plywood catboat. Charles Wittholz design. Planned for future construction.
17' lapstrake decked canoe. Iain Oughtred design. Current project.
14' plywood Micro trawler. Phil Bolger design. Built 1993.
15' strip-planked canoe. Black Duck Boats design. Built 1993.
15' plywood kayak. Mike Alford design. Built 1992.
12' lapstrake plywood skiff. Shell Boats design. Built 1992.
15' plywood dory. Black Duck Boats design. Built 1991.

Recent Repair Projects
17' wood/canvas canoe. Repairing and recanvasing. Current project.
17' Chris-Craft (1961). Replaced bottom. 1993.
25' sloop. Completely rebuilt. 1990.
15' peapod. Repaired damaged planking, stripped and refinished. 1990.

Yard Information
Retail supplies:
    Paint, fastenings, some wood. General marine supplies.

■ BOYD'S BOATS

Boyd Mefferd
P.O. Box 9
Canton, CT 06019
203-693-4811

Builder Information
Years in business: 13
Carpenters employed: 2
Shop capacity: 35'

Recent Repair Projects
17' Western Fairliner runabout (1947). Replaced bottom, stem, sternpost, keel, and chines. 1993.
26' Hacker-Craft runabout (1939). Replaced bottom, stem, and chines. Renewed engine. 1992.
23' Chris-Craft runabout (1941). Completely renewed. Replaced 90% of boat. 1991.
25' Chris-Craft runabout (1937). Completely renewed. Replaced 90% of boat. 1990.

Yard Information
Services
    Overland transport
    Engine repair
Storage
    Number of boats stored per year: 20
    Percentage of wooden boats: 100
    Inside storage facilities
    Maximum size for hauling and storing: 35' LOA
Maintenance
    Number of boats maintained per year: 20
    Percentage of wooden boats: 100
Retail supplies:
    Materials related to mahogany runabout restoration.

■ BRIGHT WATER CANOES

Ray Goudreau and Susan Keele
P.O. Box 367
Ansonia, CT 06401

Builder Information
Years in business: 8
Carpenters employed: 2

Recent New Construction
12' solo canoes (decked or open models). Ray Goudreau
    design for lapstrake plywood construction. 5 built
    1987–'91.

■ CARL'S CANVAS CANOE CARE CO.

Carl H. Williams
443 Salmonkill Rd.
Lakeville, CT 06039
203-435-9407

Builder Information
Years in business: 20
Carpenters employed: 1
Shop capacity: 18'
Willing to travel for on-the-site building projects.

Recent Repair Projects
16'–18' wood/canvas canoes. Repair work has involved
    hull restoration, recanvasing, and refinishing. 30 canoes
    repaired over last several years.

■ DENMAN BOAT CO.

Ron Denman
215 Joshuatown Rd.
Lyme, CT 06371
203-434-5546

Builder Information
Years in business: 15
Carpenters employed: 2
Shop capacity: 40'
Willing to travel for on-the-site building projects.

Recent New Construction
10' lapstrake catboat. Ron Denman design. 2 built 1992 and
    1994.

Recent Repair Projects
29' Huxford catboat (1893). Completely rebuilding. 1991–
    current.
16' Wianno Jr.-class sloop (1952). Renewed ceiling and
    bulkhead locker. Refinished. 1992.
16' Old Town sailing canoe (1944). Recanvased hull,
    renewed gunwales. Refinished. 1991.
24' power launch (1940). Replaced shaftlog, chines, and
    transom. 1990.
42' Luders ketch (1931). Replaced rudder, deck, and rails.
    1990.

■ DODSON BOAT YARD

R.J. Snyder
Box 272
Stonington, CT 06378
203-535-1507 Fax: 203-535-2163

Builder Information
Years in business: 68
Carpenters employed: 3
Shop capacity: 50'
Willing to travel for on-the-site building projects.

Recent Repair Projects
43' Nordfarer. Renewed frames and floor timbers. Ongoing
    maintenance and upgrading. 1979–'93.
39' Concordia yawl. Replaced keel, floor timbers, and
    frames. Completely refastened. 1990.

Yard Information
Services
    Marina facilities
    Launching facilities
    Moorage
    Engine repair
    Rigging
Storage
    Number of boats stored per year: 200
    Percentage of wooden boats: 5
    Maximum size for hauling and storing: 60' LOA, 9'
        draft, 35 tons
Maintenance
    Number of boats maintained per year: Varies
    Owner maintenance allowed above rail.
Retail supplies:
    Wood, fastenings, paint.

■ ESSEX BOAT WORKS

Ted Lahey
Box 37, Ferry St.
Essex, CT 06426
203-767-8276 Fax: 203-767-1729

Builder Information
Years in business: 33
Carpenters employed: 3
Shop capacity: 70'
Willing to travel for on-the-site building projects.

Recent Repair Projects
34' yawl. Renewing transom and planking. Current project.
45' yawl. Refastened bottom. 1993.
33' yawl. Replaced coamings, rear-cabin bulkhead. 1993.
22' yacht club launches. Renewed cockpit, decks, and
    rubrails. 2 boats worked on, 1992.
41' Departure ketch. Replaced planking, cabintop, and
    hatches. 1991.
63' commuter MISS ASIA. Completed extensive hull work,
    replaced cabin side. 1991–'92.
44' power cruiser. Rebuilt cabin, deckbeams, and deck.
    1990.

Yard Information
Services
  Marina facilities
  Launching facilities
  Overland transport
  Moorage
  Engine repair
  Rigging
Storage
  Number of boats stored per year: 3-5
  Percentage of wooden boats: Varies
  Inside storage facilities
  Maximum size for hauling and storing: 70' LOA, 11' draft, 50 tons
Maintenance
  Number of boats maintained per year: 100+
  Percentage of wooden boats: 15
  Owner maintenance allowed on limited basis.
Retail supplies:
  Inquire.

McCLAVE, PHILBRICK & GIBLIN

Ben Philbrick and Andy Giblin
43 Wilcox Rd.
Stonington, CT 06378
203-572-7710

Builder Information
Years in business: 13
Carpenters employed: 3-4
Shop capacity: 50'
Willing to travel for on-the-site building projects.

Recent Repair Projects
36' Newport 29-class sloop ROGUE. Replaced 57' mast. 1993.
48' Alden/Hodgdon schooner. Installed new bronze floors and frame heels. 1992–'93.
21'9" Herreshoff Fish-class sloop. Completely rebuilt 2 boats 1991, 1993.
32' Herreshoff Buzzards Bay 25-class sloop. Repaired deck and beams, renewed house and coamings, refinished. 1992.
28' Noank sloop WINSOME. Repaired and resheathed deck. 1992.
16' Herreshoff 12½-class sloops. Completely rebuilt 2 boats 1990–'92.
24'6" Watch Hill 15-class sloop. Completely rebuilt. 1990.

Yard Information
Services
  Rigging
Storage
  Number of boats stored per year: 2
  Percentage of wooden boats: 100
  Inside storage facilities
  Maximum size for hauling and storing: 50' LOA, 9' draft, 15 tons
Maintenance
  Number of boats maintained per year: 2

Percentage of wooden boats: 100
Owner maintenance allowed below rail.
Retail supplies:
  Fin-neck bolts.

OLD LYME MARINA

Todd W. Abrahamsson
34 Neck Rd.
Old Lyme, CT 06371
203-434-1272 Fax: 203-434-3068

Builder Information
Years in business: 35
Carpenters employed: 2
Shop capacity: 60'
Willing to travel for on-the-site building projects.

Recent New Construction
30' plywood/fiberglass mooring barge. Built 1986.

Recent Repair Projects
28' H-28 ketch. Renewed planking.
41' Concordia. Renewed planking on two boats, replaced stopwaters.
26' MacKenzie bassboat (1969). Completely restored. Renewed planking, chines, deck, and covering boards. Repowered.
26' Finkleday launch. Replaced 3 planks, refastened bottom, refinished. Installed new engine.
39' Rhodes 27. Completely restored. Installed new engine.

Yard Information
Services
  Marina facilities
  Launching facilities
  Moorage
  Engine repair
  Rigging
Storage
  Number of boats stored per year: 80
  Percentage of wooden boats: 20
  Maximum size for hauling and storing: 60' LOA, 8' draft, 30 tons
Maintenance
  Number of boats maintained per year: 350
  Percentage of wooden boats: 10
  Owner maintenance allowed above rail.
Retail supplies:
  Complete inventory of supplies. Wood, fastenings, paint, rope, wire, hardware, engine parts.

SETH PERSSON BOAT BUILDERS

Jon and Rick Persson
18 Riverside Ave.
Old Saybrook, CT 06475
03-388-2343

Builder Information
Years in business: 60
(continues)

(Seth Persson Boat Builders, continued)
Carpenters employed: 2-4
Shop capacity: 50'

Recent New Construction
Boats designed by Jon Persson:
15' lapstrake plywood dory skiff. Built 1992.
18' wood/canvas double-paddle canoe. Built 1992.
22' tack-and-tape plywood rowing gig. Built 1990.
10' lapstrake plywood tender. Built 1990.

Recent Repair Projects
33' Rhodes sloop. Redesigning and building main saloon. Current project.
33' Geerd Hendel power cruiser. Replacing main cabin and pilothouse. Current project.
28' Townsend cutter. Replaced stem, bowsprit, miscellaneous planking. Sistered frames, renewed caprails, and rewired. Completed 1990.

Yard Information
Services
  Rigging
Storage
  Number of boats stored per year: 15
  Percentage of wooden boats: 80
  Inside storage facilities
  Maximum size for hauling and storing: 35' LOA, 5' draft, 8 tons
Maintenance
  Number of boats maintained per year: 5
  Percentage of wooden boats: 75
  Owner maintenance allowed above and below rail.

■ PILOTS POINT MARINA

Rives Potts
63 Pilots Point Dr.
Westbrook, CT 06498
203-399-7906 Fax: 203-399-7259

Builder Information
Years in business: 20
Carpenters employed: 8-12
Shop capacity: 95'
Willing to travel for on-the-site building projects.

Recent New Construction
15' cold-molded Bermuda Fitted Dinghy. Britt Chance design. Built 1990.

Recent Repair Projects
83' Fife ketch. Building new 100' wooden mast, repairing hull damage. Refitting. Current project.
57' sloop, 65' and 75' ketches. Laid new teak decks. Refitted. 1 boat completed each year, 1991–'93.
54' Alden ketch. Completed major refit. 1990.

Yard Information
Services
  Marina facilities
  Launching facilities
  Engine repair
  Rigging

Storage
  Number of boats stored per year: 700
  Percentage of wooden boats: 5
  Inside storage facilities
  Maximum size for hauling and storing: 95' LOA, 14' draft, 80 tons
Maintenance
  Number of boats maintained per year: 1,500
  Percentage of wooden boats: 5
  Owner maintenance allowed above and below rail.
Retail supplies:
  Materials for marine repair. Engine parts, heaters, refrigeration, A/C, rope, wire, and other supplies.

■ REYNOLDS MARINE

Tucker Reynolds
10 Spring St.
Deep River, CT 06417
203-526-1055 Fax: 203-526-1055

Builder Information
Years in business: 30
Carpenters employed: 1-5
Shop capacity: 45'

Recent Repair Projects
26' MacKenzie Cuttyhunk bassboat. Completely refinished. 1993.
34' Atkin cutter. Repowered. 1992.
22' Chris-Craft Cutlass Dory. Renewed floorboards and console engine box. Repowered, refinished. 1992.
50' Elco Flattop cruiser. Repowered. 1991.
26' Chris-Craft Cutlass Cuddy. Renewed decks and sheer planks. Refinished. 1990.

Yard Information
Services
  Overland transport
  Engine repair
Storage
  Number of boats stored per year: 10
  Percentage of wooden boats: 100
  Inside storage facilities
  Maximum size for hauling and storing: 45' LOA, 4' draft, 20 tons
Maintenance
  Number of boats maintained per year: 6
  Percentage of wooden boats: 100
  Owner maintenance allowed above rail.
Retail supplies:
  Used engines, parts, and hardware.

■ TAYLOR & SNEDIKER WOODWORKING

Bill Taylor
15 Elm St.
Mystic, CT 06355
203-536-3334 Fax: same

Builder Information
Years in business: 20
Carpenters employed: 5
Shop capacity: 50'
Willing to travel for on-the-site building projects.

Recent Repair Projects
68' Sparkman & Stephens schooner BRILLIANT. Reefing and repaying all deck seams. Current project.
50' Trumpy houseboat. Renewing foredeck, frames, and interior. Current project.
42' New York 30-class sloop CARA MIA. Renewing floors, frames, and keel. Current project.
40' K40-class sloop. Renewing frames, floors, and transom. Current project.
50' Elco Flattop cruiser (1927). Renewed frames, floors, interior, foredeck, and pilothouse. 1989–'92.
30' Aage Nielsen sloop. Renewed frames, floors, cabinhouse, and cockpit. Recanvased deck. 1991.
52' schooner DEFIANCE. Built new foremast. 1991.

Yard Information
Services
    Overland transport
Storage
    Number of boats stored per year: 5
    Percentage of wooden boats: 100
    Inside storage facilities
    Maximum size for hauling and storing: 50' LOA, 8' draft, 28 tons
Maintenance
    Number of boats maintained per year: 3
    Percentage of wooden boats: 100
    Owner maintenance allowed above and below rail.

THOMSON CANOE WORKS

Schuyler Thomson
250 Bruey Rd.
Norfolk, CT 06058
203-542-5081

Builder Information
Years in business: 20
Carpenters employed: 1
Shop capacity: 34'

Recent New Construction
15'2" wood/canvas canoe. Rollin Thurlow design. Built 1993.
17'4" wood/canvas canoe. Schuyler Thomson design. 2 built 1992.

Recent Repair Projects
34' Old Town war canoe (1911). Replaced 65 ribs, 100' of planking. Recanvased. 1992.
14' Wolverine runabout (1956). Renewed veneer, deck, and transom. Refinished. 1992.
16' Rushton canoe (1904). Replaced 40 ribs, renewed planking. 1990.
About 200 other canoes have also been restored by Thomson.

Yard Information
Maintenance
    Number of boats maintained per year: 6
    Percentage of wooden boats: 100
    Owner maintenance allowed above and below rail.
Retail supplies:
    All canoe parts and most other marine supplies.

TRAVELING BOATWORKS

Aimé Ontario Fraser
24 High Point Rd.
Westport, CT 06880
203-256-1781 Fax: same

Builder Information
Years in business: 3
Carpenters employed: 1-2
Shop capacity: 25'
Willing to travel for on-the-site building projects.

Recent New Construction
16' lapstrake plywood pulling boat. Iain Oughtred design. Current project.
15' lapstrake plywood skiff. Atkin design. Built 1993.

Recent Repair Projects
26' longboat replica. Renewed gunwales, sternpost, planking. 1993.
40' ketch. Renewed shower accommodations. 1993.
30' cutter. Renewed interior joinery, replaced cabin sole. 1993.
10' Frostbite dinghy. Replaced gunwales, centerboard trunk, transom, thwarts, and knees. 1992.
45' ketch. Redesigned and built interior. 1992.

D.F. WILMES BOATBUILDER

Daniel Wilmes
120 Warner Rd.
East Haddam, CT 06249
203-873-1051

Builder Information
Years in business: 15
Carpenters employed: 1
Shop capacity: 40'

Recent New Construction
18' launch. 2 built 1991–'93.
10'–14' rowing boats. Atkin design. 3+ built 1990–'93.
18' launch. William Deed design. Built 1990.
14' plywood yard boat. Built 1990.

Recent Repair Projects
28' lobsterboat. Replaced 8 planks. 1993.
26' Groton Long Point sloop. Renewed centerboard trunk, recanvased deck. 1993.
32' Vinland 32 sloop. Completely rebuilt. 1992–'93.
34' Columbia cruiser. Renewed interior, repaired cabinsides. 1990–'92.
(continues)

(D.F. Wilmes Boatbuilder, continued)

34' Egg Harbor cruiser. Recaulked bottom, made miscellaneous repairs. 1991.

26' Lyman cruiser. Renewed decks, interior, engine. 1991.

35' Pacemaker. Renewed transom and garboards. Sistered
frames. 1990.

■ CHARLES AKERS BOATBUILDING AND REPAIR

Charles Akers
2816 Ahern Dr.
Orlando, FL 32817
407-658-0622

Builder Information
Years in business: 10
Carpenters employed: 1-3
Shop capacity: 36'
Willing to travel for on-the-site building projects.

Recent New Construction
12' plywood/epoxy Cockleshell kayak. Eric Risch design.
Built 1993.

15'6" plywood/epoxy Severn kayak. Chris Kulczycki
design. Built 1993.

16' plywood/epoxy catamaran. John Koeck design. Built
1992.

18' strip-planked Acadia 18 open launch. Eric Sommers
design. Built 1991.

20' strip-planked Elver canoe yawl. Steve Redmond
design. Built 1990.

Recent Repair Projects
32' Golden Hind sloop. Renewed rudder, keel, decks,
cabin. 1993.

20' Koeck Kat catamaran. Renewed decks and beams.
Recoated hull in epoxy and refinished. 1993.

24' Wellcraft power cruiser. Renewed stringers, cockpit,
deck, and transom. 1992.

Other numerous and varied repairs during last few years
have involved transom, floor, deck, and spar repairs.

■ BOATS, CABINETS, & JOINERY

Harold R. Richard
3712 Huntington
Scottsmoor, FL 32775

Builder Information
Years in business: 55

Carpenters employed: 1
Shop capacity: Any size

Recent New Construction
Boats designed by Harold Richard for plywood construction:

9' pram for oar and sail. Approximately 15 built 1990–'93.

16' center-cuddy shrimp boat. 5 built 1990–'93.

16' mullet/crab fishing net boats. Approximately 15 built
1990–'93.

18' lug-rigged daysailer. Built 1992.

15' sailing dory. Built 1991.

Yard Information
Services
    Sail repair
    Rigging

■ THE CANOE SHOP

Sam S. Lamar
1115-B West Orange Ave.
Tallahassee, FL 32310
904-576-5335

Builder Information
Years in business: 12
Carpenters employed: 1
Shop capacity: 34'
Willing to travel for on-the-site building projects.

Recent Repair Projects
Company specializes in the repair or restoration of canoes,
kayaks, and other small craft. Approximately 8-10
canoes are worked on each year.

Yard Information
Storage
    Number of boats stored per year: 3
    Percentage of wooden boats: Varies
    Inside storage facilities
    Maximum size for hauling and storing: Storage primar-
      ily for canoes
Retail supplies:
    Fastenings, thwarts, gunwales, planking and rib stock,
      seats, and fiberglass cloth.

■ CLASSIC BOAT RESTORATION

Philippe Delangre
2225 Idlewild Rd.
Palm Beach Gardens, FL 33410
407-625-8960

Builder Information
Years in business: 15
Carpenters employed: 2-4
Shop capacity: 132'
Willing to travel for on-the-site building projects.

Recent Repair Projects
28' Riva Aquarama Special (1979). Partially restoring;
ongoing maintenance. 1988–present.

73' Trumpy (1937). Replaced 10 frames, 12 planks, and rudder shaft timbers. 1993

42' Pacemaker (1960s). Replaced shaft timbers. 1993.

18' Chris-Craft Riviera (1953). Replaced deckbeams, deck, carlins, sheer clamps, and bullnose transom. 1993.

82' Broward motoryacht (1968). Remodeled saloon, galley, crew's quarters. 1992.

20' Chris-Craft Utility (1958). Completely restored. 1992.

18' Chris-Craft Capri (1958). Completely restored. 1991.

Yard Information
Retail supplies:
Lumber and plywood.

ERA PAST BOAT

Dale Tassell
5560 Trimble Park Rd.
Mount Dora, FL 32757
904-383-6203

Builder Information
Years in business: 30
Carpenters employed: 1
Shop capacity: 28'

Recent Repair Projects
Company specializes in full restorations of classic runabouts and utility cruisers. Projects have included boats by Chris-Craft, Gar Wood, Hacker-Craft, Century, and Correct Craft. Engine and mechanical repairs are also a specialty.

Yard Information
Services
Launching facilities
Overland transport
Engine repair
Rigging
Storage
Number of boats stored per year: 3-6
Percentage of wooden boats: 100
Inside storage facilities
Maximum size for hauling and storing: Inquire
Maintenance
Number of boats maintained per year: 35-40
Percentage of wooden boats: 100
Retail supplies:
Miscellaneous maintenance supplies and parts.

FEATHER CANOES INC.

Henry "Mac" McCarthy
3080 N. Washington Blvd. #19N
Sarasota, FL 34234
813-355-6736

Builder Information
Years in business: 14
Carpenters employed: 1
Shop capacity: 24'

Recent New Construction
Boats designed by Mac McCarthy for strip-plank construction:
16' and 18' recreational rowing shells. 3 of each size built every year.
16' sea kayak. 2 built 1993.
11'6" sailing canoe. 2 built 1993.
Boats designed by J.H. Rushton and modified by Mac McCarthy for strip-plank construction:
14' Princess tandem canoe. 2 built 1992 and '93.
10'6" and 11'6" Wee Lassie canoes. 6 of each size built 1990–'93.

Recent Repair Projects
12' Frostbite sailing dinghy. Major rebuild. 1993.

HOGTOWN BAYOU BOATWORKS

Joseph Thompson
P.O. Box 1281
Santa Rosa Beach, FL 32459
904-267-3539

Builder Information
Years in business: 14
Carpenters employed: 1
Shop capacity: 30'

Recent New Construction
Boats designed by Joseph Thompson:
21' and 25' plywood/epoxy recreational rowing shells. 4 built to date.
20' cold-molded sliding-seat Whitehall type. 12 built to date.
15' lapstrake plywood Swampscott dory. 4 built to date.
10' plywood jonboat. Built 1993.
Other new construction:
11'6" plywood Penguin-class dinghy. Philip Rhodes design. Built 1993.

Recent Repair Projects
11'6" Penguin-class dinghy. Reglued, epoxied, and refinished hull. Rerigged. 1993.
18' Chris-Craft Utility (1933). Stripped and refinished deck. 1993.

HUCKINS YACHT CORP.

3482 Lake Shore Blvd.
Jacksonville, FL 32210
904-389-1125 Fax: 904-388-2281

Builder Information
Years in business: 66
Carpenters employed: 12
Shop capacity: 90'

Recent New Construction
70' sportfisherman. Composite construction. Huckins design. Built 1992.
(continues)

(Huckins Yacht Corp., continued)

Recent Repair Projects

Approximately 300 boats (including 20 wooden boats) are repaired and/or serviced each year by Huckins. Sizes range from 22' to 80'.

Yard Information

Services
  Launching facilities
  Engine repair
Retail supplies:
  Inquire.

▊ KNOWLES BOAT CO.

Bill Knowles
5121 S.E. Sterling Circle
Stuart, FL 34997
407-286-5663 Fax: 407-286-9800

Builder Information

Years in business: 10
Carpenters employed: 6
Shop capacity: 65'

Recent New Construction

Boats design by Bill Knowles for cold-molded construction:
16' Flats boats. 4 built 1992–'93.
37' sportfisherman. 3 built 1990–'93.

Recent Repair Projects

63' Jim Smith sportfisherman. Completely redoing interior and repowering. Current project.
58' Rybovich sportfisherman (1960s). Modifying interior. Current project.

Yard Information

Services
  Launching facilities
  Engine repair
  Maximum size for hauling and storing: 65' LOA, 6' draft, 35 tons
Maintenance
  Number of boats maintained per year: 24
  Percentage of wooden boats: 25
  Owner maintenance allowed on limited basis.

▊ GEO. LUZIER BOATBUILDERS INC.

Homer Luzier
2135 Princeton St.
Sarasota, FL 34237
813-953-4989

Builder Information

Years in business: 35
Carpenters employed: 4
Shop capacity: 51'

Recent New Construction

20'6" Fish-class sloop. Rathbone/DeBuys design. Built 1993.
29' plywood/fiberglass sharpie. Bruce Kirby design. Built 1993.

20' plywood/fiberglass open fisherman/outboard bay boat. Geo. Luzier design. Built 1992.

Recent Repair Projects

26' sportfisherman WHISPER. Renewed transom and topsides. Applied AwlGrip finish. 1993.
26' power cruiser HELLO DARLIN'. Applied AwlGrip finish. 1993.
22' sportfisherman (1961). Installed new plywood deck and sheathed in Dynel. 1993.
28' Herreshoff H-28. Repaired storm damage to hull and interior. 1993.
26' sportfisherman DEFIANT. Applied AwlGrip finish. 1992.
33' sportfisherman HECTOR. Renewed cabin and transom. Sheathed cabintop and forward house with Dynel. 1991.

▊ CHARLIE MINK CUSTOM BOATS & CANOES

Charlie Mink
P.O. Box 1009
Cantonment, FL 32533
904-433-1619

Builder Information

Years in business: 6
Carpenters employed: 2
Shop capacity: 25'
Willing to travel for on-the-site building projects.

Recent New Construction

17' plywood/epoxy sculling skiff. Traditional design. Built 1993.
Strip-planked canoes. Various designs. 15 built 1990–'93.
13' plywood/epoxy pirogue. Traditional design. 7 built 1990–'93.
16' strip-planked Whitehall. Traditional design. Built 1992.
7' strip-planked tender. Built 1992.
12' wood/epoxy Tiny Mite. Glen-L Marine design. Built 1992.
10' strip-planked dinghy. Traditional design. Built 1992.

Recent Repair Projects

Fishing and sailing boats. General repairs and refinishing. Several boats worked on 1990–'93.
16' lapstrake Whitehall. Completely refinished. 1992.
Retail supplies:
  Good inventory of supplies.

▊ MONTEREY MARINE INC.

6800 S.W. Jack James Dr.
Stuart, FL 34997
407-286-2835 Fax: 407-288-4993

Builder Information

Years in business: 20
Carpenters employed: 12
Shop capacity: 125'
Willing to travel for on-the-site building projects.

Recent New Construction

58', 65', and 80' cold-molded sportfishermen. Walter Hahn designs. 6 built 1990–'93. Currently working on 65-footer.

Recent Repair Projects

58' Trumpy motoryacht. Completed minor electrical and mechanical work; renewed exterior paint. 1993.

60' St. Augustine trawler. Recaulked and refinished bottom. 1993.

80' sportfisherman. Reinstalled flying bridge, replaced engines, added stateroom and head. Renewed exterior paint. 1992.

Have also renewed teak decks on numerous sportfishermen and motoryachts. 1990–'93.

Yard Information

Services
  Marina facilities
  Engine repair
Storage
  Number of boats stored per year: 5
  Percentage of wooden boats: 20
  Maximum size for hauling and storing: 150 tons
Maintenance
  Number of boats maintained per year: 450
  Percentage of wooden boats: 10
  Owner maintenance allowed above and below rail.
Retail supplies:
  Wood, fastenings, paint, bedding compound, electrical and plumbing supplies.

■ NOA MARINE, INC.

Daniel Avoures
13030 Gandy Blvd.
St. Petersburg, FL 33702
813-576-9315 Fax: 813-576-9637

Builder Information

Years in business: 27
Carpenters employed: 2-4
Shop capacity: 80'
Willing to travel for on-the-site building projects.

Recent New Construction

16' plywood net skiff. Daniel Avoures design. Built 1990.

Recent Repair Projects

33' Alden sloop. Replaced keelbolts, section of keel, and floor timbers. Replaced or sistered frames. 1993.

34' one-design racing sloop. Rebuilt keel. 1993.

46' Chris-Craft. Replaced planking. 1992.

49' Marine Trader. Renewed topside frames, planking, transom, and transom framing. Refinished. 1992.

72' Chesapeake Bay buy boat. Renewed planking, fastenings, and part of stem. Refinished hull. 1992.

42' Matthews cruiser. Renewed topside frames and planking, refinished hull. 1992.

38' Snow schooner. Sistered frames, replaced lower stem and planking. 1992.

Yard Information

Services
  Marina facilities
  Launching facilities
  Moorage
  Engine repair
  Rigging
Maintenance
  Number of boats maintained per year: 150
  Percentage of wooden boats: 5

■ OLD TIME BOAT CO. INC.

Gary Scherb
1661D W. University Parkway
Sarasota, FL 34243
813-351-9298

Builder Information

Years in business: 14
Carpenters employed: 6
Shop capacity: 65'
Willing to travel for on-the-site building projects.

Recent New Construction

17' lapstrake Swampscott dory. Built 1993.

Recent Repair Projects

38' Chris-Craft Commuter (1929). Completely restoring. Replacing frames, planking, and mechanical systems. Current project.

28' Sea Lyon runabout (1929). Repowering, renewing upholstery, and refinishing. Current project.

24' Chris-Craft Triple-Cockpit Runabout (1928). Completely restoring. Current project.

22' Chris-Craft Sedan (1947). Refinishing. Current project.

19' Chris-Craft Barrelback (1940). Refastened and refinished hull. Renewed all systems. 1993.

20'6" Dodge Watercar runabout (1930). Completely restored. 1992.

28' Chris-Craft Triple-Cockpit Runabout (1929). Completely restored hull and engine. 1990.

Yard Information

Services
  Overland transport
  Engine repair
  Rigging
Storage
  Number of boats stored per year: 10
  Percentage of wooden boats: 100
  Inside storage facilities
  Maximum size for hauling and storing: 35' LOA, 3' draft
Maintenance
  Number of boats maintained per year: 20
  Percentage of wooden boats: 100
Retail supplies:
  Complete inventory of supplies.

■ PARKER MARINE ENTERPRISES

Reuel B. Parker
P.O. Box 3547
Fort Pierce, FL 34948
407-489-2191

Builder Information
Years in business: 30
Carpenters employed: 3
Shop capacity: 150'
Willing to travel for on-the-site building projects.

Recent New Construction
Boats designed by Reuel Parker for cold-molded construction:
60' pilot schooner. Built 1993.
44' terrapin schooner. Built 1993.
55' schooner. Built 1992.
17' crabbing skiff. 1992.
45' scow/junk. Built 1991.
25' terrapin sloop. Built 1991.

Recent Repair Projects
30' Malabar Jr. sloop. Completely rebuilt. 1990.

Yard Information
Services
    Rigging

■ HUGH SAINT INC.

Hugh Saint
1014 S.E. 9th St.
Cape Coral, FL 33990
813-574-1299 Fax: 813-574-1105

Builder Information
Years in business: 12
Carpenters employed: 4
Shop capacity: 40'

Recent New Construction
Boats built using cold-molded construction:
36' runabout. John Hacker design. Built 1994.
27' runabout. Doug Van Patten design. Built 1994.
24' runabout. Hacker/Van Patten design. Built 1994.
23' runabout. D. McCarthy design. Built 1993.
26' runabout. Hacker/McCarthy design. Built 1992.
26' and 27' runabouts. Doug Van Patten designs. 2 boats of each length built 1990–'91.

■ SCHOFIELD'S BOATWORKS

Robert Schofield
P.O. Box 352, 103 South U.S. Hwy. 1
Oak Hill, FL 32759
904-345-1215

Builder Information
Years in business: 18
Carpenters employed: 1
Shop capacity: 20'

Recent New Construction
9' plywood/epoxy modified dory. Robert Schofield design. Current project.
14' plywood bateau. Robert Schofield design. 2 built 1993.
16' plywood/epoxy Six-Hour Canoe. Mike O'Brien design. Built 1993.
12' plywood/epoxy kayak HUMMING BIRD. Richard Schofield design. Built 1993.
9' plywood/epoxy dory LARK. Ken Brown design. 11 built 1993.
14' strip-planked Puddle Duck canoe. Gil Gilpatrick design. 2 built 1990 and 1992.
12' plywood/epoxy Fisherman Skiff. H.H. Payson design. Built 1992.

Recent Repair Projects
18' Y-Flyer-class sailing scow (1967). Rebuilding forestay tang and traveler. Replacing spray guard, renewing cockpit drains. Refinishing bottom, topsides, and deck. Current project.
19'6" Grand Laker canoe (1940s). Repaired inwales and transom. Replaced outwales and deck. 1993.
13' Penn Yan cartopper (1936). Recaned seats. Stripped and refinished topsides and bottom. 1993.
15' Lee Craft runabout (1956). Stripped and refinished decks. 1993.

Yard Information
Services
    Engine repair
    Rigging
Maintenance
    Number of boats maintained per year: 10
    Percentage of wooden boats: 60
    Owner maintenance allowed on limited basis.
Retail supplies:
    Wood, fastenings, paint, and hardware, and other supplies available by special order.

■ SUMMERFIELD BOAT WORKS, INC.

Thomas Correll, General Manager
1500 S.W. 17th St.
Fort Lauderdale, FL 33315
305-525-4726 Fax: 305-525-8613

Builder Information
Years in business: 53
Carpenters employed: 4
Shop capacity: 75'

Recent Repair Projects
75' motorsailer. Renewed teak decks. 1993.
44' cutter. Replaced rubrails. 1993.
38' power cruiser (1937). Replaced garboards. 1993.
32' Grand Banks trawler. Renewed galley and interior. 1992.
65' East Coast trawler. Replaced bottom planking and refastened. 1992.

Yard Information
Services
Marina facilities
Launching facilities
Engine repair
Rigging
Storage
Number of boats stored per year: 110
Percentage of wooden boats: 20
Inside storage facilities
Maximum size for hauling and storing: 75′ LOA, 8′
draft, 70 tons
Owner maintenance only.
Retail supplies:
Complete inventory of supplies.

 ## VAN MAR BOAT CO.

Vordaman H. Van Bibber
4201 Mariner Dr.
Panama City, FL 32408
904-234-5020

Builder Information
Years in business: 20
Carpenters employed: 1
Shop capacity: 28′

Recent New Construction
18′6″ plywood hydrofoil runabout. V.H. Van Bibber
design. Current project.
23′11″ runabout. V.H. Van Bibber design. Current project.

Recent Repair Projects
21′ Century Coronado. Completely restored. 1990.
Several other 16′ and 18′ Chris-Craft runabouts completely
restored prior to 1990.

WHITICAR BOAT WORKS INC.

John C. Whiticar
3636 S.E. Old St. Lucie Blvd.
Stuart, FL 34996
407-287-2883 Fax: 407-287-2922

Builder Information
Years in business: 50
Carpenters employed: 9
Shop capacity: 80′
Willing to travel for on-the-site building projects.

Recent New Construction
Boats designed by John Whiticar for cold-molded construction:
42′ sportfisherman. Current project.
58′ sportfisherman. Built 1992.
55′ sportfisherman. Built 1990.

Recent Repair Projects
44′ sportfisherman. Renewed bottom. 1992.
53′ sportfisherman. Renewed bottom and repowered. 1990.
Numerous other small repairs and repowerings.

Yard Information
Services
Engine repair
Maintenance
Number of boats maintained per year: 300
Percentage of wooden boats: 10
Owner maintenance allowed above and below rail.
Retail supplies:
Good inventory of marine supplies.

WILDFIRE RACING TEAM

Michael Sternberg
1206 S.E. Astorwood Place
Stuart, FL 34994
407-286-1925

Builder Information
Years in business: 10
Carpenters employed: 1
Shop capacity: 60′
Willing to travel for on-the-site building projects.

Recent New Construction
35′ cold-molded/composite offshore tunnel raceboat.
Michael Sternberg desgin. Built 1989.
Wildfire offers design, construction, and rigging of cold-
molded, wood and composite boats for pleasure, sportfishing, and racing.

Recent Repair Projects
18′ power cruiser. Replaced transom and stringer. 1993.
24′ power cruiser. Renewed cockpit. 1993.
65′ motoryacht. Renewed cockpit and brightwork. 1993.
38′ deep-V power cruiser. Replaced bulkheads, stringers,
and cockpit. Renewed cabin. 1992.

Yard Information
Services
Overland transport
Engine repair
Rigging

BETULA CANOE

Jay B. Parsons
5694 Kimberly Lane
Norcross, GA 30071
404-441-2624

Builder Information
Years in business: 10
Carpenters employed: 1
Shop capacity: 16'+
Willing to travel for on-the-site building projects.

Recent New Construction
8' birchbark canoe. Traditional design for use as display
    model. Built 1991.
16' and 17' birchbark canoes. Chippewa Indian designs.
    Built 1991.

CARETTA KAYAKS

Charlie Reeves
P.O. Box 478
Tybee Island, GA 31328
912-231-0793

Builder Information
Years in business: 3
Carpenters employed: 1
Shop capacity: 23'
Willing to travel for on-the-site building projects.

Recent New Construction
Boats designed by Charlie Reeves for wood-strip/epoxy
    construction:
23' double kayak. 2 built 1993.
17' single kayak. 2 built 1993.
18'8" single kayak. 6 built 1991–'93.

Yard Information
Services
    Overland transport
    Rigging
Retail supplies:
    Wood-strip planking stock, rudder assemblies, foot-
        pegs, fastenings.

DE SILVA CO.

Ralph De Silva
335 E. Foster Ave.
Dallas, GA 30132
404-445-1821 Fax: same

Builder Information
Years in business: 45
Carpenters employed: 2
Shop capacity: 20'

Recent New Construction
Hydroplanes in lengths from 10' to 16'. Batten-seam, ply-
    wood/epoxy construction. De Silva designs.

ROBB WHITE & SONS

Robb White
P.O. Box 561
Thomasville, GA 31799
912-726-2524

Builder Information
Years in business: 33
Carpenters employed: 2
Shop capacity: 40'
Willing to travel for on-the-site building projects.

Recent New Construction
Lightweight skiffs, tenders, and small daysailers. Nesting
    skiff. Plywood or lapstrake construction. In-house
    designs.

Recent Repair Projects
26' ex-Navy motor whaleboat. Completely restored. 1990.

Yard Information
Services
    Overland transport
    Engine repair
    Sail repair
    Rigging
Retail supplies:
    Custom hardware and fittings, longleaf pine and live
        oak. Curved flitches and sawn veneer.

THE WOODEN BOATWORKS

Bob Genchi
137-D Booth Rd. SW
Marietta, GA 30060
404-425-3733

Builder Information
Years in business: 10
Carpenters employed: 1
Shop capacity: 30'

Recent Repair Projects
Over the last four years, company has done major restora-
    tion work on approximately 20 classic power craft by
    Gar Wood, Chris-Craft, Century, Correct Craft,
    Shepherd, and Grady-White. Following are their most
    recent projects:
24' Chris-Craft Sea Skiff. Renewed bottom. 1994.
20' Correct-Craft Debonaire (1956). Completely restored
    hull. 1993.
17' Chris-Craft Special Runabout (1950). Renewed bottom.
    1993.
19' Chris-Craft Capri (1957). Completely restored hull.
    1993.
16' Thompson (1962). Replaced transom. 1993.
19' Chris-Craft Holiday (1951). Completely restored hull.
    1993.

Yard Information
Maintenance
 Number of boats maintained per year: 12
 Percentage of wooden boats: 100
Retail supplies:
 Mahogany and teak, fastenings, caulking compounds,
 and paint.

■ BROOKINS BOATWORKS LTD.

Gary W. Brookins
44-354 Olina St. #4
Kaneohe, HI 96744
808-254-1091

Builder Information
Years in business: 25
Carpenters employed: 3
Shop capacity: 45'
Willing to travel for on-the-site building projects.

Recent New Construction
26' cold-molded runabout. Gary Brookins design. Built 1991.
21' cold-molded runabout. Gary Brookins design. Built 1990.
Company will also build in strip, plywood, and conven-
 tional plank-on-frame construction methods.

Recent Repair Projects
19' Chris-Craft runabout (1936). Replacing frames, bottom,
 topsides, and deck. Renewing upholstery, plumbing
 and electrical systems. Rechroming hardware and refinishing. Current project.
21' Chris-Craft Cobra runabout (1955). Completely restoring. Renewing frames, planking, deck, upholstery,
 plumbing and electrical systems. Refinishing. Current
 project.
39' Alden cutter (1937). Gutted interior. Replaced frames,
 floors, and stringers. Renewed maststep. 1992–'93.
 Rebuilding interior, 1994.

Yard Information
Maintenance
 Number of boats maintained per year: Varies

■ STAN-CRAFT/THE BOAT SHOP

Sydney H. Young
South 101 Main St.
Post Falls, ID 83854
208-667-5009 Fax: 208-664-0733

Builder Information
Years in business: 60
Carpenters employed: 2
Shop capacity: 36'

Recent New Construction
Boats designed by Sydney Young for double-planked
 mahogany construction:
30' triple-cockpit runabout. 2 built 1993.
25' double-cockpit runabout. 3 built 1991–'93.
28' triple-cockpit runabout. 3 built 1991–'92.
30' 18-passenger, high-speed water taxi. 2 built 1990.

Recent Repair Projects
Complete restoration of the following boats:
20' Ventnor Deluxe runabout (1948). 1993.
20' Chris-Craft Caravelle (1960). 1993.
22' Chris-Craft Sportsman (1946). 1992.
18'6" Gar Wood (1947). 1992.
21' Century Coronado (1956 and 1957 models). 1990 and
 1991.
21'8" Stan-Craft Torpedo (1949). 1990.

Yard Information
Services
 Overland transport
 Engine repair
 Rigging
Storage
 Number of boats stored per year: 175
 Percentage of wooden boats: 40
 Inside storage facilities
 Maximum size for hauling and storing: 36' LOA, 4'
 draft, 10 tons
Maintenance
 Number of boats maintained per year: 300
 Percentage of wooden boats: 45
Retail supplies:
 Hardware and accessories, wood, fastenings. Supplies
 for repair and refinishing.

■ GRIFFIN BOATWORKS

William R. (Bill) Hamm
1210 Buchanan St.
Rockford, IL 61101
815-964-5455 Fax: same

Builder Information
Years in business: 20
Carpenters employed: 2
Shop capacity: 30'
Willing to travel for on-the-site building projects.

Recent New Construction
Boats designed by Bill Hamm for wood/epoxy construction:
8' sailing dinghy. 5 built 1990–'94.
10' outboard dinghy. 3 built 1990–'94.
16' daysailer/overnighter. Built 1992.

Recent Repair Projects
16' Correct Craft runabout. Replaced bottom and refinished. 1993.

Yard Information
Services
    Overland transport
    Rigging
Storage
    Number of boats stored per year: 6
    Percentage of wooden boats: 50
    Inside storage facilities
    Maximum size for hauling and storing: 20' LOA
Maintenance
    Number of boats maintained per year: 6
    Percentage of wooden boats: 50
    Owner maintenance allowed above and below rail.
Retail supplies:
    Inquire.

■ WISE MARINE CO.

Paul Wise
Unit #127, 37 Sherwood Terrace
Lake Bluff, IL 60044
708-295-9612

Builder Information
Years in business: 10
Carpenters employed: 1
Shop capacity: 40'
Willing to travel for on-the-site building projects.

Recent New Construction
23' iceboat. Paul Wise design. Built 1990.

Recent Repair Projects
20' Peterborough runabout (1938). Replacing keel, stem, and frames. Building new cold-molded bottom. Current project.
26' Rainbow-class sloop. Renewed keel, rebuilt interior. 1993.
26' Luders 16-class sloop. Built new cold-molded cabin house. 1991.

16' Chris-Craft Runabout (1936). Replaced deck, bottom, and transom. Renewed interior, repowered. 1991.
18' Chris-Craft Continental (1959). Built new cold-molded bottom and refastened hull. 1990.

Yard Information
Retail supplies:
    Bruynzeel marine plywood, teak, mahogany, and WEST System supplies.

■ YACHT STANDARD

John Scully
P.O. Box 31
Plainfield, IL 60544
312-421-7703

Builder Information
Years in business: 20
Carpenters employed: 1+
Shop capacity: 100'
Willing to travel for on-the-site building projects.

Recent Repair Projects
28' Chris-Craft cabin cruiser. Extensively restored including major repairs to bottom planking, and deck and cabintop renewal. 1992–'93.
32' Chris-Craft cabin cruiser. Replaced cabin windshield. 1991.
35' Sparkman & Stephens sloop. Renewed cockpit and coaming. 1990.

Yard Information
Maintenance
    Number of boats maintained per year: 1-6
    Percentage of wooden boats: 90
    Owner maintenance allowed.

■ BIGFORK CANOE TRAILS

Jack Minehart
3016 Neola St.
Cedar Falls, IA 50613
319-266-8939

Note: See Minnesota listing for summer address and phone number.

Builder Information
Years in business: 18
Carpenters employed: 2
Shop capacity: 26'
Willing to travel for on-the-site building projects.

Recent New Construction

Birchbark canoes. Designs by Jack Minehart based on traditional Indian types.

22' Voyageur-style canoe. Built 1993.

17' Chippewa long-nose canoe. 2 built 1993.

18' Mic Mac canoe. Built 1993.

16' Algonquin-type canoe. Built 1993.

Recent Repair Projects

26' birchbark Voyageur canoe. Rebound and capped gunwales, renewed pitch. 1993.

16' Chippewa canoe. Replaced damaged bow, ribs, and sheathing. 1993.

Yard Information

Services

    Launching facilities

    Overland transport

Storage

    Number of boats stored per year: 2-3

    Percentage of wooden boats: 100

    Inside storage facilities

    Maximum size for hauling and storing: 30' LOA

Maintenance

    Number of boats maintained per year: Varies

    Percentage of wooden boats: 100

Retail supplies:

    Cedar, ash, maple.

■ OKOBOJI BOATS

Jim Jensen
P.O. Box 619
Okoboji, IA 51355
712-332-2144 Fax: 712-332-2889

Builder Information

Years in business: 10

Carpenters employed: 1

Shop capacity: 40'

Recent Repair Projects

14' Hafer rowboat. Refinished. 1993.

36' Chris-Craft cruiser (1967). Completed minor hull repairs. 1993.

27' Chris-Craft cruiser (1952). Completed minor bottom repairs. 1993.

26'6" Chris-Craft (1940). Refinished. 1992.

18' Century Resorter (1967). Renewed brightwork, reupholstered. 1991.

16' Hafer runabout (1947). Completely restored. 1990–'91.

22' Chris-Craft Sea Skiff (1957). Completely restored. 1990–'91.

Yard Information

Services

    Marina facilities

    Launching facilities

    Overland transport

    Moorage

    Engine repair

    Rigging

Storage

    Number of boats stored per year: 375

    Percentage of wooden boats: 10

    Inside storage facilities

    Maximum size for hauling and storing: 40' LOA, 4' draft

Maintenance

    Number of boats maintained per year: 600

    Percentage of wooden boats: 10

    Owner maintenance allowed above and below rail.

Retail supplies:

    Wood, paint, screws, hardware, varnish, stripper.

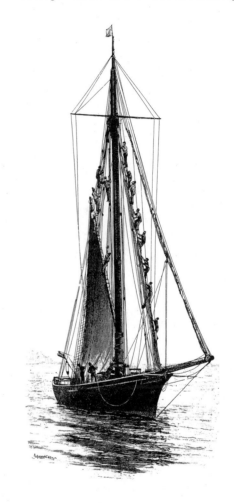

■ TERRACE WOOD WORKS

Eddy Greig
2085 Terrace Hwy.
St. Martinville, LA 70582
318-394-4485

Builder Information

Years in business: 26

Carpenters employed: 1

Shop capacity: 20'

Recent New Construction

12'–14' pirogues. Plywood or cypress planking.

■ ACADIA CANOE SHOP

Lee K. LaBelle
RFD #5, Box 372
Ellsworth, ME 04605
207-667-9433

Builder Information
Years in business: 12
Carpenters employed: 1
Shop capacity: 20'

Recent New Construction
Shop is currently open on a part-time basis. Most of work involves construction or repair of wood/canvas canoes and small boats.

Recent Repair Projects
16' Old Town square-sterned canoe (1922). Completely restored. 1993.

■ APPRENTICESHOP OF MAINE MARITIME MUSEUM

Philip Shelton
243 Washington St.
Bath, ME 04530
207-443-1316

Builder Information
Years in business: 23
Carpenters employed: 2 instructors, 10 students
Shop capacity: 65'

Recent New Construction
14' lapstrake Rangeley Lake boat. H. Ellis design. Built 1993.
18' inboard launch. Arno Day design. Built 1993.
In-house designs:
12' lapstrake Whitehall. 2 built 1992.
12' peapod. 2 built 1991.
16' plywood V-bottomed outboard boat. Built 1991.
24' lobsterboat. Built 1990.

Recent Repair Projects
21' naphtha launch. Renewed frames, sternpost, and planking. Rebuilt engine. 1993.
10' lapstrake tender. Renewed planking and transom. Refinished. 1993.
12' dory. Replaced bottom. 1993.
16' Herreshoff 12½. Renewed keel, frames, and planking. Refinished. 1993.
21' double-ended launch. Refastened hull and refinished. Rebuilt engine. 1993.
26' Northeast Harbor A-class sloop. Renewed deadwood, transom, and planking. 1991.
22' picnic launch. Renewed frames, keel, and transom. Refinished. 1990.

Yard Information
Services
  Moorage
Maintenance
  Number of boats maintained per year: 8
  Percentage of wooden boats: 100

■ APPRENTICESHOP OF NOBLEBORO

Lance Lee
P.O. Box 215
Nobleboro, ME 04555-0215
207-563-1060

Builder Information
Years in business: 3
Carpenters employed: 2 instructors, 6 apprentices
Shop capacity: 47'

Recent New Construction
38' Bantry Bay gig. Irish Sea Fisheries Board/Cyril Chisholm design. 1 built 1991; 1 under construction.
18' strip-planked West Point outboard skiff. Alton Wallace design. Current project.
16' Bahama dinghy. J. Albury design. Current project.
12' North Haven-class sailing dinghy. Built 1993.
23' Block Island Cowhorn cat-schooner. Lapstrake construction. Plans by H.I. Chapelle. Built 1993.
15' Washington Country peapod. Plans by Dave Dillion. Built 1992.
11'6" sailing dinghy. Bob Baker design. Built 1991.

Recent Repair Projects
30' Gil Smith Long Island catboat. Reframing, replacing deck. Current project.
16' Herreshoff 12½. Replaced transom, frames, garboards, and 4 planks. 1994.
9' Lawley tender. Replaced 3 planks. 1993.
10' Whitehall. Renewed frames, garboard, and centerboard trunk. 1993.
39' Azorean whaleboat. Replaced sheerstrake, thwart knees, and mast. Refastened and refinished hull. 1991.

■ THE ARTISANS SCHOOL

Stephen E. Barnes
P.O. Box 539
Rockport, ME 04856
207-236-6071

Builder Information
Years in business: 11
Carpenters employed: 4 instructors, 18 students
Shop capacity: 50'

Recent New Construction
36'10" sail-assisted power cruiser. William Garden design. Current project.
17' lapstrake Swampscott dory. Built 1993.
20' cold-molded Whitehall. John England/Steve Barnes design. Built 1993.
36' Sonder boat. Steve Barnes design. Built 1993.
38' Sonder boat. Modified N.G. Herreshoff design. Built 1992.
24' Baker 240 sloop. R.H. Baker design. Built 1992.
16' Haven 12½-class sloop. Joel White design. Built 1993.

Recent Repair Projects
Numerous small jobs by students over the last several years.

■ BALD HEAD BOATWORKS

E. Barton Chapin III and Lucy W. Hull
Bald Head Rd.
Arrowsic, ME 04530
207-443-4908 Fax: same

Builder Information
Years in business: 12
Carpenters employed: 1
Shop capacity: 35'
Willing to travel for on-the-site building projects.

Recent Repair Projects
64' ketch. Completed off-site mechanical and wood work. 1993.

Yard Information
Storage
    Number of boats stored per year: 1
    Percentage of wooden boats: 100
    Maximum size for hauling and storing: 35' LOA, 5' draft, 8 tons
Maintenance
    Number of boats maintained per year: 1-2
    Percentage of wooden boats: 100

■ BENJAMIN RIVER MARINE

Doug Hylan
Rte. 175, P.O. Box 58
Brooklin, ME 04616
207-359-2244

Builder Information
Years in business: 7
Carpenters employed: 3
Shop capacity: 55'

Recent New Construction
28' Rozinante. L.F. Herreshoff design. Current project.
16' Haven 12½. Joel White design. 2 built 1993.
13' lapstrake plywood peapod. Doug Hylan design. 2 built 1993.
15' lapstrake plywood Whitehall type. Iain Oughtred design. Built 1993.
30' strip and plywood Elderyacht cutter. Cy Hamlin design. Built 1992.
16' plywood outboard garvey. Doug Hylan design. Built 1991.
10' lapstrake plywood tender. Iain Oughtred design. Built 1990.

Recent Repair Projects
39' Concordia yawls. Sheathed decks in Dynel and epoxy and completed miscellaneous repairs. 3 boats worked on during 1991–'93.
39' Concordia yawl. Replaced keel, floors, and bottom planking. 1993.
40' Sparkman & Stephens sloop. Sheathed deck in Dynel and epoxy. Repaired horn timber. 1992.
24' Culler skiff. Replaced forward house. 1992.
32' Gray power cruiser (1929). Replaced cockpit and foredeck. 1990–'93.

38' Sparkman & Stephens yawl. Replaced frame ends and replanked bottom. 1990.
41' Concordia yawl. Replaced engine, electric panel, and icebox. 1990.

Yard Information
Services
    Launching facilities
    Moorage
    Engine repair
    Rigging
Storage
    Number of boats stored per year: 50
    Percentage of wooden boats: 80
    Inside storage facilities
    Maximum size for hauling and storing: 45' LOA, 7' draft, 12 tons
Maintenance
    Number of boats maintained per year: 50
    Percentage of wooden boats: 80
    Owner maintenance allowed on boats stored outside.
Retail supplies:
    Wood, fastenings, paint, hardware, cordage.

■ BILLINGS DIESEL & MARINE SERVICE, INC.

Harlan Billings
Moose Island
Stonington, ME 04681
207-367-2328 Fax: 207-367-5925

Builder Information
Years in business: 28
Carpenters employed: 5
Shop capacity: 150'
Willing to travel for on-the-site building projects.

Recent Repair Projects
59' motorsailer NOR'EASTER. Renewed frames, planking, rails, cabin trunk, engine, and electrical system. 1991–'92. Currently working on pilothouse, mast, and rigging.
96' motoryacht PRINCIPIA. Repairing hull, renewing top of deckhouse, completely refinishing. Renewing electrical system. Current project.
143' schooner SHERMAN ZWICKER. Renewed keel, planking, frames, fo'c's'le, and interior. 1990–'93.

Yard Information
Services
    Marina facilities
    Launching facilities
    Overland transport
    Moorage
    Engine repair
    Rigging
Storage
    Number of boats stored per year: 365
    Percentage of wooden boats: 40
(continues)

(Billings Diesel & Marine Service, Inc., continued)
Inside storage facilities
    Maximum size for hauling and storing: Inquire
Maintenance
    Number of boats maintained per year: 1,000+
    Percentage of wooden boats: 40
    Owner maintenance allowed above rail.
Retail supplies:
    Complete inventory of supplies.

■ THOMAS BLEVINS, BOATBUILDER

Thomas Blevins
Rte. 27, RR #1, Box 790
Edgecomb, ME 04556
207-882-6396 Fax: 207-882-9826

Builder Information
Years in business: 25
Carpenters employed: 1-5
Shop capacity: 60'
Willing to travel for on-the-site building projects.

Recent New Construction
40' high-performance cruising catamaran. Strip plank/
    composite construction. Thomas Blevins design.
    Current project.
12' Columbia rowing and sailing dinghy. N.G. Herreshoff
    design. Built 1993.
40' Formula 40 racing trimaran. Strip plank/composite
    construction. Adrien Thompson/Thomas Blevins
    design. Built 1992–'93.
20' Shark catamaran. Wood/composite construction. Rod
    MacAlpine-Downie design. 6 built 1990–'93.

■ BOOTHBAY REGION BOATYARD

Jeff Lowell
Ebenecook Rd., P.O. Box 179
West Southport, ME 04576
207-633-2970 Fax: 207-633-7144

Builder Information
Years in business: 20
Carpenters employed: 2
Shop capacity: 65'

Recent Repair Projects
36' Florida sportfisherman. Renewing joinerwork, refasten-
    ing, and replacing tower. Rewiring and replumbing.
    Completely refinishing. Current project.
45' Downeast sportfisherman. Renewed garboard planks
    and numerous frames, refastened. Replaced wiring and
    plumbing systems, and overhauled engine. Refinished.
    1992–'93.
65' Long Island commuter RAGTIME. Replaced frames
    and refastened. Renewed engines and all systems.
    Refinished. 1990.

Yard Information
Services
    Marina facilities
    Launching facilities
    Overland transport
    Moorage
    Engine repair
    Rigging
Storage
    Number of boats stored per year: 200
    Percentage of wooden boats: 5
    Inside storage facilities
    Maximum size for hauling and storing: 65' LOA, 12'
        draft, 35 tons
Maintenance
    Number of boats maintained per year: 200
    Percentage of wooden boats: 10
    Owner maintenance allowed on limited basis.
Retail supplies:
    Wood, fastenings, paint, hardware, engine parts. Good
        inventory of supplies on hand; will order other mate-
        rials on request.

■ BRASS TACKS CANOE SHOP

Steven Van Syckel
RR #1, Box 205C1
Hiram, ME 04041
207-625-7397

Builder Information
Years in business: 10
Carpenters employed: 1
Shop capacity: 22

Recent Repair Projects
Specializes in the restoration and recanvasing of
    wood/canvas canoes.

■ BREWER'S SOUTH FREEPORT MARINE

John S. Brewer
P.O. Box 119, Main St.
South Freeport, ME 04078
207-865-3181 Fax: 207-865-3183

Builder Information
Years in business: 10
Carpenters employed: 4
Shop capacity: 48'

Recent Repair Projects
24' Casco Bay Hampton WALRUS (Hull #1). Replacing
    sole, transom, engine box, and console. Current project.
43' Penbo cruiser ARIEL (1968). Replaced garboards, 18
    planks, 15 floor timbers, 4 frames. Refastened bottom,
    repaired cabintop. 1993.
37' Alden schooner HISPANOLA (1928). Repaired center-
    board. 1993.
12' North Haven-class sailing dinghy. Replaced center-
    board trunk. 1992.
30' Hinckley sloop ROVING KIND. Renewed frames,
    floors, planking, horn timber, and coamings.
    Refinished. 1990–'93.

30′ MacKenzie Cuttyhunk bassboat EEL. Renewed planking. 1990.

39′ Luke sloop EVENTIDE. Replaced stem and transom. Redesigned and built new cockpit and cabintop. 1990.

Yard Information
Services
  Marina facilities
  Launching facilities
  Moorage
  Engine repair
  Rigging
Storage
  Number of boats stored per year: 125
  Percentage of wooden boats: Varies
  Inside storage facilities
  Maximum size for hauling and storing: 50′ LOA, 8′ draft, 25 tons
Maintenance
  Number of boats maintained per year: 80+
  Percentage of wooden boats: 10
  Owner maintenance allowed above and below rail.

■ BROOKLIN BOAT YARD

Center Harbor Rd., P.O. Box 143
Brooklin, ME 04616
207-359-2236 Fax: 207-359-8871

Builder Information
Years in business: 33
Carpenters employed: 10
Shop capacity: 80′
Willing to travel for on-the-site building projects.

Recent New Construction
74′ cold-molded ketch DRAGONERA. Joel White design. Current project.

59′ cold-molded tug/yacht. Scott Sprague design. Current project.

46′ cold-molded sloop LUCAYO. Roger Marshall design. Built 1993.

55′ cold-molded over Airex core, IMS racing sloop AURORA. William Tripp design. Built 1992.

43′ cutter. Joel White design. Built 1991.

52′ cold-molded Swede-55 sloop VORTEX. Knud Reimers design. Built 1990.

Recent Repair Projects
36′ William Hand ketch. Extending cabin and installing new interior. Current project.

39′ Sparkman & Stephens "Finisterre" yawl. Installing new engine, refinishing topsides. Current project.

54′ William Gardner P-boat. Reframed, renewed deckhouse and toerails. Installing new engine. Ongoing project. 1990–current.

21′ Boothbay Harbor One-Design sloop. Applied cold-molded overlay, replaced wooden spar. 1992.

44′ Bunker & Ellis power cruiser. Replaced stem. 1991.

46′ Sparkman & Stephens yawl. Refastened deck and sheathed in Dynel. 1991.

26′ Herreshoff Alerion-class sloop. Laid new teak deck, refinished hull. 1991.

Yard Information
Services
  Launching facilities
  Moorage
  Engine repair
  Rigging
Storage
  Number of boats stored per year: 100
  Percentage of wooden boats: 75
  Inside storage facilities
  Maximum size for hauling and storing: 70′ LOA, 10′ draft, 25 tons
Maintenance
  Number of boats maintained per year: 100
  Percentage of wooden boats: 75
Retail supplies:
  Complete inventory of supplies.

■ J.O. BROWN & SON, INC.

Foy W. Brown
Box 525
North Haven, ME 04853
207-867-4621

Builder Information
Years in business: 10
Carpenters employed: 4
Shop capacity: 42′

Recent New Construction
42′ lobsterboat. In-house design.

Recent Repair Projects
Numerous repair projects over last several years.

Yard Information
Services
  Marina facilities
  Launching facilities
  Overland transport
  Moorage
  Engine repair
  Rigging
Storage
  Number of boats stored per year: 100
  Percentage of wooden boats: 10
  Inside storage facilities
  Maximum size for hauling and storing: 45′ LOA, 7′ draft, 15 tons
Maintenance
  Number of boats maintained per year: 100
  Percentage of wooden boats: 10
  Owner maintenance allowed above and below rail.
Retail supplies:
  Good inventory of supplies.

BULLHOUSE BOATWORKS

David Corcoran
P.O. Box 69
Kennebunkport, ME 04046
207-967-3484

Builder Information
Years in business: 4
Carpenters employed: 1
Shop capacity: 26'
Willing to travel for on-the-site building projects.

Recent New Construction
24'6" E-class sloop. Herreshoff design. 1 built 1992, 1 under
    construction.
15' lapstrake dory. Vrieland design. Built 1993.
17' lapstrake double-paddle canoe. L.F. Herreshoff design.
    Built 1991.

Recent Repair Projects
24' lobster yacht. Replaced 20 frames, stem, housetop, and
    trim. Refastened hull. 1993.
39' Concordia yawl. Replaced 30 frames, renewed mast-
    step. 1993.
33' Herreshoff Araminta ketch. Built new interior. 1992.
22' Chris-Craft Sportsman. Replaced deck and transom.
    1991.

BURT'S CANOES

Burt Libby
Rte. 1, Box 1090
Litchfield, ME 04350
207-268-4802

Builder Information
Years in business: 6
Carpenters employed: 1
Shop capacity: 20'

Recent New Construction
Wood/canvas canoes designed by Burt Libby:
13' canoe. 6 built 1990–'93.
16' canoe. 6 built 1990–'93.
18'6" canoe. 4 built 1991–'93.

Recent Repair Projects
Numerous canoe repairs, including a Kennebec (1913) and
    a 25' Old Town (1929). Restoration and recanvasing.
    1990–'93.

WM. CANNELL BOATBUILDING

W.B. (Bill) Cannell
P.O. Box 900
Camden, ME 04843
207-236-2383 Fax: 207-236-2711

Builder Information
Years in business: 18
Carpenters employed: 10
Shop capacity: 100'

Recent Repair Projects
39' Burgess/Lawley R-boat (1927). Completely restoring.
    Current project.
59' Burgess/Abeking & Rasmussen 10-Meter class.
    Completely restoring. Current project.

Yard Information
Services
    Marina facilities
    Launching facilities

THE CANOE WORKS

Guy Cyr
HCR 32, Box 3, Rte. #1
Sullivan, ME 04664
207-422-9095

Builder Information
Years in business: 33
Carpenters employed: 1
Shop capacity: 20'
Willing to travel for on-the-site building projects.

Recent New Construction
17' wood/canvas Indian Girl canoe. J.H. Rushton design.
    4 built 1992–'93.
11'6" Trapper canoe. Cyr/Grosjean design. 7 built
    1990–'93.
16' wood/canvas canoe. Cyr/Grosjean canoe. 2 built
    1990–'93.

Recent Repair Projects
15'–20' wood/canvas canoes. Old Town, Kennebec,
    Morris, Penn Yan, Kingsbury, and Arnold models.
    Complete restorations, including work on ribs, gun-
    wales, thwarts, seats, and stems, recanvasing and
    refinishing.
17' Passamaquoddy birchbark canoe (1870). Restored for
    display. Renewed lacing and spruce-gum caulking.
    Reset ribs. 1993.

Yard Information
Services
    Overland transport
Storage
    Number of boats stored per year: 35
    Percentage of wooden boats: 100
    Inside storage facilities
    Maximum size for hauling and storing: 20' LOA
Maintenance
    Number of boats maintained per year: 20-30
    Percentage of wooden boats: 90
    Owner maintenance allowed above and below rail.
Retail supplies:
    Cedar, brass canoe tacks, canvas, and stembands.

■ CAPE ELIZABETH BOAT

William S. Linnell II
P.O. Box 243
Cape Elizabeth, ME 04107-0243
207-767-4367 Fax: 207-780-1266

Builder Information
Years in business: 10
Carpenters employed: 1
Shop capacity: 40'
Willing to travel for on-the-site building projects.

Recent Repair Projects
40' lobsterboat/gillnetter. Repaired deck. Replaced shaft and keel tubes. 1992–'93.
86' longliner. Built freezer in fish hold. Remodeled galley. 1993.
40' lobsterboat. Built tank for dipping traps. 1992.
86' dragger. Converted to longliner. Resheathed fish hold, repaired deck. 1992.
40' Chinese junk. Replaced planking and frames. Recaulked hull. 1991.
35' lobsterboat. Replaced transom. 1991.
30' lobsterboat. Replaced working deck and deck framing. 1991.

Yard Information
Maintenance
  Number of boats maintained per year: 1

■ CARRYING PLACE BOAT CO.

Jonathan F. Keyes
P.O. Box 106
Phippsburg, ME 04562
207-443-5171

Builder Information
Years in business: 5
Carpenters employed: 1
Shop capacity: 24'

Recent New Construction
Boats designed by Jonathan Keyes:
12' flat-bottomed skiff. Built 1993.
15' strip-planked outboard skiff. 3 built 1992–'94.
15' flat-bottomed skiff. Built 1991.
Other new construction:
15' strip-planked West Point outboard skiff. Alton Wallace design modified by Keyes. Built 1991.
18' strip-planked West Point outboard skiff. Alton Wallace design. Built 1990.

Recent Repair Projects
18' West Point outboard skiff. Renewed frames and fastenings. 1992.

Yard Information
Maintenance
  Number of boats maintained per year: 2-4
  Percentage of wooden boats: 100
  Owner maintenance allowed above and below rail.

■ STEPHEN CAYARD

Stephen Cayard
11 Taylor Rd.
Wellington, ME 04942
207-683-2841

Builder Information
Years in business: 5
Carpenters employed: 1

Recent New Construction
14' and 19' traditional birchbark canoes. Penobscot/Malecite designs. 19-footer built 1991; 14-footer planned for 1994.

■ CEDAR LANE BOATWORKS

Capt. Dan Pease
P.O. Box 218
South Thomaston, ME 04858
207-594-9141

Builder Information
Years in business: 14
Carpenters employed: 1
Shop capacity: 50'
Willing to travel for on-the-site building projects.

Recent New Construction
12' lapstrake skiff. Built 1993.
15' sailing peapod. Jeff Smith design. Built 1992.

Recent Repair Projects
65' schooner. Renewed planking, refinished. 1993.
12' lapstrake skiff. Completely rebuilt. 1992.

Yard Information
Services
  Overland transport
Storage
  Number of boats stored per year: 5
  Percentage of wooden boats: 80
  Inside storage facilities
  Maximum size for hauling and storing: 50' LOA, 8' draft
Maintenance
  Number of boats maintained per year: 4
  Percentage of wooden boats: 100

■ CENTER HARBOR BOAT

Jack W. Powell
Rte. 175, P.O. Box 199
Brooklin, ME 04616
207-359-2512

Builder Information
Years in business: 5
Carpenters employed: 1
Shop capacity: 38'
Willing to travel for on-the-site building projects.
(continues)

(Center Harbor Boat, continued)

Recent New Construction

27' lobster yacht. Arno Day design. Built 1991.

Recent Repair Projects

18' Crocker sloop. Completely refinished. 1993.

37' ketch. Renewed paint and brightwork. 1992.

28' Friendship sloop. Refinished cabin. 1992.

30' Lawley launch. Refinished exterior. 1991.

Miscellaneous small craft. Various repairs and restoration projects, and refinishing. Several boats worked on 1990–'93.

■ CHEBEAGUE MARINE, INC.

Michael Porter
Chebeague Island, ME 04017
207-846-3145

Builder Information

Years in business: 17

Carpenters employed: 1-3

Shop capacity: 35'

Willing to travel for on-the-site building projects.

Recent New Construction

31' steam yacht. Michael Porter design. Current project.

■ DARK AGES BOATWORKS

George Emery
Box 331
Thomaston, ME 04861
207-354-6436

Builder Information

Years in business: 16

Carpenters employed: 4-8

Shop capacity: Any size

Willing to travel for on-the-site building projects.

Recent New Construction

Company has built bits and pieces as subcontractor for other builders. Work has ranged from crossarms for a 60' catamaran, to rudders, daggerboards, and weather-deck hatches for the 90' cold-molded yacht SOPHIE.

Recent Repair Projects

46' Q-class sloop. Working on 100,000-mile overhaul. Renewing floors, fastenings, deck and bottom planking. Restoration started in 1992 and is ongoing.

36' Luders ketch. Replaced keel, repaired floors and frames. 1993.

42' William Hand motorsailer. Replaced floors and frames, and rebuilt interior. Renewed mechanical systems. 1991–'92.

50' Gauntlet-class cutter. Renewed frames and refastened. Installed new bronze floors. 1990–'91.

65'–100' schooners VICTORY CHIMES, NEW WAY, BILL OF RIGHTS, STEPHEN TABER. Endless timber and planking repairs and renewals. 1989-present.

Yard Information

Storage

    Number of boats stored per year: 2

    Percentage of wooden boats: 100

    Inside storage facilities

    Maximum size for hauling and storing: Inquire

■ ERIC DOW BOAT SHOP

Eric Dow
P.O. Box 7, Reach Rd.
Brooklin, ME 04616
207-359-2277

Builder Information

Years in business: 20

Carpenters employed: 2

Shop capacity: 35'

Recent New Construction

16' Haven 12½-class sloop. Joel White design. 2 boats currently under construction.

11' lapstrake plywood Shellback dinghy. Joel White design. Built 1993.

21' Nantucket One-Design-class sloop. John Alden design. Built 1992.

14' plywood Biscayne Bay 14-class sloop. N.G. Herreshoff design. 2 built 1990.

7'6" and 9'6" Nutshell prams. Joel White design. Approximately 200 kit boats supplied 1990–'93.

Recent Repair Projects

33' Belize cutter. Rebuilt head area. Refinished cabin and decks. 1993.

24' Chris-Craft Sportsman Runabout. Replaced forefoot and completely refinished. Repowered. 1993.

18' double-ended sloop. Renewed deadwood and planking. 1993.

21' Gar Wood utility runabout. Repaired major structural damage and refinished. 1993.

10' yacht tender. Renewed garboards and frames. 1993.

26' Dark Harbor 17-class sloop. Completely rebuilt. 1991.

Yard Information

Storage

    Number of boats stored per year: 6

    Percentage of wooden boats: 100

    Inside storage facilities

    Maximum size for hauling and storing: Inquire

Maintenance

    Number of boats maintained per year: 10

    Percentage of wooden boats: 100

■ DOWNEAST PEAPODS

James Steele
P.O. Box 82
Brooklin, ME 04616
207-359-8842

Builder Information
Years in business: 30
Carpenters employed: 1

Recent New Construction
13'6" peapod. Jim Steele design. 17 boats built 1990–'93.

■ DUCK TRAP WOODWORKING

Walter J. Simmons
P.O. Box 88
Lincolnville Beach, ME 04849
207-789-5363 Fax: 208-789-5124

Builder Information
Years in business: 23
Carpenters employed: 1-3
Shop capacity: 24'

Recent New Construction
16' lapstrake outboard. R.D. Culler design. Built 1993.
10'7" lapstrake tender. Modified Herreshoff design. Built 1992.
9' lapstrake dory skiff. W.J. Simmons design. Built 1992.
16' plywood Light Dory. Phil Bolger design. Built 1992.
17' lapstrake canoe. W.J. Simmons design. Built 1992.
15' lapstrake canoe. W.J. Simmons design. Built 1992.
16' lapstrake double-ender. W.J. Simmons design. Built 1991.

Recent Repair Projects
20' Newfoundland trap skiff. Repaired storm damage, refinished. 1993.
16' Matinicus double-ender. Refinished. 1993.
10'6" Sunshine yacht tender. Repaired planking and frames. 1993.
17' lapstrake canoe. Repaired highway accident damage. 1992.
18' Old Town Otca canoe. Repaired and recanvased. 1992.
16' Matinicus double-ender. Replaced ribs and rails. Refinished. 1992.
16' Old Town sponson outboard boats. Repaired and recanvased. 2 boats completed 1992.

Yard Information
Retail supplies:
Mail-order books, plans, fastenings, and hardware. Security devices.

■ EASTPORT BOAT YARD & SUPPLY

Thomas A. MacNaughton
P.O. Box 190
Eastport, ME 04631
207-853-6049 Fax: same

Builder Information
Years in business: 25
Carpenters employed: 3-6
Shop capacity: 50'
Willing to travel for on-the-site building projects.

Recent New Construction
54' cold-molded Danish-style displacement cutter. MacNaughton Associates, Inc. design. Current project.
9' strip-planked yacht tender. MacNaughton Associates, Inc. design. Current project.
14' strip-planked peapod. Modified Joel White design. Current project.

Recent Repair Projects
32' original Atkin Eric ketch. Installing bronze floor timbers, renewing planking. Current project.
32' ketch. Completely rebuilding. Current project.
33' Giles cutter. Renewed planking and mast. 1993.
47' Colin Archer ketch. (1895). Repairs and preservation work. 1992–'93. Boat was shipped to Colin Archer Museum in Norway upon completion of work.
20' runabout. Renewed seating and console, refurbished hull. 1992.
44' cutter. Rebuilt much of underbody after grounding damage. 1990.
80' dragger. Renewed guards and rails, some planking. 1990.

Yard Information
Services
Launching facilities
Overland transport
Moorage
Engine repair
Rigging
Storage
Number of boats stored per year: 50
Percentage of wooden boats: 50
Inside storage facilities
Maximum size for hauling and storing: Any length, 12' draft, 60 tons
Maintenance
Number of boats maintained per year: 24-45
Percentage of wooden boats: 50
Owner maintenance allowed above and below rail.
Retail supplies:
Complete inventory of supplies and equipment. Will custom-design and fabricate hardware.

■ EAST/WEST CUSTOM BOATS, INC.

Ted Perry
141 Rte. 236
Eliot, ME 03903
207-439-4769

Builder Information
Years in business: 16
Carpenters employed: 3
Shop capacity: 20'

Recent New Construction
16' cold-molded peapod. Arthur Martin design. 3 built 1990–'93.
16' plywood stitch-and-glue skiff. Arthur Martin design. 50 kit boats supplied 1990–'93.

■ ELK SPAR & BOAT SHOP

Jim Elk
32 Bridge St.
Bar Harbor, ME 04609
207-288-9045

Builder Information
Years in business: 17
Carpenters employed: 1
Shop capacity: 50'
Willing to travel for on-the-site building projects.

Recent New Construction
Solid and laminated spars for the following boats:
65' schooner. Fore gaff and boom. 1994.
Catboat. 39' mast. 1993.
80' schooner. Booms, gaffs, topmasts, and bowsprit. 1992.
38' skipjack. 2 masts and bowsprit. 1992.
33' International One-Design sloop. 3 masts built 1991–'93.
Numerous masts, booms, and gaffs for small class boats
    also built 1991–'94.

Recent Repair Projects
65' commercial charter boat RANGER. Replaced 4 planks
    and refastened as needed. 1993.
33' International One-Design sloop. Completely restored.
    Replaced frames, planking, deckbeams, deck, transom,
    and cockpit. 1992–'93.
80' sardine carrier. Converted to schooner. Replaced keel, 4
    frames, 80% of sheer clamp, deckbeams and deck, and
    bulwarks. 1991–'92.
36' International 600 class. Replaced 4 planks, breasthook,
    instrument box, and dorade box. 1991.
39' Concordia yawl. Replaced 9 planks from garboard up.
    1990.
18' Alden Sakonnet One-Design class. Sistered 6 frames,
    replaced coaming. Recaulked and refinished hull. 1990.

■ FARRIN'S BOATSHOP

Bruce A. Farrin
Sproul Rd.
Walpole, ME 04573
207-563-5510 Fax: same

Builder Information
Years in business: 33
Carpenters employed: 4
Shop capacity: 50'
Willing to travel for on-the-site building projects.

Recent Repair Projects
30' Richardson power cruiser. Restoration planned for near
    future.
27' Rice Bros. launch. Restored 75% of boat. 1993.
42' Chris-Craft power cruiser. Completely rebuilt.
    1992–'93.

Yard Information
Storage
    Number of boats stored per year: 3
    Percentage of wooden boats: Varies

Maximum size for hauling and storing: 50' LOA
Maintenance
    Number of boats maintained per year: 3
    Percentage of wooden boats: 80
    Owner maintenance allowed.
Retail supplies:
    Inquire.

■ FRANKLIN CEDAR CANOES

Charles Grosjean
Rte. 200, Box 175
Franklin, ME 04634
207-565-2282

Builder Information
Years in business: 10
Carpenters employed: 1
Shop capacity: 20'

Recent New Construction
16' Bangor Salmon Pool double-ender. Wood/canvas con-
    struction. E.M. White design. Built 1993.
18' plywood skiff. R.D. Culler design. Built 1992.
16' Bangor Salmon Pool double-ender. Strip-plank con-
    struction. E.M. White design. Built 1991.
14' strip-planked canoe. E.H. Gerrish design. Built 1991.
16' wood/canvas canoe. R.E. Grosjean design. Built 1990.
16' fiberglass-sheathed canoe. R.E. Grosjean design. Built
    1990.

Recent Repair Projects
Has restored numerous canoes over the last several years.
    Repair work has included replacement of ribs, gun-
    wales, and transoms, as well as recanvasing.

■ FREEPORT SKIFFS

Victor Stango
1 Roos Hill Dr.
Freeport, ME 04032
207-865-3811 Fax: 207-865-3851

Builder Information
Years in business: 10
Carpenters employed: 1
Shop capacity: 18'
Willing to travel for on-the-site building projects.

Recent New Construction
12'6" lapstrake dory/tender. Chaisson design. Built 1993.
13'6" skiff. In-house design. Built 1992.
10' lapstrake plywood dory/tender. Chaisson design. Built
    1991.
11'6" lapstrake plywood Acorn skiff. Iain Oughtred design.
    Built 1990.

LOUIS GOODALL, BOATWRIGHT

Louis Goodall
P.O. Box 92
Kennebunkport, ME 04046
207-985-1473

Builder Information

Years in business: 3
Carpenters employed: 1
Shop capacity: 48'
Willing to travel for on-the-site building projects.

Recent Repair Projects

24' Yankee sloop. Applying cold-molded overlay. Completely restoring. Current project.
28' power cruiser. Repowering. Current project.
18' Chris-Craft Utility power cruiser. Replaced deck. 1993.
12' Chickadee daysailer. Replaced frames and refinished. 1993.
17' Chris-Craft runabout. Completely restored. 1992.
18' sailing peapod. Replaced planking, refinished. 1992.

Yard Information

Services
    Sail repair
    Rigging
Storage
    Number of boats stored per year: 5
    Percentage of wooden boats: 100
    Inside storage facilities
    Maximum size for hauling and storing: 48' LOA
Maintenance
    Number of boats maintained per year: 6
    Percentage of wooden boats: 100
    Some owner maintenance allowed.
Retail supplies:
    Authorized service center for Hood Sails.

GREENE MARINE INC.

Walter Greene
RR #1, Box 343
Yarmouth, ME 04096
207-846-3184 Fax: 207-846-1485

Builder Information

Years in business: 13
Carpenters employed: 5
Shop capacity: 60'
Willing to travel for on-the-site building projects.

Recent New Construction

35', 56', and 60' strip-planked catamarans. Walter Greene designs. Built 1992–'93.
28' plywood catamaran. Walter Greene design. Built 1993.
46' cold-molded Eight-Meter sloop. Ed Dubois design. Built 1990.

Recent Repair Projects

50' trimaran. Replaced deckhouse. 1993.
36' power cruiser. Replaced garboards and lower planks. 1992.

52' Q-boat. Laid new teak deck, rebuilt mast. 1991–'92.
53' trimaran. Replaced bow and rudder. 1992.
50' trimaran. Replaced rudder and centerboard. 1991.
35' cold-molded sloop. Repaired collision damage to hull. 1990.

Yard Information

Services
    Launching facilities
    Rigging
Storage
    Number of boats stored per year: 10
    Percentage of wooden boats: 50
    Maximum size for hauling and storing: 60' LOA, 4' draft, 12 tons
Maintenance
    Number of boats maintained per year: 15
    Percentage of wooden boats: 50
    Owner maintenance allowed.

HADDEN & STEVENS BOATBUILDERS

Robert Stevens
HCR 32, Box 301
Small Point, ME 04567
207-389-1794

Builder Information

Years in business: 7
Carpenters employed: 2
Shop capacity: 55'
Willing to travel for on-the-site building projects.

Recent New Construction

24' V-bottomed powerboat. Lapstrake topsides and herring-bone bottom. R.D. Culler design. Built 1993.
21' plywood Carolina dory skiff. Jim Orrell design. Built 1990.
12'8" Piccolo sailing canoe. R.H. Baker design. Built 1990.

Recent Repair Projects

23' Stone Horse sloop. Recanvased deck and rebuilt cockpit. 1993.
29' Friendship sloop. Replaced mast, gaff, boom, and bowsprit. 1993.
28' 2-person rowing wherry (c. 1915). Completely rebuilt. Replaced all planking, stem, and sliding seats. 1993.
20' Alden Indian-class sloop. Recanvased deck. 1993.
100' schooner SPIRIT OF MASSACHUSETTS. Rebuilt chain locker. Replanked along waterline and replaced main topmast. Fall of 1990, '91, '92.
21' Blue Jay-class sloop. Replaced keel and floor timbers. 1991.
25' Sea Bird yawl. Completely rebuilt. Renewed keel, planking, deck, cabin, and spars. 1990.

Yard Information

Services
    Marina facilities
    Launching facilities
(continues)

(Hadden & Stevens Boatbuilders, continued)

Storage

    Number of boats stored per year: 7

    Percentage of wooden boats: 100

    Maximum size for hauling and storing: 55' LOA, 7' draft, 20 tons

Maintenance

    Number of boats maintained per year: 7

    Percentage of wooden boats: 100

    Owner maintenance allowed above and below rail.

■ H & H BOATWORKS INC.

Howard Hagar and Cymbrid Hughes
Bakers Wharf Rd., P.O. Box 218
Sebasco Estates, ME 04565
207-389-1000 Fax: 207-389-1001

Builder Information

Years in business: 17
Carpenters employed: 4
Shop capacity: 65'

Recent New Construction

25' cold-molded power launch. William Hand design. Current project.

Recent Repair Projects

39'10" Concordia yawl (1955). Replaced deadwood, floor timbers, sternpost, and knee. Renewed planking and fastenings. Rewired. 1992–'93.

39' Canadian flybridge cruiser (1959). Cold-molded hull, renewed decks, sole, house, and bridge. AwlGripped. 1990–'92.

39'10" Concordia yawl (1951). Renewed deadwood, keelbolts, and floor timbers. Refastened. 1990–'91.

36' Will Frost picnic cruiser (1950). Replaced planking and refastened. Renewed transom and teak decks, veneered cabin sides. 1990–'91.

16' Herreshoff 12½ (1940s). Replaced 30% of planking, frames, floors, keel, and sternpost. Renewed deck, coamings, and seats. 1990–'91.

16' Herreshoff 12½ (1936). Completely rebuilt boat. Replaced all but lead ballast, hardware, and some deck framing. 1990–'91.

28' Hacker-Craft (1958). Replanked topsides with layer of okoume plywood and layer of Honduras mahogany planking. 1990–'91.

Yard Information

Services

    Launching facilities

    Moorage

    Engine repair

    Rigging

Storage

    Number of boats stored per year: 40

    Percentage of wooden boats: 40

    Inside storage facilities

    Maximum size for hauling and storing: 65' LOA, 9' draft, 35 tons

Maintenance

    Number of boats maintained per year: 40-50

    Percentage of wooden boats: 50

    Owner maintenance allowed above and below rail.

Retail supplies:

    Wood, fastenings, paint, resins, and fiberglassing supplies. Engines, oil and filters, hardware, safety equipment, and electrical components.

■ HODGDON YACHTS, INC.

Timothy S. Hodgdon
Murray Hill Rd.
East Boothbay, ME 04544
207-633-4194 Fax: 207-633-4668

Builder Information

Years in business: 17
Carpenters employed: 15
Shop capacity: 130'

Recent New Construction

Boats designed by Bruce King for cold-molded construction:

79'10" commuter-style motoryacht. (1930s style). Current project.

33' sportfisherman. Built 1991.

31' speedboat. Built 1990.

■ ISLAND WOODWORKING/ CRANBERRY COVE BOAT

M. Charles Liebow
Cranberry Isles, ME 04625
207-244-7225

Builder Information

Years in business: 20
Carpenters employed: 2
Shop capacity: 50'
Willing to travel for on-the-site building projects.

Recent New Construction

18'6" cold-molded launch. Miller Sommers design. 2 built 1993–'94.

11'4" yacht tender. Spurling design. 4 built 1986–'94.

Recent Repair Projects

40' Rich power cruiser. Renewing planking. 1994.

42' Bunker & Ellis power cruiser. Renewed guard and toerails. Recommissioned. 1993.

28' Luders. Renewed keelson. 1993.

42' Bunker & Ellis power cruiser. Renewed brightwork. Recommissioned. Has maintained since 1982.

24' Bunker & Ellis power cruiser. Refinished. 1990.

26' MacKenzie Cuttyhunk bassboat. Renewed woodwork, refinished. 1991–'92.

Yard Information

Services

    Marina facilities

    Launching facilities

Moorage
Rigging
Storage
Number of boats stored per year: 50
Percentage of wooden boats: 50
Inside storage facilities
Maximum size for hauling and storing: 50' LOA, 6'
draft, 40 tons
Maintenance
Number of boats maintained per year: 50
Percentage of wooden boats: 50
Owner maintenance allowed.
Retail supplies:
Complete inventory of supplies.

■ JOHN'S BAY BOAT CO.

Peter Kass
P.O. Box 58
South Bristol, ME 04568
207-644-8261

Builder Information
Years in business: 11
Carpenters employed: 2
Shop capacity: 50'

Recent New Construction
36', 38', 40', and 41' lobsterboats. Designs by Carroll
Lowell. 6 built 1990–'93.

Recent Repair Projects
48' seiner. Replaced deck. 1992.
28' lobster yacht. Renewed house and interior. 1992.

Yard Information
Maintenance
Number of boats maintained per year: 2
Percentage of wooden boats: 50
Retail supplies:
Complete inventory of supplies.

■ J.E. JONES BOAT AND PROP

Jim Jones
P.O. Box 134
East Boothbay, ME 04544
207-633-2824

Builder Information
Years in business: 33
Carpenters employed: 1
Shop capacity: 50'

Recent New Construction
40' lobsterboat. Carroll Lowell design. Built 1989.

Recent Repair Projects
36' Stevens power cruiser. Completely rebuilt. 1993.
21' Boothbay Harbor One-Design class. Completed extensive frame repairs, replaced transom and refinished.
1992.
24' Hodgdon launch. Completely rebuilt. 1991.

18' Lyman cruiser. Replaced stem, planking, deck, rails,
and windshield. Refinished. 1990.

Yard Information
Services
Moorage
Storage
Number of boats stored per year: 10
Percentage of wooden boats: 75
Maximum size for hauling and storing: 55' LOA, 5'
draft, 30 tons
Maintenance
Number of boats maintained per year: 5
Percentage of wooden boats: 50
Owner maintenance allowed above and below rail.
Retail supplies:
Complete inventory of supplies.

■ KONITZKY BOAT WORKS INC.

Gustav A. Konitzky
HC 62, Box 084
New Harbor, ME 04554
207-667-3726

Builder Information
Years in business: 15
Carpenters employed: 2
Shop capacity: 50'
Willing to travel for on-the-site building projects.

Recent New Construction
Due to demand only, Konitzky's new boat construction in
the last few years has been limited to fiberglass hulls.
Prior to 1990, the company built numerous yachts, skiffs,
and lobsterboats of wood construction, and they would
again build in wood, were the orders there.

Recent Repair Projects
38' Pequod. Repaired stern, planking, top. 1993.
32' Downeast cruiser. Repaired and refinished. 1993.
36' lobsterboat. Renewed skeg and spray rails. 1992.
36' lobsterboat. Renewed skeg and garboard planks. 1992.
36' lobsterboat. Replaced engine beds and deck.
Repowered. 1991.
42' Novi dragger. Completely rebuilt including deck and
planking renewal. Rewired. 1990.

Yard Information
Services
Launching facilities
Overland transport
Moorage
Engine repair
Rigging
Storage
Number of boats stored per year: 40
Percentage of wooden boats: 20
Maximum size for hauling and storing: 50' LOA, 8'
draft, 40 tons
(continues)

(Konitzky Boat Works Inc., continued)
Maintenance
 Number of boats maintained per year: 40
 Percentage of wooden boats: 20
 Owner maintenance by arrangement only.
Retail supplies:
 Wood, fastenings, paint, hardware.

■ LANDING SCHOOL OF BOATBUILDING & DESIGN

John Burgess, President
David van Cleef, Director
P.O. Box 1490
Kennebunkport, ME 04046-1490
207-985-7976 Fax: 207-985-7942

Builder Information
Years in business: 16
Carpenters employed: 3 instructors, 25 students
Shop capacity: 25'

Recent New Construction
18' O-Boat-class sloop. John Alden design. 3 built 1993.
21' cold-molded runabout. Nelson Zimmer design. 3 built 1990–'93.
17' lapstrake/composite Swampscott dory. Dion design. 16 built 1990–'93.
19' lapstrake/composite Buzzards Bay 19 sloop. R.D. Culler/Landing School design. 10 built 1990–'93.
18' catboat. Carter design. 2 built 1993.
18' catboat. Fenwick Williams design. 2 built 1991.
30' Malabar Jr. auxiliary sloop. John Alden design. Built 1990.

■ LOON SEA KAYAKS

Chip Chandler
HCR 32, Box 253
Sebasco Estates, ME 04565-951
207-389-1565

Builder Information
Years in business: 6
Carpenters employed: 1
Shop capacity: 22'

Recent New Construction
Sea kayaks designed by Chip Chandler for strip-plank construction:
17'8" Razorbill. 6 built 1990–'93.
9'10" Baby Loon. 3 built 1990–'92.
21'1" Skimmer. Tandem model. 5 built 1990–'92.
16'4" Dovekie. 5 built 1990–'92.
20'1" Loon. 3 built 1990–'92.
14' Hummingbird. 4 built 1990–'92.

■ MACHIASPORT MARINE RAILWAY CO.

Karl Kurz
Rte. 92
Machiasport, ME 04655
207-255-3688

Builder Information
Years in business: 14
Carpenters employed: 1
Shop capacity: 40'

Recent New Construction
12' sneakbox. Perrine design. Current project.

Recent Repair Projects
24' Nielsen/Brewer sloop (1940). Completely restoring. Current project.
21' lobsterboat (1950s). Completely restored and re-powered. 1992–'93.

Yard Information
Services
 Moorage
 Engine repair
 Rigging
Storage
 Number of boats stored per year: 5
 Percentage of wooden boats: 100
 Inside storage facilities
 Maximum size for hauling and storing: 40' LOA, 6' draft, 30 tons
Maintenance
 Number of boats maintained per year: 6
 Percentage of wooden boats: 90
 Owner maintenance allowed.
Retail supplies:
 General chandlery supplies.

■ MAINE JOURNEYS CANOE

David Mussey
RR #1, Box 130
Charleston, ME 04422
207-285-3332

Builder Information
Years in business: 3
Carpenters employed: 1
Shop capacity: 20'
Willing to travel for on-the-site building projects.

Recent New Construction
16' wood/canvas canoe. David Mussey design. Planned for 1994.
14' wood/canvas canoes. H. Packard/D. Mussey design. 3 built 1992–'93.
17'6" wood/canvas canoes. Rollin Thurlow design. 4 built 1991–'93.

■ MALONE BOATBUILDING CO., INC.

Bruce Malone
506 West St.
Rockport, ME 04843
207-236-6282

Builder Information
Years in business: 14
Carpenters employed: 3
Shop capacity: 60'

Recent New Construction
12' plywood dory. John Gardner design. Built 1993.
28' lapstrake St. Pierre dory. John Gardner design. Built 1990.

Recent Repair Projects
28' Northeast Harbor A-class sloop. Completely restored. 1993.
21' Manhassett Bay One-Design sloop. Extensive restoration. 1993.
31' Concordia sloop. Renewed wiring and engine. 1993.
15' Old Town lapstrake runabout. Extensive restoration. 1992.

Yard Information
Storage
    Number of boats stored per year: 12
    Percentage of wooden boats: 80
    Maximum size for hauling and storing: Inquire
Maintenance
    Number of boats maintained per year: 12
    Percentage of wooden boats: 80
    Owner maintenance allowed on limited basis.
Retail supplies:
    Limited supply of materials.

■ MARINE PAINTING & REFINISHING CO.

Thomas A. Gregory
385 Main St. R.
South Portland, ME 04106
207-846-4903

Builder Information
Years in business: 6
Carpenters employed: 1
Shop capacity: 40'
Willing to travel for on-the-site building projects.

Recent Repair Projects
37' Egg Harbor (1965). Renewing stem and garboard planks. Completely refinishing. Current project.
36' Bunker & Ellis lobster yacht. Recaulked bottom, completely refinished. 1993.
36' Gower lobsterboat (1968). Applied plywood deck overlay. Completely refinished hull. 1993.
46' Egg Harbor (1971). Replaced stem and rebuilt flying bridge. Cold-molded deck. Faired and refinished hull. 1992.

20' strip-planked lobsterboat/launch. Renewed frames and transom. Applied cold-molded hull overlay. 1992.
44' Alden motoryacht (1966). Renewed decks, completely refinished. 1991.
44' Herreshoff Fishers Island-class KESTREL. Completely refinished. 1990.

Yard Information
Services
    Marina facilities
    Launching facilities
    Overland transport
Maintenance
    Number of boats maintained per year: 10-15
    Percentage of wooden boats: 90
    Owner maintenance allowed above and below rail.

■ L.A. McCARTHY, BOATSHOP

Lucy McCarthy
East Main St., P.O. Box 102
Vinalhaven, ME 04863
207-863-4962

Builder Information
Years in business: 15
Carpenters employed: 1
Shop capacity: 16'

Recent New Construction
10'6" lapstrake dory tender. Chaisson design. 9 boats built to date.

Recent Repair Projects
13'6" peapod. Renewing frames, refastening and recaulking, refinishing. Current project.
7' child's punt. Replacing plank and transom. Current project.
10'6" dory tender. Wooded hull, recaulked, and refinished. 1993.
12' flat-bottomed punt. Replaced thwarts, some frames. Refastened and recaulked. 1992.
12' Beetle Cat. Renewed frames, fastenings, and caulking. Recanvased deck, renewed rails.

Yard Information
Storage
    Number of boats stored per year: 8
    Percentage of wooden boats: 75
    Maximum size for hauling and storing: 20' LOA
Maintenance
    Number of boats maintained per year: 5
    Percentage of wooden boats: 75

■ MILE CREEK BOAT SHOP

John D. Little
RFD Box 257, Bill Luce Rd.
Washington, ME 04574
207-845-2708
(continues)

(Mile Creek Boat Shop, continued)

Builder Information
Years in business: 30
Carpenters employed: 1
Shop capacity: 45'

Recent New Construction
18' catboat. G. Follet design. Built 1990–'92.
11' lapstrake tender. J.D. Little design. Built 1990.

Recent Repair Projects
16' catboat. Renewed frames and planking. 1992–'93.
20'6" catboat. Recanvased decks and cuddy, replaced
  hatch. Installed Yanmar diesel. 1992.

Yard Information
Services
  Rigging

■ MILL COVE SMALL BOAT WORKS

Roy Jenkins and Jerry St. Clair
153 Commercial St.
Boothbay Harbor, ME 04538
207-882-6024

Builder Information
Years in business: 8
Carpenters employed: 2
Shop capacity: 15'
Willing to travel for on-the-site building projects.

Recent New Construction
14' lapstrake Navy Whitehall. Plans by Howard Chapelle.
  Built 1993.
9'3" lapstrake tender. Lawley design. 2 built 1992.

Yard Information
Services
  Overland transport
  Rigging

■ MISTY MOUNTAIN BOAT SHOP

Gary Leeman
P.O. Box 1447
Ellsworth, ME 04605
207-422-4770

Builder Information
Years in business: 16
Carpenters employed: 2
Shop capacity: 32'
Willing to travel for on-the-site building projects.

Recent Repair Projects
23' Century power cruiser. Sheathing bottom in fiberglass
  and epoxy and replacing keel. Replacing frames and refastening. Restoring interior brightwork. Current project.
15' runabout. Completely restored. Renewed planking,
  frames, decks, keel, and windshield. Sheathed bottom
  in fiberglass and epoxy, refinished exterior. Varnished
  decks and interior. 1993.

18' Old Town canoe (1940). Repaired ribs, renewed paint
  and varnish. 1993.
16' Old Town canoe (1936). Renewed planking, ribs, and
  gunwales. Recanvased and refinished. 1993.

Yard Information
Services
  Overland transport
  Engine repair
  Rigging
Storage
  Number of boats stored per year: 5-7
  Percentage of wooden boats: 50
  Inside storage facilities
  Maximum size for hauling and storing: 32' LOA, 6'
    draft
Maintenance
  Number of boats maintained per year: 10-12
  Percentage of wooden boats: 80
  Owner maintenance allowed above and below rail.

■ MOOSE ISLAND MARINE

Dean Pike
108 Water St.
Eastport, ME 04631
207-853-6058

Builder Information
Years in business: 18
Carpenters employed: 1
Shop capacity: 30'

Recent Repair Projects
20' canoe (1910). Repairing planking, sheathing hull in
  fiberglass and epoxy. 1994.
27' runabout (1970). Repowered and rewired. 1993.
16' runabout (1958). Replaced bottom planking. 1993.
23' Lyman runabout (1959). Renewed planking.
  Repowered. 1992.
23' cuddy-cabin cruiser (1968). Repowered and rewired.
  1992.

Yard Information
Services
  Launching facilities
  Overland transport
  Moorage
  Engine repair
Storage
  Number of boats stored per year: 15
  Percentage of wooden boats: 10
  Maximum size for hauling and storing: 30' LOA, 3'
    draft, 4 tons
Maintenance
  Number of boats maintained per year: 50
  Percentage of wooden boats: 15
  Owner maintenance allowed above and below rail.
Retail supplies:
  Complete inventory of supplies. Engines, paint, fiber-
    glass, epoxy, hardware, safety gear.

NORTH END SHIPYARD INC.

Doug and Linda Lee, and John Foss
P.O. Box 482, Front St.
Rockland, ME 04841
207-594-8007 Fax: 207-594-8015

Builder Information
Years in business: 21
Shop capacity: 100'

Yard Information
Storage
  Number of boats stored per year: 14
  Percentage of wooden boats: 100
  Inside storage facilities
  Maximum size for hauling and storing: 100' LOA, 11'
    draft, 153 tons
Maintenance
  Number of boats maintained per year: 30
  Percentage of wooden boats: 100
  Owner maintenance allowed above and below rail.
Retail supplies:
  Good inventory of supplies. North End Shipyard is a
    facility for large-vessel owners to do their own work.

NORTHERN BAY BOATS

Richard Washburn
HC 80, Box 23
Penobscot, ME 04476
207-326-4850

Builder Information
Years in business: 15
Carpenters employed: 1
Shop capacity: 24'
Willing to travel for on-the-site building projects.

Recent New Construction
10' lapstrake rowboat. Current project.

Recent Repair Projects
36' lobsterboat. Refastened bottom. 1993.
14' Old Town lapstrake skiff. Replaced 3 planks. 1993.
34' lobster yacht. Renewed interior joinery. 1992.
36' Pacemaker power cruiser. Replaced garboard. 1991.
32' Laurent Giles cutter. Renewed cabinhouse sheathing.
  1990.
31' Swedish sloop. Renewed cabinhouse sheathing. 1990.

Yard Information
Services
  Rigging

NORTHWOODS CANOE CO.

Rollin Thurlow
336 Range Rd.
Atkinson, ME 04426
207-564-3667

Builder Information
Years in business: 17
Carpenters employed: 2
Shop capacity: 25'

Recent New Construction
Wood/canvas canoes:
20' Grand Lake Stream square-sterned canoe. Mick Fahey
  design. 2 built 1993.
17' pleasure canoe. B.N. Morris design. 2 built 1993.
17' wilderness canoe. Rollin Thurlow design. 6 built 1993.
15' square-sterned motor canoe. Rollin Thurlow design. 2
  built 1993.
15' solo canoe. Rollin Thurlow design. 2 built 1993.

Recent Repair Projects
Specializes in the restoration of wood/canvas and all-
  wood canoes. Repair projects have involved a wide
  variety of types, including 25' and 35' war canoes.
  Approximately 15 restorations were completed in 1993.

Yard Information
Retail supplies:
  Canoe plans and books for building canoes. White
    cedar, canoe hardware, tacks, canvas (including extra-
    wide widths), and filler.

DAVID NUTT BOATBUILDER, INC.

David Nutt
Rte. 27, Box 320
West Southport, ME 04576
207-633-6009 Fax: same

Builder Information
Years in business: 20
Carpenters employed: 5
Shop capacity: 50'
Willing to travel for on-the-site building projects.

Recent New Construction
36' DuraKore/epoxy trimaran. Dick Newick design. Built
  1991.

Recent Repair Projects
39' Concordia yawl (1953). Replaced transom, coaming,
  and planking below waterline. Recanvased deck and
  refastened chainplates. 1993. Recanvasing cabintop,
  renewing planking, rebuilding rudder, refinishing
  brightwork. Current project.
39' Concordia yawl. Replacing keelbolts, planking, and
  floor timbers. Recanvasing cabintop, installing galley
  stove, rewiring mast. Current project.
22' Pulsifer Hampton boat. Refinished all brightwork. 1993.

Yard Information
Services
  Overland transport
  Engine repair
  Rigging
Storage
  Number of boats stored per year: 40
  Percentage of wooden boats: 50
(continues)

(David Nutt Boatbuilder, Inc., continued)
    Inside storage facilities
    Maximum size for hauling and storing: 50' LOA, 8'
      beam, 30 tons
Maintenance
    Number of boats maintained per year: 40
    Percentage of wooden boats: 50
    Owner maintenance allowed above rail.
Retail supplies:
    Wood, paint, fastenings, and hardware available on
      custom-order basis.

■ OAT CANOE CO.

Jeff Hanna
RR #2, Box 1900, Belgrade Rd.
Mount Vernon, ME 04352
207-293-2694

Builder Information
Years in business: 15
Carpenters employed: 1
Shop capacity: 25'

Recent Repair Projects
Company has repaired or restored approximately 40
    canoes, dinghies, or runabouts since 1990. Projects com-
    pleted in 1993: 1 canoe, 1 dinghy, 2 skiffs, 3 runabouts,
    and 1 Whitehall. All types of construction involved.

Yard Information
Retail supplies:
    Good inventory of supplies for building or repair.

■ OLD TOWN CANOE COMPANY

58 Middle St.
Old Town, ME 04468
207-827-5513 Fax: 207-827-2779

Builder Information
Years in business: 94
Carpenters employed: 4
Shop capacity: 20'

Recent New Construction
Wood/canvas or wood/fiberglass canoe models currently
    in production:
15' Trapper.
16' and 17' Otcas.
17' Molitor.
16', 18', and 20' Guide canoes.

■ PADEBCO CUSTOM BOATS

S. Bruce Cunningham
Anchor Inn Rd.
Round Pond, ME 04564
207-529-5106 Fax: same

Builder Information
Years in business: 33
Carpenters employed: 2
Shop capacity: 50'

Recent Repair Projects
36' lobsterboat. Refastened hull. 1993.
35' Cheoy Lee Rob. Refinished. 1992.

Yard Information
Services
    Launching facilities
    Overland transport
    Moorage
    Engine repair
Storage
    Number of boats stored per year: 80
    Percentage of wooden boats: 5
    Maximum size for hauling and storing: 42' LOA, 6'
      draft, 15 tons
Maintenance
    Number of boats maintained per year: 50
    Percentage of wooden boats: 5
    Owner maintenance allowed on limited basis.
Retail supplies:
    Teak, mahogany, fastenings, paint.

■ PETERSON CANOE & PADDLE

Jeffrey Peterson
Summit Hill Rd., RR #2, Box 217
Harrison, ME 04040
207-583-4070

Builder Information
Years in business: 5
Carpenters employed: 1
Shop capacity: 24'
Willing to travel for on-the-site building projects.

Recent New Construction
Traditional wood/canvas canoes, including the following
    models:
16' Prospector canoe. Chestnut Canoe Co./Ted Moores
    design. Several built 1991–'93.
17'6" guide canoe. Modified Atkinson Traveler design.
    Built 1993.

Recent Repair Projects
Wood/canvas canoes. Work ranges from minor repairs to
    complete restorations. Currently working on the fol-
    lowing:
18' Old Town Charles River canoe (1923).
18' and 20' Old Town guide canoes.
17' Kennebec sailing canoe.
16' Old Town Otca canoe (1921).
15' Peterborough canoe.
15' Old Town Trapper canoe.

Yard Information
Retail supplies:
    Canoe paddles. Traditional patterns in figured maple
      and cherry.

E. TYLER PROCTOR, JR., CUSTOM BOATBUILDER

E. Tyler Proctor, Jr.
16 Shannon Rd.
Bar Harbor, ME 04609
207-288-3679

Builder Information
Years in business: 20
Carpenters employed: 1
Shop capacity: 30′

Recent New Construction
Company specializes in construction of small, traditional boats for oar and sail in lengths from 8′ to 28′. Over the last several years, boats have been built to order from designs of Herreshoff, Chapelle, Atkin, Alden, Steward, Culler, and Proctor. A modified Herreshoff 8′ lapstrake pram is a stock item, available in rowing and sailing models. Construction for most projects has been cedar lapstrake.

Recent Repair Projects
12′ New Brunswick skiff. Replaced stem and breasthook. 1993.
18′ sponson canoe. Recanvased. 1990.

R.S. PULSIFER

R.S. (Dick) Pulsifer
3045 Merepoint Rd.
Brunswick, ME 04011
207-725-5457

Builder Information
Years in business: 21
Carpenters employed: 1
Shop capacity: 22′

Recent New Construction
22′ Pulsifer Hampton power launch. Strip-plank construction. Charlie Gomes design based on early Maine lobsterboats, and modified by Pulsifer. 3-4 boats built each year, 10 built 1991–’93.

Recent Repair Projects
Several Hamptons repaired and/or refinished each year.

Yard Information
Services
    Launching facilities
    Overland transport
    Engine repair
Storage
    Number of boats stored per year: 7
    Percentage of wooden boats: 100
    Inside storage facilities
    Maximum size for hauling and storing: 22′ LOA, 3′ draft, 1 ton
Maintenance
    Number of boats maintained per year: 10
    Percentage of wooden boats: 100
    Owner maintenance allowed above and below rail.

JAMES H. RICH BOAT YARD

James H. Rich
HC 33, Box 163
West Tremont, ME 04690
207-244-3208

Builder Information
Years in business: 37
Carpenters employed: 3
Shop capacity: 46′

Recent Repair Projects
43′ Maine-built pleasure boat. Extensively repaired cabin and superstructure. 1992–’93.
30′ sailboat. Renewed frames and planking. Resheathed deck and cabintop with fiberglass, and refinished brightwork. 1991–’92.
24′ Maine-built pleasure boat. Replaced deck, windshield, and coamings. 1990–’91.

Yard Information
Services
    Launching facilities
    Engine repair
Storage
    Number of boats stored per year: 50
    Percentage of wooden boats: 10
    Inside storage facilities
    Maximum size for hauling and storing: 46′ LOA, 6′ draft, 20 tons
Maintenance
    Number of boats maintained per year: 75
    Percentage of wooden boats: 10
Retail supplies:
    Wood, fastenings, paint, marine hardware, and other supplies.

RIVERSIDE BOAT COMPANY

Paul S. Bryant
Liberty St.
Newcastle, ME 04553
207-563-3398

Builder Information
Years in business: 48
Carpenters employed: 2
Shop capacity: 40′

Recent New Construction
24′ Zephyr class. C.D. Mower design. Built 1990–’91.

Recent Repair Projects
30′ Friendship sloop. Replaced deck and cabin. 1992–’93.
28′ Rozinante canoe yawl. Replaced deadwood and frames. 1992–’93.
31′ Friendship sloop. Replaced cabin and repowered. 1992–’93.
36′ power cruiser. Remodeled interior. 1992–’93.
16′ Herreshoff 12½. Completely rebuilt. 1991–’92.
(continues)

(Riverside Boat Company, continued)
34' power cruiser. Replaced flying bridge. 1991–'92.
31' Friendship sloop. Replaced spars. 1991–'92.

Yard Information
Services
    Launching facilities
    Moorage
    Engine repair
Storage
    Number of boats stored per year: 80
    Percentage of wooden boats: 70
    Inside storage facilities
    Maximum size for hauling and storing: 40' LOA, 5'6"
       draft, 15 tons
Maintenance
    Number of boats maintained per year: 75
    Percentage of wooden boats: 70
    Owner maintenance allowed above and below rail.
Retail supplies:
    Paint.

■ RIVER VALLEY BOATWORKS, INC.

Richard Alderette
58 Fore St.
Portland, ME 04101
207-761-4344

Builder Information
Years in business: 19
Carpenters employed: 1
Shop capacity: 42'
Willing to travel for on-the-site building projects.

Recent Repair Projects
35' and 36' lobsterboats. Installed new engines. 1993.
12' daysailer. Refinished. 1993.
40' sportfisherman. Installed new fuel tanks, renewed
    decks, completed other general repairs. 1992.
28' lobsterboat. Installed new hauling house. 1992.

Yard Information
Services
    Marina facilities
    Moorage
    Engine repair
Storage
    Number of boats stored per year: 10
    Percentage of wooden boats: 50
    Inside storage facilities
    Maximum size for hauling and storing: 42' LOA
Maintenance
    Number of boats maintained per year: 28
    Percentage of wooden boats: 4
    Owner maintenance allowed above and below rail.
Retail supplies:
    Marine engines, pumps, mechanical components, and
      electrical supplies.

■ ROBINHOOD MARINE CENTER

Robinhood Rd.
Georgetown, ME 04530
207-371-2525 Fax: 207-371-2024

Builder Information
Years in business: 30
Carpenters employed: 5
Shop capacity: 50'

Recent Repair Projects
40' Elco sedan cruiser. Refitting and refinishing. Current
    project.
53' cutter. Laid new teak deck. 1993.
38' Alden Challenger. Rebuilt house. 1993.
35' Pilot yawl. Completely refinished exterior. 1990–'93.
45' Alberg ketch. Refitted. 1992.
45' Monk ketch. Phased restoration. 1992.

Yard Information
Services
    Marina facilities
    Launching facilities
    Overland transport
    Moorage
    Engine repair
    Sail repair
    Rigging
Storage
    Number of boats stored per year: 125
    Percentage of wooden boats: Varies
    Inside storage facilities
    Maximum size for hauling and storing: 55' LOA, 8'
      draft, 30 tons
Maintenance
    Number of boats maintained per year: 200
    Percentage of wooden boats: 10
    Owner maintenance allowed above and below rail.
Retail supplies:
    Good inventory of commonly used materials.

■ ROCKPORT MARINE, INC.

Taylor Allen
1 Main St., P.O. Box 203
Rockport, ME 04856
207-236-9651 Fax: 207-236-0758

Builder Information
Years in business: 30
Carpenters employed: 6
Shop capacity: 120'
Willing to travel for on-the-site building projects.

Recent New Construction
16' Herreshoff 12½. N.G. Herreshoff design. 3 built
    1991–'93.
28' Rozinante ketch. L.F. Herreshoff design. Built 1992.

Recent Repair Projects
39'10" Concordia yawl. Rebuilt maststep, sternpost, and
deadwood area. Reinforced floor timbers, renewed
keelbolts and 8 planks. Installed new engine. 1993.
39'10" Concordia yawl. Sheathed deck with Dynel,
replaced cockpit coamings and winch bases. 1993.
50' Concordia schooner. Renewed floor timbers and keelbolts, toerails, coamings, planking, and fastenings. Laid
new teak deck. 1993.
40' Warner cutter. Sheathed deck and cabintop with Dynel,
renewed transom. 1993.
36' McIntosh schooner. Renewed floor timbers, keelbolts,
planking, and cabin sole. Refastened bottom. 1993.
60' Sparkman & Stephens yawl. Rewired vessel and
renewed planking. Sandblasted mainmast. 1992.
36' Nielsen cutter. Replaced ballast keel, floor timbers, and
deadwood. Renewed and refastened planking.
Stripped and refinished spars, refurbished interior.
1992–'93.

Yard Information
Services
Marina facilities
Launching facilities
Moorage
Engine repair
Rigging
Storage
Number of boats stored per year: 35
Percentage of wooden boats: 95
Inside storage facilities
Maximum size for hauling and storing: 60' LOA, 9'
draft, 35 tons
Maintenance
Number of boats maintained per year: 35
Percentage of wooden boats: 97
Owner maintenance allowed on boats stored outside.

■ PAUL E. ROLLINS

Paul E. Rollins
2 Scotland Bridge Rd.
York, ME 03909
207-363-6237

Builder Information
Years in business: 20
Carpenters employed: 1-3
Shop capacity: 60'
Willing to travel for on-the-site building projects.

Recent New Construction
18' lapstrake plywood camp-cruiser sloop. P.E. Rollins
design. Built 1993.
33' International One-Design sloop. Bjarne Aas design.
Built 1992–'93.
56' schooner. McIntosh/Rollins design. Built 1991–'92.

Recent Repair Projects
42' Elco Flattop cruiser. Rebuilt hull. 1992.
42' Geerd Hendel sloop. Completely rebuilt. 1990.

Yard Information
Services
Rigging
Storage
Number of boats stored per year: 5-8
Percentage of wooden boats: Varies
Inside storage facilities
Maximum size for hauling and storing: 60' LOA, 7'
draft, 35 tons
Maintenance
Number of boats maintained per year: 5-8
Percentage of wooden boats: Varies

■ GREG RÖSSEL BOAT CARPENTRY

Greg Rössel
Bangor Rd.
Troy, ME 04987
207-948-2841

Builder Information
Years in business: 10
Carpenters employed: 1
Shop capacity: 20'
Willing to travel for on-the-site building projects.

Recent New Construction
11' lapstrake sailing dinghy. George Chaisson design. Built
1990.
14' strip-planked Whitehall-type pulling boat. Built 1990.

Recent Repair Projects
18' Grand Lake Stream canoe. Completely restored. 1993.
12' Old Town tender. Recanvased. 1993.
12' Wolverine runabout. Replaced transom. 1993.
45' Sparkman & Stephens yawl. Completely restored deckhouse. 1993.
16'–18' canoes. White, Kennebec, Old Town, and Lincoln
designs. Repairs have included rail, breasthook, and
thwart replacement, recanvasing and refinishing. 7
boats worked on 1991–'92.
19' West Coast seal-hunting boat. Repaired stem, breasthook, knees, thwarts, and hood ends of planking. 1991.
14' Old Town runabout (c. 1950). Renewed transom, keel,
and knees. 1990.

Yard Information
Retail supplies:
Services offered: custom lofting, lines taking, and draft-
ing. Custom half models.

■ ROYALL BOAT WORKS

Thomas B. Royall
P.O. Box 324, Rte. 1
Freeport, ME 04032

Builder Information
Years in business: 2
Carpenters employed: 1
(continues)

(Royall Boat Works, continued)
Shop capacity: 28'
Willing to travel for on-the-site building projects.

Recent New Construction

9' lapstrake tender. Arno Day design. 2 under construction.
10'6" cold-molded Cosine wherry. Current project.

Recent Repair Projects

9'6" Lowell tender. Completely refinishing. Current project.
13' Herreshoff tender. Replaced plank, recaulked.
   Completely refinished. 1993.

Yard Information

Services
   Engine repair
   Rigging
Storage
   Number of boats stored per year: 2
   Percentage of wooden boats: 100
   Maximum size for hauling and storing: 28' LOA, 6'
      draft
Maintenance
   Number of boats maintained per year: 3
   Percentage of wooden boats: 100
   Owner maintenance allowed above and below rail.

RUSSELL BOATWORKS

Kevin D. Russell
P.O. Box 14, Main Rd.
Great Cranberry Island, ME 04625
207-244-5757

Builder Information

Years in business: 8
Carpenters employed: 1
Shop capacity: 42'
Willing to travel for on-the-site building projects.

Recent New Construction

22' cold-molded power cruiser. Spencer Lincoln design.
   Current project.
9'6" lapstrake plywood Nutshell pram. Joel White design.
   2 built 1993.
19' strip-planked/cold-molded launch. Eric Sommers
   design. 2 built 1992–'93.
11'6" tender. Arthur Spurling & Charles Liebow design. 2
   built 1991 and 1993.
22' strip-planked sloop. Ken Hankinson design. Built 1990.

Recent Repair Projects

19' Culler-designed Concordia sloop-boat. Renewing rudder, centerboard, spars, stem, and framing. Current
   project.
14' Bracy lapstrake rowboat. Completely restoring. Current
   project.
14' lapstrake sailing peapod. Replaced rudder and some
   framing. 1993.
12' Spurling rowboat (1943). Completely restored.
   Renewed frames and planking. 1992.
14' lapstrake rowboat. Replaced frames and planking. 1991.

26' Hinckley inboard launch. Renewed frames, platform,
   and ceiling. 1990.

Yard Information

Services
   Marina facilities
   Launching facilities
   Overland transport
   Moorage
   Engine repair
   Sail repair
   Rigging
Storage
Maintenance
   Number of boats maintained per year: 35
   Percentage of wooden boats: 90
Retail supplies:
   Paint, fastenings, some wood.

SAMPLES SHIPYARD

Joseph Jackimovicz, Yard Manager
P.O. Box 462, 120 Commercial St.
Boothbay Harbor, ME 04538
207-633-3171 Fax: 207-633-3824

Builder Information

Years in business: 50
Carpenters employed: 4
Shop capacity: 140'
Willing to travel for on-the-site building projects.

Recent New Construction

16' plywood rowing dory. 4 built 1991.

Recent Repair Projects

85' Trumpy motoryacht (1935). Renewing bottom.
   Repairing frames and topside planking. Current project.
17' yawlboat. Repairing planking. Current project.
95' Baltic trading schooner. Renewed frames and topside
   planking. 1990.

Yard Information

Services
   Launching facilities
   Overland transport
   Moorage
   Engine repair
   Rigging
Storage
   Number of boats stored per year: 60
   Percentage of wooden boats: 50
   Inside storage facilities
   Maximum size for hauling and storing: 70' LOA, 10'
      draft, 50 tons
Maintenance
   Number of boats maintained per year: 60
   Percentage of wooden boats: 50
   Inquire.
Retail supplies:
   Charts, fastenings, paint, glue, fiberglass materials.

SEA HOSS SKIFFS

Mark R. Murray
RR #2, Box 98A
South Harpswell, ME 04079
207-725-7297

Builder Information
Years in business: 15
Carpenters employed: 1
Shop capacity: 28'
Willing to travel for on-the-site building projects.

Recent New Construction
12' and 16' lapstrake skiffs. M.R. Murray designs. 2 built 1992.
18' strip-planked skiff. M.R. Murray design. Built 1991.
9' lapstrake Norse pram. Built 1990.

Recent Repair Projects
23' lobsterboat. Refitted for private ferry island service. 1993.
24' lobsterboat. Replaced house. 1992.
28' lobster yacht. Completed boat from bare hull. 1991.
28' lobsterboat. Replaced house. 1990.

SEAL COVE BOATYARD, INC.

Robert Vaughn
Box 99
Harborside, ME 04642
207-326-4422

Builder Information
Years in business: 45
Carpenters employed: 3
Shop capacity: 60'

Recent Repair Projects
40' Alden yawl. Replaced keel, forefoot, some hull planking, frames, and floors. 1992–'93.
21' picnic launch (1913). Completely rebuilt. 1992–'93.
41' Concordia. Replaced frames and planking. Renewed interior. 1991–'92.
34' Winslow ketch. Replaced planking, frames, floors, and cabin trunk. Renewed interior. 1990–'92.
20' Crowninshield Dark Harbor 12½. Completely rebuilt. 1990–'91.

Yard Information
Services
    Launching facilities
    Moorage
    Engine repair
Storage
    Number of boats stored per year: 140
    Percentage of wooden boats: 50
    Inside storage facilities
    Maximum size for hauling and storing: 60' LOA, 10' draft, 30 tons
Maintenance
    Number of boats maintained per year: 135
    Percentage of wooden boats: 50
    Owner maintenance allowed above and below rail.
Retail supplies:
    Complete inventory of supplies.

SHEW & BURNHAM

Cecil Burnham
P.O. Box 131
South Bristol, ME 04568
207-644-8120

Builder Information
Years in business: 25
Carpenters employed: 2
Shop capacity: 40'

Recent New Construction
Boats designed by William Shew:
39'6" cold-molded lobsterboat. Current project.
12' and 14' lapstrake Whitehall skiffs. Eighty-five 12-footers and three 14-footers built to date. Ongoing construction.
28' cold-molded utility cruiser. Built 1992.

Recent Repair Projects
16' Herreshoff 12½. Renewed floors and frame ends. 1993.
21' Herreshoff Fish-class sloop. Renewed transom, floors, and frame ends. 1991.
26' Hacker-Craft. Completely restored. 1990.

Yard Information
Storage
    Number of boats stored per year: 3
    Percentage of wooden boats: 80
    Inside storage facilities
    Maximum size for hauling and storing: 28' LOA
Maintenance
    Number of boats maintained per year: 4
    Percentage of wooden boats: 100

RALPH W. STANLEY, INC.

Ralph W. Stanley
Box 458
Southwest Harbor, ME 04679
207-244-3795

Builder Information
Years in business: 42
Carpenters employed: 5
Shop capacity: 50'

Recent New Construction
Boats designed by Ralph Stanley:
25' plywood open launch. Built 1993.
36' cabin cruiser. Built 1992.
30' cabin launch. Built 1991.
29' cabin launch. Built 1990.
(continues)

(Ralph W. Stanley, Inc., continued)

Recent Repair Projects

26′ lobsterboat. Replaced frames aft of bulkhead. 1993.

39′ yacht club committee boat. Repaired collision damage. 1992.

33′ lobsterboat. Sistered frames, renewed top strakes. Replaced deck, cabin, and shelter. 1991.

33′ Friendship sloop. Replaced deck. 1990.

Yard Information

Services
    Launching facilities
    Moorage
    Rigging
Storage
    Number of boats stored per year: 20
    Percentage of wooden boats: 100
    Inside storage facilities
    Maximum size for hauling and storing: 45′ LOA, 6′ draft
Maintenance
    Number of boats maintained per year: 20
    Percentage of wooden boats: 100
    Owner maintenance allowed above and below rail.
Retail supplies:
    Paint and general hardware.

STAR BOAT CO.

Peter C. Clapp
Rte. 73, FR 201, P.O. Box 26
Spruce Head, ME 04859
207-594-5600

Builder Information

Years in business: 5
Carpenters employed: 1-3
Shop capacity: 40′
Willing to travel for on-the-site building projects.

Recent New Construction

12′ plywood Trifle pram. Fred Bingham design. 2 built 1993.

16′ Haven 12½-class sloop. Joel White design. Built 1992.

15′6″ plywood Sweet Pea peapod. Phil Bolger design. Built 1992.

14′ plywood June Bug sailing skiff. Phil Bolger design. Built 1991.

9′6″ lapstrake Norwegian pram. Dave Foster design. 2 built 1991.

Recent Repair Projects

19′ Century Raven. Replaced ribs and planking, rebuilt windshield. 1993.

15′6″ Snipe-class sloop. Replaced centerboard trunk and mast. 1993.

44′ Alden sloop. Renewed cockpit floor. 1993.

18′ Old Town canoe. Recanvased and revarnished. 1992.

38′ Friendship sloop. Rebuilt cabin sole, built new interior doors and tables. 1992.

18′ sloop (1946). Repaired standing rigging, recanvased deck, and renewed coaming. Refinished. 1991.

Yard Information

Storage
    Number of boats stored per year: 3-5
    Percentage of wooden boats: 50
    Maximum size for hauling and storing: 40′ LOA
Maintenance
    Number of boats maintained per year: 3
    Percentage of wooden boats: 50
    Owner maintenance allowed.

C. STICKNEY, BOATBUILDERS, LTD.

Chris Stickney
P.O. Box 1146
St. George, ME 04857
207-372-8543

Builder Information

Years in business: 18
Carpenters employed: 2
Shop capacity: 36′
Willing to travel for on-the-site building projects.

Recent New Construction

10′6″ lapstrake tender. 2 built 1993.

9′ lapstrake sailing dinghy. Frederick Goeller design. Built 1993.

Recent Repair Projects

32′ Post cutter. Replacing backbone and sections of planking. Current project.

28′ Palmer Scott sloop. Repairing structural timbers below waterline. Current project.

13′ Old Town Whitecap sloop. Replacing frames and bottom planking. Current project.

23′ International 110-class sloop. Replacing keel and deck. Refinishing. Current project.

70′ sardine carrier DOUBLE EAGLE. Replaced bulkheads and pilothouse. 1992–′93.

65′ Alden schooner WENDAMEEN. Renewed bulwarks and deck joinery. 1992.

37′ Crocker ketch SEACREST. Replaced deck and sheerstrakes. 1991.

STIMSON MARINE, INC.

David Stimson
RR #1, Box 524, River Rd.
Boothbay, ME 04537
207-633-7252 Fax: 207-633-6058

Builder Information

Years in business: 23
Carpenters employed: 1
Shop capacity: 60′
Willing to travel for on-the-site building projects.

Recent New Construction
11'8" Geodesic Airolite Snowshoe 12 canoe. Platt Monfort design. Built 1993.

13'6" lapstrake Amesbury skiff. John Gardner design. 4 built 1993.

17'4" skin-on-frame Spoondrift 17 sea kayak. David Stimson design. 2 built 1992–'93.

11'5" Geodesic Airolite Nimrod 12 canoe. Platt Monfort design. 15 built 1990–'93.

11'5" lapstrake Sea Urchin skiff. Stimson design. 3 built 1990–'93.

22' Geodesic Airolite racing kayak. Stimson design. Built 1992.

13'6" lapstrake wherry. Stimson design. 3 built 1992.

Recent Repair Projects
27' King's Cruiser sloop. Repaired planking, frames, and forefoot. Replaced deck framing and deck. 1993.

14' Old Town Whitecap sloop. Refastened hull, repaired centerboard trunk. 1993.

32' International 500-class sloop. Repaired frames and bottom planking. 1990, 1993.

38' power cruiser. Refastened and recaulked hull. 1992.

15' Coast Guard peapod. Replaced frames, refastened, recaulked, and faired hull. 1991.

20' sloop. Replaced transom, deck framing, deck, and coamings. 1991.

38' Alden schooner. Repaired frames, refastened and recaulked bottom. 1990.

Yard Information
Maintenance

Number of boats maintained per year: Varies

Percentage of wooden boats: 100

Owner maintenance allowed above and below rail.

Retail supplies:

Plans and materials for Geodesic boats.

■ SWANSON CARPENTRY & BOATWORKS

Mark Swanson
P.O. Box 129
Warren, ME 04864
207-273-3362

Builder Information
Years in business: 17
Carpenters employed: 1
Shop capacity: 20'
Willing to travel for on-the-site building projects.

Recent New Construction
Mark Swanson adaptations of traditional designs:
15' lapstrake Danish sailing pram. Built 1993.

9'6" and 10' lapstrake Norwegian prams. One of each size built 1990 and 1992.

Recent Repair Projects
54' Chris-Craft power cruiser (1958). Refinished both interior and exterior. 1991.

■ DAVID SWEET, BOATBUILDER

David Sweet
Sargent Dr.
Northeast Harbor, ME 04662
207-276-3950 Fax: 207-276-3272

Builder Information
Years in business: 20
Carpenters employed: 1+
Shop capacity: Any size
Willing to travel for on-the-site building projects.

Recent New Construction
13' lapstrake peapod. David Sweet design. 2 built 1993.

Yard Information
Services
Moorage

■ MICHAEL WARR WOODWORK

Michael P. Warr
Burnt Cove Rd.
Stonington, ME 04681
207-367-2360

Builder Information
Years in business: 21
Carpenters employed: 1-2
Shop capacity: 50'
Willing to travel for on-the-site building projects.

Recent Repair Projects
32' Alden cutter. Sheathed deck and cockpit with Dynel. Built new interior. 1993.

21' Century Coronado. Replaced stem, chines, frames, floors, and planking. 1993.

17' Chris-Craft Barrelback runabout. Replaced topside planking and sheathed bottom in Dynel. Refinished. 1992.

38' Sparkman & Stephens sloop. Replaced frames, floors, and maststep. Partially refastened. 1990–'93.

47' A.C.F. motoryacht. Realigned cockpit framing. Renewed sole and hatches. Repaired aft bulkhead. 1991.

16' Herreshoff 12½. Sistered 9 frames, replaced 3 planks. Replaced transom and coaming. 1991.

38' Rhodes cutter. Replaced keelbolts, floors, and frames. Renewed stem apron, transom, cabin sole, and interior joinery. Refastened hull and refinished. Completed 1990.

Yard Information
Services
Rigging
Storage
Number of boats stored per year: 10
Percentage of wooden boats: 100
Inside storage facilities
Maximum size for hauling and storing: Inquire
(continues)

(Michael Warr Woodwork, continued)
Maintenance
    Number of boats maintained per year: 2-3
    Percentage of wooden boats: 100
    Owner maintenance allowed above and below rail.

■ WASHINGTON COUNTY TECHNICAL COLLEGE

Marine Trades Center
RR #1, Box 74, Deep Cove Rd.
Eastport, ME 04631-9618
207-853-2518 Fax: 207-853-2577

Builder Information
Years in business: 20
Carpenters employed: 4 instructors, 36 students

Recent New Construction
21' cold-molded outboard skiff. Marine Trades Center
    design. Current project.
15' Whitehall pulling boat. Traditional design. Built 1993.
19' Downeast outboard skiff. Strip-planked/cold-molded
    construction. John Gardner design. 2 built 1991–'93.
17' Buzzards Bay 14 sloop. L.F. Herreshoff design.
    Completed 1990.

■ WEST COVE BOAT YARD

Stephen McMullen
Waukeag Ave., P.O. Box 383
Sorrento, ME 04677
207-422-3137 Fax: same

Builder Information
Years in business: 13
Carpenters employed: 1-2
Shop capacity: 45'

Recent New Construction
18' strip-planked Barbara Anne launch. Robert Steward
    design. Current project.

Recent Repair Projects
31' Wicks Bros. power cruiser. Replaced fuel tanks. 1993.
43' Swan sloop. Renewed teak deck. 1993.
30' Northeast Harbor A-class sloop WHISTLER. Reframed
    and renewed deck. 1992.
30' Northeast Harbor A-class sloop ARIEL. Renewed
    frames and refastened. 1990.

Yard Information
Services
    Launching facilities
    Moorage
    Engine repair
    Rigging
Storage
    Number of boats stored per year: 120
    Percentage of wooden boats: 25
    Inside storage facilities
    Maximum size for hauling and storing: 45' LOA

Maintenance
    Number of boats maintained per year: 120
    Percentage of wooden boats: 25
Retail supplies:
    Fastenings, paint, hardware, line, and engine parts.

■ WILLIS BOAT YARD

Willis A. Beal
P.O. Box 146
Beals, ME 04611
207-497-5630

Builder Information
Years in business: 29
Carpenters employed: 1
Shop capacity: 42'

Recent New Construction
30' strip-planked lobsterboat. Willis Beal design. Current
    project.
35' strip-planked lobsterboat. Willis Beal design. Built 1993.

■ WINTERPORT MARINE & BOATYARD

Jim Griffiths
Water St., P.O. Box 130
Winterport, ME 04496
207-223-8885

Builder Information
Years in business: 5
Carpenters employed: 2
Shop capacity: 50'

Recent Repair Projects
41' Chris-Craft power cruiser. Repairing and refinishing
    hull. Current project.
30' Bunker & Ellis day cruiser. Replaced plank, refinished
    hull. 1993.
16' Old Town sailing dinghy. Completely rebuilt. 1992.

Yard Information
Services
    Marina facilities
    Launching facilities
    Overland transport
    Moorage
    Engine repair
    Rigging
Storage
    Number of boats stored per year: 100
    Percentage of wooden boats: 25
    Inside storage facilities
    Maximum size for hauling and storing: 45' LOA, 8'
      draft, 25 tons
Maintenance
    Number of boats maintained per year: 100
    Percentage of wooden boats: 25
    Owner maintenance allowed.

Retail supplies:

Wood, hardware, materials for repair and refinishing. Cleaning supplies.

■ THE WOODEN BOAT COMPANY

Nigel Bower
4684 Upper Mechanic St.
Camden, ME 04843
207-236-8605

Builder Information

Years in business: 8
Carpenters employed: 1
Shop capacity: 50'
Willing to travel for on-the-site building projects.

Recent New Construction

13'6" lapstrake peapod. Havilah Hawkins design. Built 1993.
7'6" pram. Nigel Bower design. Built 1993.
16' Herreshoff 12½. Built 1990.
9'6" pram. Nigel Bower design. Built 1990.

Recent Repair Projects

26' Lyman cruiser. Laid teak deck overlay and refinished. 1993.
39'8" Rhodes sloop. Completely restored. 1990–'93.
37' U.S. One-Design class. Renewed bottom planking, floors, and keelbolts. Refastened and refinished hull. 1992.
60' Alden schooner. Replaced booms, gaffs, and bowsprits. 1990.
27' Quincy Adams 17-class sloop. Renewed frames, floors, and backbone. Recanvased deck, replaced covering boards, and refinished. 1990.
86' McIntosh schooner. Repaired spars. 1990.

Yard Information

Services
    Moorage
    Engine repair
    Rigging
Storage
    Number of boats stored per year: 10
    Percentage of wooden boats: 100
    Inside storage facilities
    Maximum size for hauling and storing: 50' LOA, 8' draft, 20 tons
Maintenance
    Number of boats maintained per year: 10
    Percentage of wooden boats: 100
    Owner maintenance allowed above and below rail.

■ ZENDIGO BOAT WORKS

Arthur L. Poole
RR #2, Box 390
Mount Vernon, ME 04352
207-293-2788

Builder Information

Years in business: 10
Carpenters employed: 1
Shop capacity: 20'

Recent New Construction

Boats designed by Arthur Poole for lapstrake construction:
16' Sea Bright light-racing skiff. Built 1993.
18' Sea Bright light-racing skiff. 2 built 1991–'92.
20' Sea Bright surf-racing skiff. Built 1990–'91.
Other new construction:
16' Sea Bright sailing skiff. Lapstrake construction. Traditional design circa 1900. Built 1990.

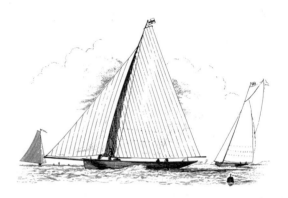

■ BARRY W. BEALS

Barry W. Beals
9178 Centerway Rd.
Gaithersburg, MD 20879
301-926-0911

Builder Information

Years in business: 4
Carpenters employed: 1
Shop capacity: 16'

Recent New Construction

16' strip canoe. William English design. Built 1993.

Yard Information

Retail supplies:
    Cherry, ash, and maple canoe paddles, designed and built by Beals.

■ BELKOV YACHT CARPENTRY CO.

Larry Belkov
311 Third St.
Annapolis, MD 21403
410-269-1777 Fax: 410-269-8477

Builder Information

Years in business: 14
Carpenters employed: 7
Shop capacity: 55'
(continues)

(Belkov Yacht Carpentry Co., continued)

Recent New Construction

32' cold-molded Chesapeake Bay boat. Gary Van Tassel and Larry Belkov design. Built 1990.

■ CLUBHOUSE BOATWORKS

Robert W. MacAdam
217 S. River Clubhouse Rd.
Harwood, MD 20776
410-798-5356

Builder Information
Years in business: 5
Carpenters employed: 1
Shop capacity: 20'
Willing to travel for on-the-site building projects.

Recent New Construction
10' plywood sailing skiff. Atkin design. 7 built 1990–'93.
15'6" lapstrake plywood Whisp skiff. Steve Redmond design. Built 1992.
12' lapstrake plywood Acorn sailing dinghy. Iain Oughtred design. Built 1992.
8' lapstrake plywood Acorn sailing dinghy. Iain Oughtred design. Built 1991.
13'6" plywood Little Gem skiff. Ken Swan design. Built 1991.

Recent Repair Projects
20' Chesapeake 20-class sloops. Four restored 1990–'93.
Dyer dinghies and tenders. Repairs and refurbishing. Numerous jobs 1990–'93.

■ COASTAL COMPOSITES, LTD.

Anthony Delima
303 Cannon St.
Chestertown, MD 21620
800-398-7556 Fax: 410-778-0012

Builder Information
Years in business: 6
Carpenters employed: 1
Shop capacity: 70'
Willing to travel for on-the-site building projects.

Recent New Construction
18' cold-molded runabout. Elco design. Current project.
40' cold-molded cutter. Alden design. Built 1993.
8' cold-molded catboat. M. Barto design. 2 built 1993.
34' cold-molded sloop. Hinckley design. Built 1993.

Recent Repair Projects
Current projects:
26' sloop. Renewing planking.
33' sloop. Replacing teak cockpit.
24' power cruiser. Replacing engine.
26' sloop. Completely restoring.
39' sloop. Renewing keel.

Yard Information
Retail supplies:
Materials for cold-molding. Catalog available.

■ CRAFTWORKS/ELECTRA-GHOST CANOES

Allen Cady
7117 Bembe Beach Rd.
Annapolis, MD 21403
410-268-1808 Fax: same

Builder Information
Years in business: 15
Carpenters employed: 2
Shop capacity: 42'
Willing to travel for on-the-site building projects.

Recent Repair Projects
32' Pacemaker (1955). Replaced keel and garboards. 1993.
20' Chesapeake 20 sloop. Renewed framing and deck. 1993.
42' deadrise boat (1936). Replaced chine logs, renewed planking and decks. 1992.
30' Oxford 400 sloop. Replaced sternpost, renewed planking and refastened. 1992.
44' Fishers Island 31 (1927). Completely rebuilt. Renewed keel, frames, decks. 1987–'91.
26' Fay & Bowen launch. Completely restored. 1991.
Has also restored several Old Town canoes. 1991–'93.

■ CROCKETT BROS. BOATYARD, INC.

Philip Conner
202 Bank St., P.O. Box 369
Oxford, MD 21654
410-226-5113 Fax: 410-226-5602

Builder Information
Years in business: 15
Carpenters employed: 1-2
Shop capacity: 55'

Recent Repair Projects
40' Smith/Hodgdon trawler. Renewed cabin, decks, planking, and electrical system. Refinished. 1993.

Yard Information
Services
Marina facilities
Launching facilities
Engine repair
Rigging
Storage
Number of boats stored per year: 100
Percentage of wooden boats: 5
Inside storage facilities
Maximum size for hauling and storing: 55' LOA, 6.5' draft, 30 tons
Maintenance
Number of boats maintained per year: 300
Percentage of wooden boats: 5
Owner maintenance allowed above and below rail.
Retail supplies:
WEST System supplies, stainless and bronze fastenings. Extensive inventory of other materials for maintenance and repair.

CYPRESS MARINE INC.

Allen J. Flinchum
730 Cypress Rd.
Severna Park, MD 21146
410-647-7940 Fax: 410-647-0000

Builder Information
Years in business: 25
Carpenters employed: 2
Shop capacity: 75'
Willing to travel for on-the-site building projects.

Recent New Construction
21' plywood Caroline skiff. Phil Bolger design. Built 1993.
16' wood/epoxy ultralight bassboat. Paul Reed Smith design. Built 1992.
40' barge/pile driver. Designed by owner. Built 1991.
20'4" Chincoteague scow. Wood/epoxy construction. A.J. Flinchum design. 18 built 1990–'93.
70' strip/cold-molded sportfisherman. A.J. Flinchum design. Built 1990.

Recent Repair Projects
35' Richardson sportfisherman. Replaced numerous frames, bulkhead, and cockpit. Installed new engine, and refinished hull. 1993–'94.
37' Egg Harbor sportfisherman. Renewed hull caulking, refinished. 1993.
25' Annie ketch. Laminated stem, renewed horn timber and butt blocks. Recaulked and refinished hull. Replaced engine, fuel tank, and wiring. 1993.
18' catboat. Renewed deck and horn timber. Applied AwlGrip finish. 1991.

Yard Information
Services
    Marina facilities
    Launching facilities
    Overland transport
    Engine repair
    Rigging
Storage
    Maximum size for hauling and storing: 75' LOA, 12' draft, 50 tons
Maintenance
    Number of boats maintained per year: 300
    Percentage of wooden boats: 5
    Owner maintenance allowed above rail.
Retail supplies:
    Some general repair materials. Limited supply of retail items.

FIDDLEHEAD BOATWORKS

Mike Collins
2905 Overland Ave.
Baltimore, MD 21244

Builder Information
Years in business: 30
Carpenters employed: 2
Shop capacity: 36'
Willing to travel for on-the-site building projects.

Recent New Construction
7' wood/epoxy child's canoe Kidkano. Glen-L Marine and Phil Bolger design. 6 built 1990–'92.
17' wood/canvas Butternut canoe. Traditional design. 2 built 1992–'93.

Recent Repair Projects
13'–18' wood/canvas canoes. Completely restored 30 boats 1990–'93.
19' Century Resorter. Renewed transom, frames, and engine bed. Stripped and varnished exterior. 1990.

Yard Information
Services
Maintenance
    Number of boats maintained per year: 2-3
    Percentage of wooden boats: 100

HUDDLESTUN COLD-MOLDED CATBOATS

Bernard P. Huddlestun
14041 Triadelphia Rd.
Glenelg, MD 21737
410-489-5289

Builder Information
Years in business: 20
Carpenters employed: 1
Shop capacity: 24'

Recent New Construction
16' cold-molded catboat. Bernard Huddlestun design. Current project.
20' cold-molded catboat. Bernard Huddlestun design. Built 1992.
7' plywood pram. Schott design. Built 1992.

Recent Repair Projects
18' catboat. Redesigned and built cabintop and hatch. 1990.

INT'L. HISTORICAL WATERCRAFT SOCIETY

Melbourne Smith
P.O. Box 54
Annapolis, MD 21404
410-544-2591 Fax: 410-544-2698

Builder Information
Years in business: 30
Carpenters employed: 1-30
Shop capacity: Any size
Willing to travel for on-the-site building projects.

Recent New Construction
114' 3-ton brigantine. Melbourne Smith design. Built 1990–'91.
(continues)

(Int'l. Historical Watercraft Society, continued)
Yard Information
Services
 Sail repair
 Rigging

◼ ISLAND POINT CONSTRUCTION

Stephen Marks
2428 Lodge Farm Rd.
Baltimore, MD 21219

Builder Information
Years in business: 10
Carpenters employed: 1
Shop capacity: 40'
Willing to travel for on-the-site building projects.

Recent New Construction
Company specializes in the construction of wooden boats
 under 25'. All methods of construction utilized.

Recent Repair Projects
28' Herreshoff Rozinante canoe yawl. Renewing planking,
 deck, house, cockpit. Refinishing interior. Current
 project.
36' Tor sloop. Repaired hull and deck and refinished. 1992.

Yard Information
Services
 Marina facilities
 Launching facilities
Storage
 Number of boats stored per year: 40
 Percentage of wooden boats: 15
 Maximum size for hauling and storing: 30' LOA, 2'6"
  draft, 8 tons
Maintenance
 Number of boats maintained per year: 2-3
 Percentage of wooden boats: 100
 Owner maintenance allowed above and below rail.

◼ JAMES BOATWORKS

Gary James
5831 Hudson Wharf Rd.
Cambridge, MD 21613
410-221-0744

Builder Information
Years in business: 16
Carpenters employed: 1-3
Shop capacity: 45'

Recent New Construction
20' deadrise sailing skiff. 1918 design. Current project.
16' lapstrake plywood Whisp skiff. Steve Redmond design.
 Built 1991.

Recent Repair Projects
39' deadrise workboat. Replacing stem, forward deck, rail,
 and guard. Current project.

36' deadrise cruiser. Recanvased decks and cabintop.
 Refinished. 1993.
36' Egg Harbor cruiser. Refastened hull and completely
 refinished exterior. Rebuilt pilothouse windshield.
 1993.
38' Chris-Craft power cruiser. Rebuilt interior. 1992.
42' sportfisherman. Repaired and modified cabin and pilothouse. 1992.
36' Chris-Craft Constellation (1957). Replaced teak deck
 and rebuilt lower windshields. Sheathed cabintop in
 fiberglass and AwlGripped. 1991.
40' deadrise sportfisherman. Renewed stem, windshield,
 cabintop, bottom planking, chine log, and guardrail.
 Repowered. 1990.

Yard Information
Services
 Maximum size for hauling and storing: 45' LOA, 3'6"
  draft, 12 tons
Maintenance
 Number of boats maintained per year: 12
 Percentage of wooden boats: 75
 Owner maintenance allowed on limited basis.
Retail supplies:
 Materials for boatbuilding and repair.

◼ TIMOTHY M. KERNS

Timothy M. Kerns
49 College Ave.
Annapolis, MD 21401
410-267-8360 Fax: same

Builder Information
Years in business: 15
Carpenters employed: 2
Shop capacity: Any size
Willing to travel for on-the-site building projects.

Recent Repair Projects
Company offers both hands-on work and complete project
 management for power and sailing vessels. Expertise in
 refinishing with all types of varnish, stain, and paint,
 including AwlGrip. Current/recent projects:
57' Trumpy motoryacht (1958). Various repairs and complete refinishing. Renewing electrical and plumbing
 systems, and repowering.
22' Crosby tugboat. Completely refinishing.
30' Herreshoff. Completely refinishing.
45' Chris-Craft power cruiser. Replaced bottom planking
 as needed.

Yard Information
Services
 Marina facilities
 Moorage
 Engine repair
 Rigging
Storage
 Number of boats stored per year: varies
 Inside storage facilities
 Maximum size for hauling and storing: Inquire

Maintenance
Number of boats maintained per year: 20
Percentage of wooden boats: 40

 ## M.W. LOWERY BOAT YARD

Maynard W. Lowery
Box 266
Tilghman, MD 21671
410-886-2268

Builder Information
Years in business: 44
Carpenters employed: 1
Shop capacity: 53′

Recent New Construction
16′ catboat. Fenwick Williams design. 2 built 1993.

Recent Repair Projects
38′ crab/oyster boat. Replaced decks and cabin. 1993.

 ## MAROLINA YACHTS

Bo Toeffer
1410 Foxtail Lane
Prince Frederick, MD 20678
410-257-9075

Builder Information
Years in business: 4
Carpenters employed: 1
Shop capacity: 43′
Willing to travel for on-the-site building projects.

Recent New Construction
12′6″ plywood duckboat. Glen-L Marine design. Built 1994.
29′ cold-molded sportfisherman. David Martin design. Built 1993.

Recent Repair Projects
57′ motoryacht. Renewed companionway. 1993.

Yard Information
Services
Overland transport
Maintenance
Number of boats maintained per year: Varies
Retail supplies:
Wood, epoxy, paint.

 ## MAST AND MALLET, INC.

Joe Reid
1014 Benning Rd., P.O. Box 151
Galesville, MD 20765
410-867-1587 Fax: same

Builder Information
Years in business: 9
Carpenters employed: 4
Shop capacity: 40′
Willing to travel for on-the-site building projects.

Recent New Construction
30′ cold-molded Chesapeake Bay lobster yacht. Mike Kaufman design. Built 1993.
22′ modified Chesapeake crab-scrape boat. Cold-molded bottom and planked topsides. Joe Reid design. 4 built to date.
24′ Martha Green power cruiser. William Atkin design. Built 1990.

Recent Repair Projects
68′ Trumpy motoryacht (1955). Renewed frames and 50% of planking. 1993.
17′ Chris-Craft Deluxe Runabout (1948). Renewed topsides, deck, and transom. 1993.
47′ ketch (1954). Installed new hull blocks and deck carlins. Renewed spars. 1993.
17′ Chris-Craft Barrelback Runabout. Completely restored. Cold-molded bottom, renewed deck and interior. 1992.

Yard Information
Services
Overland transport
Storage
Number of boats stored per year: 4
Percentage of wooden boats: Varies
Maximum size for hauling and storing: 40′ LOA, 6′ draft
Maintenance
Number of boats maintained per year: 40-60
Percentage of wooden boats: 75
Owner maintenance allowed.
Retail supplies:
Wood.

O'CONNELL'S WOODEN BOATS

Marc Barto
303 Cannon St.
Chestertown, MD 21620
410-778-0012

Builder Information
Years in business: 10
Carpenters employed: 2
Shop capacity: 30′
Willing to travel for on-the-site building projects.

Recent New Construction
15′ cold-molded catboat. Joel White design. 2 built 1990 and 1993.
8′ cold-molded sailing dinghy. Marc Barto design. 4 built 1993.
17′ lapstrake pulling boat. Herreshoff design. Built 1992.
10′ lapstrake tender. Herreshoff design. Built 1992.
13′6″ lapstrake Melon Seed sailing skiff. Traditional design. 3 built 1990–'92.
14′ plywood garvey. Marc Barto design. Built 1992.
12′ lapstrake Acorn skiff. Iain Oughtred design. Built 1991.
(continues)

(O'Connell's Wooden Boats, continued)

Recent Repair Projects

25' Folkboat KIMBERLY. Renewing frames, 2 planks, and keelbolts. Refinishing. Current project.

36' Alden ketch. Renewing cabin joinery, refinishing. Current project.

64' racing shell. Structural cold-molding. 1993.

85' schooner ALEXANDRIA. Replaced 2 planks. 1993.

12' Beetle Cat. Renewed stem, centerboard, rudder. 1993.

19' catboat BUXOM LASS. Replaced spars. 1992.

19' power dory. Replaced bottom and garboard planks. 1992.

Yard Information

Retail supplies:

Bronze hardware. Custom patternmaking and casting.

■ R.J. PELASARA

R.J. Pelasara
15708 Thompson Rd.
Silver Spring, MD 20905
301-384-4464 Fax: 301-384-5871

Builder Information

Years in business: 10
Carpenters employed: 1
Shop capacity: 30'
Willing to travel for on-the-site building projects.

Recent New Construction

13', 15', and 17' strip-planked canoes. J.H. Rushton designs. 3 built 1992–'93.

Recent Repair Projects

19' Lightning-class sloops. Repair work has involved deck, frame, and plank replacement, rig renewal, and refinishing. 3 boats repaired during 1993.

Yard Information

Services
    Rigging
Storage
    Number of boats stored per year: 4
    Percentage of wooden boats: 50
    Maximum size for hauling and storing: 25' LOA, 3' draft, 2 tons
Maintenance
    Number of boats maintained per year: 2
    Percentage of wooden boats: 100

■ PEREGRINE WOODWORKS, INC.

Peter Boudreau, Paul Powichroski, and
LeRoy Surosky
1000 Key Highway East
Baltimore, MD 21230
410-727-7472 Fax: 410-727-1396

Builder Information

Years in business: 10
Carpenters employed: 5

Shop capacity: 150'
Willing to travel for on-the-site building projects.

Recent New Construction

100' topsail schooner PRIDE OF BALTIMORE II. Thomas Gillmer design.

Recent Repair Projects

36' Ohlson 36 yawl. Replacing stem, repairing cockpit and spar. Current project.

56' Pacemaker motoryacht. Renewing planks and floor timbers. Current project.

100' topsail schooner PRIDE OF BALTIMORE II. Laminated new main topmast, installed miscellaneous equipment, aligned shaft. Repaired foremast, recaulked aft cabintop, completed miscellaneous repairs. Winters, 1991–'93.

130' schooner NEW WAY (formerly WESTERN UNION). Replaced portions of shelf and clamp. Repaired planking and decks. 1990 and 1993.

45' skipjack MINNIE V. Laminated new fir mast, renewed bulwarks, foredeck, and maststep. 1992–'93.

131' barkentine GAZELA PHILADELPHIA. Replaced stem, frames, planking, transom, and mizzenmast. Major restoration project. 1991–'92.

75' pungy schooner LADY MARYLAND. Repaired mainmast and foremast. Renewed deck. 1991–'92.

Yard Information

Services
    Rigging
Maintenance
    Number of boats maintained per year: 4-5
    Percentage of wooden boats: 100

■ CLARK POSTON

Clark Poston
P.O. Box 1452
Annapolis, MD 21401
410-867-0042

Builder Information

Years in business: 12
Carpenters employed: 1
Shop capacity: Any size
Willing to travel for on-the-site building projects.

Recent New Construction

18' hunting skiff. Clark Poston design. Built 1993.

8' and 10' lapstrake prams. L.F. Herreshoff designs. 2 built 1993.

16'10" lapstrake Piscataqua River wherry. Traditional design. Built 1993.

46' strip-planked sloop. Interior finishing. C.W. Payne design. 1992.

36' sloop. Nat Benjamin design. Built 1991.

10' tender. Nat Benjamin design. 4 built 1990.

Recent Repair Projects

60' motoryacht. Renewed interior. 1993.

50' Hooper Island Draketail launch. Renewed frames, planking, caulking, deck, stem, and rails. 1993.

35' Hooper Island Draketail launch. Renewed planking and caulking, horn timber, and stem. 1993.

60' C.E. Nicholson gaff cutter (1896). Complete restoration. Renewed frames, fastenings, caulking, deck, interior, stem, sternpost, and rig. 1991.

225' C.E. Nicholson schooner CREOLE. Repaired forward bulwarks, reseated bowsprit. 1990.

14' C.E. Nicholson lapstrake tender. Renewed frames and garboards. 1990.

28' cutter. Renewed stem, planking, deck, interior, rig, and engine. 1990.

■ ALLEN C. RAWL, INC.

Allen C. Rawl
11314 Reynolds Rd., P.O. Box 2
Bradshaw, MD 21021
410-592-2170 Fax: 410-592-3344

Builder Information
Years in business: 17
Carpenters employed: 1-16
Shop capacity: Any size
Willing to travel for on-the-site building projects.

Recent New Construction
90' 17th-century, 3-masted bark replica SUSAN CON-STANT. Stanley Potter design. Built 1991.

Recent Repair Projects
Repair or restoration of the following boats:
49' Chesapeake Bay skipjack (1955). 1993.
74' yawl (1947). 1993.
74' ketch (1920). 1992.

Yard Information
Services
 Engine repair
 Sail repair
 Rigging

■ RIVERS EDGE BOATS

John E. Swain
31638 W. Edge Rd.
Millington, MD 21651
410-928-3553

Builder Information
Years in business: 27
Carpenters employed: 1-4
Shop capacity: 60'
Willing to travel for on-the-site building projects.

Recent New Construction
45' plywood/epoxy 3-masted sharpie-schooner. John Swain design. Current project.

23' strip-planked Blue Moon cutter. Thomas Gillmer design. Third boat completed in 1990.

Recent Repair Projects
50' Nova Scotia schooner. Replacing 40 frames, transom, sternpost, deck, sheer clamp, and cabin. 1991-current.

25'3" Iversen International 25. Replaced keel, floors, and frames. Resheathed deck and cabintop. 1993.

28' Winslow Four-Sum sloop. Replaced keel, floors, frames, and transom. Resheathed deck. 1992.

45' Chesapeake Bay buy boat. Replaced bottom and garboard planks. Renewed interior, engine, masts, and rigging. 1992.

30' Winslow ketch. Replaced planks, rubrail, and toerail. 1992.

40' ketch. Renewed cabintop. 1992.

50' trawler. Built pilot berth, TV cabinet, and icebox. 1991.

Yard Information
Services
 Rigging
Storage
 Number of boats stored per year: 3
 Percentage of wooden boats: 100
 Maximum size for hauling and storing: 60' LOA, 4' draft, 18 tons
Maintenance
 Number of boats maintained per year: 10
 Percentage of wooden boats: 100
 Owner maintenance allowed above and below rail.

■ RUMERY'S BOAT YARD

Gregory C. Carroll
P.O. Box L, 109 Cleaves St.
Biddeford, MD 04005
207-282-0408 Fax: 207-283-0057

Builder Information
Years in business: 30
Carpenters employed: 2
Shop capacity: 55'

Recent Repair Projects
41' Concordia sloop. Repairing broken frames, replacing floors, keelbolts, some deadwood, and planking. Current project.

39' Concordia yawl. Repaired broken frames. Installed longer maststep. Repowered and rewired. 1993.

36' Aage Nielsen double-ended sloop. Replaced after deck and structural members. Built custom teak cockpit and new coamings. 1992.

40' Rhodes/Cheoy Lee Reliant sloop. Renewed cabin sides and coamings. Reseamed teak decks. Built new boom, installed new engine, wiring, and plumbing. 1992.

33' Herreshoff Araminta ketch. Built interior to a design by Robert Mason. Installed engine and systems. 1991-'92.

Yard Information
Services
 Marina facilities
 Launching facilities
 Engine repair
 Rigging
Storage
 Number of boats stored per year: 65
 Percentage of wooden boats: 15
(continues)

(Rumery's Boat Yard, continued)
    Inside storage facilities
    Maximum size for hauling and storing: 55' LOA, 25
       tons
Maintenance
    Number of boats maintained per year: 15-20
    Percentage of wooden boats: 70
    Owner maintenance allowed above rail.
Retail supplies:
    Fully stocked ship's store.

■ UP THE CREEK BOATWORKS

Charles Gilless
Riverside Dr., Box 265
Galesville, MD 20765
410-867-1318

Builder Information
Years in business: 18
Carpenters employed: 2-3
Shop capacity: 50'
Willing to travel for on-the-site building projects.

Recent New Construction
20' vacuum-bagged, vari-camber trailerable trimaran.
    Chris White design. 3 built 1987–'89.

Recent Repair Projects
32' Stadel/Jones gaff sloop. Renewed bulwarks, caprail,
    covering boards, cockpit, afterdeck, transom, and tran-
    som framing. 1993.
26' Herreshoff Alerion-class sloop. Replaced centerboard
    trunk and sections of deck. Recaulked. 1993.
38' Chesapeake Bay workboat. Replaced bad bottom
    planking and recaulked. 1993.
39'11" Wiley trawler SWEET & LOW. Renewed sheer in
    cockpit area and sheathed decks with plywood and
    fiberglass. Renewed bulwarks, toerails, and bowsprit.
    Refinished hull. 1993.

Yard Information
Services
    Marina facilities
    Launching facilities
    Engine repair
    Rigging
Storage
    Number of boats stored per year: 120
    Percentage of wooden boats: 10
    Inside storage facilities
    Maximum size for hauling and storing: 50' LOA, 6'6"
      draft, 30 tons
Maintenance
    Number of boats maintained per year: 20
    Percentage of wooden boats: 50
    Owner maintenance allowed above and below rail.
Retail supplies:
    Wood, fastenings, paint, and fiberglassing supplies.

■ WIKANDER YACHT YARD, INC.

Stuart A. Wikander
3178 Windrows Way
Eden, MD 21822
410-749-9521

Builder Information
Years in business: 14
Carpenters employed: 1
Shop capacity: 45'

Recent New Construction
16' Wicomico River rowing skiff. Wood/epoxy construc-
    tion. Stuart Wikander design. Built 1994.

Recent Repair Projects
41' Chris-Craft double-cabin cruiser. Replacing sections of
    hull and refastening. Completely refinishing topsides
    and superstructure. Current project.
30' Owens (1966). Refastened and recaulked bottom.
    Refinished topsides. 1993.

Yard Information
Services
    Marina facilities
    Launching facilities
    Engine repair
    Rigging
Storage
    Number of boats stored per year: 30
    Percentage of wooden boats: 10
    Maximum size for hauling and storing: 45' LOA, 6'
      draft, 25 tons
Maintenance
    Number of boats maintained per year: 70
    Percentage of wooden boats: 10
    Owner maintenance allowed above and below rail.
Retail supplies:
    Fastenings, paint, and other supplies.

■ YACHT MAINTENANCE CO. INC.

Charles R. Smith III
101 Hayward St.
Cambridge, MD 21613
410-228-8878 Fax: 410-228-4216

Builder Information
Years in business: 20
Carpenters employed: 3-10
Shop capacity: 125'
Willing to travel for on-the-site building projects.

Recent Repair Projects
70' Trumpy motoryacht. Replaced sternpost. Completely
    refinished. 1993.
85' Trumpy motoryacht. Replaced garboards, 45 frames.
    Refastened. 1993.
65' converted shrimp trawler. Repaired extensive fire dam-
    age, installed new flying bridge, refinished. 1993.
56' Elco cruiser. Repaired extensive rot in cabin and deck,
    completely refinished. 1993.

Yard Information

Services

Marina facilities

Launching facilities

Moorage

Engine repair

Rigging

Storage

Number of boats stored per year: 100

Percentage of wooden boats: 10

Inside storage facilities

Maximum size for hauling and storing: 120' LOA, 10' draft, 200 tons

Maintenance

Number of boats maintained per year: 200

Percentage of wooden boats: 15

Owner maintenance allowed above and below rail.

Retail supplies:

Extensive inventory of supplies.

■ AREY'S POND BOATYARD

Tony Davis
45 Arey's Lane
South Orleans, MA 02662
508-255-0994 Fax: 508-255-8977

Builder Information

Years in business: 12

Carpenters employed: 3

Shop capacity: 30'

Recent New Construction

9'6" plywood/epoxy flat-bottomed skiff. Arno Day design. 12 built 1991–'93.

11' plywood/epoxy flat-bottomed rowing and sailing skiff. Arno Day design. 3 built 1991–'93.

Recent Repair Projects

Company has completed over 29 major restoration projects in last several years, including the following:

15' Barber runabout. Current project.

19' Simmons Sea Skiff. Renewing stem and deck, sheathing bottom in fiberglass and refinishing. Current project.

23' Dunbar Monomoy sloop. Renewed frames, keel, transom, and 40% of planking. 1992–'93, and ongoing.

20' Controversy sloop. Completed hull, bottom, and deck repairs. Refinished. 1992–'93.

35' Dickerson ketch. Replaced bilge stringer and bottom planking. 1992.

24' Lyman cruiser. Refinished brightwork, built doors and shelves. 1991–'92.

Yard Information

Services

Launching facilities

Overland transport

Moorage

Engine repair

Sail repair

Rigging

Storage

Number of boats stored per year: 65

Percentage of wooden boats: 5

Inside storage facilities

Maximum size for hauling and storing: 50' LOA, 5' draft, 20 tons

Maintenance

Number of boats maintained per year: 300

Percentage of wooden boats: 30

Owner maintenance allowed above and below rail.

Retail supplies:

Full line of sailboat hardware, fastenings, paint, varnish, engine parts, cleaning equipment, and cordage.

■ ATLANTIC BOAT WORKS

Bill McLearn
7 "Y" St.
Hull, MA 02045
617-925-0708 Fax: 617-925-9686

Builder Information

Years in business: 18

Carpenters employed: 1

Shop capacity: 36'

Willing to travel for on-the-site building projects.

Recent New Construction

26' Thunderbird-class sloop. Plywood/fiberglass construction. Ben Seaborn design. Built 1993.

12' DN iceboat. Planked/plywood construction. 4 built 1991–'92.

(continues)

(Atlantic Boat Works, continued)
Yard Information
Services
  Rigging
Maintenance
  Number of boats maintained per year: 12
  Percentage of wooden boats: 90

■ BALLENTINE'S BOAT SHOP, INC.

Stephen Ballentine
1104 Rte. 28A
Cataumet, MA 02534
508-563-2800 Fax: 508-564-5412

Builder Information
Years in business: 20
Carpenters employed: 2
Shop capacity: 45'

Recent New Construction
32' Buzzards Bay 25-class sloop. N.G. Herreshoff design.
  Current project.

Recent Repair Projects
36' Herreshoff Newport 29-class sloop. Completely
  rebuilding, including keel replacement and renewal of
  frames and planking. Current project.
16' Herreshoff 12-1/2s. Complete restoration of 4 boats,
  1990–'93.
33' Nielsen yawl. Repaired planking, refastened bottom.
  Renewed housetop, sheathed with Dynel, replaced
  moldings. 1992.
24' catboat. Renewed keel, frames, centerboard, trunk, and
  rudder. 1992.

Yard Information
Services
  Engine repair
  Rigging
Storage
  Number of boats stored per year: 75
  Percentage of wooden boats: 60
  Inside storage facilities
  Maximum size for hauling and storing: 45' LOA, 6'
    draft, 15 tons
Maintenance
  Number of boats maintained per year: 80
  Percentage of wooden boats: 60

■ LESLIE BEAVAN

Leslie Beavan
607 Setucket Rd.
South Dennis, MA 02660
508-385-3470

Builder Information
Years in business: 18
Carpenters employed: 1
Shop capacity: 35'

Recent New Construction
8' plywood pram. John Gardner design. Built 1991.
Recent new construction has been mostly subcontract carpentry work for other boatshops in the area.

Recent Repair Projects
47' yawl. Remodeled cabin. 1993.
16' catboat. Refastened hull, refinished. 1992.

■ BEETLE, INC.

Charles F. York
313 Smith Neck Rd.
South Dartmouth, MA 02748
508-996-9971

Builder Information
Years in business: 73
Carpenters employed: 4
Shop capacity: 12'4"

Recent New Construction
12'4" Beetle Cat catboats. John Beetle design from 1920.
  15 built 1993.

Recent Repair Projects
Beetle Cats. Everything from minor repairs to complete
  rebuilding.

Yard Information
Services
  Launching facilities
  Overland transport
  Sail repair
  Rigging
Storage
  Number of boats stored per year: 60
  Percentage of wooden boats: 100
  Inside storage facilities
  Maximum size for hauling and storing: 12'4"; storage
    for Beetle Cats only
Maintenance
  Number of boats maintained per year: 80
  Percentage of wooden boats: 100
Retail supplies:
  All parts, supplies, and accessories for Beetle Cats.

■ BROWNELL BOAT YARD INC.

Jay Parker
1 Park St., P.O. Box 744
Mattapoisett, MA 02739-0744
508-758-3671 Fax: 508-758-3574

Builder Information
Years in business: 40
Carpenters employed: 3
Shop capacity: 52'+

Recent New Construction
52' cold-molded sportfisherman. McInnis & Brownell
  design. Current project.

Recent Repair Projects

44' BBY 44 sportfisherman. Completely renewed and repowered. 1993.

50' BBY 50 sportfisherman. Repowered and upgraded. 1992.

Yard Information

Services
Launching facilities
Overland transport
Moorage
Engine repair
Rigging
Storage
Number of boats stored per year: 75
Percentage of wooden boats: 20
Inside storage facilities
Maximum size for hauling and storing: 50' LOA, 7' draft, 60 tons
Maintenance
Number of boats maintained per year: 100
Percentage of wooden boats: 50
Retail supplies:
Complete inventory of supplies.

■ WILLIAM CLEMENTS BOATBUILDER

William Clements
18 Mt. Pleasant St., P.O. Box 87
North Billerica, MA 01862
508-663-3103

Builder Information

Years in business: 13
Carpenters employed: 1
Shop capacity: 20'

Recent New Construction

Boats of lapstrake plywood construction:
12'10" Rob Roy-type, decked, double-paddle canoe. R.D. Culler/William Clements design. Built 1993.
13' open double-paddle canoe. R.D. Culler design. Built 1993.
13' canoe yawl. George Holmes design. 2 built 1991–'92.
15'8" sailing canoe. J.H. Rushton design. Built 1992.
18' sailing canoe. Lines from W.P. Stephens. Built 1990.

Recent Repair Projects

13'–25' canoes. Work ranges from minor repairs to major restorations. About 15 projects a year.

■ CONCORDIA CO., INC.

Bob Ackland
South Wharf, P.O. Box P-203
South Dartmouth, MA 02748
508-999-1381 Fax: 508-999-0450

Builder Information

Years in business: 55
Carpenters employed: 5

Shop capacity: 60'
Willing to travel for on-the-site building projects.

Recent New Construction

12'4" Beetle Cat. John Beetle design. 13 built 1992–'93.

Recent Repair Projects

47' Stevens 47 sloop. Modified cabin, renewed all mechanical systems, refinished. 1993.
39'10" Concordia yawl. Completely rebuilt. 1993.
41' Concordia yawl. Renewed cockpit, planking, and frames. 1993.
39'10" Concordia yawl. Renewed cockpit. 1992.
48' Cheoy Lee ketch. Renewed bowsprit and metal work. Refinished. 1993.
Various repairs to other Concordia yawls. Several boats worked on, 1991–'93.

Yard Information

Services
Marina facilities
Launching facilities
Overland transport
Moorage
Engine repair
Sail repair
Rigging
Storage
Number of boats stored per year: 120
Percentage of wooden boats: 25
Inside storage facilities
Maximum size for hauling and storing: 60' LOA, 10' draft, 30 tons
Maintenance
Number of boats maintained per year: 200
Percentage of wooden boats: 15
Owner maintenance allowed on limited basis.
Retail supplies:
Wood, fastenings, paint, rigging supplies, and engine parts.

■ CROCKER'S BOAT YARD, INC.

Samuel Sturgis Crocker
15 Ashland Ave., P.O. Box 268
Manchester, MA 01944-0268
508-526-1971 Fax: 508-526-7625

Builder Information

Years in business: 49
Carpenters employed: 2
Shop capacity: 55'

Recent New Construction

30' tugboat. S.S. Crocker design. Built 1993.
34' sloop. S.S. Crocker design. Built 1991.
16' tender. Reproduction of classic design. Built 1991.

Recent Repair Projects

52' Eldredge-McInnis trawler-yacht. Replaced frames and bottom planking. 1993.
(continues)

(Crocker's Boat Yard, Inc., continued)

30'6" Yankee One-Design class. Replaced deckbeams and deck canvas. 1992–'93.

23' Crocker Stonehorse. Restored for Peabody Museum exhibit. 1992.

34' Hinckley Sou'wester. Replaced teak deck, stem, and some planking. 1991–'92.

Yard Information

Services
   Marina facilities
   Launching facilities
   Overland transport
   Moorage
   Engine repair
   Sail repair
   Rigging
Storage
   Number of boats stored per year: 85
   Percentage of wooden boats: 25
   Inside storage facilities
   Maximum size for hauling and storing: 55' LOA, 8' draft, 30 tons
Maintenance
   Number of boats maintained per year: 125
   Percentage of wooden boats: 25
   Owner maintenance allowed on limited basis.
Retail supplies:
   Complete inventory of supplies.

◾ F. J. DION YACHT YARD

Fred Atkins
23 Glendale St.
Salem, MA 01970
508-744-0844 Fax: 508-745-7258

Builder Information

Years in business: 80
Carpenters employed: 4
Shop capacity: 75'

Recent Repair Projects

46' Rhodes/Abeking sloop. Replaced deckbeams, teak housetop, galley, icebox, several interior bulkheads, and rudder. 1992–'93.

52' Luke/Nielsen yawl. Renewed bulwarks, railcaps, transom, and much of bottom planking. 1991–'92.

50' Hinckley 50. Laid new teak decks. 1992.

16' Herreshoff 12½. Repaired frames, refastened. Replaced coamings, sheathed foredeck with Dynel, completely refinished. 1991.

48' Abeking yawl (1946). Renewed interior, bulkheads, wiring, and plumbing. Refinished. 1990–'92.

36' Derecktor Gulfstream 36. Sheathed decks with Dynel, renewed floor timbers, engine bed, keelbolts, 25% of bottom planking, transom, coamings, and boom. 1990–'92.

53' Luke Bros. cutter (1938). Rebuilt new fo'c's'le, head, and related cabinetry. Refinished. 1990.

Yard Information

Services
   Launching facilities
   Overland transport
   Moorage
   Engine repair
   Sail repair
   Rigging
Storage
   Number of boats stored per year: 100
   Percentage of wooden boats: 15
   Inside storage facilities
   Maximum size for hauling and storing: 60' LOA, 6' draft, 50 tons
Maintenance
   Number of boats maintained per year: 50
   Percentage of wooden boats: 30
Retail supplies:
   Complete inventory of supplies.

◾ ELDRED - COOPER BOATBUILDERS

Douglas E. Cooper
267 Sippewissett Rd.
Falmouth, MA 02540
508-548-2297

Builder Information

Years in business: 97
Carpenters employed: 3
Shop capacity: 45'

Recent New Construction

11'6" utility skiff. Lapstrake topsides and plywood bottom. W. Cooper design. 2 built 1992.

9'10" plywood/epoxy DC-10 sailing dinghy. D. Cooper design. 5 built 1990–'91.

Other new construction prior to 1990 included Gold Cup replica raceboat MISS COLUMBIA, a 38' Newick trimaran, and a 23' Cooper-designed catamaran.

Recent Repair Projects

26' cabin cruiser (1960). Replaced bottom planking, renewed teak cockpit sole, renewed brightwork. 1993.

16' Herreshoff 12½s. Complete or partial restorations. Frame, deck, transom, and coaming repairs. Refinishing. 4 boats rebuilt 1990–'93.

45' cruising sloop. Built new 56' hollow wooden mast. Renewed rigging. 1990.

32' raceboat SISTER SYN. Replaced engine beds and deckbeams. 1990.

Yard Information

Services
   Rigging
Maintenance
   Number of boats maintained per year: 12
   Percentage of wooden boats: 80

■ ROBERT ELLIOTT

Robert Elliott
47 Pleasant St., P.O. Box 796
Rowley, MA 01969
508-948-2389

Builder Information
Years in business: 19
Carpenters employed: 1
Shop capacity: 24′

Recent New Construction
14′ lapstrake dory. Traditional design. 4 built with students between 1990 and 1993.

Recent Repair Projects
13′6″ strip-planked Thompson lake skiff. Replaced planking, stem, skeg, and splash rail. 1993.

■ EUROPEAN CUSTOM YACHTS LTD.

Kaz Zatek
2358 Cranberry Highway
West Wareham, MA 02576
508-295-7445 Fax: same

Builder Information
Years in business: 30
Carpenters employed: 3
Shop capacity: 50′
Willing to travel for on-the-site building projects.

Recent New Construction
32′ cold-molded sharpie. Bruce Kirby design. Built 1993.

Recent Repair Projects
Complete refitting to Bristol condition of the following boats:
42′ New York 30-class sloop LINNET (1905). 1992-current.
46′ Palmer Johnson/Frers WHITE EAGLE (1976). 1990–'94.
42′ Wheeler sedan cruiser. 1990–'93.
40′ Rhodes 27 sloop. 1990–'92.
30′ Atlantic 30. 1991.
41′ Pacemaker power cruiser. 1990.

Yard Information
Services
 Engine repair
Storage
 Number of boats stored per year: 10
 Percentage of wooden boats: 50
 Inside storage facilities
 Maximum size for hauling and storing: 50′ LOA, 6′ draft, 25 tons
Maintenance
 Number of boats maintained per year: 10
 Percentage of wooden boats: 50
 Owner maintenance allowed on boats stored outside.

■ FLYER'S

Francis J. Santos
131A Commercial St., P.O. Box 561
Provincetown, MA 02657
508-487-0518

Builder Information
Years in business: 49
Carpenters employed: 2
Shop capacity: 65′

Recent Repair Projects
56′ commercial fishing vessel LIBERTY BELLE. Renewing stem, floor timbers, and planking. Current project.
60′ Desco commercial fishing vessel HIZZONNER. Retimbered and replanked port side. Replaced aft garboards. 1993.
56′ Lawley cabin cruiser VALJORA (1922). Recaulked and refastened struts as needed. Retimbered and rebuilt after compartment. 1992.

Yard Information
Services
 Marina facilities
 Launching facilities
 Moorage
 Engine repair
 Rigging
Storage
 Number of boats stored per year: 35
 Percentage of wooden boats: 45
 Maximum size for hauling and storing: 65′ LOA, 10′ draft, 70 tons
Maintenance
 Number of boats maintained per year: 60
 Percentage of wooden boats: 60
 Owner maintenance allowed above and below rail.
Retail supplies:
 Materials for boat repair and maintenance.

■ GANNON & BENJAMIN MARINE RAILWAY INC.

Ross M. Gannon and Nathaniel P. Benjamin
Beach Rd., Box 1095
Vineyard Haven, MA 02568
503-693-4658 Fax: 508-693-1818

Builder Information
Years in business: 20
Carpenters employed: 6
Shop capacity: 70′
Willing to travel for on-the-site building projects.

Recent New Construction
Boats designed by Nat Benjamin:
11′ lapstrake sailing skiff. Built 1993.
10′ tender for oar and sail. 3 built 1991–'92.
9′ tender. Built 1991.
(continues)

(Gannon & Benjamin Marine Railway Inc., continued)
30' yawl. Built 1991.
37' ketch. Built 1990.

Recent Repair Projects

22' Crosby catboat. Renewing keel, stem, frames, cockpit, planking, and engine. Current project.
28' bassboat. Replaced frames, transom, floors, keel, stem, cabin, and engine. 1993.
34' Burgess Six-Meter-class sloop. Renewed deck, frames, and keel. 1993.
30' Alden sloop. Renewed keelbolts and floor timbers. Sistered frames. 1992.
64' Alden schooner. Reframed 30' of hull and replaced 70% of planking. Renewed interior and tanks. Total rebuild. 1990–'94.
50' Alden schooner. Reframed 30' and replanked 70% of hull. Renewed clamps, hanging knees, and deckhouses. 1992.
72' Illingsworth yawl. Renewed deckhouses, hatches, engine, wiring, deck, and cockpit. Major restoration. 1987–'93.

Yard Information

Services
  Marina facilities
  Launching facilities
  Moorage
  Engine repair
  Sail repair
  Rigging
Storage
  Number of boats stored per year: 9
  Percentage of wooden boats: 100
  Maximum size for hauling and storing: 60' LOA, 8½' draft, 40 tons
Maintenance
  Number of boats maintained per year: 10
  Percentage of wooden boats: 100
  Owner maintenance allowed above and below rail.
Retail supplies:
  Good inventory of bronze, wood, and paint.

■ GILES RACING HYDROS

Bill Giles
626 School St.
North Dighton, MA 02764
508-823-5653 Fax: 508-824-5149

Builder Information

Years in business: 34
Carpenters employed: 1
Shop capacity: 24'

Recent New Construction

9'–11'6" APBA-class racing hydroplanes. Bill Giles designs. 13 built 1990–'93.

Recent Repair Projects

Specializes in the repair of 11'–13' APBA-class racing hydroplanes and runabouts. Several boats worked on each year.

■ HAVE TOOLS WILL TRAVEL

Gary Grinnell
Northampton, MA 01060
413-586-2007

Builder Information

Years in business: 7
Carpenters employed: 1
Willing to travel for on-the-site building projects.

Recent Repair Projects

19' center-console skiff. Renewed floor and center console. 1993.
18' Shark-class sloop. Replaced planking, bilge stringers, deck, transom, and bulkheads. Refinished. 1993.
37' Ohlson yawl. Renewed stem, transom, transom framing, planking, and frames. 1993.
40' Navy launch. Renewed planking. 1993.
16' Penn Yan skiff. Replaced floorboards and seats. Sheathed bottom in fiberglass. Refinished. 1992.
16' Chris-Craft runabout. Replaced planking, deck and deck framing, stem, and keel. 1992.
36' Chris-Craft power cruiser. Sistered frames. Renewed planking, bulkheads, transom and frame, deck and deck framing, cabin, and flying bridge. 1991–'92.

■ HINGHAM BOAT WORKS INC.

Robert E. Murray
2G Shipyard Dr.
Hingham, MA 02043
617-749-8868

Builder Information

Years in business: 14
Carpenters employed: 2
Shop capacity: 45'
Willing to travel for on-the-site building projects.

Recent Repair Projects

37' Uhlrichson power cruiser. Replacing 7 frames and 4 planks. Current project.
58' Chris-Craft power cruiser. Extensively restored. Renewed forward cabin, pilothouse, and flying bridge. 1993.
26' Lyman cruiser. Renewed deck, coaming, and windshield. 1993.
32' Dickerson ketch. Replaced 'midship planking and section of sheer clamp. 1992.
22' Lyman Sleeper. Replaced 6 frames and 5 planks. Repaired bow damage. 1991.
38' Jonesport lobsterboat. Repaired bilge fire damage. Renewed frames, planking, and section of keel. 1990.

■ LAUGHING LOON CUSTOM CANOES & KAYAKS

Rob Macks
833 Colrain Rd.
Greenfield, MA 01301
413-773-5375 Fax: same

Builder Information
Years in business: 2
Carpenters employed: 1
Shop capacity: 19'

Recent New Construction
Boats designed by Rob Macks for strip-planked construction:
18'4" baidarka-type sea kayak. Built 1993.
16'6" and 18'4" sea kayaks. Built 1991.
Other new construction:
10'8" strip-planked double-paddle canoe. J.H. Rushton design. Built 1991.

■ PERT LOWELL CO., INC.

Ralph F. Johnson, Jr.
Lane's End
Newburyport, MA 01951
508-462-7409 Fax: 508-465-1064

Builder Information
Years in business: 26
Carpenters employed: 2
Shop capacity: 24'

Recent New Construction
Company specializes in construction of 16'6" Town-class sloop. Lapstrake construction. Pert Lowell design.

Recent Repair Projects
Repair work has involved a little bit of everything.

Yard Information
Services
    Launching facilities
    Overland transport
    Engine repair
    Rigging
Storage
    Number of boats stored per year: 22
    Percentage of wooden boats: 50
    Maximum size for hauling and storing: 30' LOA, 5' draft, 2 tons
Maintenance
    Number of boats maintained per year: 12
    Percentage of wooden boats: 75
    Owner maintenance allowed above and below rail.
Retail supplies:
    Wood, fastenings, paint, hardware.

■ LOWELL'S BOAT SHOP

Gary Kincaid
459 Main St.
Amesbury, MA 01913
508-388-0162

Builder Information
Years in business: 20
Carpenters employed: 4
Shop capacity: 30'

Recent New Construction
8'9"-21' lapstrake dories. Lowell designs. 67 built 1990–'93.

Recent Repair Projects
Restoration and/or refinishing of the following boats during 1993:
16' Dodge Watercar (1926).
26' Monomoy Surfboat.
12' Penn Yan.
13' Whitehall.
22' steamboat (1910).
10' Captain's Gig.

Yard Information
Maintenance
    Number of boats maintained per year: 6-10
    Percentage of wooden boats: 100
Retail supplies:
    Complete inventory of supplies.

■ MANCHESTER MARINE

John Winder
17 Ashland Ave., Box 1469
Manchester, MA 01944
508-526-7911 Fax: 508-526-8638

Builder Information
Years in business: 50
Carpenters employed: 5
Shop capacity: 60'
Willing to travel for on-the-site building projects.

Recent Repair Projects
32' Norge sloop. Replacing deck and sheathing with Dynel. Current project.
39' Concordia yawl. Renewing keelbolts, maststep, and tierods. Installing carbon-fiber mast. Current project.
48' Alden Lady Helene ketch. Replacing 10 frames. Current project.
35' Hinckley Sou'wester. Laying new plywood deck with teak overlay, and sheathing housetop with Dynel. Replacing engine. Current project.
32' Norge sloop. Replaced keelbolts, refastened hull. Renewed house beams. 1992–'93.
46' Sparkman & Stephens sloop. Replaced housetop sheathing. Renewed cockpit seats and coamings. 1992–'93.
(continues)

(Manchester Marine, continued)
39′ Concordia yawl. Replaced 7 planks, 8 frames, covering board, toerails, and coamings. Sheathed deck with Dynel. 1991–′92.

Yard Information
Services
    Marina facilities
    Launching facilities
    Moorage
    Engine repair
    Rigging
Storage
    Number of boats stored per year: 180
    Percentage of wooden boats: 20
    Inside storage facilities
    Maximum size for hauling and storing: 70′ LOA, 12′ draft, 100 tons
Maintenance
    Number of boats maintained per year: 100
    Percentage of wooden boats: 30
    Owner maintenance allowed above and below rail.
Retail supplies:
    Ship's store. Complete inventory of supplies.

■ MARTHA'S VINEYARD SHIPYARD, INC.

Philip P. Hale, President
P.O. Box 1119, Beach Rd.
Vineyard Haven, MA 02568
508-693-0400 Fax: 508-693-4100

Builder Information
Years in business: 10
Carpenters employed: 1
Shop capacity: 50′
Willing to travel for on-the-site building projects.

Recent Repair Projects
16′ Herreshoff 12½. Plank and frame repairs, deck recanvasing. Approximately one boat worked on each year.
48′ Tancook schooner. Replaced planking and knees. 1992–′93.
42′ Stonington motorsailers. Plank, frame, and cockpit repairs. A few boats worked on each year.
32′ lobsterboat. Replaced foredeck and cabin superstructure. 1991.
18′–42′ sail and power boats. Rewiring and engine replacements. Several boats worked on each year.

Yard Information
Services
    Launching facilities
    Overland transport
    Moorage
    Engine repair
    Sail repair
    Rigging

Storage
    Number of boats stored per year: 65
    Percentage of wooden boats: 15
    Inside storage facilities
    Maximum size for hauling and storing: 50′ LOA, 8′ draft, 22½ tons
Maintenance
    Number of boats maintained per year: 125
    Percentage of wooden boats: 15
    Owner maintenance allowed above and below rail.
Retail supplies:
    Wood, fastenings, paint, charts, engine parts, rope, wire, electrical and plumbing parts.

■ G.S. MAYNARD & CO.

Gary S. Maynard
1 Water St., P.O. Box 2079
Vineyard Haven, MA 02568
508-693-5597

Builder Information
Years in business: 7
Carpenters employed: 2-4
Shop capacity: Any size
Willing to travel for on-the-site building projects.

Recent New Construction
14′ work skiffs. Maynard design. 3 built 1990.

Recent Repair Projects
8′ Bahama dinghy CHASER. Completely rebuilding. Current project.
48′ cutter MACNAB. Completely rebuilding. Current project.
30′ launch ACTIVE. Replaced floors and planking. 1993.
108′ passenger schooner SHENANDOAH. Rebuilt galley, made various repairs. 1992–′93.
80′ passenger schooner SYLVINA W. BEAL. Renewed interior joinerwork, hatches, and rigging. 1992.
45′ Scots Zulu VIOLET. Completely rebuilt and rerigged. Completed 1991.
63′ schooner WHEN & IF. Refastened hull, recaulked decks, renewed cockpit. Completely refinished. 1990.

Yard Information
Services
    Launching facilities
    Engine repair
    Sail repair
    Rigging
Storage
    Number of boats stored per year: 3
    Percentage of wooden boats: 100
    Inside storage facilities
    Maximum size for hauling and storing: 45′ LOA, 6′ draft, 25 tons
Maintenance
    Number of boats maintained per year: 5
    Percentage of wooden boats: 100
    Owner maintenance allowed above and below rail.

Retail supplies:
   Native and other lumber, stainless and bronze fastenings, paint, and other supplies.

■ DAMIAN McLAUGHLIN JR.

Damian McLaughlin
294 Sam Turner Rd., Box 538
North Falmouth, MA 02556
508-563-3075 Fax: 508-563-6542

Builder Information
Years in business: 23
Carpenters employed: 1-15
Shop capacity: 50'

Recent New Construction
30' cold-molded trimaran. Kurt Hughes design. Current project.
43' cold-molded cutter. Chuck Paine design. Built 1993.
15'6" plywood dory. Phil Bolger design. 3 built 1993.
12' cold-molded sailing dinghy. Modified N.G. Herreshoff design. Built 1992.

Yard Information
Services
   Engine repair
   Rigging

■ MONTGOMERY BOAT YARD

David H. Montgomery
29 Ferry St.
Gloucester, MA 01930
508-281-6524

Builder Information
Years in business: 89
Carpenters employed: 3
Shop capacity: 40'

Recent New Construction
8' plywood step-sharpie FLYING CLOUD. Phil Bolger design. Built 1993.
14'6" plywood Microtrawler step-sharpie. Phil Bolger design. Built 1993.
16' lapstrake plywood Spur II pulling boat. Phil Bolger design. Built 1992.
15'4" lapstrake plywood catboat SPARTINA. Phil Bolger design. Built 1992.
11' lapstrake sampan. R.D. Culler design. Built 1991.
19'6" plywood cat-yawl. Phil Bolger design. Built 1991.
30'4" gaff yawl. John Alden design. Built 1990.

Recent Repair Projects
15' Fish-class catboat. Recanvased deck. 1993.
18' Annisquam catboat. Refastened and recaulked hull. Renewed rig. 1993.
15' Fish-class catboat. Replaced planks, refastened and recaulked. 1992.
28' Friendship sloop. Renewed deck, cockpit, bulwarks. 1991.

Yard Information
Services
   Launching facilities
   Moorage
   Engine repair
   Sail repair
   Rigging
Storage
   Number of boats stored per year: 50
   Percentage of wooden boats: 60
   Inside storage facilities
   Maximum size for hauling and storing: 40' LOA, 6' draft, 12 tons
Maintenance
   Number of boats maintained per year: 12
   Percentage of wooden boats: 100
   Owner maintenance allowed above and below rail.

■ OLD WHARF DORY CO.

Walter Baron
RR #1, Old Chequessett Neck Rd.
Wellfleet, MA 02667
508-349-2383

Builder Information
Years in business: 16
Carpenters employed: 1
Shop capacity: 30'

Recent New Construction
11' Asa Thompson skiff. Lapstrake sides and plywood bottom. Built 1993.
16' plywood work skiff. Walter Baron design. Built 1993.
17' composite pulling boat. Jon Aborn design. Built 1993.
18' Greenland-style sea kayak. Composite construction. Walter Baron design. Built 1992.
8' plywood pram. Walter Baron design. 3 built 1990–'93.
10' plywood/epoxy V-bottomed skiff. Tracy O'Brien design. Built 1992.
18' plywood Norwalk Islands sharpie. Bruce Kirby design. Built 1990.

Recent Repair Projects
35' dragger. Rebuilt deck. 1993.
12' Beetle Cat. Recanvased deck, sistered frames. 1991.

Yard Information
Maintenance
   Number of boats maintained per year: 2
   Percentage of wooden boats: 100
Retail supplies:
   Wood, fastenings.

■ PRESERVATION SHIPYARD

Thomas A. Cavanaugh
44R Merrimac St.
Newburyport, MA 01950
508-463-0012 Fax: same

Builder Information
Years in business: 8
Carpenters employed: 2
Shop capacity: 65'

Recent Repair Projects
41' Chris-Craft power cruiser (1959). Renewing planking and joinerwork in bridge cabin. Refastening bottom. Current project.
35' Friendship sloop (1941). Renewing planking, stem, and rudder. Reginishing and refitting. Current project.
32' Trojan power cruiser (1962). Repairing chines, planking, and transom. Current project.
34' Elco Cruisette (1924). Completely restoring. Current project.
44' Palmer Johnson motorsailer. Replaced 12 planks and repaired stem. 1993.
27' William Hand power cruiser. Replaced cockpit roof, and installed new head and galley. 1990. Replaced aft keelson, rudder shaft, shaftlog, and cabin sides. 1993.
24' Crosby Striper bassboat (1957). Replaced chine logs, cockpit sole, and floor timbers. Partially refastened. Renewed engine. 1992.

■ REDD'S POND BOATWORKS

Thad Danielson
1 Norman St.
Marblehead, MA 01945
617-631-3443

Builder Information
Years in business: 13
Carpenters employed: 1
Shop capacity: 80'
Willing to travel for on-the-site building projects.

Recent New Construction
10'4" and 11'7" lapstrake Norwegian prams. Thad Danielson designs. Built 1992–'93.
9' lapstrake Norwegian design. A.E. Christensen design. Built 1991.
11'7" Columbia dinghy. N.G. Herreshoff design. 2 built 1993.

Recent Repair Projects
28' S-class sloop. Renewed coaming and cabin trunk. 1993.
12'4" Beetle Cat. Sistered frames, repaired carlin. Renewed planking and fastenings, deck, and canvas. 1993.
24' sloop. Restored companionway. 1993.
24' Alden/Gamage cutter. Renewed floors and engine bed. 1992.
30'6" Atlantic-class sloop. Renewed frames, floors, planking, deckbeams, deck, and canvas. 1991.

Yard Information
Services
    Rigging
Retail supplies:
    Wood and fastenings.

■ RIVENDELL MARINE

Tom Wolstenholme
304 Shore Rd., Box 926
Monument Beach, MA 02553
508-759-0330 Fax: same

Builder Information
Years in business: 18
Carpenters employed: 2
Shop capacity: 40'

Recent Repair Projects
34' Hinckley Sou'wester (1947). Replaced keel, deadwood, 32 frames, 16 floors. Repowered. 1993.
56' Hand schooner LOTUS (1917). Renewed stem, deckbeams and deck, knees, planks, frames, and bulwarks. Repowered and rewired. 1992–'93.
36' Giles ketch. Replaced frames, recanvased cabintop, repowered. 1992.
46' Granks Banks trawler-yacht ALASKAN. Rebuilt starboard teak deck, cold-molded breakwater, and planked up bulwarks. Renewed much of planking. 1991.
35' Concordia sloop. Renewed frames and floors, replaced deck, covering boards, and cabintops. 1991.

■ ROSS BROS.

Robert P. Ross
28 N. Maple St.
Florence, MA 01060
413-586-3875 Fax: 413-586-5686

Builder Information
Years in business: 10
Carpenters employed: 2
Shop capacity: 20'

Recent Repair Projects
Complete restoration of the following boats:
7'6" Old Town dinghy. 2 boats repaired. Current project and 1993.
17' Gerrish canoe. Current project.
16' Old Town Abercrombie. Current project.
11'6" Old Town dinghy. 1993.
16' Waltham canoe. 1993.

Yard Information
Services
    Overland transport
Storage
    Number of boats stored per year: 40
    Percentage of wooden boats: 95
    Maximum size for hauling and storing: 20' LOA, 3' draft, 2 tons

Maintenance
    Number of boats maintained per year: 10
    Percentage of wooden boats: 100
Retail supplies:
    Hardware for antique wooden boats.

■ SHAW'S BOAT YARD, INC.

Thomas and Guy Ransley
86 Main St.
Dighton, MA 02715
508-669-5714 Fax: 508-669-6885

Builder Information
Years in business: 62
Carpenters employed: 3
Shop capacity: 60'
42' Matthews Sedan cruiser (1959). Renewing planking, frames, transom, and deck. Current project.
26' MacKenzie Cuttyhunk bassboat. Renewed cockpit, stern, rails, windshield, and engine. AwlGripped hull. 1991–'93.
40' Fleetwing cruiser (1929). Replaced stem, keel, stern, planking.
36' Egg Harbor Sedan cruiser (1962). Renewed planking and deck. Installed stove, plumbing, and windlass. AwlGripped hull.

Yard Information
Services
    Marina facilities
    Moorage
    Engine repair
Storage
    Number of boats stored per year: 125
    Percentage of wooden boats: 50
    Maximum size for hauling and storing: 50' LOA, 6' draft, 30 tons
Maintenance
    Number of boats maintained per year: 25
    Percentage of wooden boats: 50
    Owner maintenance allowed.
Retail supplies:
    Wood, fastenings, paint, hardware, WEST System supplies, rope, engine parts, accessories. Special orders welcome.

■ SOUTH SHORE BOATWORKS

Bob Fuller
Elm St., P.O. Box 29
Hanson, MA 02341
617-293-2293 Fax: 617-293-7370

Builder Information
Years in business: 4
Carpenters employed: 2
Shop capacity: 25'
Willing to travel for on-the-site building projects.

Recent New Construction
14' plywood/epoxy Sea-Tamer sea kayak. Alan Lutz design. 3 built 1993.
17' plywood/epoxy Sea-Tamer sea kayak. Charles and Bob Fuller design. 50 built 1990–'93.
21' plywood/epoxy Sea-Tamer II tandem sea kayak. Alan Lutz design. 4 built 1993.
11' plywood/epoxy Lutz 3.4m cartopper sailing dinghy. Alan Lutz design. Built 1993.
19' plywood/epoxy Big Dory Banks dory. Phil Bolger design. Built 1992.
20' plywood/cold-molded steam launch. H.K. Anderson design. Built 1992.

Recent Repair Projects
11' peapod. Replaced seats. 1993.
26' Dutch ketch. Repaired keel, replaced hatches. 1993.

Yard Information
Maintenance
    Number of boats maintained per year: 4
    Percentage of wooden boats: 50
Retail supplies:
    Wood, fiberglass, epoxy, fastenings. Plans and kits for Sea-Tamer kayaks and Lutz cartopper dinghy.

■ STORY BOATBUILDING

Brad Story
66 John Wise Ave., Box 231
Essex, MA 01929
508-768-6291

Builder Information
Years in business: 18
Carpenters employed: 2
Shop capacity: 50'

Recent New Construction
53' strip/cold-molded power cruiser. Andre Mauric design. Current project.
24' plywood trimaran. Phil Bolger design. Built 1993.
32' carvel/glued plywood liveaboard power cruiser. Phil Bolger design. Built 1993.
20' lapstrake plywood Ov'nighter cat-ketch. Phil Bolger design. 2 built 1991.
17' knockabout. L.F. Herreshoff design. Built 1991.
42' lobsterboat/gillnetter. John Gilbert design. Built 1990.

Recent Repair Projects
25' Cape Cod catboat. Renewed deck, cockpit, cabintop. 1993.
48' lugger. Renewed deck and companionway shelter. 1992–'93.
51' lobsterboat. Replaced pilothouse and deck. 1992.
36' catboat. Rebuilt interior, renewed cockpit and trunk. Installed new engine. 1991–'92.

TRIAD BOATWORKS INC.

Seth Kohn, Greg Tuxworth, and Peter Costa
4 Fairhaven Rd., P.O. Box 1148
Mattapoisett, MA 02739
508-758-4224 Fax: 508-758-3882

Builder Information
Years in business: 20
Carpenters employed: 3
Shop capacity: 80'
Willing to travel for on-the-site building projects.

Recent New Construction
11' lapstrake sailing dinghy. N.G. Herreshoff design.
    Current project.
17' cold-molded Buzzards Bay 14. L.F. Herreshoff design.
    Current project.

Recent Repair Projects
25' Chris-Craft runabout. Built inlaid deck, replaced electrical system, refastened, and refinished. 1993.
39' Concordia yawl. Renewed teak deck, mast tie-rod system, deadwood, floors, cabin sole, and electronics. Refinished. 1990–'93.
41' Concordia sloop. Replaced mast. 1992.
52' Concordia schooner. Replaced masts. 1992.
33' Concordia sloop. Renewed cockpit, planking, and toerail. 1991–'92.
36' Sparkman & Stephens cold-molded sloop. Renewed cockpit, keel, deadwood, and planking. Refinished. 1991–'92.
39' Concordia yawl. Renewed cockpit, sheathed plywood deck with fiberglass. 1991–'92.

Yard Information
Services
    Overland transport
    Engine repair
    Rigging
Storage
    Number of boats stored per year: 50
    Percentage of wooden boats: 60
    Inside storage facilities
    Maximum size for hauling and storing: 60' LOA, 7½' draft, 30 tons
Maintenance
    Number of boats maintained per year: 20
    Percentage of wooden boats: 60
    Owner maintenance allowed above and below rail.

TRI-WERX

George M. Williams
324 Blacksmith Shop Rd.
East Falmouth, MA 02536
508-540-3608

Builder Information
Years in business: 11
Carpenters employed: 1
Shop capacity: 36'
Willing to travel for on-the-site building projects.

Recent New Construction
14'–24' plywood commercial work skiffs. George Williams design. 104 built to date.

Recent Repair Projects
14'–24' work skiffs. Rigging for different types of fishing gear, rail and stem repairs, hull fiberglassing.

Yard Information
Services
    Launching facilities
    Overland transport
    Engine repair
    Rigging
Storage
    Number of boats stored per year: 8
    Percentage of wooden boats: 100
    Maximum size for hauling and storing: 36' LOA
Maintenance
    Number of boats maintained per year: 6
    Percentage of wooden boats: 100
    Owner maintenance allowed above and below rail.
Retail supplies:
    Cleats, oarlocks, rope, resin, glue, and other materials.

VICTORY BOAT CO.

Gary Vantol
RR #2, Warwick Rd.
Athol, MA 01331
508-249-2121

Builder Information
Years in business: 20
Carpenters employed: 2-3
Shop capacity: 36'

Recent New Construction
16' Swampscott dory. Traditional design and construction.
9' cold-molded sailing pram. Modified H.I. Chapelle design.

Recent Repair Projects
14' True Amesbury skiff (1930s). Renewing bottom and refinishing. Current project.

WELLING BOAT CO.

Mark Welling
P.O. Box 483
Ipswich, MA 01938
508-356-1123

Builder Information
Years in business: 15
Carpenters employed: 2
Shop capacity: 60'
Willing to travel for on-the-site building projects.

Recent New Construction

15' batten-seamed mahogany runabout. Tom Doane design. Built 1993.

11'6" lapstrake plywood Shellback dinghy. Joel White design. 5 built 1993.

17' Buzzards Bay 14-class sloop. L.F. Herreshoff design. Built 1992.

Recent Repair Projects

38' Slocum Spray. Renewed deck, cabin, and interior. Repowered. 1993.

75' Fredonia schooner LETTIE G. HOWARD. Supervised planking crew. 1992.

36' Bolger trawler-yacht ODD LOT. Renewed deck, cabin, and interior. Repowered. 1991.

43' Chris-Craft Constellation. Replaced and AwlGripped superstructure. 1990.

71' Fife yawl HALLOWEEN. Installed interior systems and related joinerwork. 1990.

WOODEN TANGENT

David W. Peterson
60 Marion Rd.
Mattapoisett, MA 02739
508-758-9662

Builder Information

Years in business: 20
Carpenters employed: 1
Shop capacity: 60'
Willing to travel for on-the-site building projects.

Recent Repair Projects

24'10" Herreshoff E class. Rebuilding. Current project.

27'6" Herreshoff S-boat. Rebuilding. Current project.

39' Casey yawl (1940). Rebuilt house and cockpit. Sistered 46 frames, renewed planking, and recanvased deck. 1991–'93.

16' Herreshoff 12½s. 10 boats restored or repaired 1990–'93.

12'6" Beetle Cats. Various types of repair including plank and deck renewal. Several boats worked on 1990–'93.

24'10" Herreshoff E class. Completely rebuilt 2 boats, 1991–'93.

9' hydroplane (1954). Rebuilt cockpit and recanvased deck. 1990.

Yard Information

Services
    Rigging
Storage
    Number of boats stored per year: 10
    Percentage of wooden boats: 90
    Inside storage facilities
Maintenance
    Number of boats maintained per year: 10
    Percentage of wooden boats: 100
    Owner maintenance allowed on limited basis.

AU SABLE RIVERBOAT SHOP

Gary Willoughby
1678 Michelson
Ann Arbor, MI 49738
517-348-8485

Builder Information

Years in business: 12
Carpenters employed: 2
Shop capacity: 24'

Recent New Construction

24' plywood drift boat. 14 built to date.
14'–18' strip-planked canoes.

Recent Repair Projects

Repair work has involved wood/canvas canoes.

Yard Information

Services
    Launching facilities
Maintenance
    Number of boats maintained per year: 40
    Percentage of wooden boats: 40
Retail supplies:
    Wood.

BAD RIVER BOATWORKS

James M. Taber
17013 Marion
Brant, MI 48614
517-585-3514

Builder Information

Years in business: 8
Carpenters employed: 1
Shop capacity: 30'

Recent New Construction

10'8" strip-planked solo canoe. Built 1993.

Recent Repair Projects

Chris-Craft runabout (1947). Repaired chines, transom and deck framing. Replaced original hull planking with mahogany planking over plywood and epoxy, and finished bright. Renewed engine, rechromed hardware. 1991–'93.

(continues)

(Bad River Boatworks, continued)

Old Town runabout (1953). Repaired framing. Replaced hull canvas with epoxy and fiberglass, and finished bright. 1991.

21' Duke runabout (1956). Renewed keel, chines, and floors. Replaced bottom planking with plywood and fiberglass. Refastened, faired, and varnished topsides. 1989–'91.

BAKER'S CUSTOM CANOES & BOATS

Brian Baker
2670 Walter Rd.
Coleman, MI 48618
517-465-1497

Builder Information
Years in business: 40
Carpenters employed: 1
Shop capacity: Any size

Recent New Construction
34' Voyageur canoe replica. Brian Baker design. Built 1992.

Recent Repair Projects
12'–18' wood/canvas canoes and kayaks. Completely restores and refinishes approximately 6 or 7 boats each year.

Yard Information
Services
   Overland transport
Retail supplies:
   Paint, varnish, canvas, canoe paddles.

BETSIE BAY KAYAK

Alan R. Anderson
P.O. Box 1706
Frankfort, MI 49635
616-352-7774

Builder Information
Years in business: 8
Carpenters employed: 1
Shop capacity: 19'

Recent New Construction
Greenland-type sea kayaks designed by Alan Anderson for plywood construction:
19' Recluse kayak. 20 built 1990–'93.
17'11" Manitou kayak. 18 built 1990–'93.
17' Valkyrie kayak. 18 built 1990–'93.
16' Idun kayak. Built 1990–'93.
13'6" children's Miko kayak. 5 built 1990–'93.

BINGHAM BOAT WORKS LTD.

Joseph Bingham
HC 01, Box 58
Marquette, MI 49855
906-225-0050 Fax: 906-225-0604

Builder Information
Years in business: 64
Carpenters employed: 4
Shop capacity: 70'
Willing to travel for on-the-site building projects.

Recent Repair Projects
35' lobsterboat/cruiser. Replaced cabin, deck, and engine. 1993.
35' Chris-Craft Corinthian. Replaced bad wood on deck and cabintop. Renewed vinyl. Completely restored. 1993.
35' yawl. Replaced bulwarks, spindles, and taffrail. 1992.
44' Alden sloop. Replaced interior and deck. 1990.

Yard Information
Services
   Engine repair
   Rigging
Storage
   Number of boats stored per year: 32
   Percentage of wooden boats: 10
   Inside storage facilities
   Maximum size for hauling and storing: Inquire
Maintenance
   Number of boats maintained per year: 70-80
   Percentage of wooden boats: 15

CADILLAC BOAT SHOP

Russ Arrand
4081 E. 30 Rd.
Cadillac, MI 49601
616-779-0764

Builder Information
Years in business: 15
Carpenters employed: 1
Shop capacity: 24'

Recent Repair Projects
17' Chris-Craft Barrelstern (1941). Refastened sides, epoxied bottom. Rebuilt engine. Current project.
24' Chris-Craft Triple-Cockpit (1929). Refastened deck, replaced topside planking, refinished. 1992.
18' Century Arabian (1957). Tuned up, refinished. 1993.
20' Chris-Craft Riviera (1952). Replaced engine hatch, completely refinished. 1993.
20' Chris-Craft Continental (1961). Completely refinished. 1993.
22' Chris-Craft Utility (1950). Completely refinished. 1993.
17' Chris-Craft Utility. Restored to show quality. 1992.

Yard Information
Services
   Overland transport
   Engine repair
Storage
   Number of boats stored per year: 3
   Percentage of wooden boats: 100

Inside storage facilities
Maximum size for hauling and storing: 24' LOA, 3'
    draft, 2 tons
Maintenance
    Number of boats maintained per year: 12
    Percentage of wooden boats: 100
Retail supplies:
    Will order materials on request.

■ CANOESPORT

Roger G. Possley
940 N. Main St.
Ann Arbor, MI 48104
313-996-1393 Fax: 313-996-1946

Builder Information
Years in business: 14
Carpenters employed: 1
Shop capacity: 30'

Recent Repair Projects
15' Chestnut canoe (c. 1930s). Replaced 20' of planking, 15
    ribs, stems, and gunwales. Recanvased and refinished.
    1993.
18' Old Town H.W. Model sailing canoe (1946). Replaced
    10' of planking, 8 ribs, stems, and gunwales.
    Recanvased and refinished. 1993.
18' Old Town guide canoe (1948). Renewed stem and
    recanvased. Refinished to custom Old Town paint spec-
    ifications. 1993.
15' Thompson canoe (pre-1940). Replaced 20' of planking, 6
    ribs, stem, and gunwales. Recanvased and refinished.
    1993.
17' Arrowhead canoe. Replaced garboard planks, recan-
    vased, and refinished. 1993.
15' Old Town Trapper canoe (1952). Recaned seats.
    Recanvased and refinished. 1993.
18' St. Lawrence River skiff (ca. 1930). Restored deck and
    refinished. 1993.

Yard Information
Services
    Launching facilities
    Overland transport
    Rigging
Storage
    Number of boats stored per year: 160
    Percentage of wooden boats: Varies
    Inside storage facilities
    Maximum size for hauling and storing: Storage primar-
        ily for canoes
Maintenance
    Number of boats maintained per year: 55
    Percentage of wooden boats: 60
    Owner maintenance allowed.
Retail supplies:
    Paint, varnish, fastenings, planking and rib stock. WEST
        System products.

■ CLASSIC WATERCRAFT

William G. Nungester
11993 East U.S. 223
Blissfield, MI 49228
517-486-4288

Builder Information
Years in business: 6
Carpenters employed: 1
Shop capacity: 40'
Willing to travel for on-the-site building projects.

Recent Repair Projects
32' Nova Scotian sloop (1948). Completely restoring.
    Current project.
20' Chris-Craft runabout (1948). Refinished. 1994.
50' power commuter (1940). Completed general mainte-
    nance work. 1993.
15' Whitehall (1976). Renewed planking and frames.
    Refinished. 1993.
37' Alden sloop (1938). Replaced stem and keelson. 1992.

Yard Information
Services
    Sail repair
    Rigging
Storage
    Number of boats stored per year: varies
    Percentage of wooden boats: 60
    Maximum size for hauling and storing: 40' LOA
Maintenance
    Number of boats maintained per year: varies
    Percentage of wooden boats: 90

■ DIAMOND BOAT WORKS INC.

Mark and Nancy Edmonson
P.O. Box 85
St. Clair, MI 48079-0085
313-984-4060

Builder Information
Years in business: 5
Carpenters employed: 2
Shop capacity: 35'
Willing to travel for on-the-site building projects.

Recent Repair Projects
Complete restorations of approximately 30 classic power
    craft in the last 4 years, including the following most
    recent projects:
18' Chris-Craft Riviera (1951). 1993.
22' Hacker-Craft runabout (1947). 1993.
26' Hacker-Craft Triple (1929). 1993.
18' Gar Wood Utility (1947). 1993.
22' Chris-Craft Utility cruisers (1951). 2 restored in 1993.
30' Lyman power cruiser (1969). 1992.

Yard Information
Services
    Engine repair
(continues)

(Diamond Boat Works Inc., continued)

Storage
>Number of boats stored per year: 8
>Percentage of wooden boats: 100
>Inside storage facilities
>Maximum size for hauling and storing: 33′ LOA

Maintenance
>Number of boats maintained per year: 125
>Percentage of wooden boats: 100

Retail supplies:
>Limited inventory of supplies. Paint, fastenings, oak, mahogany, and other wood.

■ FOX FARM REPAIR SERVICE

Mark Pleune
10582 E. Eckerle Rd.
Suttons Bay, MI 49682
616-271-3640 Fax: 616-271-4884

Builder Information
Years in business: 10
Carpenters employed: 2
Shop capacity: 35′
Willing to travel for on-the-site building projects.

Recent New Construction
9′ Geodesic Airolite. Platt Monfort design. Built 1993.
14′ strip-planked runabout. Replica of 1951 Thompson. Built 1990.

Recent Repair Projects
14′ Thompson (1951). Complete renewal. Current project.
14′ Shell Lake boat (1951). Complete renewal. Current project.
16′ Old Town canoe (1940). Renewed canvas, refinished. 1993.
19′ Lightning-class sloop (1960). Repaired hull, refinished. 1992.
18′ Century runabout (1963). Refinished. 1992.
27′ St. Pierre dory (1971). Built custom interior. 1992.
17′ Penn Yan runabout (1948). Recanvased hull and refinished. 1990.

Yard Information
Services
>Launching facilities
>Overland transport
>Engine repair
>Rigging

Storage
>Number of boats stored per year: 20
>Percentage of wooden boats: 50
>Inside storage facilities
>Maximum size for hauling and storing: 35′ LOA, 5′ draft, 10 tons

Maintenance
>Number of boats maintained per year: 50
>Percentage of wooden boats: 50
>Owner maintenance allowed above and below rail.

Retail supplies:
>WEST System products, fastenings, paints.

■ GRAND CRAFT CORP.

Richard Sligh
430 W. 21st St.
Holland, MI 49423
616-396-5450 Fax: 616-396-6210

Builder Information
Years in business: 14
Carpenters employed: 7
Shop capacity: 50′

Recent New Construction
Boats designed by Richard Sligh for cold-molded construction:
36′ commuter. Built 1993.
30′ commuter. Built 1993.
24′ triple-cockpit runabout. Built 1993.

Recent Repair Projects
Extensively rebuilt and repowered the following boats during 1993:
32′ Consolidated launch (1923).
29′ Chris-Craft Sportsman Runabout (1938).
27′ Chris-Craft Semi-Enclosed Cruiser (1960).

■ GREAT LAKES BOAT BUILDING CO.

Michael J. Kiefer
7066 103rd Ave.
South Haven, MI 49090
616-637-6805

Builder Information
Years in business: 7
Carpenters employed: 1
Shop capacity: 22′

Recent New Construction
Boats designed by Michael Kiefer for lapstrake plywood construction:
14′ fishing semi-dory. Built 1993.
12′ catboat. 2 built 1993.
7′6″, 9′, and 10′ rowing/sailing dinghies. 4 built 1993.
Other new construction:
16′ plywood lapstrake sailing Whitehall. R.D. Culler design, construction modified by Kiefer. 3 built 1993.
14′ plywood lapstrake Whitehall. H.I. Chapelle design, construction modified by Kiefer. Built 1993.

■ HARBOR CRAFT

Larry Ketten
P.O. Box 21, 100 McBride Park Dr.
Harbor Springs, MI 49740
616-348-3737

Builder Information
Years in business: 4
Carpenters employed: 1
Shop capacity: 50′
Willing to travel for on-the-site building projects.

Recent New Construction

40′ trimaran. Strip-plank construction. Tony Grainger
design. Current project.

Recent Repair Projects

34′ Hutchinson cruiser. Renewed topsides and deck. 1993.
32′ Consolidated launch (1922). Restored 75% of boat. 1992.

Yard Information

Storage
    Number of boats stored per year: 25
    Percentage of wooden boats: 39
    Inside storage facilities
    Maximum size for hauling and storing: 50′ LOA.
Maintenance
    Number of boats maintained per year: 8
    Percentage of wooden boats: 75
    Owner maintenance allowed above and below rail.
Retail supplies:
    Special-order items only.

■ KLONDIKE WOODWORKS

Elmer L. Johnson
RR #1, Box 19
Lake Linden, MI 49945
906-296-0691

Builder Information

Years in business: 18
Carpenters employed: 1
Shop capacity: 18′

Recent New Construction

Wood/canvas canoes in lengths of 14′3″, 16′, and 17′4″.
Elmer Johnson designs. Several built each winter.

Recent Repair Projects

Wood/canvas canoes. Repair, restoration, recanvasing,
and refinishing.

■ KOSS KLASSIC BOATS

Michael and James Koss
197 N. Mattesen Lake Rd.
Bronson, MI 49028
517-369-8885

Builder Information

Years in business: 4
Carpenters employed: 1
Shop capacity: 26′

Recent New Construction

13′ strip-planked canoe. Koss design. Built 1992.

Recent Repair Projects

16′ Chris-Craft Deluxe Runabout (1941). Renewed topsides, deck, transom, and upholstery. Renewed bottom
with WEST System. Repowered. 1992.
17′ Chris-Craft Deluxe Runabout (1954). Replaced topside
and deck planking. Repowered. 1991.

16′ Chris-Craft Deluxe Runabout (1941). Renewed upholstery and engine. Completely refinished. 1990.

Yard Information

Services
    Engine repair
Storage
    Number of boats stored per year: 12
    Percentage of wooden boats: 100
    Inside storage facilities
    Maximum size for hauling and storing: Inquire
Maintenance
    Number of boats maintained per year: 6
    Percentage of wooden boats: 100

■ MacKERCHER ANTIQUE & CLASSIC MARINE SPECIALTIES

R. Scott MacKercher
925 Industrial Park Dr.
Whitehall, MI 49461
616-893-8187

Builder Information

Years in business: 13
Carpenters employed: 2
Shop capacity: 29′
Willing to travel for on-the-site building projects.

Recent Repair Projects

Complete restorations of the following classic power craft:
16′ Chris-Craft Special Race Boat (1938).
18′ Chris-Craft Deluxe Utility (1940).
17′ Chris-Craft Custom Sportsman Utility (1955).
17′ Chris-Craft Deluxe Runabout (1948).
17′ Hacker-Craft Custom Split Cockpit (1935).
26′ Great Lakes Custom Triple-Cockpit Runabout (1925).

Yard Information

Services
    Engine repair
Storage
    Number of boats stored per year: 30
    Percentage of wooden boats: 100
    Inside storage facilities
    Maximum size for hauling and storing: 29′ LOA, 20″
    draft, 6,500 lbs.
Maintenance
    Number of boats maintained per year: 30-50
    Percentage of wooden boats: 100
    Owner maintenance allowed above and below rail.
Retail supplies:
    Wood, fastenings, paint, varnish, engine parts. Custom-
built trailers and custom-sewn mooring covers.

■ MACKIE BOAT WORKS

Alan Mackie
P.O. Box 219
Algonac, MI 48001
810-794-4120

Builder Information

Years in business: 22
Carpenters employed: 2
Shop capacity: 50'
Willing to travel for on-the-site building projects.

Recent New Construction

17' Whitehall. Traditional design. Built 1992.

Recent Repair Projects

18' Chris-Craft Cobra. Rebuilding. Current project.
49' Matthews power cruiser. Repaired rot in cabin side. 1993.
34' Pacemaker power cruiser. Replaced transom. 1993.
21' Lyman power cruiser (1956). Replaced transom and bottom planking. 1993.
35' Chris-Craft cruiser. Renewed teak deck, side planks, and sheer clamp. 1993.
20' Chris-Craft Custom Runabout (1948). Completely refinished and refitted. 1992-'93.
Numerous other antique runabouts restored in last few years.

Yard Information

Services
    Marina facilities
    Engine repair
Storage
    Number of boats stored per year: 30
    Percentage of wooden boats: 20
    Maximum size for hauling and storing: 45' LOA, 4' draft, 15 tons
Maintenance
    Number of boats maintained per year: 20
    Percentage of wooden boats: 95

■ MARSHALL MARINE & WOODWORKING

Thomas F. Marshall
5599 Scenic Dr.
Sault Ste. Marie, MI 49783
906-635-9106

Builder Information

Years in business: 10
Carpenters employed: 2
Shop capacity: 25'
Willing to travel for on-the-site building projects.

Recent New Construction

7'2" lapstrake Cabin Boy dinghy. Atkin design. Built 1992.

Recent Repair Projects

18' Old Town guide canoe (1928). Renewed decks, outwales, and thwarts. Recanvased and refinished. 1992.
16' Old Town guide canoe (1922). Replaced 3 ribs. Renewed decks, inwales, outwales, and thwarts. Recanvased and refinished. 1992.
16' Comet-class sloop (1947). Renewed decks and canvas, floorboards and centerboard trunk. Fiberglassed hull, refinished. 1991.
22' modified Sea Bird yawl (1932). Complete restoration. Renewed 3 frames, 5 floors, centerboard trunk, cockpit, decks, and interior. Replaced bowsprit and standing rigging. Refinished. 1990.

Yard Information

Services
    Overland transport
    Moorage
    Rigging
Storage
    Number of boats stored per year: 4
    Percentage of wooden boats: 50
    Inside storage facilities
    Maximum size for hauling and storing: 25' LOA, 2.5 tons
Maintenance
    Number of boats maintained per year: 3
    Percentage of wooden boats: 66
    Owner maintenance allowed above and below rail.
Retail supplies:
    Very limited supply of materials for canoe restoration.

■ MERRYMAN BOATS

Craig K. Thompson
4915 Delta River Dr.
Lansing, MI 48906
517-482-9333 Fax: 517-323-0132

Builder Information

Years in business: 8
Carpenters employed: 1
Shop capacity: 12'

Recent New Construction

6' and 8' lapstrake plywood prams. Designs by Merryman Boats. Available as kits.

■ MERTAUGH BOAT WORKS INC.

Bruce Glupker
Hessel Point Rd., P.O. Box 40
Hessel, MI 49745
906-484-2434 Fax: 906-484-2501

Builder Information

Years in business: 65
Carpenters employed: 3
Shop capacity: 40'

Recent Repair Projects

Runabouts, launches, power cruisers, and sailboats in lengths from 10' to 40'. Work has involved keel, frame, deck, and hull repairs, as well as renewal of electrical, plumbing, electronic, and power systems. Approximately 30 boats worked on between 1990 and 1993.

Yard Information
Services
    Marina facilities
    Launching facilities
    Overland transport
    Engine repair
    Rigging
Storage
    Number of boats stored per year: 200
    Percentage of wooden boats: 25-30
    Inside storage facilities
    Maximum size for hauling and storing: 42' LOA, 7'
        draft, 20 tons
Maintenance
    Number of boats maintained per year: 250
    Percentage of wooden boats: 35
    Owner maintenance allowed above and below rail.
Retail supplies:
    Complete inventory of supplies.

NEW ERA DESIGN

Patrick Owen
6408 Swamp Rd.
Frankfort, MI 49635
616-882-5945 Fax: same

Builder Information
Years in business: 9
Carpenters employed: 1
Shop capacity: Any size
Willing to travel for on-the-site building projects.

Recent New Construction
24' cold-molded, high-performance luxury power cruiser.
    Patrick Owen design. Built 1994.

NORTHWOOD BOATWORKS

Dave Moore
7680 Dundas Rd. NW
Alden, MI 49612
616-331-6516 Fax: 616-331-4193

Builder Information
Years in business: 16
Carpenters employed: 2
Shop capacity: 35'

Recent Repair Projects
Rebuilding, restoration, and/or refinishing of the follow-
    ing craft:
25' Chris-Craft Sportsman (1946). 1993.
25' Faering sailboat (1986). 1993.
17' Chris-Craft Barrelback Deluxe (1942). 1992.
21' Century Coronado (1966). 1991.
24' Chris-Craft Holiday (1953). 1991.
18' Thompson wood/canvas canoe (1930). 1990.

Yard Information
Services
    Engine repair

Storage
    Number of boats stored per year: 7
    Percentage of wooden boats: 100
Maintenance
    Number of boats maintained per year: 12
    Percentage of wooden boats: 100
    Owner maintenance allowed above rail.
Retail supplies:
    Paints, varnish, fastenings, wood, and other supplies.

PATRICK'S LANDING

Bruce W. Patrick
Rural Route, Box 28
Cedarville, MI 49719
906-484-3398

Builder Information
Years in business: 60
Carpenters employed: 1
Shop capacity: 26'

Recent New Construction
23' fantail-sterned launch. Bruce Patrick design. Built 1990.

Recent Repair Projects
21' Patrick Craft. Replaced keel, frames, some planking. 1993.
18' Chris-Craft. Renewed decks, engine stringers. 1993.
14' Chris-Craft outboard cruiser. Renewed keel and fiber-
    glass sheathing. 1993.
26' Lyman Hardtop day cruiser. Renewed decks. 1993.
24' Truscott launch. Replaced stem and stem knee.
    Renewed deck and interior. 1992.

Yard Information
Services
    Marina facilities
    Launching facilities
    Moorage
    Engine repair
Storage
    Number of boats stored per year: 40
    Percentage of wooden boats: 75
    Inside storage facilities
    Maximum size for hauling and storing: 26' LOA, 2'
        draft
Maintenance
    Number of boats maintained per year: 20
    Percentage of wooden boats: 100

SKYWOODS

Scott Ira Barkdoll
Oakley Rd.
Honor, MI 49640

Builder Information
Years in business: 2
Carpenters employed: 1
Willing to travel for on-the-site building projects.
(continues)

(Skywoods, continued)

Recent New Construction

17' strip-planked Red Bird canoe. Ted Moores design. Built 1992.

Recent Repair Projects

17' Old Town guide canoe. Repairing gunwale, recanvas- ing hull, refinishing brightwork. Current project.

15' Old Town canoe. Renewed ribs and gunwales. 1993.

17' Old Town H.W. Model canoe (1923). Replaced about 50% of wood. Renewed ribs, planking, decks, and gun- wales. 1992–'93.

Yard Information

Services

Overland transport

Maintenance

Number of boats maintained per year: 3

Percentage of wooden boats: 100

Retail supplies:

Cedar, ash, walnut, and cherry. Epoxy, canvas.

■ TASSIER BOAT SHOP

Gary Tassier
RR #1, Box 5
Cedarville, MI 49719
906-484-2573

Builder Information

Years in business: 53

Carpenters employed: 3

Shop capacity: 35'

Willing to travel for on-the-site building projects.

Recent Repair Projects

25' Chris-Craft Sportsman. Renewing bottom, decks, and cabin. Ongoing project. 1992-current.

24' Chris-Craft Cadet. Renewing decks and refinishing top- sides. Repowering. Current project.

30' Chris-Craft Cruiser. Completely refinished interior and exterior. 1992–'93.

16' and 18' lapstrake pulling boats. Replaced frames and planking. 1992–'93.

20' Century runabout. Replaced frames, bottom planking, and decks. Refinished. 1991–'92.

28' Luedtke L-class sloop. Replaced frames and planking. Refinished cabin and mast. 1990–'91.

Yard Information

Services

Marina facilities

Launching facilities

Moorage

Engine repair

Rigging

Storage

Number of boats stored per year: 125

Percentage of wooden boats: 75

Inside storage facilities

Maximum size for hauling and storing: 30' LOA

Maintenance

Number of boats maintained per year: 200

Percentage of wooden boats: 75

Retail supplies:

Wood, fastenings, paint, rope, hardware, new and used engine parts.

■ THORNAPPLE RIVER CANOES

Scott DeVoll
9135 68th St. SE
Alto, MI 49302
616-868-7679

Builder Information

Years in business: 6

Carpenters employed: 1

Shop capacity: 20'

Recent New Construction

15'6" strip-planked solo canoe. Scott DeVoll design. Built 1993.

Recent Repair Projects

16' wood/canvas Old Town canoe. Repairing gunwales and recanvasing. Current project.

15' Old Town canoe. Renewing ribs and planking, resheathing in fiberglass. Current project.

17' wood/canvas Old Town canoe (1920). Renewed gun- wales and decks, recanvased. 1993.

18' wood/canvas canoe. Replaced thwarts, seats, gun- wales, and decks. 1993.

16' wood/canvas canoe. Renewed ribs and planking, recanvased. 1992.

■ VAN DAM WOOD CRAFT

Stephen Van Dam
970 E. Division St.
Boyne City, MI 49712
616-582-2323 Fax: 616-582-3561

Builder Information

Years in business: 17

Carpenters employed: 5-6

Shop capacity: 120'

Recent New Construction

Boats of cold-molded construction:

35' replica launch. Current project.

26' speedboat. John Hacker design. Built 1993.

30' speedboat. George Crouch design. Built 1991.

33' sloop. F. Ford design. Built 1990–'91.

Recent Repair Projects

22' speedboat (1947). Completely restoring. Current project.

64' 75-Square-Meter class. Laid new teak decks. Refinished. 1991–'93.

58' Alden ketch. Completely refitted, refinished. 1992–'93.

Yard Information

Services
Launching facilities
Engine repair
Rigging
Storage
Number of boats stored per year: 120
Percentage of wooden boats: 10-20
Inside storage facilities
Maximum size for hauling and storing: 9' draft, 35 tons
Maintenance
Number of boats maintained per year: 50-80
Percentage of wooden boats: 25
Owner maintenance allowed.

■ VINTAGE BOAT WORKS, INC.

Jed Mooney
5110 M-72 West
Traverse City, MI 49684
616-929-9814

Builder Information

Years in business: 25
Carpenters employed: 1-3
Shop capacity: 50'

Recent New Construction

22' sloop Mist. Stitch-and-glue plywood construction. Karl Stambaugh design. Built 1993.

Capable of new construction in traditional and contemporary/composite methods; replica and reproduction building.

Recent Repair Projects

16' Old Town canoes (1925 and 1962 models). Repaired ribs and wales, recanvased and refinished. 1993.

22' Chris-Craft Continental. Repaired or replaced damaged planks and shelf. Refastened and refinished. Renewed upholstery, rechromed hardware, converted to 12-volt DC. Restored to show condition. 1992.

17' Chris-Craft Sportsman Utility (1955). Renewed bottom with WEST System. Replaced planking and made custom modifications. Rebuilt engine, rechromed hardware, and reupholstered. Refinished to "Award Winning" show condition. 1992.

14'6" Lane Lifeboat & Davit Co. launch (1937). Repaired planking, replaced frames, fabricated new motor box, floorboards, rudder and tiller. Installed rebuilt original motor. Refinished to "Award Winning" show condition. 1992.

20' Chris-Craft Grand Prix runabout (1968). Repaired or replaced planking, and refastened. Reupholstered and refinished to show condition. 1991.

22' Gar Wood triple-cockpit runabout (1936). Replaced frames and planking, and refastened. Renewed bottom with WEST system. Repowered and refinished. 1991.

Yard Information

Services
Overland transport
Engine repair
Rigging
Storage
Number of boats stored per year: 10
Percentage of wooden boats: 100
Inside storage facilities
Maintenance
Number of boats maintained per year: 10
Percentage of wooden boats: 100
Owner maintenance allowed on case basis.
Retail supplies:
Plywood and lumber, fastenings, varnish, paint, and other materials for refinishing. Hardware, original and reproduction parts, engines and parts, WEST System epoxy products.

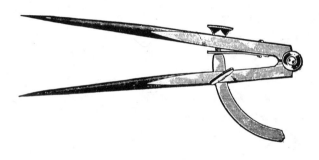

■ J.W. BELTMAN WOODWORKING

John Kavanagh-Beltman
799 Birch Dr.
Bovey, MN 55709
218-245-2678

Builder Information

Years in business: 10
Carpenters employed: 1
Shop capacity: 40'
Willing to travel for on-the-site building projects.

Recent New Construction

17' wood/canvas canoe. John Kavanagh-Beltman design. 2 built 1990–'93.

30' lapstrake bateau. Traditional design. Built 1990.

Yard Information

Retail supplies:
Paddles and oars a specialty — custom and standard designs.

BIGFORK CANOE TRAILS

Jack Minehart
Rte. 1
Max, MN 56659
218-798-2735

Builder Information
For information on company, see Bigfork Canoe Trails listing in the state of Iowa. Use Minnesota address and phone number for the months of June, July, and August.

BOURQUIN BOATS

Jeanne Bourquin
1568 McMahan Blvd.
Ely, MN 55731
218-365-5499

Builder Information
Years in business: 10
Carpenters employed: 2
Shop capacity: 20'
Willing to travel for on-the-site building projects.

Recent New Construction
16½' wood/canvas canoe. Otter model for tandem or solo use. Jeanne Bourquin design. 6 built to date.
17½' wood/canvas expedition-tandem canoe. Atkinson Traveler design by Rollin Thurlow. 4 built to date.

Recent Repair Projects
15'–20' wood/canvas canoes. Old Town, Chestnut, Peterborough, White, and Seliga designs. Various types of repair; approximately 4-6 canoes worked on each year.

Yard Information
Services
    Marina facilities
    Launching facilities
    Overland transport
Maintenance
    Number of boats maintained per year: 4-10
    Percentage of wooden boats: 100
    Owner maintenance allowed.
Retail supplies:
    Milled-wood replacement parts for canoes. Fastenings, stembands, canvas, etc.

BRISTOL CLASSICS

F. Todd Warner
2511 State Hwy. #7
Excelsior, MN 55331
612-470-7851 Fax: 612-474-9609

Builder Information
Years in business: 17
Carpenters employed: 3
Shop capacity: 35'

Recent New Construction
242-class hydroplanes. In-house design based on John Hacker hydroplane. Currently in planning stage.

Recent Repair Projects
Recent repair projects have included restoration of the following classic power craft:
19'6" Gar Wood (1947).
18' Century Sea Maid (1953).
30' Morgan/Hacker (1985).
21' Century Coronado (1957).
33' Gar Wood (1925).
27' Fay & Bowen (1939).

Yard Information
Services
    Overland transport
    Engine repair
Storage
    Number of boats stored per year: 50
    Percentage of wooden boats: 100
    Inside storage facilities
    Maximum size for hauling and storing: 35' LOA
Maintenance
    Number of boats maintained per year: 20
    Percentage of wooden boats: 100
Retail supplies:
    Refinishing supplies on special-order basis.

DAVID CHRISTOFFERSON DESIGN

David Christofferson
267 Goodhue/Uppertown
St. Paul, MN 55102
612-222-0261

Builder Information
Years in business: 20
Carpenters employed: 1
Shop capacity: 30'

Recent New Construction
18'9" plywood/fiberglass canoe for paddle and oar. Christofferson design, based on 19th-century bark canoe from the Athabasca region. Built 1993.
17'6" lapstrake bateau. Christofferson design, based on lumberman's bateau. Built 1990.

Recent Repair Projects
22' 18th-century bateau replica. Repaired planking. Designed and built traditional sailing rig. 1990–'92.

HAFEMAN BOAT WORKS

Ray and Christie Boessel
RR #1, Box 187
Bigfork, MN 56628
218-743-3709

Builder Information
Years in business: 73

Carpenters employed: 1
Shop capacity: 26'

Recent New Construction

Birchbark and cedar canoes available in the following models. Approximately 12 boats built each year.

17', 20', and 26' fur trade freight canoes. Designs based on Algonquin and French models used in early 1600s.

13' and 16' Chippewa Long-Nose canoes. Chippewa Indian designs.

16' old-style Algonquin canoe. Algonquin Indian design.

Also build Chippewa canoe display models in variety of lengths from 2' to 10'.

Recent Repair Projects

16' Chippewa Long-Nose canoe. Renewed spruce root bindings and pitch. 2 canoes repaired 1990–'93.

26' fur trade freight canoe. Renewed spruce root bindings and pitch. 1991 and 1993.

17' fur trade canoe. Repaired gunwale. 1990.

Yard Information

Services
Launching facilities
Maintenance
Number of boats maintained per year: 6
Percentage of wooden boats: 100
Owner maintenance allowed.

■ INLAND YACHT

Christian W. Dahl
749 Spring Hill Dr.
Woodbury, MN 55125
612-738-0199

Builder Information

Years in business: 40
Carpenters employed: 1
Shop capacity: 30'

Recent New Construction

Boats designed by Christian Dahl:
16' French dory. Built 1992.
30' schooner. Built 1990.

Recent Repair Projects

46' ketch. Renewed planking. 1992.
47' houseboat. Renewed trim. 1991.

Yard Information

Services
Overland transport
Engine repair
Rigging

■ ROB MYHRE DESIGN/BOAT RESTORATION

Rob Myhre
3210 Snelling Ave.
Minneapolis, MN 55406
612-729-8159

Builder Information

Years in business: 9
Carpenters employed: 2
Shop capacity: 73'
Willing to travel for on-the-site building projects.

Recent Repair Projects

28' Carver (1968). Renewed deck and superstructure. 1993.
19' Chris-Craft (1952). Completely rebuilt. 1993.
17' Chris-Craft (1939). Completely rebuilt. 1993.
17' Lyman (1964). Refinished. 1992.
21' Century (1960). Renewed hull planking. 1992.
26' Carver (1970). Renewed deck. 1991.
36' Chris-Craft (1964). Renewed planking. 1991.

■ RAVEN BOATS

Scott Mills
9 North Yukon Dr.
Ely, MN 55731
218-365-4322

Builder Information

Years in business: 7
Carpenters employed: 1
Shop capacity: 22'

Recent New Construction

14'6" and 17' wood/canvas canoes. Scott Mills designs. 4 of each size built 1990–'93.

Recent Repair Projects

Specializes in restoration of wood/canvas canoes. Several boats worked on 1990–'93.

■ L.J. RONNING BOATWORKS/ LAURENTIAN KAYAKS

Larry J. Ronning
N. Star Rte., Box 230-B
Two Harbors, MN 55616
218-834-3249

Builder Information

Years in business: 16
Carpenters employed: 1
Shop capacity: 48'
Willing to travel for on-the-site building projects.

Recent New Construction

18' lapstrake plywood Seiche sea kayak. L.J. Ronning design. 2 built 1993.

12'8" lapstrake Catspaw dinghy. Joel White/N.G. Herreshoff design. 3 built 1990–'93.

12'4" lapstrake Yankee Tender skiff. Joel White/WoodenBoat design. 2 built 1992.

16'4" lapstrake plywood Voyager sea kayak. L.J. Ronning design. 2 built 1992.

11' lapstrake tender. L.J. Ronning design. 3 built 1990–'91.

(continues)

(L.J. Ronning Boatworks/Laurentian Kayaks, continued)

Recent Repair Projects

45' 3-masted Zeeto schooner. Designed and built new galley, settee, and quarter berth. 1993.

16' lapstrake pulling boats for oar and power (1936). Restoring 17-boat rental fleet from Isle Royale. 2 boats per year. 1991–'93.

42' lapstrake, Knarr-type Viking boat LEIF ERICKSON. Completely restored. 1990-current.

35'–40' lapstrake Chris-Craft power cruisers. Various types of repair work, including new decks, and plank and transom repair. 1990–'93.

14' and 16' strip-planked Shell Lake boats for oar and power. Renewed frames. 1991–'92.

■ STEWART RIVER BOATWORKS

Alex Comb
Rte. 1, Box 203-B
Two Harbors, MN 55616
218-834-5037 Fax: 218-834-2506

Builder Information
Years in business: 14
Carpenters employed: 1
Shop capacity: 26'

Recent New Construction
Boats designed by Alex Comb:
14'10" wood/canvas Unity canoe. 6 built 1992–'93.
15'6" wood/canvas Traveler canoe. 4 built 1993.
17'10" kayaks. Strip-planked or plywood construction. 2 boats built 1992–'93.
Other new construction:
16' wood/canvas Prospector canoe. Chestnut Canoe Co. design. 12 built 1988–'93.
17'10" guide canoe. E.M. White/Alex Comb design. 4 built 1992–'93.

Recent Repair Projects
Repair or restoration of wood/canvas canoes and skiffs from 12' to 18'. Several projects since 1990.
16' inboard runabout. Replaced bottom planking. 1992.

■ VINTAGE BOAT WORKS

Jim Biersach
P.O. Box 391
Nisswa, MN 56468
218-963-4403

Builder Information
Years in business: 20
Carpenters employed: 1
Shop capacity: 40'

Recent Repair Projects
14' Larson Falls Flyer (1937). Completely restored. 1993.
16' Gar Wood Utility (1948). Replaced bottom with WEST System and renewed topside planking. Rebuilt engine. 1993.

14' Switzer Craft (1954). Applied new plywood skin, renewed framing. 1992.

19' Higgins (1948). Renewed plywood planking, framing, and upholstery. Refinished boat. 1992.

20' Johnson C-scow (1962). Replaced framing and planking, recanvased deck and refinished. 1992.

19' Chris-Craft Capri (1958). Renewed bottom with WEST System and refinished. 1991.

20' Century Restorter (1956). Replaced stem and forefoot, and some bottom planking. 1991.

Yard Information
Services
    Marina facilities
    Launching facilities
    Overland transport
    Moorage
    Engine repair
    Sail repair
    Rigging
Storage
    Number of boats stored per year: 130
    Percentage of wooden boats: 20
    Inside storage facilities
    Maximum size for hauling and storing: 30' LOA
Maintenance
    Number of boats maintained per year: 300
    Percentage of wooden boats: 10
    Owner maintenance allowed above and below rail.
Retail supplies:
    Wood, fastenings, paint, and accessories.

■ MORLEY CEDAR CANOES

Greg Morley
P.O. Box 5147
Swan Lake, MT 59911
406-886-2242

Builder Information
Years in business: 21
Carpenters employed: 1
Shop capacity: 26'
Willing to travel for on-the-site building projects.

Recent New Construction

Boats designed by Greg Morley for composite/wood-strip construction:

13', 15', 16', 17', and 18' canoes. 18 boats built 1992–'93.

18' rowing shell. Built 1993.

14' Swan Lake skiff. 2 built 1992.

18' touring kayak. 2 built 1991–'92.

Other new construction:

18' Adirondack guideboat. Grant design. Built 1993.

Recent Repair Projects

Strip-planked and wood/canvas canoes. Minor repairs to major restorations.

◼ BARRINGTON BOAT SHOP

Jeffrey R. Fogman, DBA
97 Swain Rd.
Barrington, NH 03825
603-664-9752

Builder Information

Years in business: 20

Carpenters employed: 2-10

Shop capacity: Any size

Willing to travel for on-the-site building projects.

Recent New Construction

52' staysail schooner. Bud McIntosh design. Current project.

Recent Repair Projects

46' ketch. Completed major structural repairs from keel up. 1993.

85' ketch. Rebuilt keel, deckbeams, decks, houses, hatches. 1990.

Yard Information

Services

Rigging

◼ GEOFFREY BURKE, BOATBUILDER

Geoffrey Burke
P.O. Box 212
Chocorua, NH 03817-0212
603-323-8702

Builder Information

Years in business: 12

Carpenters employed: 1

Shop capacity: 20'

Willing to travel for on-the-site building projects.

Recent New Construction

Company specializes in the construction of white cedar lapstrake canoes and pulling boats. Designs are by Walter Simmons (some modified by Geoffrey Burke) and J.H. Rushton.

Canoes are available in several lengths from 10'6" to 18' and are designed for use as solo or tandem, cruising and tripping canoes. Models 15' or longer can be equipped with fixed or sliding seats; several sailing rigs are also available.

Pulling boat designs offered are Walt Simmons's 16' Duck Trap wherry and a 12' Buyce-designed Adirondack guideboat. Both are equipped for recreational rowing.

Yard Information

Services

Rigging

Storage

Number of boats stored per year: 2-5

Percentage of wooden boats: 100

Maximum size for hauling and storing: 20' LOA

Maintenance

Number of boats maintained per year: 1-5

Percentage of wooden boats: 100

Owner maintenance allowed above and below rail.

Retail supplies:

Select Northern white cedar, red and white oak, and cherry. Oars, single and double paddles, yokes, variety of sailing rigs for canoes.

◼ CONNECTICUT RIVER BOAT WORKS

Mitchell Ross
Stony Brook Rd.
Lebanon, NH 03766
603-448-4568

Builder Information

Years in business: 4

Carpenters employed: 1

Shop capacity: 20'

Recent New Construction

24' True Rocket sloop. Completing boat (last hull built by A.R. True). Current project.

15' Sweet Pea peapod. Stitch-and-glue construction. Phil Bolger design. Built 1992.

10' lapstrake plywood Flipper skiff. John Atkin design. Built 1990.

Yard Information

Services

Sail repair

Retail supplies:

Materials for stitch-and-glue construction, marine hardware, sails.

HARPER & SONS' BOAT SALES & RESTORATION

Jerry W. Harper, Sr. & Jr.
55 Daniel Webster Highway, Rte. 3
Meredith, NH 03253
603-279-8841 Fax: 603-279-6535

Builder Information
Years in business: 16
Carpenters employed: 2
Shop capacity: 50'

Recent New Construction
45' triple-cockpit, torpedo-sterned runabout. In-house design. Current project.

Recent Repair Projects
17' Dart double-cockpit runabout (1930). Replaced bottom with WEST System. Replaced decks and planking. Renewed upholstery. 1993.

32' long-decker launch (1929). Replaced floors, seats, and decks. Renewed upholstery and repowered. 1992–'93.

28' Hacker-Craft (1939). Increased length with 4' stepped, barrel stern. Renewed decks and planking. Repowered. 1992–'93.

20' Dodge Water Car runabout. Increased length with 3' stepped, barrel stern.

45' Chris-Craft Constellation tri-cabin cruiser (1960). Completely restored boat. Renewed engine and canvas. 1992.

22' Century Coronado (1963). Replaced bottom with WEST System. Renewed frames, planking, decks, and upholstery. Repaired engine. 1991.

17' Century Sea Maid runabout (1942). Replaced bottom with WEST System. Renewed planking and decks. Repowered. 1990.

Yard Information
Services
  Marina facilities
  Overland transport
  Engine repair
Storage
  Number of boats stored per year: 60
  Percentage of wooden boats: 90
  Inside storage facilities
  Maximum size for hauling and storing: 50' LOA
Maintenance
  Number of boats maintained per year: Varies
  Percentage of wooden boats: 90
  Owner maintenance allowed.
Retail supplies:
  Complete inventory of supplies.

PHILIP A. KENDALL CUSTOM BOATBUILDERS

Philip A. Kendall
Middle Rd.
North Sandwich, NH 03259
603-284-7058

Builder Information
Years in business: 45
Carpenters employed: 1-3
Shop capacity: 45'

Recent New Construction
14' lapstrake Whitehall. One built 1991; one currently under construction.

Recent Repair Projects
19' Chris-Craft Continental. Replacing decks and hull planking. Refinishing. Current project.

10' Rushton canoe. Replacing decks and hull planking. Current project.

15'5"–18' wood/canvas canoes. Replaced ribs, planking, and canvas. 12 canoes repaired between 1990 and 1993.

16' Grady-White. Renewed transom, deck, and bilge stringers. 1991.

18' Lyman. Renewed deck and transom. Refastened and refinished hull. 1991.

23' Chris-Craft Continental. Refinished. 1990.

Yard Information
Maintenance
  Number of boats maintained per year: 10
  Percentage of wooden boats: 50
Retail supplies:
  Wood, paint, fastenings.

LAKES REGION RESTORATIONS, INC.

Philip K. Spencer
P.O. Box 163, Bay St.
Wolfeboro Falls, NH 03896
603-569-5038 Fax: same

Builder Information
Years in business: 11
Carpenters employed: 1-2
Shop capacity: 34'
Willing to travel for on-the-site building projects.

Recent New Construction
19'7" Chris-Craft replica. Carvel topsides with plywood/epoxy bottom. Chris Smith design. Built 1993.

Recent Repair Projects
21' Century Coronado. Renewed side planking and knees. 1993.

25' Gar Wood runabout. Renewed topside planking, deck, and interior. 1992–'93.

21' Hacker Raceboat (1925). Totally rebuilt, repowered. 1993.

26' Chris-Craft (1930). Completely refinished, repowered. 1993.

18' Whitehall pulling boat (1895). Completely refinished. 1992.

17'–33' antique and classic runabouts. Refinishing to major rebuilds. Numerous projects to date.

Yard Information
Services
    Launching facilities
    Overland transport
    Engine repair
Storage
    Number of boats stored per year: 10
    Percentage of wooden boats: 100
    Inside storage facilities
    Maximum size for hauling and storing: 34' LOA, 2'
        draft, 3-4 tons
Maintenance
    Number of boats maintained per year: 20
    Percentage of wooden boats: 100
    Owner maintenance allowed above and below rail.

KEVIN MARTIN, BOATBUILDER

Kevin Martin
4 Windsor Lane
Epping, NH 03042
603-679-5153

Builder Information
Years in business: 14
Carpenters employed: 2
Shop capacity: 30'
Willing to travel for on-the-site building projects.

Recent New Construction
16' wood/canvas Charles River canoe. Kingsbury design.
    Built 1993.
16' lapstrake Ugo canoe. J.H. Rushton design. Built 1992.
16' Adirondack guideboat. Grant design. 2 built 1990 and
    1992.
11'6" lapstrake Vaux Jr. canoe. J.H. Rushton design. 4 built
    1990–'91.
16' lapstrake Piscataqua River wherry. Built 1990.

Recent Repair Projects
15' Old Town lapstrake outboard. Completely refinished.
    1993.
17' Rangeley Lake boats. Completely restored 4 boats.
    1991–'93.
12'–18' wood/canvas canoes and boats. Worked on
    approximately 45 boats from 1990 to 1993. Repairs
    involved woodworking and recanvasing.
24' Shepherd runabout. Replaced frames, chines, and
    planking. Refinished. 1991–'92.
12' and 16' Peterborough canoes. Replaced decks and rails.
    Refinished. 1992.
12' Lymington scow. Replaced frames and planking.
    Recanvased deck and refinished. 1991.
17' St. Lawrence River skiff. Replaced frames and planking.
    Refinished. 1991.
Retail supplies:
    Materials for canoe restoration. Lumber, canvas, fasten-
        ings, and other supplies.

MULLER BOATWORKS

Bo and Kathy Muller
Rte. 103, Box 45
Sunapee, NH 03782
603-863-8146

Builder Information
Years in business: 13
Carpenters employed: 2
Shop capacity: 33'

Recent New Construction
27' runabout. Reproduction of 1936 Chris-Craft Custom
    Runabout. Current project.
19' runabout. Reproduction of 1936 Chris-Craft Blue &
    White Racing Runabout. Built 1993.

Recent Repair Projects
21' Chris-Craft Deluxe Utility (1936). Renewed bottom and
    frames. Completed other restoration work. 1993.
21' Century Coronado (1955). Renewed bottom and
    frames. 1993.
19' Chris-Craft Sportsman (1938). Restored hull, renewed
    bottom. 1993.
24' Chris-Craft runabout (1929). Replaced planking and
    frames. 1992.
22' Chris-Craft runabout (1927). Renewed decks and
    interior. 1991.
27' Chris-Craft racing runabout (1939). Restored hull.
    Replaced all planking and frames. 1990.
21' Fay & Bowen launch (1910). Restored hull. 1990.

Yard Information
Storage
    Number of boats stored per year: 9
    Percentage of wooden boats: 100
    Inside storage facilities
Maintenance
    Number of boats maintained per year: 45
    Percentage of wooden boats: 100

NEW ENGLAND BOAT & MOTOR, INC.

Mark P. Mason
28 Center St., P.O. Box 1283
Laconia, NH 03246
617-528-3411 Fax: 617-528-3436

Builder Information
Years in business: 30
Carpenters employed: 3
Shop capacity: 40'
Willing to travel for on-the-site building projects.

Recent New Construction
33'6" cold-molded speedboat. George Crouch design. Built
    1992.

Recent Repair Projects
35' Gold Cup racer (1927). Replaced decks, bulkheads, and
    interior. 1993.
(continues)

(New England Boat & Motor, Inc., continued)
Yard Information
Services
Overland transport
Engine repair
Storage
Number of boats stored per year: 12
Percentage of wooden boats: 100
Inside storage facilities
Maximum size for hauling and storing: 35' LOA, 4 tons
Maintenance
Number of boats maintained per year: 20
Percentage of wooden boats: 100
Owner maintenance allowed above and below rail.
Retail supplies:
Limited inventory.

■ ONION RIVER BOATWORKS

Ken Bassett
55 River St.
Franklin, NH 03235
603-934-3034 Fax: same

Builder Information
Years in business: 15
Carpenters employed: 2
Shop capacity: 30'
Willing to travel for on-the-site building projects.

Recent New Construction
15' cold-molded runabout. Ken Bassett design. 2 built 1991
and 1993.
18' plywood, sliding-seat pulling boat. Ken Bassett design.
Built 1991.
20' cold-molded Gold Cup raceboat replica. Chris Smith
design. Built 1990.

Recent Repair Projects
16'–18' canoes. Repairs, recanvasing, and refinishing.
1990–'93.
13' Curtiss hydroplane. Renewed bottom, recanvased
deck, and refinished. 1993.
21' Century runabout. Renewed bottom, transom, and topside planking. Refinished. 1993.
17' Chris-Craft runabout. Replaced stem, keel, transom,
and bottom. Refinished. 1992.
26' Chris-Craft raceboat. Replaced stem, keel, transom, and
bottom. Refastened topsides. 1992.
16' Hickman runabout. Completely restored from frame up.
Renewed upholstery, repowered, and refinished. 1991.
16' Lyman runabout. Renewed stem, keel, and transom.
Refinished. 1990.

■ OWL BROOK BOATWORKS

David S. Baer and Whitney Perry
P.O. Box 346
Holderness, NH 03245
603-968-3828

Builder Information
Years in business: 8
Carpenters employed: 2-3
Shop capacity: 35'

Recent New Construction
19' cold-molded replica of 1967 Century Arabian. Built
1992.
15'7" lapstrake plywood rowing skiff. Steve Redmond
design. Built 1991.
Currently working on developing line of small fishing and
sport boats.

Recent Repair Projects
22' Alden One-Design class (c. 1955). Replacing keelbolts
and boom. Recaulking hull. Current project.
26' Hutchinson Longdecker runabout (1927). Replaced
bow planks and battens, renewed bottom, and refinished. 1993.
24' Chris-Craft Sportsman (1959). Renewed brightwork
and partially refinished. 1993.
30' oyster river boat (1911). Replaced engine stringers and
some planking. Refinished. 1993.
18' Chris-Craft Riviera (1953). Renewed deck and planking,
hull finish and chrome. 1993.
22' Shepard runabout (1952). Completely restored boat and
engine. 1992.
28' Riva Super Aquarama (1984). Completely restored
including woodwork, finish, upholstery, and chrome.
1992.

Yard Information
Services
Engine repair
Sail repair
Rigging
Storage
Number of boats stored per year: 10
Percentage of wooden boats: 100
Inside storage facilities
Maximum size for hauling and storing: Inquire
Maintenance
Number of boats maintained per year: 25+
Percentage of wooden boats: 100
Retail supplies:
Products on hand available for purchase. Will special-
order anything on request.

■ TRAYNER'S BOATSHOP

Jay Trayner
RR #1, Box 117
Warner, NH 03278
603-456-3418 Fax: 603-938-2673

Builder Information
Years in business: 10
Carpenters employed: 2
Shop capacity: 35'
Willing to travel for on-the-site building projects.

Recent New Construction

16' lapstrake Rangeley Lake boat. Charles Barrett design. Current project.

14' plywood Winter Hawk daysailer. Built 1992.

Recent Repair Projects

18' Chris-Craft Utility cruiser. Refinishing. Current project.

15', 16', and 17' Old Town canoes. Four boats restored. 1991–'93.

16' Comet-class sloop. Replaced bottom frames, transom, deck, and centerboard trunk. Refinished. 1993.

19' Lightning-class sloop. Replaced bottom frames and centerboard trunk. Refastened bottom and refinished. 1993.

16' Century Resorter. Replaced two planks and refinished hull. 1990.

16' Old Town double-ended rowing boat. Replaced everything but stems. 1990.

18' Chris-Craft Utility cruiser. Renewed stem and transom, refastened deck, and refinished boat. 1990.

Yard Information

Services
Rigging
Maintenance
Number of boats maintained per year: 12
Percentage of wooden boats: 100

◼ HENRI VAILLANCOURT

Henri Vaillancourt
Box 142
Greenville, NH 03048
603-878-2944

Builder Information

Years in business: 23
Carpenters employed: 1
Shop capacity: 37'

Recent New Construction

Birchbark canoes. Traditional St. Lawrence River Malecite Indian designs, including the following:

20' freight canoe. Built 1993.

14' freight canoe. Built 1993.

16' traveling canoe. Built 1992.

12' one-man hunting canoe. Built 1992.

Recent Repair Projects

18' Penobscot canoe (late 19th century). Major hull repair and reconstruction. 1993.

14' Algonquin canoe (1940s). Repaired ribs and thwarts. 1993.

Yard Information

Retail supplies:
Birchbark in very limited quantities. Videos on birch-bark canoe construction.

◼ WILD MEADOW CANOES

Tom Whalen
P.O. Box 517, Rte. 25
Center Harbor, NH 03226
603-253-7536

Builder Information

Years in business: 5
Carpenters employed: 1
Shop capacity: 18'

Recent Repair Projects

Repair and recanvasing of the following canoes:

16' Old Town (1959). 1993.

16' Old Town (1924). 1993.

18' Old Town (1926). 1993.

17' B.N. Morris. 1992.

17' Old Town (1937). 1992.

Current project is a 17' Racine/McGreivey canoe. Repairing a double puncture, repainting, and revarnishing.

◼ ZEBCRAFT

Harvard Forden
RFD #1, Box 312
Ashland, NH 03217
603-279-7336

Builder Information

Years in business: 19
Carpenters employed: 1-2
Shop capacity: 36'
Willing to travel for on-the-site building projects.

Recent New Construction

26' cold-molded two-step hydroplane. Harvard Forden design. 1 built 1993, 1 planned for 1994.

24' cold-molded single-step hydroplane. Harvard Forden design. Built 1990.

Recent Repair Projects

35' lake launch (1910). Replaced keel, forefoot, garboards, and some bottom planking. Refabricated hardware. 1992.

14' Thompson outboard runabout (1953). Completely restored. Renewed bottom, decks, and transom. 1992.

16' Thompson outboard runabout (1956). Replaced framing, gunwales, deck, transom. Refinished. 1991.

34' Owens flying-bridge cruiser (1960). Replaced chines, some framing and bottom planking. Renewed topsides. 1991.

Yard Information

Services
Overland transport
Engine repair
Storage
Number of boats stored per year: 6
Percentage of wooden boats: 100

(continues)

(Zebcraft, continued)
 Inside storage facilities
 Maximum size for hauling and storing: 36' LOA, 2'6"
  draft, 3½ tons
Maintenance
 Number of boats maintained per year: 3-4
 Percentage of wooden boats: 100

■ ASAY BOATS

Robert Asay
1001 Boardwalk
Asbury Park, NJ 07712
908-776-5424

Builder Information
Years in business: 10
Carpenters employed: 1
Shop capacity: 19'

Recent New Construction
17½' and 19' Sea Bright skiffs designed by Robert Asay for
 lapstrake plywood construction. 10 boats built between
 1990 and 1993.

■ CHERUBINI BOAT CO., INC.

Lee Cherubini
51 Norman Ave.
Delran, NJ 08075
609-764-1112 Fax: 609-764-8240

Builder Information
Years in business: 35
Carpenters employed: 3
Shop capacity: 80'
Willing to travel for on-the-site building projects.

Recent Repair Projects
53' yawl. Renewed frames, planking, and fastenings. 1993.
19' Chris-Craft Capri (1947). Renewed planking and fastenings, replaced transom. 1993.
34' Herreshoff Fishers Island 23 class. Renewed planking
 and rig. Refinished. 1990.

Yard Information
Services
 Engine repair
 Rigging
Storage
 Number of boats stored per year: 30
 Percentage of wooden boats: 5

Maximum size for hauling and storing: 75' LOA, 9'
 draft, 40 tons
Maintenance
 Number of boats maintained per year: 15
 Percentage of wooden boats: 5
 Owner maintenance allowed above rail.
Retail supplies:
 Fastenings, wood, epoxy.

■ G.F.C. BOATS

Gary F. Clements
490 Hagan Rd.
Cape May Court House, NJ 0821
609-861-2171

Builder Information
Years in business: 5
Carpenters employed: 1
Shop capacity: 30'

Recent New Construction
30' shoal-draft Bahama Mama cruising ketch.
 Plywood/epoxy construction. Karl Stambaugh design.
 Planned for near future.
16' plywood/epoxy Shoestring center-console fishing skiff.
 Karl Stambaugh design. Built 1993.
15' strip-planked/epoxy Titmouse trailerable sloop. Sam
 Rabl design. Built 1992–'93.
11'6" plywood/epoxy Cartopper skiff. Phil Bolger design.
 6 built in kit form or as completed boats, 1991–'93.

■ CHARLES HANKINS

Charles Hankins
504 Grand Central Ave.
Lavallette, NJ 08735
908-793-7443

Builder Information
Years in business: 80
Carpenters employed: 2
Shop capacity: 18'

Recent New Construction
Boats designed by Charles Hankins:
15' plywood rowboat. 10 built 1993.
17' lapstrake surf boat. 5 built 1993.

Recent Repair Projects
16'–18' surf boats. Repair work has included frame and
 planking renewal, refinishing.

■ JONES BOATS

Thomas Firth Jones
Box 391
Tuckahoe, NJ 08250
609-628-2063

Builder Information
Years in business: 12

Carpenters employed: 1-2
Shop capacity: 35'

Recent New Construction

15' lapstrake plywood runabout. Robert Stephens design.
  Built 1993.
10' plywood sailing garvey. T.F. Jones design. Built 1993.
25' plywood biplane catamaran. T.F. Jones design. Built
  1992.
9' plywood nesting pram. T.F. Jones design. Built 1992.
8' plywood El Toro sailing pram. MacGregor design. 2
  built 1991.
14' lapstrake runabout. T.F. Jones design. Built 1990.

Recent Repair Projects

24' Atkin motorsailer. Renewed cockpit sole, repaired hull.
  1993.
17' Tuckahoe catboat. Replaced mast. 1993.
23' Hinemoa catamaran. Completed construction. 1990.
14' lapstrake inboard. Renewed hull. 1990.

■ ERIC R. KINDERVATER

Eric R. Kindervater
North St., P.O. Box 2
West Creek, NJ 08092
609-296-1659

Builder Information

Years in business: 35
Carpenters employed: 1
Shop capacity: 70'
Willing to travel for on-the-site building projects.

Recent New Construction

12' Barnegat Bay sneakbox (sailing model). Traditional
  design. Built 1993.
12' Barnegat Bay sneakbox (gunning model). Traditional
  design. 8 built 1990–'92.
24' and 28' clamming garveys. Eric Kindervater designs. 6
  built 1990–'92.
28' Barnegat Bay cabin garvey. Eric Kindervater design. 4
  built 1990–'92.

Recent Repair Projects

56' Chris-Craft power cruiser. Currently restoring.
55' Chris-Craft yacht/fisherman. Currently restoring.
42' Matthews double-cabin cruiser (1949). Renewed 40% of
  frames, bottom planking, and transom. 1992.

Yard Information

Services
  Overland transport
  Engine repair
  Rigging
Storage
  Number of boats stored per year: 35
  Percentage of wooden boats: 90
  Maximum size for hauling and storing: 40' LOA, 6'
    draft
Maintenance
  Number of boats maintained per year: 40-50

Percentage of wooden boats: 75
Owner maintenance allowed above rail.

■ THE LOON WORKS

Tom MacKenzie
24 Lake Shore Dr.
Parsippany, NJ 07054-3939
201-503-9492

Builder Information

Years in business: 20
Carpenters employed: 1
Shop capacity: 20'
Willing to travel for on-the-site building projects.

Recent New Construction

11'–15' wood/canvas canoes. David Yost designs. 18 built
  over last several years.

Recent Repair Projects

Restoration or repair of various wood/canvas canoes. 15
  boats worked on 1990–'93.

Yard Information

Storage
  Number of boats stored per year: 6-8
  Percentage of wooden boats: 100
  Inside storage facilities
  Maximum size for hauling and storing: Canoes to 20'
Maintenance
  Number of boats maintained per year: 12
  Percentage of wooden boats: 100
  Owner maintenance allowed.
Retail supplies:
  Materials for canoe construction and repair.

■ PERRINE BOAT WORKS

John M. Chadwick, Jr.
143 Brook St., Box 18
Barnegat, NJ 08005
609-698-2280

Builder Information

Years in business: 94
Carpenters employed: 1-3
Shop capacity: 30'
Willing to travel for on-the-site building projects.

Recent New Construction

Boats designed by Perrine:
12' gunning sneakbox. 3 built 1992.
15'6" sailing sneakbox. Built 1991.

Recent Repair Projects

12' Cranmer sneakbox. Replacing keel, planking, frames,
  and centerboard trunk. Sheathing hull in fiberglass.
  Current project.
(continues)

(Perrine Boat Works, continued)

15'6" Perrine sneakbox. Completely restoring. Current project.

12' Lang sneakbox. Refastened and recaulked hull. Sheathed in fiberglass and refinished. Renewed mast, rudder, boom, sprit pole, and daggerboard. 1993.

42' Novi boat. Refastened bottom and transom. Installed shaft tube to stop leak. 1992.

22' catboat. Reglued and refinished mast, boom, and gaff. 1992.

34' charter boat. Renewed cabin and rebuilt interior. 1991.

Yard Information
Services
 Sail repair
 Rigging
Maintenance
 Number of boats maintained per year: 8
 Percentage of wooden boats: 80
 Owner maintenance allowed above and below rail.

◼ STERLING MARINE

Newton S. Sterling
7 Bates Lane
Port Republic, NJ 08241
609-652-1950 Fax: 609-748-8982

Builder Information
Years in business: 25
Carpenters employed: 1-2
Shop capacity: 40'
Willing to travel for on-the-site building projects.

Recent New Construction
Boats designed by Newton Sterling:
12' plywood/epoxy garvey. 2 built 1993.
16' plywood/epoxy garvey. 15 built 1992–'93.
14' garvey. Built 1991.
10' stitch-and-glue plywood sneakbox. Built 1990.

Recent Repair Projects
Complete restoration of the following boats:
19' and 20' speed garveys. 2 boats restored 1990–'94.
19' Chris-Craft runabout. 1990–'93.
37' Wheeler sportfisherman. 1990–'91.
19' Lightning-class sloop. 1990.

Yard Information
Services
 Engine repair
Storage
 Number of boats stored per year: 4
 Percentage of wooden boats: 100
 Inside storage facilities
 Maximum size for hauling and storing: 38' LOA
Maintenance
 Number of boats maintained per year: 6
 Percentage of wooden boats: 100
Retail supplies:
 Wood, paint, fastenings. Available on order basis.

◼ BLUE STREAK MARINE

Seth Rolland and Chris Mullen
HCR 74, Box 22203
El Prado, NM 87529
505-751-0923

Builder Information
Years in business: 7
Carpenters employed: 1
Shop capacity: 24'
Willing to travel for on-the-site building projects.

Recent New Construction
16' plywood Tursiops sea kayak. Mike Alford design. 4 built 1992–'93.
16' lapstrake Swampscott dory. John Gardner design. Built 1990.

Recent Repair Projects
14' Icelandic fishing boat. Completely restored; replaced 60% of wood. 1991.

THE ADIRONDACK GUIDE BOAT SHOP

John B. Spring
Blue Mountain Lake Rd.
Indian Lake, NY 12842
518-648-5455 Fax: same

Builder Information
Years in business: 30
Carpenters employed: 2
Shop capacity: 20'

Recent New Construction
16' guideboats and 15' or 17' wood/canvas canoes. Company usually builds one guideboat each year and several canoes.

Recent Repair Projects
16' Austin Adirondack guideboat. Refastening and refinishing. Current project.

16' Adirondack guideboat (builder unknown). Complete restoration. Renewing ribs and planking, refinishing. Current project.

16' Old Town wood/canvas runabout. Replaced transom and deck. Recanvased. 1993.

14' catboat. Completely restored. Replaced frames, transom, cabintop. 1993.

16' Parsons Adirondack guideboat (1893). Completely restored. Renewed ribs and planking. 1993.

16' Peterborough canoe (1890s). Replaced ribs, plank battens and some planking, keel, keelson, and stems. 1993.

11' Rushton Wee Lassie canoe. Completely restored. 1993.

AGB — ADIRONDACK GOODBOAT

Mason Smith
HC 01, Box 44
Long Lake, NY 12847
518-624-6398

Builder Information
Years in business: 21
Carpenters employed: 2
Shop capacity: 24'
Willing to travel for on-the-site building projects.

Recent New Construction
Boats designed by Mason Smith for Constant Camber construction:

17' Adirondack Goodboats and 16' Goodboat kits. Two 17-footers under construction; 2 kits supplied 1993.

16' Chipmunk canoe. 1 kit supplied 1993.

15' superlight canoe. Built 1993.

16' tandem canoe. 2 built 1993.

17' paddling/sailing canoes. 4 built 1992–'93.

17' lug-rigged rowing/sailing boats. 25 built 1990–'93.

Recent Repair Projects
14' Penn Yan outboard runabout. Completely restoring. Current project.

17' Adirondack Goodboats. Refurbishing hulls and refinishing. Current projects.

15' and 16' Rushton Indian Girl canoes. Rebuilt and restored hulls, recanvased and refinished. 2 boats worked on during 1993.

11'–15' Rushton lapstrake canoes. Rebuilt or restored 3 boats 1992–'93.

16' Adirondack guideboats. 4 boats restored 1990–'93.

18' Old Town centerboard daysailers. Completely rebuilt or restored 6 boats 1990–'93.

ALDER CREEK BOAT WORKS

Carol Hanna
10511 Joslin Rd.
Remsen, NY 13438
315-831-5321

Builder Information
Years in business: 12
Carpenters employed: 1
Shop capacity: 17'

Recent New Construction
Boats designed by Peterborough Canoe Co.:

12' strip-planked solo canoe. 2 built 1992–'93.

16' strip-planked, solo or tandem canoe. 2 built 1991–'93.

15' wood/canvas solo or tandem canoe. 3 built 1990–'93.

17' wood/canvas tandem canoe. 2 built 1990–'93.

Recent Repair Projects
10'–19' wood/canvas canoes. Restoration, recanvasing, and refinishing. Approximately 50 canoes worked on between 1990–'93.

14' Penn Yan Swift runabout. Recanvased. 1992.

15'–16' wood/canvas rowing boats. Completely restored 6 boats, 1990 and 1993.

16' guideboats. Repaired and refinished 2 boats, 1990–'93.

12'–16' skiffs. Repaired and refinished 2 boats, 1990–'93.

Yard Information
Maintenance
    Number of boats maintained per year: 1-2
    Percentage of wooden boats: 100
Retail supplies:
    Hardware, paint, varnish, canvas.

ALEUT WOOD & SKIN KAYAK

R. Bruce Lemon
P.O. Box 54
Jacksonville, NY 14854
607-387-8000

Builder Information
Years in business: 2
Carpenters employed: 1
Shop capacity: 21'
Willing to travel for on-the-site building projects.

Recent New Construction
17' and 21' Aleut kayaks. Hand-stitched skins on hand-lashed wood frames. R. Bruce Lemon designs based on authentic Aleut baidarka kayaks. Eleven 17-footers built 1992–'94; three 21-footers built 1993–'94.

■ ARNOTTS BOAT YARD

Bruce A. Dante
15 Athasca Rd.
Islip, NY 11751
516-581-5808 Fax: same

Builder Information
Years in business: 15
Carpenters employed: 1-2
Shop capacity: 45'

Recent Repair Projects
18' Harless ice scooter. Renewing frames and bottom
   planking. Replacing deck. Current project.
37' Knutson sloop. Stripped and refinished hull and brightwork. Replaced frames as necessary. 1993.
43' Richardson cruiser. Renewed decks and guardrails.
   Replaced planking, reframed transom. Stripped and
   refinished hull. 1991.

Yard Information
Services
   Launching facilities
   Overland transport
   Engine repair
Storage
   Number of boats stored per year: 85
   Percentage of wooden boats: 10
   Maximum size for hauling and storing: 45' LOA,
      18 tons
Maintenance
   Number of boats maintained per year: 100
   Percentage of wooden boats: 20
   Owner maintenance allowed above and below rail.
Retail supplies:
   Paint, varnish, fastenings, hardware, engine parts.

■ BATTENKILL BOATWORKS

Michael McEvoy
The Mill on Mill St.
Greenwich, NY 12834
518-692-9623

Builder Information
Years in business: 5
Carpenters employed: 1
Shop capacity: 26'
Willing to travel for on-the-site building projects.

Recent New Construction
Boats designed by Michael McEvoy for lapstrake
   construction:
15' catboat. Current project.
12' racing/sailing dinghy. Current project.
16' sailing skiff. Built 1993.
16' work scow. Built 1992.
12' outboard duckboat. Built 1992.
10'6" rowing skiff. Built 1991.

Recent Repair Projects
26' Crocker flush-decked cruising sloop. Completely
   rebuilding. Current project.

■ BOATHOUSE WOODWORKS

James Cameron
Upper Saint Regis
Lake Clear, NY 12945
518-327-3470 Fax: same

Builder Information
Years in business: 16
Carpenters employed: 1
Shop capacity: 32'
Willing to travel for on-the-site building projects.

Recent New Construction
14' guideboat. Smooth-lap construction. 3 built 1992–'93,
   one under construction.
15' strip-planked Electra-Craft. Reproduction of Syracuse
   Boat Co. design. Built 1991.
16' Adirondack guideboat. Vassar design. Built 1990.

Recent Repair Projects
32' Clinton Crane Idem-class sloop (1902). Replaced cockpit and recanvased deck. Renewed brightwork. 1994.
14' and 16' guideboats. Repairs have included bottom
   board replacement, storm damage repair, and renewal
   of stems, decks, gunwales, and finish. 3 boats worked
   on 1993–'94.
17' Electra-Craft cruiser. Replaced decks and interior floor.
   Refinished. 1993.
32' Idem-class sloop. Replaced keelson, centerboard trunk,
   stem, transom, and planking. 1992.
18' Gar Wood Sedan cruiser. Renewed bottom, transom,
   stem, decks, and canvas sheathing. 1991.

Yard Information
Storage
   Number of boats stored per year: 10
   Percentage of wooden boats: 95
   Inside storage facilities
   Maximum size for hauling and storing: 10' LOA, 1 ton
Maintenance
   Number of boats maintained per year: 40
   Percentage of wooden boats: 98

■ CAYUGA WOODEN BOATWORKS

6301 Water St., P.O. Box 301
Cayuga, NY 13034
315-253-7447

Builder Information
Years in business: 8
Carpenters employed: 3-6
Shop capacity: 65'
Willing to travel for on-the-site building projects.

Recent New Construction
7'6" lapstrake plywood tender. Current project.

Recent Repair Projects

31' Fishers Island 23 (1931). Renewing frames, floors, and bottom planking. Planned for 1994.

20' Century Resorter (1954). Completely rebuilding. Renewing frames, floors, planking, deck, engine, and upholstery. Current project.

38' Atkin schooner (1927). Ongoing project — renewal of cabin sole, galley, engine box, and interior trim. 1991–'94.

43' Richardson power cruiser (1956). Renewed frames, planking, decks, stem, transom, cabin sides, windshields. 1992–'93.

65' Thousand Islands tour boat (1917). Replaced frames, planking, section of keel, and shaftlog. 1993.

30' Jim Brown trimaran (1970). Repaired deck, bulkheads, cockpit floor. 1993.

65' fantail passenger ferry (1913). Replaced 60 frames, 5 floors, 20% of planking. Refastened hull and refinished. 1992.

Yard Information

Services
  Marina facilities
  Launching facilities
  Engine repair
  Rigging
Storage
  Number of boats stored per year: 70
  Percentage of wooden boats: 50
  Inside storage facilities
  Maximum size for hauling and storing: 65' LOA, 8' draft, 50 tons
Maintenance
  Number of boats maintained per year: Varies
  Percentage of wooden boats: 50
  Owner maintenance allowed above and below rail.
Retail supplies:
  Wood, fastenings, hardware, paint, caulk. Good inventory of supplies.

■ H. CHALK & SON INC.

Duane J. Chalk
Box 35, Main St.
Fishers Landing, NY 13641
315-686-4125 Fax: 315-686-0051

Builder Information

Years in business: 46
Carpenters employed: 1
Shop capacity: 26'
Willing to travel for on-the-site building projects.

Recent Repair Projects

Complete refinishing of the following classic power craft:
22' Shepard. Current project.
17' Chris-Craft. Rebuilding. Current project.
19' Lyman. Current project.
23' Hutchinson. 1993.
26' Hacker-Craft. 1992.
23' Fitzgerald & Lee. 1992.

Yard Information

Services
  Marina facilities
  Launching facilities
  Overland transport
  Moorage
  Engine repair
  Rigging
Storage
  Number of boats stored per year: 375
  Percentage of wooden boats: 5
  Inside storage facilities
  Maximum size for hauling and storing: 30' LOA
Maintenance
  Number of boats maintained per year: 100's
  Percentage of wooden boats: 5
Retail supplies:
  Complete inventory of supplies.

■ CLEAR ROCK BOATS

Peter Watson
5325 Barber Rd.
Avon, NY 14414
716-226-6874

Builder Information

Years in business: 8
Carpenters employed: 1
Shop capacity: 40'
Willing to travel for on-the-site building projects.

Recent New Construction

18'6" lapstrake Grand Banks dory for oar and sail. Traditional design. Built 1989.

20' lapstrake sailing bateau. R.D. Culler design. Built 1988.

Recent Repair Projects

16' wood/canvas Old Town canoe. Renewed stems, decks, gunwales, and caned seats. Recanvased and refinished hull. 1993.

14' lapstrake Thompson runabout. Renewed keel, transom, framing, stern planking, splash rails, and windshield. Refinished. 1992–'93.

24' Norwegian Honeymoon sloop. Pulled and checked keelbolts. Replaced some planking and frames, and refastened. Renewed decks and cabin, refinished. 1992.

15' wood/canvas Chestnut canoe. Replaced 9 ribs, 30% of planking, stems, gunwales, and seats. Recanvased and refinished hull. 1992.

17'6" wood/canvas Kennebec canoe. Replaced 12 ribs and gunwales. Recanvased and refinished hull. 1991.

17'6" cold-molded Danish racing canoe. Replaced gunwales and refinished. 1990.

Yard Information

Services
  Engine repair
(continues)

(Clear Rock Boats, continued)

Storage
Number of boats stored per year: 2
Maximum size for hauling and storing: 40' LOA, 6' draft, 20 tons

Maintenance
Number of boats maintained per year: Varies
Percentage of wooden boats: 100
Owner maintenance allowed above and below rail.

Retail supplies:
Complete inventory of supplies. Will special-order by request.

■ COECLES HARBOR MARINA & BOATYARD INC.

John and Peter Needham
Box 1670, Hudson Ave.
Shelter Island, NY 11964
516-749-0700 Fax: 516-749-0593

Builder Information
Years in business: 20
Carpenters employed: 5-6
Shop capacity: 55'
Willing to travel for on-the-site building projects.

Recent New Construction
11' lapstrake Susan skiff. Robert Steward design. 2 built 1993.
35' speedboat. John Hacker design. Built 1992.

Recent Repair Projects
33' Richardson cruiser. Replaced foredeck, forward hatch, and rails. 1993.
36' Baltzer Voyager. Replaced transom, recanvased cabin-top. 1993.
36' Rob Rich lobster picnic boat. Renewed stem, forward topside planking, and cabin trunk. 1993.
41' cutter. Converted and rebuilt main cabin interior and galley. 1993.
55' Scheel/Van Dam sloop PATRICIAN. Refinished exterior, renewed rig. 1993.
26' Pennant sloop. Built new mainmast. 1992.

Yard Information
Services
Marina facilities
Launching facilities
Overland transport
Moorage
Engine repair
Rigging
Storage
Number of boats stored per year: 120
Percentage of wooden boats: 30
Inside storage facilities
Maximum size for hauling and storing: 60' LOA, 7' draft, 30 tons

Maintenance
Number of boats maintained per year: 500
Percentage of wooden boats: 25
Owner maintenance allowed above rail.

Retail supplies:
Marine supplies, Evinrude motors.

■ DANO CANOES

Donald and Pamela Dano
102 Sweeting St.
Syracuse, NY 13203
315-476-8919

Builder Information
Years in business: 16
Carpenters employed: 1
Shop capacity: 20'

Recent New Construction
Boats designed by Donald Dano and built during 1990–'94:
10'2", 11'2", 12'6", and 13'6" strip-planked canoes. 6 built.
14'6" tandem canoe. 1 built.
18'3" skiff for oar and sail. 1 built.

Recent Repair Projects
17' canoes. Several repaired over last four years.

Yard Information
Services
Overland transport
Sail repair
Rigging
Storage
Number of boats stored per year: 8
Percentage of wooden boats: 100
Inside storage facilities
Maximum size for hauling and storing: 20' LOA, 1' draft, 1,000 lbs.

Maintenance
Number of boats maintained per year: Varies
Percentage of wooden boats: 80

Retail supplies:
Brass foundry and forge work for canoes. Custom hardware and fittings.

■ ANTONIO DIAS/MARINE DESIGN & CONSTRUCTION

Antonio Dias and Katherine Mehls
193 Tillson Lake Rd.
Wallkill, NY 12589-3214
914-895-9165

Builder Information
Years in business: 10
Carpenters employed: 1
Shop capacity: 26'
Willing to travel for on-the-site building projects.

Recent New Construction

Boats designed by Antonio Dias for glued-lapstrake construction:

18′ Beach Point 18 canoe yawl. Built 1993.

16′ Spar'hawk sailing canoe. Built 1993.

14′ Little Cat sailing dinghy. 2 built 1992.

■ ELCO — ELECTRIC LAUNCH COMPANY, INC.

Joseph W. Fleming II
261 Upper North Rd.
Highland, NY 12528
914-691-3777 Fax: 914-691-3799

Builder Information

Years in business: 10
Carpenters employed: 6
Shop capacity: 50′

Recent New Construction

24′ and 30′ electric launches. Cold-molded construction. Vintage 1890s Elco designs. Available on custom-order basis.

Recent Repair Projects

15′ raceboat (1930s). Completely rebuilding. Current project.

27′ runabout. Completed various repairs. 1994.

14′ electric launch. Repaired and rewired 3 boats. 1993.

18′ Cape Dory launch. Repaired and refinished. 1993.

■ FIVE POINTS INC.

Carolyn Tocha
RD #1, Box 12
Little Valley, NY 14755
716-938-6315 Fax: same

Builder Information

Years in business: 9
Carpenters employed: 3
Shop capacity: 36′
Willing to travel for on-the-site building projects.

Recent New Construction

23′ plywood Birdwatcher camp-cruiser. Phil Bolger design. Built 1993.

7′6″ plywood dinghy. Five Points Inc. design. 2 built 1992.

Recent Repair Projects

19′ Chris-Craft Capri. Replaced section of keel, repaired frames and bottom planking. 1993.

13′ guideboat (1920s). Renewed ribs and several planks. 1993.

18′ Gar Wood (1934). Completely restored including transom frame, bottom and side planking, and deck. Rebuilt engine. 1993.

15′ Century Resorter (1951). Replaced port chine, several planks, and transom frame. Refinished. 1993.

25′ Alden sloop (1912). Recanvased deck, recaulked hull, renewed paint and varnish. 1992–'93.

19′ Lyman (1961). Repaired stem and planking, refinished. 1991–'92.

36′ Alden yawl. Replaced keel timber and rebuilt deck and cockpit. Renewed planking. 1990–'91.

Yard Information

Services
  Overland transport
  Engine repair
Storage
  Number of boats stored per year: 10
  Percentage of wooden boats: 100
  Inside storage facilities
  Maximum size for hauling and storing: Inquire
Maintenance
  Number of boats maintained per year: 5-20
  Percentage of wooden boats: 75
Retail supplies:
  Paint, varnish, fastenings, caulking, preservatives, wood.

■ FORESTPORT BOAT CO. INC.

Parker Snead, President
River St.
Forestport, NY 13338
315-392-4898

Builder Information

Years in business: 12
Carpenters employed: 3
Shop capacity: 25′

Recent New Construction

13′ single-cockpit outboard runabout. Planked sides and plywood bottom. Parker Snead design. 3 built 1991–'93.

16′ double-cockpit outboard or jet runabout. Planked sides and plywood bottom. Parker Snead design. In planning stage.

Recent Repair Projects

Complete restoration of the following boats:

19′ Chris-Craft Custom Runabout (1939). Current project.

21′ Century Coronado (1968). Current project.

18′ Century Utility (1946). Current project.

16′ Century Resorter. Current project.

17′ Chris-Craft Deluxe Runabout (1940). 1993, for shipment to Hawaii.

25′ Chris-Craft Sportsman (1940, Ser. #1). 1992.

Yard Information

Services
  Overland transport
  Engine repair
Storage
  Number of boats stored per year: 70
  Percentage of wooden boats: 80
  Inside storage facilities
  Maximum size for hauling and storing: Inquire
Maintenance
  Number of boats maintained per year: 100
  Percentage of wooden boats: 80

GARWOOD BOAT CO., INC.

Thomas R. and Lawrence A. Turcotte
329 Broadway
Watervliet, NY 12189
518-273-2654

Builder Information
Years in business: 20
Carpenters employed: 8
Shop capacity: 50'

Recent New Construction
Between 1990 and present, the GarWood Boat Company has built over 50 runabouts using double-planked, cold-molded WEST System construction. Their new boat production has a 16'–40' size range.
The specific models are as follows: 16' Split Cockpit; 16' Speedster; 19' Deluxe Runabout (twin cockpit forward); 22' Deluxe Runabout (triple cockpit); 22' Streamliner (rear engine); 22' Speedster (aft cockpit); 25' Deluxe Runabout (triple cockpit); 28' and 33' Commemorative Baby Gars; 40' Ocean Runabout; and Gold Cup racing boats (construction and restoration).

Recent Repair Projects
Maintenance, restoration, and rebuilding of vintage 16' to 33' Gar Woods built between 1922 and 1948.

Yard Information
Services
    Launching facilities
    Overland transport
    Engine repair
Storage
    Number of boats stored per year: 24
    Percentage of wooden boats: 100
    Inside storage facilities
    Maximum size for hauling and storing: 50' LOA, 3' draft, 6 tons
Maintenance
    Number of boats maintained per year: 24
    Percentage of wooden boats: 100
Retail supplies:
    Paint, varnish, hardware, and other supplies.

HACKER CRAFT BOAT CO.

Rte. 9 North
Silver Bay, NY 12874
518-543-6731 Fax: 518-543-6732

Builder Information
Years in business: 41
Carpenters employed: 16-20
Shop capacity: 55'
Willing to travel for on-the-site building projects.

Recent New Construction
Company specializes in the construction of 20' to 44' runabouts, cabin cruisers, raceboats, launches, and commuters. Wood/epoxy construction. About 25 boats are built each year. Shipped world-wide.

HALL'S BOAT CORPORATION

Mary O. Hall
Box 312
Lake George, NY 12845
518-668-5437

Builder Information
Years in business: 66
Carpenters employed: 3

Recent Repair Projects
Chris-Crafts, Gar Woods, and other antique powerboats. Minor repairs to complete restorations. Approximately 50 boats repaired a year.

Yard Information
Services
    Marina facilities
    Launching facilities
    Engine repair
    Rigging
Storage
    Number of boats stored per year: 125
    Percentage of wooden boats: 60
    Inside storage facilities
    Maximum size for hauling and storing: 30' LOA
Maintenance
    Number of boats maintained per year: 125
    Percentage of wooden boats: 60
Retail supplies:
    Paint, sandpaper, fittings, and other marine supplies.

HATHAWAY BOAT SHOP

Christopher Woodward
9 Algonquin Ave.
Saranac Lake, NY 12983
518-891-3961 Fax: 518-327-3313

Builder Information
Years in business: 60
Carpenters employed: 1
Shop capacity: 35'

Recent New Construction
Traditionally built Adirondack guideboats have been a specialty for the last 60 years. Recent projects have included a 15'6" Vassar-designed guideboat, a 13'6" Will Martin design, and a 16' Hanmer design. One boat built each year.

Recent Repair Projects
13'–18' Adirondack guideboats. Cole, Smith, Seeber, and Parsons designs. Repair work has involved renewing planking and ribs, as well as recanvasing and refinishing. Approximately 12 boats repaired 1991–'93.
Old Town, Kennebec, and Morris canoes. Recanvasing and refinishing. 10 boats restored 1990–'93.
18' Penn Yan Baby Buzz cruiser. Recanvased and refinished. 1990.
26' Century runabout. Renewed bottom and refinished. 1990.

Yard Information

Retail supplies:

Fastenings, hardware, paint, canvas, oars, paddles, caned seats.

ROGER H. HOLZMACHER

Roger H. Holzmacher
31 Willow St.
Babylon, NY 11702
516-669-3540

Builder Information

Years in business: 12
Carpenters employed: 1
Shop capacity: 25'

Recent New Construction

16' lapstrake outboard skiff. Roger Holzmacher design. 2 built 1990 and 1993.

Recent Repair Projects

Boats worked on from 1990–'93:

18' G.F. Carter sloop. Replaced keel, centerboard trunk, rudder post trunk, 50% of planking, coamings, and rails.

20' G.F. Carter catboat. Replaced transom and deadwood.

26' Wilbur Ketcham launch. Sistered frames, replaced floor timbers and sternpost.

24' daysailer. Replaced keel.

43' Richardson cruiser. Replaced sections of planking, transom framing, and main deck. Joint project with Arnotts Boatyard, Islip, NY.

45' Cy Hamlin center-cockpit yawl. Replaced transom framing, aft deckbeams, clamps, and rails. Joint project with Arnotts Boatyard, Islip, NY.

BILL KALLUSCH BOATS

William Kallusch
7410 Rte. 14
Sodus Point, NY 14555
315-483-6371

Builder Information

Years in business: 70
Carpenters employed: 3
Shop capacity: 55'
Willing to travel for on-the-site building projects.

Recent New Construction

Boats of plywood construction:

9' Sharpie skiff. Todd Kallusch design. 8 built 1990–'93.

12' Fantam skiff for oar and sail. Todd Kallusch design. 1 rowing model and 1 sailing model built 1992.

14' Bantam-class sloop. Philip Rhodes design. Built 1990.

Recent Repair Projects

30' Pacemaker. Renewing transom, decks, and windshield. Current project.

24' Crosby lobsterboat. Completely restoring. Current project.

21' Cruisers Inc. runabout. Renewing decks and rail. Completely refinishing. Current project.

17' Chris-Craft runabout (1942). Completely restoring. Current project.

17' and 18' Lyman runabouts (1960 and 1958 models). Completely restored. 1991–'92.

17' Penn Yan canoe (1948). Renewed ribs. Recanvased hull and replaced gunwales. 1992.

17' and 18' Chris-Craft runabouts (1937 and 1940 models). Completely restored. 1990.

Yard Information

Services

Marina facilities

Launching facilities

Overland transport

Moorage

Engine repair

Rigging

Storage

Number of boats stored per year: 20

Percentage of wooden boats: 75

Inside storage facilities

Maximum size for hauling and storing: 55' LOA, 10' draft, 30 tons

Maintenance

Number of boats maintained per year: 50

Percentage of wooden boats: 75

Owner maintenance allowed above and below rail.

Retail supplies:

Paint, fastenings, mahogany, marine plywood, seam and bedding compounds, and other materials related to boatbuilding and repair. Full-service yard.

KORTCHMAR & WILLNER

Michael Kortchmar
Box 2096, Sterling Ave.
Greenport, NY 11944
516-477-2466 Fax: 516-765-3153

Builder Information

Years in business: 9
Carpenters employed: 3
Shop capacity: 80'
Willing to travel for on-the-site building projects.

Recent Repair Projects

40' Nevins 40 PRIMA DONNA (1956). Repaired shaftlog, frames and floors. Reinstalled engine. Rebuilt forward cabin, installed windlass. 1993.

28' Wittholz catboat. Renewed various structural members, refinished. 1992–'93.

42' custom motor launch (1920). Renewed backbone, planking, floors, and foredeck. 1992–'93.

46' New York 32 SIRIUS. Completed structural work on keel, floors, and framing. Rebuilt interior, replaced boom. 1989–'93.

(continues)

(Kortchmar & Willner, continued)

37′ Alden U.S. One-Design sloop. Replaced teak deck, deck framing, and clamp. Refastened hull, renewed cockpit, and installed engine. 1989–'90.

Yard Information

Services
Launching facilities
Overland transport
Rigging
Storage
Number of boats stored per year: 50
Inside storage facilities
Maximum size for hauling and storing: 45′ LOA, 7′ draft, 20 tons
Owner maintenance allowed.
Retail supplies:
Hauling, storage, and maintenance to be offered starting in 1994. Company will also be opening a bronze foundry in 1994, and carrying retail supplies as demand exists.

■ TOM KRIEG'S BOAT SHOP

Thomas F. Krieg
P.O. Box 1007, Westlake Rd.
Cooperstown, NY 13326
607-547-2658

Builder Information

Years in business: 10
Carpenters employed: 1
Shop capacity: 55′

Recent Repair Projects

16′ Anchorage Boat Works launch (1950s). Replaced decks, rails, coaming, and seats. Renewed engine. 1993.
17′ Morris canoe (c. 1916). Recanvased and refinished. 1993.
55′ Elco cruiser (1912). Replaced transom and planking. Repaired forward canopy. 1992.
22′ catboat (1939). Replaced planking. Modified and rebuilt interior, refinished hull and deck. 1992.
16′ J.R. Robertson canoe. Replaced 4 ribs and planking. Recanvased and refinished hull. 1991.
25′ Gazely destroyer-type stern launch (c. 1895). Replaced keel, shaftlog, planking, and ceiling. 1989–'91.
18′ Dodge Boat & Plane Works sloop (1935). Renewed garboards, transom, centerboard trunk, and decks. Refinished. 1990.

Yard Information

Services
Engine repair
Sail repair
Rigging
Maintenance
Number of boats maintained per year: 15
Percentage of wooden boats: 95
Owner maintenance allowed.
Retail supplies:
Paint, hardware, fastenings, rigging and mooring supplies.

■ LEILANI BOATWORKS

Brian Kearney
2601 Ave. X
Brooklyn, NY 11235
718-332-2717

Builder Information

Years in business: 15
Carpenters employed: 1
Shop capacity: 50′
Willing to travel for on-the-site building projects.

Recent Repair Projects

50′ Lawley yawl (1903). Renewed hull with cold-molded overlay. 1992.

Yard Information

Services
Engine repair
Rigging

■ McGREIVEY'S CANOE SHOP

John McGreivey
1379 Old State Rd.
Cato, NY 13033
315-626-6635

Builder Information

Years in business: 17
Carpenters employed: 2
Shop capacity: 25′
Willing to travel for on-the-site building projects.

Recent New Construction

15′ wood/canvas canoe. Detroit Boat Co. design. 2 built 1993.
17′ wood/canvas canoe. Racine Boat Mfg. Co. design. 15 built 1989–'93.

Recent Repair Projects

Restoration or repair of wood/canvas canoes, rowboats, outboards, and Adirondack guideboats. Numerous projects each year.

Yard Information

Retail supplies:
Hardware and custom parts for wood/canvas canoes and guideboats. Canvas, filler, varnish, and paint.

■ A.B. MEANOR'S WOODWORKS

Allen B. Meanor
RD #3, Box 411A, Cole Rd.
Delanson, NY 12053
518-895-2255

Builder Information

Years in business: 20
Carpenters employed: 1
Shop capacity: 28′

Recent New Construction

22'6" runabout. Cold-molded topsides, plywood and mahogany bottom. Allen Meanor design. Built 1991–'92.

24' runabout. Cold-molded topsides, plywood and mahogany bottom. John Hacker design. 2 built 1990.

Recent Repair Projects

Repair work has included bottom, transom, and deck renewal on several power cruisers, ranging in size from 28' to 36'. 4 boats restored 1991–'93.

Retail supplies:

Stainless-steel fastenings, mahogany, oak, paint, WEST System products.

■ MORROW'S BOAT SHOP

Ralph Morrow
46 Duprey St.
Saranac Lake, NY 12983
518-891-0432

Builder Information

Years in business: 35
Carpenters employed: 1
Shop capacity: 24'

Recent New Construction

Specializes in construction of Adirondack guideboats. Builds about 2 boats each year — 41 completed to date.

Recent Repair Projects

Repairs Chris-Crafts, Hacker-Crafts, canoes, and guide-boats.

Yard Information

Maintenance

Number of boats maintained per year: 10-20
Percentage of wooden boats: 100

Retail supplies:

Inquire.

■ NORTH RIVER BOATWORKS

Howard Mittleman
6 Elm St.
Albany, NY 12202
518-434-4414 Fax: 518-432-8984

Builder Information

Years in business: 14
Carpenters employed: 4
Shop capacity: 22'
Willing to travel for on-the-site building projects.

Recent New Construction

14' lapstrake pulling boat. Rushton Model 109. 7 built 1990–'93.

15' lapstrake North River skiff. Howard Mittleman design. 4 built 1990–'93.

18' lapstrake St. Lawrence River sailing skiff. A. Bain & Co. design (1893). Built 1992.

13'6" lapstrake Amesbury skiff. John Gardner design. 2 built 1992.

13'9" Keuka Lake trout boat. Sutherland design. 2 built 1990.

Recent Repair Projects

15'–18' wood/canvas canoes. Repair, restoration and recanvasing. Several completed 1990–'93.

16' Smith & Sons Lake George skiff. Replaced keel and stem. 1992.

16' Rushton Vesper sailing canoe. Restored to museum quality for display at The Adirondack Museum. 1990.

18' Rushton Iowa canoe. Major restoration. 1990.

26' Friendship sloop. Replaced bowsprit and cockpit coaming. 1990.

15' North River skiff. Replaced damaged planks and fittings. 1990.

■ OLIVER CANOES

Oliver K. Clark
8657 Rebecca Dr.
Williamsville, NY 14221
716-632-4336

Builder Information

Years in business: 1
Carpenters employed: 1
Shop capacity: 16'

Recent New Construction

Company specializes in the building and repair of 14' and 16' custom wood/canvas canoes.

■ CARL PICKHARDT, BOATBUILDER

Carl Pickhardt
P.O. Box 95
Halcottville, NY 12438
607-326-4071

Builder Information

Years in business: 5
Carpenters employed: 1
Shop capacity: 30'
Willing to travel for on-the-site building projects.

Recent New Construction

19' cold-molded Lightning-class sloop. Sparkman & Stephens design. Current project.

13'6" plywood rowing skiff. C. Pickhardt design. Built 1993.

10'6" strip/composite double-paddle canoe. J.H. Rushton design. 2 built 1991–'92.

Recent Repair Projects

17' Old Town sailing canoe. Renewing deck, recanvasing hull and sponsons, and refinishing. Current project.

12' Penguin-class dinghy. Replaced keelson and some frames and planking. Taped seams and epoxied hull exterior, faired and refinished. 1993.

(continues)

(Cark Pickhardt, Boatbuilder, continued)
7'6" Old Town dinghy. Scarfed section of guardrail, sheathed hull in fiberglass and epoxy. 1993.
12' lapstrake skiff. Replaced chine, bottom, and planking. 1991.

Yard Information
Services
Overland transport
Maintenance
Number of boats maintained per year: 5
Percentage of wooden boats: 100
Owner maintenance allowed above and below rail.
Retail supplies:
Miscellaneous hardware, fastenings, paint. Bahama dinghy cradle boats.

■ PORT BAY BOATS

James H. Mayo
7736 Hapeman Rd., P.O. Box 242
Wolcott, NY 14590
315-594-2952

Builder Information
Years in business: 10
Carpenters employed: 1
Shop capacity: 24'
Willing to travel for on-the-site building projects.

Recent New Construction
22' strip-planked Blue Moon cutter. Thomas Gillmer design. Built 1992–'93.
9' lapstrake tender. Lawley design. 4 built 1992–'93.
11'6" lapstrake Columbia dinghy. N.G. Herreshoff design. Built 1990.

Recent Repair Projects
Complete restorations of the following boats:
16' Rushton canoe. 1993.
16' Adirondack guideboat. 1992.
16' Chris-Craft. 1991.
18' Chris-Craft. 1991.
18' Chris-Craft Riviera. 1990.

Yard Information
Maintenance
Number of boats maintained per year: 6
Percentage of wooden boats: 100

■ ROCK CITY RESTORATIONS

Scott Dorrer
RD #1, Box 36
Cropseyville, NY 12052
518-279-3676

Builder Information
Years in business: 7
Carpenters employed: 2
Shop capacity: 45'
Willing to travel for on-the-site building projects.

Recent New Construction
14'6" batten-seam hydroplane. John Hacker design. Built 1993.
22' wood/epoxy runabout. Gar Wood design. 2 built 1989.
28' wood/epoxy runabout. Gar Wood design. 2 built 1989.

Recent Repair Projects
22' Chris-Craft utility. Refinished. 1993.
22' Chris-Craft runabout. Replaced bottom. 1992.
21' Dodge utility. Replaced bottom. 1992.
16' Chris-Craft runabout. Completely reconstructed. 1992.
18' Hacker-Craft runabout. Renewed transom framing. 1992.
16' Adirondack guideboat. Replaced ribs, renewed seats, refinished. 1991.
21' Gesswein runabout. Completely reconstructed. 1991.

Yard Information
Services
Overland transport
Engine repair
Storage
Number of boats stored per year: 5
Percentage of wooden boats: 100
Maximum size for hauling and storing: 35' LOA, 2½' draft, 4-5 tons
Maintenance
Number of boats maintained per year: 15-20
Percentage of wooden boats: 100
Owner maintenance allowed above and below rail.
Retail supplies:
Building supplies, some lumber.

■ JOHN A. ROGERS, BUILDER

John Rogers
4880 County Rd. 11
Rushville, NY 14544
716-554-6778

Builder Information
Years in business: 13
Carpenters employed: 1
Shop capacity: 25'
Willing to travel for on-the-site building projects.

Recent New Construction
20' cold-molded Shark-class catamarans built on a custom-order basis. Rod Macalpine-Downie design. 3 built 1991–'94.

Recent Repair Projects
20' Shark. Repaired collision damage to hull. 1993.
22' Ensign. Replaced maststep on two boats. Renewed coaming and cabin interior on a third boat. 1991–'93.

■ SAILBOAT SHOP INC.

1322 E. Geneseo St.
Skaneateles, NY 13152
315-685-7558

Builder Information

Years in business: 15
Carpenters employed: 2
Shop capacity: 28'
Willing to travel for on-the-site building projects.

Recent Repair Projects

16' catboat. Built new mast. 1993.
19' Lightning-class sloop. Repaired mast and centerboard trunk, recaulked bottom, recanvased deck. 1991–'93.
16' Comet-class sloop. Replaced bottom planking. 1993.
20' Long Island Jr. sloop. Replaced sections of keel and keelson, renewed some planking. 1991.

Yard Information

Services
  Launching facilities
  Overland transport
  Moorage
  Rigging
Storage
  Number of boats stored per year: 50
  Percentage of wooden boats: 5
  Inside storage facilities
  Maximum size for hauling and storing: 26' LOA, 3½' draft, 4 tons
Maintenance
  Number of boats maintained per year: 250
  Percentage of wooden boats: 5
  Owner maintenance allowed above and below rail.
Retail supplies:
  Wood, paint, fastenings, epoxy, fiberglass, rigging supplies.

■ ST. LAWRENCE RESTORATION

Marilyn Cook, Jim Brown, and Donald Price
411 Franklin St., P.O. Box 310
Clayton, NY 13624
315-686-5950 Fax: 315-686-5939

Builder Information

Years in business: 21
Carpenters employed: 3
Shop capacity: 55'

Recent New Construction

11' plywood skiff. Traditional design. 14 built 1992–'93.

Recent Repair Projects

26' Lyman Sportsman utility. Completely refinishing. Current project.
28' Rochester runabout (1928). Completely restoring. Current project.
34' Hubert Johnson utility cruiser. Completely restored. 1990–'91.

Yard Information

Services
  Marina facilities
  Launching facilities
  Overland transport
  Moorage
  Engine repair
Storage
  Number of boats stored per year: 100
  Percentage of wooden boats: 25
  Inside storage facilities
  Maximum size for hauling and storing: 55' LOA, 6' draft, 25 tons
Maintenance
  Number of boats maintained per year: 200
  Percentage of wooden boats: 50
  Owner maintenance allowed above rail.
Retail supplies:
  Complete inventory of supplies.

■ SCARANO BOAT BUILDING

Richard Scarano
Port of Albany
Albany, NY 12202
518-463-3401 Fax: 518-463-3403

Builder Information

Years in business: 17
Carpenters employed: 6
Shop capacity: 90'
Willing to travel for on-the-site building projects.

Recent New Construction

Boats designed by Richard Scarano for composite wood/epoxy construction:
75' schooner. Built 1993.
70' schooner. Built 1992.
48' tour boat. Built 1992.
115' historic vessel replica. Built 1991.
60' tour boat. Built 1990.
31'6" sloop. 2 built 1990.

Recent Repair Projects

55' Elco (1929). Completely replaced deck and superstructure. Sheathed and epoxied topsides and bottom planking. Renewed all systems, repowered. 1993.
38' Chris-Craft (1956). Repaired hull, renewed all systems. 1992.
22' Chris-Craft (1956). General repairs and refinishing. 1990.

Yard Information

Services
  Launching facilities
  Overland transport
  Rigging
Storage
  Number of boats stored per year: 12
  Percentage of wooden boats: 60
  Inside storage facilities
  Maximum size for hauling and storing: 50' LOA, 7' draft, 22 tons
Maintenance
  Number of boats maintained per year: 8
  Percentage of wooden boats: 50
Retail supplies:
  Materials for construction and repair.

■ THE SECOND CENTURY

Milo B. Williams
P.O. Box 8
Old Forge, NY 13420

Builder Information
Years in business: 20
Carpenters employed: 1
Shop capacity: 20'

Recent New Construction
13'6" and 17' plywood/epoxy Brown's Tract scows. Traditional Adirondack designs. Three 13½-footers and four 17-footers built 1990–'93.

Recent Repair Projects
In the last four years, company has worked on approximately 25 Adirondack guideboats, 6 wood and wood/canvas canoes, and 5 Barnegat Bay sneakboxes.

Yard Information
Services
  Overland transport
Storage
  Number of boats stored per year: 30
  Percentage of wooden boats: 95
  Inside storage facilities
  Maximum size for hauling and storing: 20' LOA, 8" draft
Maintenance
  Number of boats maintained per year: 20
  Percentage of wooden boats: 100
  Owner maintenance allowed.
Retail supplies:
  Wood, fastenings, and paint.

■ SILVER BAY GUIDEBOAT AND CANOE CO.

Thomas M. James
86 Lakeshore Dr.
Silver Bay, NY 12874

Builder Information
Years in business: 14
Carpenters employed: 1
Shop capacity: 24'

Recent Repair Projects
17' Lake George rowing skiff. Major restoration. 1993.
15' kayak (1920s). Completely rebuilt. 1993.
17' Lyman runabout (1941). Completely rebuilt. 1991.
16'–18' Old Town canoes. Repairs and recanvasing. 5 canoes worked on 1991-present.

Yard Information
Services
  Marina facilities
  Launching facilities
  Engine repair
Maintenance
  Number of boats maintained per year: 65
  Percentage of wooden boats: 50

Retail supplies:
  Wood, paint, fastenings, canvas, hardware.

■ SPENCER BOATWORKS INC.

Spencer R. Jenkins
P.O. Box 144
Rte. 3, Bloomingdale Rd.
Saranac Lake, NY 12983-0144
518-891-5828 Fax: 518-483-1746

Builder Information
Years in business: 10
Carpenters employed: 4
Shop capacity: 40'

Recent New Construction
15' plywood/epoxy California Cracker Box. Glen-L Marine design. Built 1992.
20' wood/fiberglass electric launch. Spencer Jenkins design. Built 1990.
18' plywood/epoxy raceboat. Spencer Jenkins design. Built 1990.

Recent Repair Projects
Repair, restoration, and refinishing of antique and classic power craft, early one-design class boats, and canoes, skiffs, and dinghies. Approximately 75 boats worked on during last several years.

Yard Information
Services
  Overland transport
  Engine repair
Storage
  Number of boats stored per year: 100
  Percentage of wooden boats: 70
  Inside storage facilities
  Maximum size for hauling and storing: 40' LOA
Maintenance
  Number of boats maintained per year: 200
  Percentage of wooden boats: 90
Retail supplies:
  Paint, sandpaper, fastenings, wood, hardware, and epoxy.

■ SUTHERLAND BOAT & COACH, INC.

Daniel R. Sutherland
416½ West Lake Rd.
Hammondsport, NY 14840
607-868-3993

Builder Information
Years in business: 10
Carpenters employed: 2
Shop capacity: 40'

Recent New Construction
14' rowing/trout fishing boat. T. Todd design. Current project.

22' St. Lawrence skiff. Lapstrake construction. L.E. Fry design. Built 1991.

14' lapstrake double-ended pulling boat. J.H. Rushton design. 2 built 1990–'91.

14' rowing/trout fishing boat. H.J. Sutherland design. Built 1990.

Recent Repair Projects

30' iceboat (1890). Replacing side rails, repairing spar and bowsprit. Current project.

25' Springstead launch (1912). Refinishing hull, rebuilding engine. Current project.

21' Chris-Craft Capri (1956). Replacing deck and refinishing. Rebuilding engine. 1993.

22' Johnson C-scow. Repaired backbone and sistered ribs. Replaced bownose. 1993.

16' Murray Wright K-boats. Renewed keels, frames, decks, and spars. Refinished. 6 boats restored 1990–'93.

12'–16' Penn Yan dinghies/runabouts. Replaced frames, planking, and gunwales. Recanvased hulls. 12 different models restored 1990–'93.

38' Johnson A-scows. Renewed deck framing and decks, planking, frames, and spars. Refinished. 3 boats restored 1991–'93.

■ VIKING BOATBUILDERS

Steve Gould
102 Mill Rd.
Riverhead, NY 11901
516-727-6478 Fax: 516-727-7710

Builder Information

Years in business: 15
Carpenters employed: 2
Shop capacity: 40'
Willing to travel for on-the-site building projects.

Recent New Construction

26' cold-molded Noank sloop. Charles Wittholz design. Current project.

17' cold-molded Appledore-type, double-ended rowboat. John Gardner design. Built 1993.

12' strip-planked Spurling rowboat. Plans by John Gardner. 3 built 1992–'93.

17' strip-planked Whitehall. John Gardner design. Built 1992.

Recent Repair Projects

30' Richardson cruiser. Renewed deck and framing. 1993.

34' Hinckley Sou'wester. Replaced keelbolts, floors, and cockpit. 1993.

36' Owens power cruiser. Cold-molded hull, renewed cabin, deck, and interior. 1992–'93.

18' catboat. Replaced deck and coaming. 1990.

Yard Information

Services
    Overland transport
    Rigging

Storage
    Number of boats stored per year: 6
    Percentage of wooden boats: 100
    Maximum size for hauling and storing: Inquire
Maintenance
    Number of boats maintained per year: 3
    Percentage of wooden boats: Varies
    Owner maintenance allowed above and below rail.

■ FRANK M. WEEKS YACHT YARD

Brian Weeks
10 Riverview Ct.
Patchogue, NY 11772
516-475-1675

Builder Information

Years in business: 96
Carpenters employed: 4
Shop capacity: 55'
Willing to travel for on-the-site building projects.

Recent New Construction

12' cold-molded DN iceboat. DN class/Archie Aroll design. 22 built 1991–'93.

14' strip-planked sailing dinghy. Brian Weeks design. 2 built 1993.

Recent Repair Projects

Company specializes in the restoration of traditional sail and power craft. Currently working on a 1959 Matthews cruiser, two 1969 Egg Harbor power cruisers, and a 26' Patchogue One-Design class boat.

Over the years, they've also worked on numerous runabouts, many of which have been boat show award winners.

Yard Information

Services
    Marina facilities
    Launching facilities
    Overland transport
    Moorage
    Engine repair
    Rigging
Storage
    Number of boats stored per year: 150
    Percentage of wooden boats: 20
    Inside storage facilities
    Maximum size for hauling and storing: 55' LOA, 8' draft, 40 tons
Retail supplies:
    Available on walk-in and mail-order basis. Engine sales, machine shop, and WEST System products.

◼ WILLIAMS WOOD BOAT SHOP

Bill Williams
4914 Seneca St.
West Seneca, NY 14224
716-674-7455

Builder Information
Years in business: 52
Carpenters employed: 1
Shop capacity: 48'
Willing to travel for on-the-site building projects.

Recent Repair Projects
38' Pacemaker (1968). Renewing transom and planking. Current project.
35' Chris-Craft Futura (1956). Restoring hull and refinishing. Current project.
32' Trojan (1964). Replacing bottom and bow. Current project.
41' Matthews Sedan Cruiser. Replacing transom, resheathing deck. Current project.
38' Chris-Craft Sea Skiff (1968). Renewed frames and planking. 1993–'94.
25' Century Coronado (1958). Replaced bottom planking, frames, keel, chines, and stem. Completely restored. 1992–'93.

Yard Information
Services
    Marina facilities
    Launching facilities
    Moorage
    Engine repair
Storage
    Number of boats stored per year: 75
    Percentage of wooden boats: 10
    Inside storage facilities
    Maximum size for hauling and storing: 50' LOA, 7' draft, 35 tons
Maintenance
    Number of boats maintained per year: 25-50
    Percentage of wooden boats: 5
    Owner maintenance allowed above and below rail.

◼ BISCAYNE BAY BOAT WORKS

Michael M. Matheson
Rte. 4, Box 412
Murphy, NC 28906
704-644-5325

Builder Information
Years in business: 18
Carpenters employed: 1
Shop capacity: 48'

Recent Repair Projects
20' motorized canoe. Completely restored. 1993.
22' Prowler power cruiser. Completely rebuilt and repowered. 1992.
36' commuter. Completely restored. 1990–'91.

Yard Information
Services
    Overland transport
Storage
    Number of boats stored per year: 12
    Percentage of wooden boats: 100
    Inside storage facilities
    Maximum size for hauling and storing: 48' LOA, 4' draft, 10 tons
Maintenance
    Number of boats maintained per year: 8
    Percentage of wooden boats: 100
Retail supplies:
    Wood, paint, and other supplies. Will special-order anything on request.

◼ BLACK RIVER BOATS

Douglas Little
Rte. 1, Box 173D
Rose Hill, NC 28458
910-532-4217

Builder Information
Years in business: 11
Carpenters employed: 2
Shop capacity: 18'

Recent New Construction
Electric-powered boats designed by Douglas Little:
16' river boat. Current project.
16'4" Bullet launch. 2 built 1993.
13'6" Asria kayak. 2 built 1992.
15'11" Companion canoe. 3 built 1992.
14'6" Guide canoe. 12 built 1990–'93.
11'11" Lucy canoe. 8 built 1990.

Recent Repair Projects
15' Lumberton Boat Co. runabout PLAYBOY (1950). Replaced stem. Completely restored. 1993.

■ BLAKE BOATWORKS

Bryan Blake
P.O. Box 91
Gloucester, NC 28528
919-729-8021

Builder Information
Years in business: 18
Carpenters employed: 1-4
Shop capacity: 60'

Recent New Construction
40' strip-planked motorsailer/fishing boat. Bryan Blake
    design. Built 1992.

Recent Repair Projects
Completely refurbished the following boats:
38' skipjack. 1993–'94.
26' MacKenzie Cuttyhunk bassboat. 1992–'93.

Yard Information
Services
    Overland transport
    Rigging
Maintenance
    Number of boats maintained per year: 5-10
    Percentage of wooden boats: 100

■ BUDSIN WOOD CRAFT

Tom Hesselink
P.O. Box 279
Marshallberg, NC 28853
919-729-1540

Builder Information
Years in business: 8
Carpenters employed: 1-2
Shop capacity: 35'

Recent New Construction
33' cold-molded touring launch. Modified Nelson Zimmer
    design. Built 1992–'93.
15' cold-molded electric launch. Tom Hesselink design. 11
    built 1990–'93.

Recent Repair Projects
15' and 18' Electra-Craft launches (1936 and 1937 models).
    Restored decks and interiors. Renewed drive systems,
    sheathed hulls with epoxy/fiberglass. 1993.

■ CAPE FEAR COMMUNITY COLLEGE

David Flagler, Lead Instructor
411 N. Front St.
Wilmington, NC 28401
910-251-5651 Fax: 910-763-2279

Builder Information
Years in business: 20
Carpenters employed: 4 instructors, 13 students

Shop capacity: 36'
Willing to travel for on-the-site building projects.

Recent New Construction
8' plywood pram. Herreshoff/Gardner design. 25 built
    1990–'93.
12' cold-molded dinghy. Spurling design. Built 1993.
12'6" Catspaw dinghy. Herreshoff/White design. 2 built
    1990.

■ CLASSIC CANOES

Tom Barrett
10925 Raven Rock Rd.
Raleigh, NC 27614
919-870-8758

Builder Information
Years in business: 6
Carpenters employed: 1
Shop capacity: 25'

Recent Repair Projects
Company specializes in the repair and recanvasing of
    canoes and small wooden boats.

Yard Information
Maintenance
    Number of boats maintained per year: 8-10
    Percentage of wooden boats: 95

■ EAST BAY BOAT WORKS, INC.

Ricky Gillikin
P.O. Box 220
Harkers Island, NC 28531
919-728-2004 Fax: 919-728-3771

Builder Information
Years in business: 23
Carpenters employed: 10
Shop capacity: 125'
Willing to travel for on-the-site building projects.

Recent New Construction
78' strip-planked excursion/dinner vessel. James Gillikin
    design. Built 1993.
34' cold-molded express cruiser. Ricky Gillikin design.
    Built 1993.
36' cold-molded express cruiser. Bob Hull design. Built 1993.
28' and 39' cold-molded sportfishing boats. Ricky Gillikin
    designs. Built 1991 and 1992.
20' cold-molded deadrise skiff. Ricky Gillikin design. Built
    1990.
30' strip-planked day boat. Ricky Gillikin design. Built 1990.

Recent Repair Projects
Refurbishing and general maintenance of the following
    boats during 1990–'93:
28', 40', and 48' sportfishing boats.
48' and 56' ferryboats.
(continues)

(East Bay Boat Works, continued)
40' commercial fishing boat.
65' head boat.
63' yacht.
43' charter vessel.

Yard Information
Services
 Marina facilities
 Launching facilities
 Overland transport
 Moorage
 Engine repair
 Rigging
Storage
 Number of boats stored per year: 10
 Percentage of wooden boats: 90
 Maximum size for hauling and storing: 65' LOA, 5'
  draft, 50 tons
Maintenance
 Number of boats maintained per year: 20
 Percentage of wooden boats: 80
 Owner maintenance allowed above and below rail.
Retail supplies:
 Lumber, plywood, fastenings, paint, hardware, and
  engines.

■ ELY TRAIL CRAFTS

Ronald R. "Ron" Ely
3464 Murray Town Rd.
Burgaw, NC 28425
910-259-4120

Builder Information
Years in business: 6
Carpenters employed: 1
Shop capacity: 17'

Recent New Construction
Boats designed by Ron Ely for plywood construction:
8' fishing boat for electric motor. Built 1993.
14' one-person sea kayak. 6-8 kit boats supplied 1990.

■ HIGH ROCK BOAT YARD

Clayton Gray
Owen Rd., P.O. Drawer I
Southmont, NC 27351
704-798-1338

Builder Information
Years in business: 14
Carpenters employed: 1
Shop capacity: 30'

Recent Repair Projects
Old Town wood/canvas canoes and sailing canoes a specialty. Approximately 15 canoes restored and refinished
 each year. Company also restores Chris-Craft and
 Century power craft, and Lightning-class sloops.

Yard Information
Services
 Sail repair
 Rigging
Maintenance
 Number of boats maintained per year: Varies
 Owner maintenance allowed on special basis.
Retail supplies:
 Materials in stock. White oak, holly, and red elm.

■ MIERKE'S YACHT SERVICE

Bruce Mierke
Rte. 4, Bear Paw 813
Murphy, NC 28906
704-644-5014

Builder Information
Years in business: 13
Carpenters employed: 1
Shop capacity: 40'
Willing to travel for on-the-site building projects.

Recent New Construction
22' cold-molded sportfisherman. Forrest Johnson design.
 Built 1992.
20' cold-molded runabout. John Hacker design. Built 1990.

Recent Repair Projects
Boats worked on during 1990–'93:
36' commuter (1939). Renewed bottom, deck, transom, and
 cabin. Refinished topsides.
25' Old Town war canoe (1949). Repaired ribs and planking. Renewed decks and rails, refinished interior.
 Recanvased hull.
24' Hacker runabout. Renewed bottom and transom.
20' Chris-Craft Custom runabout. Renewed frames and
 bottom, refinished topsides and deck.
20' White motorized canoe (1910). Refinished interior,
 recanvased hull.

Yard Information
Services
 Overland transport
 Rigging
Maintenance
 Number of boats maintained per year: 3-5
 Percentage of wooden boats: 50

■ RUSSELL YACHTS

Tommy Russell
903 Shepard St., P.O. Box 3488
Morehead City, NC 28557
919-240-2848 Fax: 919-247-5069

Builder Information
Years in business: 20
Carpenters employed: 2
Shop capacity: 70'

Recent New Construction

47′ cold-molded ketch. Craig Walters design. Built 1990.

■ SCOTT BOATYARD INC.

Michael Scott
Box 312
Buxton, NC 27920
919-995-4331

Builder Information

Years in business: 17
Carpenters employed: 2
Shop capacity: 55′

Recent Repair Projects

Work has involved repairs and renovations to many boats over the last 4 years including deck renewal, repowering, cabin extensions, all types of hull repairs, drivetrain repairs, alterations and replacements, and polyurethane painting.

Yard Information

Services
    Marina facilities
    Launching facilities
    Engine repair
Storage
    Number of boats stored per year: 14
    Percentage of wooden boats: 50
    Maximum size for hauling and storing: 55′ LOA, 6′ draft, 30 tons
Maintenance
    Number of boats maintained per year: 300
    Percentage of wooden boats: 50
    Owner maintenance allowed above and below rail.
Retail supplies:
    Good inventory of supplies including fastenings, resins, and fiberglass cloth. Will do custom ordering for next-day delivery.

■ SHIP CREEK BOAT WORKS

Ed Verge
25 Fork Point Rd.
Oriental, NC 28571
919-249-1902 Fax: same

Builder Information

Years in business: 25
Carpenters employed: 1
Shop capacity: 45′
Willing to travel for on-the-site building projects.

Recent New Construction

32′ cold-molded Norwalk Islands sharpie. Bruce Kirby design. Built 1990.

Recent Repair Projects

36′ Winslow/McIntosh yawl. Renewed keel and keelbolts, bulwarks, cockpit, coaming, and rubrail. Replaced rudder and mainmast, recaulked decks. 1993.

92′ replica of HALF MOON. Resheathed exterior planking, replaced sheer. Renewed floors, refastened bottom. 1992.

Concordia 41. Replaced steel floors and adjacent frames. Renewed floors under engine bed and rebuilt bed. Replaced 24 planks, refastened and recaulked teak decks. 1992.

Concordia 39. Renewed deck, sheathed with Dynel and epoxy, renewed caprail. Refinished. 1991.

Yard Information

Services
    Moorage
    Rigging
Retail supplies:
    Complete inventory of supplies.

■ N.L. SILVA & CO.

Nelson L. Silva
7980 Market St. (Hwy. 17N)
Wilmington, NC 28405
910-686-4356

Builder Information

Years in business: 20
Carpenters employed: 2-5
Shop capacity: 40′

Recent New Construction

21′ strip-planked lobster skiff. N.L. Silva design. Current project.

22′ strip-planked sharpie ketch. N.L. Silva design. Built 1993.

17′, 20′, and 22′ lapstrake plywood skiffs. Designs by T.N. Simmons. Over 40 built 1988–'93.

Recent Repair Projects

20′ Simmons skiff (1970). Renewed transom and decks. 1993.

22′ Simmons skiff (1968). Replaced windshield. 1993.

21′ Grady-White power cruiser (1961). Totally rebuilt. 1991.

■ TAYLOR BOAT WORKS

John H. McCallum
P.O. Box 1346, 200 Pensacola Ave.
Morehead City, NC 28557
919-726-6374 Fax: 919-726-2602

Builder Information

Years in business: 29
Carpenters employed: 3
Shop capacity: 60′
Willing to travel for on-the-site building projects.

Recent Repair Projects

34′ Huckins Fairform Flyer express cruiser. Fabricated interior, installed engines, wiring, electronics, outriggers. 1993.

(continues)

(Taylor Boat Works, continued)
44' Pacemaker double-cabin motoryacht. Installed rubrails, toerails, and handrails. Extended hardtop and installed dodgerboards. Replaced rudderport backing blocks, shaftlogs, and associated planking. Refinished exterior.

Yard Information
Services
  Marina facilities
  Rigging
Storage
Maintenance
  Number of boats maintained per year: 150
  Percentage of wooden boats: 25
  Owner maintenance allowed on limited basis.
Retail supplies:
  Wood, fastenings, paint, shop supplies, and electrical supplies.

■ CLASSIC BOAT WORKS

Debbie Jones
3239 Old Oxford Rd.
Hamilton, OH 45013
513-896-1517

Builder Information
Years in business: 12
Carpenters employed: 1
Shop capacity: 21'

Recent Repair Projects
17' Chris-Craft ski boat (1960). Replaced several planks. Refinished hull and decks. 1992.
21' Century Coronado (1964). Rebuilt transom. Refinished hull and interior. 1992.
18' Century Sabre utility cruiser. Restored hull and engine. 1991.
21' Century Coronado (1965). Replaced bottom and topside planking, refinished hull and interior. Rebuilt engine. 1990.

Yard Information
Services
  Engine repair

Maintenance
  Number of boats maintained per year: 3-5
  Percentage of wooden boats: 100
  Owner maintenance allowed above and below rail.

■ CLASSIC MARINE

Dwight Davis
5719 Wahl Rd.
Vickery, OH 43464
419-684-9804

Builder Information
Years in business: 8
Carpenters employed: 1-4
Shop capacity: 50'
Willing to travel for on-the-site building projects.

Recent New Construction
14' plywood/composite jetboat. Classic Marine design. Built 1993.

Recent Repair Projects
25' Chris-Craft. Replaced transom and 6 planks, refinished. 1993.
26' Lyman. Replaced garboards, renewed cabinetry. Epoxied and refinished hull. 1993.
25' Lyman. Renewed keel, transom, and 16 planks. 1993.
38' Chris-Craft. Replaced keel, knee, forward planking. 1993.
37' Egg Harbor. Completely restored. 1992–'93.
30' Lyman. Completely restored. 1991.
Company specializes in Chris-Craft and Lyman repairs. Numerous other boats restored in last few years.

Yard Information
Retail supplies:
  Fastenings, wood, epoxy.

■ HURON LAGOONS MARINA

Thomas Solberg
100 Laguna Dr., P.O. Box 231
Huron, OH 44839
419-433-3200 Fax: 419-433-7616

Builder Information
Years in business: 25
Carpenters employed: 2
Shop capacity: 50'

Recent Repair Projects
40' Chris-Craft Conqueror (1959). Stem to transom refinishing. Current project.
34' Post sportfisherman (1966). Repairing fire damage. Completely rebuilding boat. Ongoing project.

Yard Information
Services
  Marina facilities
  Launching facilities
  Moorage
  Engine repair

Storage
  Number of boats stored per year: 225
  Percentage of wooden boats: 5
  Inside storage facilities
  Maximum size for hauling and storing: 50' LOA, 5'
    draft, 20 tons
Maintenance
  Number of boats maintained per year: 100+
  Percentage of wooden boats: 10
  Owner maintenance allowed above and below rail.
Retail supplies:
  Complete inventory of supplies.

■ KOROKNAY'S MARINE WOODWORKING

Tom Koroknay
3718 Lindsey Rd.
Lexington, OH 44904
419-884-0222

Builder Information
Years in business: 13
Carpenters employed: 1
Shop capacity: 30'

Recent Repair Projects
Specializes in the restoration and repair of Lyman boats,
  including the following projects:
28' Lyman Soft Top. Renewed bottom planking and interi-
  or brightwork. 1993.
26' Lyman Hardtop. Repaired frames and bottom planking. 1993.
30' Lyman Islander. Completely restored. 1993.
26' Lyman Hardtop. Completely restored. 1993.
20' Lyman runabout. Replaced transom and 60' of bottom
  planking. 1992.
23' Lyman runabout. Completely restored. 1991.

Yard Information
Services
  Engine repair
Storage
  Number of boats stored per year: 3-5
  Percentage of wooden boats: 100
  Inside storage facilities
  Maximum size for hauling and storing: 30' LOA, 3'
    draft, 4 tons
Maintenance
  Number of boats maintained per year: 3-5
  Percentage of wooden boats: 100
  Owner maintenance allowed above rail.
Retail supplies:
  Paint, varnish, fastenings. All parts and specialty items
    for Lyman boats. Can reproduce original wood parts.

■ MEREDITH MARINE, INC.

W.R. "Spike" Meredith
16040 Wake Robin Dr.
Newbury, OH 44065
216-564-7173 Fax: 216-564-7175

Builder Information
Years in business: 25
Carpenters employed: 1
Shop capacity: 40'

Recent New Construction
Boats designed by Spike Meredith for cold-molded or
  wood/epoxy construction:
25' center-console fishing boat. Built 1992.
25' runabout. Built 1992.
25' speedboat. Built 1991.

Recent Repair Projects
22' Chris-Craft speedboat. Restored and repowered.
  1992-'93.

Yard Information
Services
  Engine repair
  Rigging
Maintenance
  Number of boats maintained per year: 3
  Percentage of wooden boats: 100

■ NOAH'S BOAT SHOP

Charlie Cassell
P.O. Box 284
Kinsman, OH 44428
216-876-9004

Builder Information
Years in business: 24
Carpenters employed: 1
Shop capacity: 45'
Willing to travel for on-the-site building projects.

Recent Repair Projects
Complete restorations of the following boats:
19' Lyman (1953). Current project.
17' Chris-Craft Deluxe Runabout (1947). 1993.
18' Chris-Craft Riviera (1950). 1993.
38' Chris-Craft Constellation Convertible (1956). 1993.
16' Century Imperial (1952). 1993.

Yard Information
Services
  Overland transport
  Engine repair
Storage
  Number of boats stored per year: 15
  Percentage of wooden boats: 95
  Maximum size for hauling and storing: 36' LOA, 15'
    draft, 25 tons
(continues)

(Noah's Boat Shop, continued)
Maintenance
Number of boats maintained per year: 5
Percentage of wooden boats: 100
Owner maintenance allowed above and below rail.
Retail supplies:
Complete inventory of supplies for building and repair,
plus trailers and hitches.

■ SAYRE BROTHERS/ARGO WOOD BOAT RESTORATION

Zenna and Bud Sayre
P.O. Box 65, 5171 North Bank S.E.
Buckeye Lake, OH 43008
614-928-3691

Builder Information
Years in business: 90
Carpenters employed: 2
Shop capacity: 26'

Recent Repair Projects
15'–25' runabouts. Models by Chris-Craft, Century,
Higgins, Hacker-Craft, and Gar Wood. Restoration
work has included replacing planks and other wooden
members, engine rebuilding, and hull refinishing.

Yard Information
Services
Marina facilities
Launching facilities
Overland transport
Moorage
Engine repair
Storage
Number of boats stored per year: 100
Percentage of wooden boats: 50
Inside storage facilities
Maximum size for hauling and storing: 26' LOA
Maintenance
Number of boats maintained per year: 200
Percentage of wooden boats: 35
Retail supplies:
On-the-water marine store. Paints, marine plywood,
mahogany, hardware, canvas. Complete line of prod-
ucts to repair and refinish wooden boats. Full service
for inboard and I/O boats.

■ SKIFF CRAFT

Ed Peters
P.O. Box 115, Guy St.
Plain City, OH 43064
614-873-4664

Builder Information
Years in business: 10
Carpenters employed: 7
Shop capacity: 35'
Willing to travel for on-the-site building projects.

Recent New Construction
Boats designed by Skiff Craft for lapstrake construction:
24' Sports Hardtop cruiser. Current project.
26' Sports Run-a-bout. 1 built 1992, 1 under construction.
33' Commercial Sportfisherman. Built 1992.
Other new construction:
22' lapstrake Fox Island-class sloop. Joel White design.
Built 1993.
16' strip-planked fishing boats. 5 built 1993.

Recent Repair Projects
Complete restoration of the following boats:
26' Lyman (1957). Current project.
16' Chris-Craft (1956). Current project.
14' Bowman cruiser (1955). 1993.
14' Henry (1956). 1993.
22' Chris-Craft (1952). 1991.
Company also repaired or restored approximately 60 Skiff
Crafts over the last year. Work included hull painting,
vinyl replacement, and total restorations.

Yard Information
Services
Overland transport
Rigging
Storage
Number of boats stored per year: 20
Percentage of wooden boats: 100
Inside storage facilities
Maximum size for hauling and storing: 35' LOA, 4'
draft, 6 tons
Maintenance
Number of boats maintained per year: 40
Percentage of wooden boats: 100
Retail supplies:
Catalog available. Parts, wood, paint, varnish. Gifts.

■ VINTAGE BOATWORKS

Tim Martin
546 Southard Ave.
Toledo, OH 43624
419-255-2628 Fax: 419-255-2628

Builder Information
Years in business: 4
Carpenters employed: 2
Shop capacity: 38'

Recent New Construction
Boats of wood/epoxy construction:
31' 1:12 scale DD-class destroyer. Built 1990.
14'6" runabout. Replica of 1957 Chris-Craft kit boat. Built
1990.
23'7" Bartender powerboat. George Calkins design. Built
1990.

Recent Repair Projects
Complete restorations of the following classic power craft:
17' Chris-Craft Deluxe Runabout (1946 and 1947 models).
Current project.
15'6" Thompson. Current project.

21' Lyman (1960 and 1961 models). 1992–'94.
17' Chris-Craft Deluxe Runabout (1948). 1993.

Yard Information
Services
  Overland transport
  Engine repair
Storage
  Number of boats stored per year: 50
  Percentage of wooden boats: 98
  Inside storage facilities
  Maximum size for hauling and storing: 38' LOA
Maintenance
  Number of boats maintained per year: Varies
  Percentage of wooden boats: 100
  Owner maintenance allowed above and below rail.

■ THE WOODEN CANOE SHOP INC.

Gilbert Cramer
RR #4, 03583 Rd. 13
Bryan, OH 43506
419-636-1689

Builder Information
Years in business: 10
Carpenters employed: 1
Shop capacity: 25
Willing to travel for on-the-site building projects.

Recent Repair Projects
Specializes in the repair and restoration of wood/canvas
  canoes. In the last 4 years, over 40 canoes have been
  completed, including the following models:
16' Detroit canoe.
18' Kennebec canoe.
16' and 17' Morris canoes.
13'–18' Old Town canoes.
14' and 15' Peterborough canoes.
17' Carleton canoe.

■ ZIMMERMAN BOAT WORKS

D. Matthew Zimmerman
1403 Chambers Rd.
Columbus, OH 43212
614-488-7921

Builder Information
Years in business: 10
Carpenters employed: 1
Shop capacity: 33'
Willing to travel for on-the-site building projects.

Recent Repair Projects
28' Chris-Craft Model 14 (1929). Completely rebuilding.
  Current project.
22' catboat (1937). Replaced frames, renewed deck canvas
  and coamings, refinished hull. 1993.

Yard Information
Services
  Overland transport
Storage
  Number of boats stored per year: 20
  Percentage of wooden boats: 100
  Inside storage facilities
  Maximum size for hauling and storing: 30' LOA
Maintenance
  Number of boats maintained per year: 25
  Percentage of wooden boats: 100
  Owner maintenance allowed above rail.
Retail supplies:
  Wood, fastenings, paint, varnish, epoxy, and caulking
  materials.

■ APPLEGATE BOATWORKS

John and Laura McCallum
25380 Fleck Rd.
Veneta, OR 97487
503-935-2370

Builder Information
Years in business: 18
Carpenters employed: 1
Shop capacity: 22'
Willing to travel for on-the-site building projects.

Recent New Construction
9'10" farm punt. John McCallum design. Built 1993.
14' taped-seam plywood duckboat. John McCallum
  design. Built 1993.
36' strip-planked trimaran hull. Dick Newick design. Built
  1991.
19' taped-seam plywood canoe. John McCallum design
  (replica of Makah Indian dugout canoe). Built 1990.
(continues)

(Applegate Boatworks, continued)

Recent Repair Projects

16' plywood runabout (1959). Repaired rot, renewed deck, and refinished. 1993.

36" sloop-rigged model (1933). Reassembled sailing rig. 1993.

16' Old Town canoe. Repaired deck, recanvased hull. 1993.

19' Lightning-class sloops. Renewed decks, centerboards, and keels. Built 28' hollow spruce spar. 4 different boats worked on 1992–'93.

18' Thistle-class sloops. Repaired mast and centerboard trunks. Refinished. 4 boats worked on 1990–'93.

16' bateau. Repaired plank, revarnished. 1990.

16' McKenzie River drift boat. Completed structural repairs, recaulked, and refinished. Several boats worked on 1990–'93.

Yard Information

Services

Rigging

CHARLOT MARINE WORKS INC.

Deny Charlot, President
303 N.E. Tomahawk Island Dr.
Portland, OR 97217
503-289-1855 Fax: 503-289-9358

Builder Information

Years in business: 18

Carpenters employed: 9

Shop capacity: 85'

Willing to travel for on-the-site building projects.

Recent New Construction

7' plywood dinghy. D. Smith design. Built 1993.

29' Charlot SeaSkif I/O powerboat. Lapstrake construction. Harvy/Charlot design. Built 1992.

28' Columbia River Sportsman powerboat. Westerlund/Charlot design. Built 1990.

Recent Repair Projects

50' Alden yawl ALTAIR (1916). Renewing interior, mechanical and electrical systems, and rig. Refinishing. Current project.

48' Stevens commuter SCOTCH MIST (1930). Renewing mechanical and electrical systems. Restoring and refinishing hull. Current project.

34' Chris-Craft Connie (1964). Rebuilt transom. Renewed running gear. Refinished. 1993.

32' Taylor cutter JENERIO (1948). Completely restored hull. Renewed mechanical and electrical system, and rig. 1992–'94.

36' Chris-Craft Sea Skiff. Replanked and refastened bottom. Renewed frames. 1993.

24' Chris-Craft Sea Skiff (1962). Completely restored. Renewed electrical and mechanical systems. Refinished. 1993.

16' and 18' Chris-Craft runabouts. Completely restored 3 boats to original condition. 1990–'93.

Yard Information

Services

Launching facilities

Overland transport

Engine repair

Rigging

Storage

Number of boats stored per year: 22

Percentage of wooden boats: 70

Maximum size for hauling and storing: 42' LOA, 4' draft

Maintenance

Number of boats maintained per year: 10

Percentage of wooden boats: 90

Owner maintenance allowed.

CLIPPER CRAFT MFG. CO. INC.

Tao Trinh
10130 N. Portland Rd.
Portland, OR 97203
503-286-3013

Builder Information

Years in business: 40

Carpenters employed: 2

Shop capacity: 28'

Recent New Construction

23', 26', and 28' lapstrake plywood dories with cabins. Jim Stayley designs. 5 built 1993, 3 currently under construction.

Recent Repair Projects

20' lapstrake skiff. Replaced chine stiffeners, renewed bottom, and installed bow tank. Replaced forward floor, repaired leaking transom. 1993.

CUSTOM CANOES

Phil and Sally Wald
88 Shady Loop
Springfield, OR 97477
503-726-8750

Builder Information

Years in business: 4

Carpenters employed: 1

Shop capacity: 20'

Recent Repair Projects

17' Old Town canoe. Renewing ribs and planking, recanvasing and refinishing. Current project.

15' Thompson Bros. canoe. Renewing ribs and planking, recanvasing and refinishing. Current project.

Yard Information

Maintenance

Number of boats maintained per year: 2

Percentage of wooden boats: 100

■ FLYNN & FLYNN CUSTOM BOAT WORKS

Rik Flynn
3005 Bay Ocean Rd.
Tillamook, OR 97141

Builder Information
Years in business: 20
Carpenters employed: 1-3
Shop capacity: 100'
Willing to travel for on-the-site building projects.

Recent New Construction
16' plywood/epoxy rowing skiff. Built 1993.
18' plywood/epoxy Bay skiff. Glen-L Marine design. Built 1992.

Recent Repair Projects
75' tugboat (1939). Completely restored. Replaced bulwarks and rails, recaulked deck, and refinished. Repaired engine. 1991.

Yard Information
Services
  Marina facilities
  Moorage
  Engine repair
  Rigging
Storage
  Number of boats stored per year: 10
  Percentage of wooden boats: 25
  Maximum size for hauling and storing: Inquire
Maintenance
  Number of boats maintained per year: 4
  Percentage of wooden boats: 25
  Owner maintenance allowed above and below rail.
Retail supplies:
  Complete inventory of supplies.

■ DON HILL RIVER BOATS

Don Hill
P.O. Box CC
Springfield, OR 97477
503-747-7430

Builder Information
Years in business: 30
Shop capacity: 16'

Recent New Construction
10', 13', and 15' river drift boats. Plywood construction. Don Hill designs. Available as kits or completed boats.
Retail supplies:
  Marine plywood, fastenings, oars and oarlocks, trailers, and boat covers. Plans and kit boats.

■ RAY'S RIVER DORIES

C. Ray Heater
3345 N.E. 84
Portland, OR 97220
503-254-5847

Builder Information
Years in business: 20
Carpenters employed: 2
Shop capacity: 20'

Recent New Construction
Boats designed by Ray Heater for plywood/epoxy construction:
14'10" Rogue River drift boat. 5 built 1990–'93.
15'5" Rogue River drift boat. 10 built 1990–'93.
8' river pram. 3 built 1990–'93.
13'3" McKenzie River drift boat. 7 built 1990–'93.
11'3" McKenzie River drift boat. 3 built 1990–'93.
14'10" McKenzie River drift boat. 2 built 1990–'93.

Yard Information
Storage
  Number of boats stored per year: 6
  Percentage of wooden boats: 100
  Inside storage facilities
  Maximum size for hauling and storing: 20' LOA, 6" draft
Maintenance
  Number of boats maintained per year: 4
  Percentage of wooden boats: 100
  Owner maintenance allowed.
Retail supplies:
  Kit boats, epoxy, paint, fastenings.

■ STEELE'S BOATS

Keith D. Steele
44976 McKenzie Hwy.
Leaburg, OR 97489
503-896-3279

Builder Information
Years in business: 43
Carpenters employed: 1-2
Shop capacity: 20'

Recent New Construction
McKenzie River drift boats. Designed by Keith Steele for plywood construction. Over 2,600 boats built to date; currently building 20-30 boats each year.

Recent Repair Projects
Drift boats. All types of repair.

SWAN DESIGN & SWAN BOATS

Ken Swan
P.O. Box 267
Hubbard, OR 97032
503-982-5062

Builder Information
Years in business: 10
Carpenters employed: 1
Shop capacity: 16'

Recent New Construction
Boats designed by Ken Swan for plywood construction:
13'6" rowboat. 2 built 1993 –'94; 3 kit boats supplied
   1992–'93.
13'4" drift boat. Built 1992–'93.

 TENMILE MARINA INC.

Stan Russell
P.O. Box 275, 7th & Park Sts.
Lakeside, OR 97449
503-759-3137

Builder Information
Years in business: 30
Carpenters employed: 1
Shop capacity: 25'

Recent New Construction
15' plywood Bay Boat. Alden design. 2 built 1990.

Recent Repair Projects
12' rowing boat (1900). Completely restoring. Current
   project.
17' Chris-Craft runabout. Replaced transom and topside
   planking. 1993.
16' canoe. Repaired bow and stern damage. 1993.
25' Chris-Craft runabout. Completely restored. 1993.
18' salmon boat (c. 1930). Completely restored. 1992.
17' Chris-Craft runabout. Replaced bottom. 1992.

Yard Information
Services
   Marina facilities
   Launching facilities
   Overland transport
   Moorage
   Engine repair
   Rigging
Storage
   Number of boats stored per year: 95
   Percentage of wooden boats: 5
   Inside storage facilities
   Maximum size for hauling and storing: 25' LOA
Maintenance
   Number of boats maintained per year: 130
   Percentage of wooden boats: 10
Retail supplies:
   Fastenings and other marine supplies.

 DOUBLE J. BOATWORKS

Jim Troyan
210 Hickory St.
Sharpsville, PA 16150
412-962-3220

Builder Information
Years in business: 10
Carpenters employed: 1
Shop capacity: 25'
Willing to travel for on-the-site building projects.

Recent Repair Projects
23' Lyman runabout (1958). Completely rebuilding.
   Renewing stem, keel, frames, transom, and deck.
   Current project.
12' cold-molded runabout (1950s). Renewing framing and
   hull. Completely refinish ing. Current project.
19' Skiff-Craft outboard power cruiser (1965). Renewed
   transom. 1993.
19' Chris-Craft Holiday (1952). Completely rebuilt and
   refinished. 1990–'91.
20' Grady-White Atlantic (1964). Completely rebuilt and
   refinished. Completed 1990.

Yard Information
Services
   Engine repair
   Rigging
Maintenance
   Number of boats maintained per year: 6-10
   Percentage of wooden boats: 95
Retail supplies:
   Marine plywood, lumber, fastenings, hardware, paint.

 MIDDLE PATH BOATS

Andre de Bardelaben
Box 8881
Pittsburgh, PA 15221
412-247-4860

Builder Information
Years in business: 17
Carpenters employed: 2
Shop capacity: 30'

Recent New Construction
Lightweight wood/epoxy canoes and rowing craft. Line
   includes 12 rowing models (both fixed and sliding seat,
   with sail and outboard options), 5 solo canoes, and 3
   tandem canoes.

■ MOBILE MARINE

Dan H. Lindrooth
2924 Orchard Lane
Huntingdon Valley, PA 19006
215-947-9731

Builder Information
Years in business: 38
Carpenters employed: 1
Shop capacity: 18'
Willing to travel for on-the-site building projects.

Recent New Construction
15' plywood Chippewa 15 canoe. Weston Farmer design. Built 1993.
15' plywood Lake Master 15 fishing skiff. Ken Swan design. Built 1992.
18'3" strip-planked Micmac 18 canoe. David Hazen design. 2 built 1991.
12'9" strip-planked Wee Laddie solo canoe. R.D. Culler/Dan Lindrooth design. 4 built 1991.
14'5" plywood sailing Amesbury dory-skiff. Dan Lindrooth design. Built 1990.

Recent Repair Projects
17' Thistle-class sloop. Replacing guardrails, refinishing interior bright. Current project.
18' canoe. Replaced outer gunwales and refinished exterior. 1993.
12' fishing boat. Completely refinished. 1992.

Yard Information
Storage
    Number of boats stored per year: 6
    Percentage of wooden boats: 100
    Maximum size for hauling and storing: 20' LOA; trailerable
Maintenance
    Number of boats maintained per year: 6
    Percentage of wooden boats: 100
    Owner maintenance allowed above and below rail.
Retail supplies:
    Plywood and lumber, including teak, mahogany, spruce, oak, ash. Stainless-steel and bronze fastenings.

■ A. WAYNE MOWERY

A. Wayne Mowery
210 Ridgewood Rd.
Wallingford, PA 19086
215-566-2493

Builder Information
Years in business: 7
Carpenters employed: 1
Shop capacity: 20'

Recent Repair Projects
Repair work has included total restorations of the following wood/canvas lake boats and canoes:
15' Skowhegan Laker. 1993.
12' Penn Yan lake boat. 1992.

16' Kennebec canoe (1918). 1992.
17' Old Town canoe. 1991.
16' Old Town Yankee (1924). 1990.
18' Old Town Guide Special. 1990.

■ SOUTH COVE BOAT SHOP

Robert Barker
615 Moyers Lane
Easton, PA 18042
215-253-9210 Fax: same

Builder Information
Years in business: 12
Carpenters employed: 1
Shop capacity: 30'
Willing to travel for on-the-site building projects.

Recent New Construction
22' Muscongus Bay sloop. Current project.
20' lapstrake Swampscott sailing dory. G. Chaisson design. Built 1993.
15' dory skiff. John Gardner design. Built 1993.
16' Swampscott dory. John Gardner design. Built 1991.
11' lapstrake sailing Whitehall. Traditional design. Built 1990.

Recent Repair Projects
24' sloop. Renewing interior, decks and hatches. Current project.
19' Lightning-class sloop. Replaced rudder. Reset centerboard trunk. 1993.
18' catboat. Replaced rubrail. 1993.
13' Penguin-class dinghy. Renewed plywood planking. 1992.

■ WOODSTRIP WATERCRAFT CO.

Al Bratton
1818 Swamp Pike
Gilbertsville, PA 19525
610-326-9282

Builder Information
Years in business: 7
Carpenters employed: 1
Shop capacity: 25'

Recent New Construction
15'10" plywood kayak. Dennis Davis design. 2 built 1991 and 1993.
16'6" strip-planked kayak. Chip Chandler design. 2 built 1992–'93.
14', 16', and 17' strip-planked canoes. Al Bratton designs. 9 built 1990–'93.
15' plywood kayak. Mike Alford design. Built 1990.
15' plywood dory. Phil Bolger design. Built 1990.
(continues)

(Woodstrip Watercraft Co., continued)
Recent Repair Projects
Wood/canvas canoes. Morris, Old Town, Kennebec,
  Chestnut, White, and Peterborough models.
  Approximately 35 canoes restored 1990–'93.
14' Penn Yan Swift runabout. Completely restored.

Yard Information
Maintenance
  Number of boats maintained per year: 15
  Percentage of wooden boats: 100
Retail supplies:
  Paint, fiberglass, epoxy, canvas, tacks.

■ CONANICUT MARINE SERVICES

William Munger
1 Ferry Wharf
Jamestown, RI 02835
401-423-1556 Fax: 401-423-7152

Builder Information
Years in business: 30
Carpenters employed: 2-3
Shop capacity: 45'

Recent Repair Projects
39' Concordia yawl. Completely refinished. 1993.
40' Hinckley. Renewed toerails, some reconstruction, refinished. 1992.
39' Concordia yawl. Completely refinished. 1992.
26' Lyman. Completely restored. 1992.
41' Concordia. Modified forward cabin. 1992.
39' Rhodes 27. Refinished, rechromed hardware. 1991.
41' Concordia. Upgraded mechanical systems and refitted.
  1991.

Yard Information
Services
  Marina facilities
  Launching facilities
  Overland transport
  Moorage
  Engine repair
  Rigging
Storage
  Number of boats stored per year: 175
  Percentage of wooden boats: 4
  Inside storage facilities
  Maximum size for hauling and storing: 47' LOA, 7'
    draft, 15 tons
Maintenance
  Number of boats maintained per year: 200
  Percentage of wooden boats: 4
  Owner maintenance allowed on boats stored outside.
Retail supplies:
  Materials for maintenance, marine lumber, engines and
    parts, electronics, refrigeration, and other supplies.

■ DUGAN SMALL BOAT SHOP

Bill Kelley
543 West Side Rd.
Block Island, RI 02807
401-466-2412

Builder Information
Years in business: 5
Carpenters employed: 1
Shop capacity: 25'
Willing to travel for on-the-site building projects.

Recent New Construction
16' strip-planked Kingston lobsterboat. Traditional design.
  Current project.
13' lapstrake Salisbury Point skiff. Lowell design. Built 1991.

Yard Information
Services
  Overland transport
  Rigging
Storage
  Number of boats stored per year: 3
  Percentage of wooden boats: 100
  Maximum size for hauling and storing: Inquire
Maintenance
  Number of boats maintained per year: 3
  Percentage of wooden boats: 100

■ DUTCH HARBOR BOAT YARD

Fred Lorensen
252 Narragansett Ave., P.O. Box 175
Jamestown, RI 02835
401-423-0630 Fax: 401-423-3834

Builder Information
Years in business: 12
Carpenters employed: 2
Shop capacity: 60'

Recent Repair Projects
25' Friendship sloop (1978). Renewing stem and billethead.
  Current project.
55' Scheel cold-molded sloop. Completed structural deck
  work, renewed cabin molding, applied teak overlay on
  cabin sides. 1992–'93. Currently repairing delaminated
  deck around mast partners and replacing teak sheerstrake.
39' Concordia yawl. Stripped and refinished exterior,
  1992–'93. Currently renewing brightwork, replacing
  garboards.
38' Alden motorsailer (1957). Renewing bad areas around
  maststep and transom knees. Installing new deckbeams
  in bridge deck. 1992-current.
16' Herreshoff 12½ (1947). Replaced keelbolts and garboards, refinished. 1993.
39' Concordia yawl. Replaced keelbolts and planking,
  renewed bottom caulking. 1993.
40' Huckins power cruiser. Replaced front windows and
  molding, repaired settee berth. 1992–'93.

Yard Information
Services
Marina facilities
Launching facilities
Moorage
Engine repair
Rigging
Storage
Number of boats stored per year: 55
Percentage of wooden boats: 20
Inside storage facilities
Maximum size for hauling and storing: 55′ LOA, 7′ draft, 25 tons
Maintenance
Number of boats maintained per year: 75
Percentage of wooden boats: 20
Owner maintenance allowed above and below rail.

■ GARDINER MARINE, INC.

Paul D. Gardiner
125 Steamboat Ave.
Wickford, RI 02852
401-294-1000

Builder Information
Years in business: 12
Carpenters employed: 3-5
Shop capacity: 60′
Willing to travel for on-the-site building projects.

Recent New Construction
26′ Hampton-type launch. Built 1993.

Recent Repair Projects
50′ Elco cruiser, QUEEN O′ SCOTS. Renewing to USCG Certificate requirements. Exterior restored 1993; currently working on interior.
35′ Colin Archer ketch. Replaced rudder, renewing other sections of boat. Current project.
38′ William Garden ketch. Repairing deck, renewing finish. Current project.
53′ Huckins Fairform Flyer. Making numerous repairs, applying AwlGrip finish. Current project.
134′ J-class sloop ENDEAVOUR. AwlGripped dorades, renewed hatch and cockpit. 1993.

Yard Information
Services
Marina facilities
Launching facilities
Overland transport
Engine repair
Rigging
Storage
Number of boats stored per year: 5
Percentage of wooden boats: 80
Maximum size for hauling and storing: 60′ LOA, 7′ draft, 60 tons

Maintenance
Number of boats maintained per year: 25
Percentage of wooden boats: 75
Owner maintenance allowed.
Retail supplies:
Complete inventory of supplies. Special orders welcome.

■ NARRAGANSETT SHIPWRIGHTS INC.

Frank McCaffrey
215 Third St.
Newport, RI 02840
401-846-3312

Builder Information
Years in business: 16
Carpenters employed: 4
Shop capacity: 70′
Willing to travel for on-the-site building projects.

Recent New Construction
10′ tender. Lawton design. Built 1993.

Recent Repair Projects
65′ Alden/Hinckley yawl NIRVANA. Replaced sections of deck framing and teak deck. 1993.
50′ Crowninshield schooner FORTUNE. Renewed frames, bottom planking, and transom. Built new mainmast. 1993.
20′ Herreshoff Fish-class ANCHOVY (1916). Completely rebuilt. 1992.
28′ Herreshoff S-boat OSPREY. Renewed sheerstrakes, cabin, and deck. 1992.
43′6″ Herreshoff New York 30-class sloop NAUTILUS (1905). Replanked hull. 1991.
Herreshoff 30-Square-Meter ORIOLE II. Completely rebuilt. 1991.
28′ Herreshoff S-boat DANAE. Completely rebuilt. 1990.

Yard Information
Storage
Number of boats stored per year: 10
Percentage of wooden boats: 100
Inside storage facilities
Maximum size for hauling and storing: 50′ LOA
Maintenance
Number of boats maintained per year: 5
Percentage of wooden boats: 100
Owner maintenance allowed above and below rail.
Retail supplies:
Wood, fastenings, paint, hardware.

◼ C.R. SCOTT MARINE WOODWORKING CO., INC.

Christopher R. Scott
1 Little Harbor Landing
Portsmouth, RI 02871
401-683-6878 Fax: same

Builder Information
Years in business: 14
Carpenters employed: 2-4
Shop capacity: 70'
Willing to travel for on-the-site building projects.

Recent Repair Projects
46' Little Harbor. Modified aft stateroom. 1993.
57' Chris-Craft Constellation. Refitted. 1993.
50' ketch. Renewed caprails, taffrail, and transom. 1992.
150' Tall Ship. Replaced decks. 1992.
200' minesweeper. Renewed planks and decking. 1991.
187' motoryacht. Laid 11,000 linear feet of teak deck. 1990.
92' sloop. Laid new teak deck, renewed caprail and handrail. 1990.

Yard Information
Storage
　　Number of boats stored per year: 3-5
　　Inside storage facilities
　　Maximum size for hauling and storing: 70' LOA, 16' draft, 170 tons
Maintenance
　　Number of boats maintained per year: 4
　　Percentage of wooden boats: 50
　　Owner maintenance allowed above and below rail.
Retail supplies:
　　Wood and chandlery supplies.

◼ GEORGE W. ZACHORNE, JR.

George W. Zachorne, Jr.
160 Pleasant St.
Wickford, RI 02852
401-294-4472

Builder Information
Years in business: 18
Carpenters employed: 1
Shop capacity: 45'
Willing to travel for on-the-site building projects.

Recent New Construction
12' lapstrake Whitehall. Built 1992.
14' plywood outboard work skiff. Built 1991.

Recent Repair Projects
28' Herreshoff S-boat AQUILA (1919). Completely restoring. Current project.
16' Herreshoff 12½s. 4 boats completely restored since 1990.
42' ketch DOVEKIE (1974). Renewed keelbolts, modernized interior. Repowered and refinished. 1993.
42' Grand Banks trawler-yacht. Rebuilt bulwarks and replaced aft-cabin bulkhead. 1993.

35' Concordia sloop. Replaced cockpit and interior. Repowered and rewired. 1992–'93.
32' Alden sloop (1933). Sistered frames, renewed 700' of planking. Rebuilt cockpit and repowered. 1992–'93.
26' bassboat (1961). Replaced afterdeck, toerail, and guardrail. 1992.

Yard Information
Services
　　Marina facilities
　　Launching facilities
　　Overland transport
　　Moorage
Storage
　　Number of boats stored per year: 60
　　Percentage of wooden boats: 10
　　Maximum size for hauling and storing: 45' LOA, 6' draft, 15 tons
Maintenance
　　Number of boats maintained per year: 9-10
　　Percentage of wooden boats: 100
　　Owner maintenance allowed above and below rail.
Retail supplies:
　　Ship's store — complete inventory of supplies.

◼ AMBLER BOAT WORKS

John Smith
P.O. Box 194
Sheldon, SC 29941
803-846-9561 Fax: same

Builder Information
Years in business: 32
Carpenters employed: 2
Shop capacity: 34'
Willing to travel for on-the-site building projects.

Recent New Construction
16' cold-molded St. Lawrence River skiff. 3 built 1990–'93.
14' lapstrake Rob Roy canoe. MacGregor design. Built 1992.

Recent Repair Projects
18' Thompson runabout. Renewed stern and keel, refinished.
14' Lyman runabout. Renewed transom, refinished.
Numerous wood rowing shells and gigs. Repairs due to accidents and neglect.

Yard Information
Services
　　Overland transport
　　Engine repair
　　Rigging
Maintenance
　　Number of boats maintained per year: 100
　　Percentage of wooden boats: 70

BLACKWATER BOATWORKS

Jay Devenny
677 Pawley Rd.
Mt. Pleasant, SC 29464
803-884-7089

Builder Information
Years in business: 3
Carpenters employed: 1
Shop capacity: 25'
Willing to travel for on-the-site building projects.

Recent New Construction
Boats designed by Jay Devenny for strip-plank construction:
12' double-paddle solo canoe.
14' fly fishing skiff. Built 1993.
14', 16', and 17' canoes. 4 built 1991–'93.
Other new construction:
14' strip-planked Rob Roy kayak. Daryl Graves design. Built 1993.

Recent Repair Projects
14' plywood skiff (1959). Replacing chines, gunwales, and deck. Refinishing. Current project.
18' Old Town canoe (1953). Completely restoring. Current project.
13' Penn Yan cartopper (1955). Completely restored. 1992.
68' tour boat MAJOR ANDERSON. Repaired non-structural rot, replaced 63 windows! 1993.
Retail supplies:
Epoxy and fiberglass cloth. Custom-milled, bead-and-cove cedar strip planking.

SAWDUST BOATWORKS

Mark Bayne
2205 Middle St.
Sullivans Island, SC 29482
803-884-4896

Builder Information
Years in business: 16
Carpenters employed: 3-5
Shop capacity: 50'
Willing to travel for on-the-site building projects.

Recent New Construction
30' strip-planked/cold-molded lobsterboat. Nelson Zimmer design. Current project.
35' strip-planked/cold-molded schooner. William Hand design. Current project.
16' clam skiff. John Gardner design. 2 built 1993.
16' lapstrake plywood creek skiff. Traditional design. 2 built each year.
16' plywood Gloucester Light Dory. Phil Bolger design. Built 1993.
20' strip-planked Abaco runabout. Albury/Bayne design. 2 built 1991–'92.
29' plywood/fiberglass cat-ketch sharpie. Bruce Kirby design. Built 1992.

Recent Repair Projects
18' Chris-Craft Holiday. Renewed sheer planks, engine box, seats, and decks. 1993.
25' Folkboat. Renewed keel, hatches, and other areas. 1993.
50' South Carolina Wildlife Dept. research boat. Replaced stem, rails, planking. 1993.
72' Citadel yacht MARIAH. Laid new teak decks, renewed forward end of pilothouse. 1992–'93.
68' tour boat MAJOR ANDERSON. Replaced upper deck, some framing, 300' of planking, and all butt blocks. 1990.

Yard Information
Services
  Rigging
Maintenance
  Number of boats maintained per year: Varies
  Percentage of wooden boats: 90
  Owner maintenance allowed above rail.

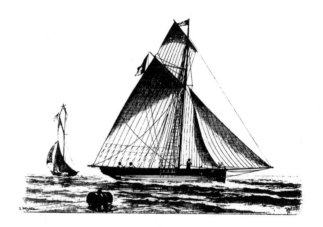

HOLLIS BROS. INC.

R.B. "Bobby" Hollis
652 N. Trezevant
Memphis, TN 38112
901-454-7669 Fax: 901-458-4527

Builder Information
Years in business: 10
Carpenters employed: 1-3
Shop capacity: 55'
Willing to travel for on-the-site building projects.

Recent New Construction
7' and 8' plywood tenders. R.B. Hollis designs. One of each size built 1993.

Recent Repair Projects
47' Egg Harbor power cruiser. Replaced stem, toerails, rubrails, and splash rails. Refastened some of planking. 1993.
26' Chris-Craft runabout cruiser. Replaced deck, toerails, and 4 planks. 1993.
26' Chris-Craft power cruiser. Replaced chine and 2 planks. 1993.

■ FLEETWOOD BOATS

Jim Frechette
8504 Bear Creek Dr.
Austin, TX 78737
512-288-5359

Builder Information
Years in business: 12
Carpenters employed: 1
Shop capacity: 26′

Recent Repair Projects
25′ Chris-Craft Express Cruiser (1941). Completely
    restored. Replaced frames and planking, repaired
    engine. 1992–'93.
19′ Chris-Craft Capri (1955). Repaired plank. 1993.
17′ Century Resorter (1960). Completely refinished. 1993.
36′ Chris-Craft Commander (1955). Renewed all bright-
    work. 1992.

Yard Information
Services
    Engine repair
Maintenance
    Number of boats maintained per year: 6
    Percentage of wooden boats: 100
    Owner maintenance allowed.

■ WILLIAM GEISLER

William Geisler
13511 Janwood
Farmers Branch, TX 75234
214-241-3009

Builder Information
Years in business: 7
Carpenters employed: 1
Shop capacity: 24′
Willing to travel for on-the-site building projects.

Recent New Construction
18′6″ wood/canvas Greenland kayak. Built 1993.
16′ lapstrake tandem canoe. W.P. Stephens design. Built 1991.

Recent Repair Projects
15′6″ Light Dory. Renewed plywood hull, replaced gun-
    wales, and section of transom. 1994.

■ HOLMES BOAT WORKS

Robert C. Holmes II
4404 Garrow
Houston, TX 77011
713-923-6435

Builder Information
Years in business: 53
Carpenters employed: 2
Shop capacity: 30′

Recent New Construction
Boats designed by Robert C. Holmes, Sr. for plywood
    construction:
16′ center-console, semi-V runabout/fishing boat. Current
    project.
19′ double-cockpit inboard runabout/skiboat. Current
    project.

Recent Repair Projects
Complete restoration or refinishing of the following boats:
17′ Chris-Craft Utility (1956). 1993.
18′ Holmes (1965). 1993.
17′ Chris-Craft (1962). 1993.
18′ Century (1965). 1993.
14′ Helton (1932). 1992.
16′ Holmes (1952). 1992.

Yard Information
Services
    Rigging
Maintenance
    Number of boats maintained per year: 100
    Percentage of wooden boats: 60
Retail supplies:
    Inquire.

■ HUNDLEY BOAT CO.

Byron Kibler Hundley
708 Hundley Dr.
Lake Dallas, TX 75065
817-497-6024

Builder Information
Years in business: 54
Carpenters employed: 1
Shop capacity: 65′

Recent New Construction
19′ aft-cockpit runabout. Carvel/cold-molded construc-
    tion. Replica of 1936 Chris-Craft Racer. Built 1991.
21′ Cobra runabout. Replica of Chris-Craft design. Built 1990.

Recent Repair Projects

23′ Chris-Craft Day Cruiser (1942). Completely restoring. Current project.

19′ Chris-Craft Silver Arrow. Completely restoring. Current project.

29′ Chris-Craft Sportsman (1939). Replacing bottom, completely restoring. Current project.

52′ Chris-Craft Connie. Renewing planking, refinishing. Current project.

26′ Chris-Craft Enclosed Cruiser. Completely refinished. 1994.

17′ Chris-Craft Sportsman. Replaced bottom with WEST System. Refinished and renewed upholstery. 1994.

35′ Chris-Craft Sea Skiff. Replaced teak decks and swim platform. Installed two new engines and refinished. 1993.

Yard Information

Services
  Engine repair
Storage
  Number of boats stored per year: 40
  Percentage of wooden boats: 95
  Inside storage facilities
  Maximum size for hauling and storing: 65′ LOA, 5′ draft, 35 tons
Maintenance
  Number of boats maintained per year: 48
  Percentage of wooden boats: 95
  Owner maintenance allowed above and below rail.
Retail supplies:
  Mill work, paint, fastenings, used parts.

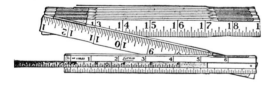

■ GOLD COAST YACHTS INC.

Richard A. Difede and Roger Hatfield
P.O. Box 1980
Kingshill, U.S.V.I. 00851
809-778-1004 Fax: 809-778-2859

Builder Information

Years in business: 20
Carpenters employed: 16
Shop capacity: 80′
Willing to travel for on-the-site building projects.

Recent New Construction

Company specializes in the design and construction of sailing or power catamarans, for use as commercial charter vessels, ferryboats, or water taxis. Boats are designed by Roger Hatfield for composite epoxy/strip-plank construction.

Hulls range in size from 38′ to 61′; the company builds, on average, 5-6 boats each year.

Recent Repair Projects

57′ Gold Coast 57 catamaran. Completely rebuilt. 1990.

■ BUFFALO BATEAUS

Jim Boone
1570 W. 1600 South
Lewiston, UT 84320
801-258-5254

Builder Information

Years in business: 10
Carpenters employed: 1
Shop capacity: 24′

Recent New Construction

18′ plywood gunning dory. John Gardner design. Current project.

11′ lapstrake plywood Charlotte canoe. Tom Hill design. Built 1993.

13′ plywood/fiberglass pirogue. Glen-L Marine design. Built 1992.

22′ plywood/fiberglass punt. Jim Boone design. Built 1990.

Recent Repair Projects

18′ bateau. Replaced planked bottom with plywood and sheathed in fiberglass. 1990.

Numerous small wooden boats. Minor repairs and modifications, and refinishing.

THE ADIRONDACK GUIDE-BOAT

Steve Kaulback
Box 144
Charlotte, VT 05445
802-425-3926

Builder Information
Years in business: 14
Carpenters employed: 1-2
Shop capacity: 18'

Recent New Construction
Adirondack guideboats in 13', 14', 15' and 17'9" lengths.
Strip-plank construction, designs by Steve Kaulback. 11
built 1990–'93.

Recent Repair Projects
16' Adirondack guideboat. Renewed planking, completely
refinished. 1992.
13' Lyman rowboat. Replaced 50% of the frames, gunwales, thwarts, and hardware. Refinished. 1992.
17' St. Lawrence River skiff. Repaired planking and refinished. 1991.

Yard Information
Retail supplies:
Anything related to Adirondack guideboats.

D.P. COOPER BOAT BUILDING INC.

Dexter Cooper
RR #1, Box 267
Hartland, VT 05048
802-436-2640 Fax: same

Builder Information
Years in business: 18
Carpenters employed: 1
Shop capacity: 40'

Recent Repair Projects
Company specializes in the building of wooden spars and
has built spars for a wide variety of boats, from 8'
prams to 80' cutters. The following are recent projects:
96' motoryacht PRINCIPIA. Building two 40' hollow
masts. Current project.
70' cutter BLOODHOUND. Solid spars — 63' mainmast,
33' topmast, 50' boom, and 30' gaff. 1993.
50' motorsailer NOR'EASTER. Hollow spars — 48' mainmast, 40' foremast, booms, and gaffs. 1991.
30' sloop. Restoring. Current project.

Yard Information
Services
Overland transport
Rigging

DARLING'S BOATWORKS INC.

George Darling
Ferry Rd.
Charlotte, VT 05445
802-425-2004 Fax: same

Builder Information
Years in business: 16
Carpenters employed: 2
Shop capacity: 40'

Recent Repair Projects
40' WWI Captain's launch. Replaced bottom planking. 1993.
18' cold-molded runabout. Sheathed hull in fiberglass and
epoxy, applied AwlGrip finish. 1993.
18' St. Lawrence River skiff. Completely refinished hull
and brightwork. 1993.
27' bassboat (1950). Repaired planking and frames, completely refinished. 1992.
39' Alden cutter. Minor repairs and refinishing. Annual
project.
32' Hess-designed Bristol Channel cutter. Minor repairs
and refinishing. Annual project.
16' Century runabout (1953). Minor repairs and refinishing. Annual project.

Yard Information
Services
Overland transport
Rigging
Storage
Number of boats stored per year: 30
Percentage of wooden boats: 30
Maximum size for hauling and storing: 40' LOA, 6'
draft, 10 tons
Maintenance
Number of boats maintained per year: 100
Percentage of wooden boats: 30
Owner maintenance allowed on limited basis.

FAERING DESIGN INC.

Chip Stulen
P.O. Box 805
Shelburne, VT 05482
802-462-2126

Builder Information
Years in business: 18
Carpenters employed: 1
Shop capacity: 30'

Recent New Construction
12'3" lapstrake tender. William Crosby design. Built
1991–'92.
13' lapstrake double-paddle canoe. Chip Stulen design.
Built 1991.
18' lapstrake St. Lawrence River skiff. Traditional design.
Built 1990–'91.
19'6" lapstrake Fjording 19.5 sloop. Chip Stulen design.
Built 1990.

Recent Repair Projects

30' St. Pierre dory. Renewed interior. 1991–'92.

16' faering for oar and sail. Repaired planking, refinished. 1991.

Currently, Chip is working as project manager for the restoration of the 1906 sidewheeler TICONDEROGA at the Shelburne Museum, Shelburne, Vermont. Anticipated completion date for the project is 1996 or 1997.

 HILL FAMILY BOATBUILDING CO.

Thomas J. Hill
RR #1, Box 2310
Huntington, VT 05462

Builder Information

Years in business: 22
Carpenters employed: 1
Shop capacity: Any size
Willing to travel for on-the-site building projects.

Recent New Construction

Tom specializes in the design and construction of lapstrake-plywood ultralight skiffs, dories, and canoes. He has built approximately 30 small craft over the last 3 years.

Recent Repair Projects

Currently involved in restoration of the Shelburne Museum's 220' sidewheeler TICONDEROGA.

 KING BOAT WORKS

Graeme King
P.O. Box 234
Putney, VT 05346
802-387-5373

Builder Information

Years in business: 25
Carpenters employed: 3
Shop capacity: 60'

Recent New Construction

Rowing shells designed by Graeme King for stressed-skin construction:

58' eight-oared shell. 8 built 1990–'93.

43' four-oared shell. Built 1993.

32' double scull. 2 built 1993.

27' single scull. 60 built 1990–'93.

Recent Repair Projects

Company has repaired numerous shells over the last several years, including the following recent projects:

59' eight-oared shell. Repaired 24' hole. 1993.

27' single shell. Restored hull — had been broken in half.

27' single shell. Replaced forward 6' of hull.

Also recently restored a 26' Thames skiff, built in 1880.

Yard Information

Launching facilities
Retail supplies:
Fittings and materials for rowing shells.

 FUAT LATIF, BOATBUILDER

Fuat Latif
RFD 1, Box 20E
Orwell, VT 05760
802-948-2753

Builder Information

Years in business: 10
Carpenters employed: 1
Shop capacity: 20'

Recent New Construction

11'6" lapstrake double-paddle Vaux Jr. canoe. J.H. Rushton design. Current project.

16' Adirondack guideboat. Grant design. 2 under construction.

16' lapstrake tandem Ugo canoe. J.H. Rushton design. Built 1993.

10'6" lapstrake Wee Lassie canoe. J.H. Rushton design. 6 built 1990–'93.

16' lapstrake St. Lawrence River skiff. Built 1990.

 PATCH & CO. BOAT REPAIR INC.

Nick Patch
Box 2661, Thompson Point Rd.
Charlotte, VT 05445
802-425-3227

Builder Information

Years in business: 10
Carpenters employed: 3
Shop capacity: Any size
Willing to travel for on-the-site building projects.

Recent Repair Projects

35' Chris-Craft cruiser. Renewed frames and bottom planking. Refinished. 1993.

16' Lakefield skiff. Completely restored. 1993.

17' Old Town canoe. Completely restored. 1993.

30' Hacker-Craft. Repaired rotten structural timbers, refinished. 1992.

40' custom excursion boat. Replaced deck, transom, and cockpit sole. Refinished. 1991–'93.

28' Herreshoff S-boat. Completely restored. 1991–'92.

28' Lyman. Renewed joinerwork, refinished. 1991–'92.

 SHADY RILL BOATWORKS

Ed Epstein
P.O. Box 1089
Montpelier, VT 05601
802-229-5123

Builder Information

Years in business: 9
Carpenters employed: 1
Shop capacity: 36'
(continues)

(Shady Rill Boatworks, continued)

Recent New Construction

36' plywood gaff-rigged schooner. Thomas Colvin design. Current project.

21' plywood catamaran. Wharram design. Built 1991–'92.

22' lapstrake Sharptown barge. R.D. Culler design. Built 1990.

25' skipjack. Joe Gregory design. Completed 1989.

18' lapstrake yawl. Ed Epstein design. Built 1989.

■ SHELBURNE SHIPYARD

Mary M. Griswold
P.O. Box 610, Harbor Rd.
Shelburne, VT 05482
802-985-3326 Fax: 802-985-9510

Builder Information
Years in business: 20
Carpenters employed: 2
Shop capacity: 55'

Recent Repair Projects
32' Pembroke cruiser. Replaced plank. 1993.

40' 30-Square-Meter class. Replaced deadwood, reattached ballast keel. 1993.

35' Chris-Craft power cruiser. Renewed transom. 1993.

33' tugboat. Replaced planking, several frames, and deck. 1992–'93.

Yard Information
Services
    Marina facilities
    Overland transport
    Moorage
    Engine repair
    Rigging
Storage
    Number of boats stored per year: 550
    Percentage of wooden boats: 5
    Inside storage facilities
    Maximum size for hauling and storing: 70' LOA, 10' draft, 55 tons
Maintenance
    Number of boats maintained per year: 200
    Percentage of wooden boats: 5
    Owner maintenance allowed above and below rail.
Retail supplies:
    Inquire.

■ SHELL BOATS

Fred Shell
RD #2, Box 289C
St. Albans, VT 05478
802-524-9645

Builder Information
Years in business: 11
Carpenters employed: 1
Shop capacity: 28'

Recent New Construction
Boats designed by Fred Shell for lapstrake plywood construction:

15' trailerable micro-cruiser trimaran. Current project.

7' cat-rigged Leif tender. 2 built 1990–'93.

13' Swifty 13 micro-cruiser. 2 built 1992–'93.

15' Swifty 15 micro-cruiser. Built 1993.

19' Great Blue Heron cat-ketch. 4 built 1990–'93.

Company also supplies kits for 7'–19' sailboats. About 30-35 kits sold each year during 1990–'93.

Recent Repair Projects
16' canoe. Completely restored. 1992.

12' Vermont Moppet daysailers. Restored 3 boats 1990–'93.

Yard Information
Retail supplies:
    Kit boats.

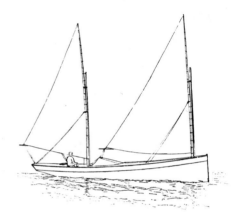

■ HORN HARBOR BOATWORKS INC.

Norman Turner
P.O. Box 37
Port Haywood, VA 23138
804-725-3223

Builder Information
Years in business: 50
Carpenters employed: 2
Shop capacity: 70'

Recent New Construction
Last two boats built in 1990 and 1991 were a 47' deadrise crabber and a 50' deadrise lobsterboat. E. Diggs/in-house designs. Since 1991, company has been operating mainly as a repair and service yard.

Recent Repair Projects
Repairwork has included 20'–30' wooden boats and 30'–65' deadrise workboats. Projects have involved hull, deck, cabin, and running gear repair and replacement.

Yard Information
Services
    Marina facilities
    Launching facilities

Storage
  Number of boats stored per year: 10
  Percentage of wooden boats: 10
  Maximum size for hauling and storing: 35' LOA, 5'
    draft, 15 tons
Maintenance
  Number of boats maintained per year: 75-80
  Percentage of wooden boats: 50
  Owner maintenance allowed below rail.
Retail supplies:
  Paint, fastenings, fiberglassing materials, lumber, and
    other supplies.

■ JUDSON BOATS

David Judson
Box 416
Grimstead, VA 23064
804-725-4195

Builder Information
Years in business: 20
Carpenters employed: 1
Shop capacity: 45'

Recent New Construction
22' lapstrake/cross-planked outboard skiff. David Judson
  design. Current project.
12' and 15' rowing skiffs. David Judson designs. 3 built
  1991.
7'6" lapstrake plywood Nutshell pram. Joel White design.
  2 built 1991.

Recent Repair Projects
26' Luders 16-class sloop. Completely rebuilding. Current
  project.
18' Hampton One-Design sloop. Recanvased decks,
  renewed paint and brightwork. 1992.
34' McIntosh sloop. Modified interior, rebuilt galley.
  Completed various hull repairs. 1991.
127' motoryacht (1927). Repaired wheelhouse and captain's cabin. Renewed deck. 1990–'91.

■ OCRAN BOAT SHOP, INC.

Fred Ajootian
Box 4005
White Stone, VA 22578
804-435-6305

Builder Information
Years in business: 34
Carpenters employed: 2
Shop capacity: 50'

Recent New Construction
Boats designed by Fred Ajootian:
16' flat-bottomed rowing skiff. Current project.
20' inboard fishing launch. Built 1992–'93.

Recent Repair Projects
32' Owens power cruiser. Rebuilt transom, replaced garboard planks. 1993–'94.
31' lobsterboat. Rebuilt cabin. 1993–'94.
30' workboat. Replaced horn timbers and keelbolts. 1993.
34' workboat. Replaced keel and deadwood. 1993.
38' Egg Harbor power cruiser. Replaced keelbolts, floor
  timbers, and garboard planks. 1993.

Yard Information
Services
  Engine repair
  Rigging
Maintenance
  Number of boats maintained per year: 100
  Percentage of wooden boats: 50
Retail supplies:
  Stainless-steel propeller shafts.

■ ROCK HALL BOAT SHOP

David Scarbrough
P.O. Box 185
Burgess, VA 22432
804-453-5574

Builder Information
Years in business: 15
Carpenters employed: 1
Shop capacity: 25'

Recent New Construction
18' lobsterboat-type skiff. Eric Dow design. Built 1993.
Boats designed by David Scarbrough:
15'4" lapstrake Coot sloop. 2 built 1991–'92.
14' rowing skiff. Built 1991.
16' lapstrake Vireo sloop. 2 built 1990.

Recent Repair Projects
34' cruising auxiliary. Renewed mast. 1993.
24' Atkin Maid of Endor cutter. Renewed bowsprit. 1993.
17' cold-molded Olympic kayak. Strengthened hull,
  renewed deck, restored. 1993.
15' lapstrake Whitehall. Renewed planking and frames,
  restored. 1991.
14' Penn Yan outboard runabout. Restored. 1990.

■ TIFFANY YACHTS INC.

Rebecca C. Jones
Rte. 3, Box 133
Burgess, VA 22432
804-453-3437 Fax: 804-453-3837

Builder Information
Years in business: 50
Carpenters employed: 4
Shop capacity: 80'
(continues)

(Tiffany Yachts Inc., continued)

Recent New Construction

40' cold-molded sportfisherman. T.R. Cockrell, Jr. design. Built 1993.

34' cabin cruiser. Chesapeake deadrise construction. T.R. Cockrell, Jr. design. Built 1993.

Recent Repair Projects

Have completed a variety of projects over last several years.

Yard Information

Services
    Marina facilities
    Launching facilities
    Engine repair
    Sail repair
    Rigging
Storage
    Number of boats stored per year: 15
    Percentage of wooden boats: 25
    Maximum size for hauling and storing: 80' LOA, 10' draft, 60 tons
Maintenance
    Number of boats maintained per year: 200
    Percentage of wooden boats: 30
Retail supplies:
    Teak, mahogany, plywood, fastenings, fiberglass, paint, adhesives.

■ ZIMMERMAN MARINE INC.

Steve Zimmerman
Rte. 650, Box 10
Cardinal, VA 23025
804-725-3440 Fax: 804-725-7904

Builder Information

Years in business: 13
Carpenters employed: 7
Shop capacity: 100'

Recent New Construction

52' cold-molded ketch. Bruce King design. Current project.

Recent Repair Projects

38' William Atkin ketch. Recaulked above and below waterline. 1993.

40' Hinckley ketch. Sistered frames, renewed caulking. 1993.

84' Broward motoryacht. Renewed systems, repaired decks. Annually upgrading. 1991–'93.

41' Rosenblatt/Luke ketch (1960). Repaired bottom and cabinside. Annually upgrading. 1990–'93.

46' Pacemaker motoryacht. Renewed keel and bottom planking. 1990.

Yard Information

Services
    Overland transport
    Engine repair
    Rigging

Storage
    Number of boats stored per year: 18
    Percentage of wooden boats: 15
    Inside storage facilities
    Maximum size for hauling and storing: 50' LOA, 6'6" draft, 25 tons
Maintenance
    Number of boats maintained per year: 40
    Percentage of wooden boats: 15
    Owner maintenance allowed.

■ ASPOYA BOATS

F. Jay Smith
1346 Thompson Rd.
Anacortes, WA 98221
206-293-2034

Builder Information

Years in business: 15
Carpenters employed: 1
Shop capacity: 60'
Willing to travel for on-the-site building projects.

Recent New Construction

Boats of lapstrake construction:

22' Norwegian faering. F. Jay Smith design. Current project.

7'10" Norwegian pram. Nils O. Ulset design. Current project.

24' gunter-rigged Norwegian seksaering. F. Jay Smith design. Built 1992.

9' and 10' Norwegian prams. Nils O. Ulset designs. One of each size built 1990–'91.

Recent Repair Projects

50' Sparkman & Stephens motoryacht (1927). Built 5-piece locker/desk/bookshelf unit for main saloon. Modified and rebuilt forward stateroom, renewed teak brightwork. 1993.

45' Jones/Goodell power cruiser. Renewed 7 planks and 29 frames. 1992.

10' Oslo dinghy. Completely rebuilt. 1992.

73' Robinson barkentine VARUA. Replaced engineroom doghouse, repaired aft companionway and covering board. 1991.

42' Grand Banks trawler-yacht (1963). Replaced lazarette hatch and framing. Renewed deck and framing, partially replaced cabin side. 1991.

■ BAIRD BOAT CO., INC.

Ernie Baird
305 8th St.
Port Townsend, WA 98368
206-385-5727

Builder Information
Years in business: 15
Carpenters employed: 6-10
Shop capacity: 100′

Recent Repair Projects
45′ staysail schooner ELSITA. Renewed foremast, standing rigging, bulwark, railcap, and planking. 1993.
27′ Folkboat CHLOE. Renewed mast and rig, house, deck fittings, engine and tanks. 1993.
50′ sloop COURAGEOUS. Replaced frames, refastened and recaulked. 1993.
46′ sloop HAIDA. Splined hull seams below waterline. Renewed framing and floor, installed bronze maststep. 1993.
57′ fishing vessel BERGEN. Repaired keel. Renewed forefoot and planking, aligned shaft. 1993.
100′ topsail schooner RAGLAND. Renewed bulwark, railcap, planks, covering board, and rudder. 1991 and 1993.
38′ cutter PHOENIX. Lengthened mast and renewed bowsprit. Repaired house and interior. Recaulked hull. 1991 and 1993.

Yard Information
Services
    Marina facilities
    Launching facilities
    Engine repair
    Rigging
    Maximum size for hauling and storing: 65′ LOA, 18′ draft, 70 tons
Retail supplies:
    Wood, paint, zincs, fastenings.

■ BAXTER BOAT CO.

David E. Baxter
Star Rte., Box 13, P.O. Box 127
Olga, WA 98279
206-376-2472

Builder Information
Years in business: 45
Carpenters employed: 2
Shop capacity: 120′
Willing to travel for on-the-site building projects.

Recent New Construction
Hollow wooden spars and masts built to customer specifications or in-house designs.

Recent Repair Projects
Rebuilding and/or general overhaul of the following boats:
72′ tug. Renewed planking, decks, and bulwarks. 1993.
18′ and 20′ power launches. 1991 and 1992.

52′ schooner. 1992.
95′ tugboat. 1990.
19′6″ speedboat. 1990.

Yard Information
Services
    Marina facilities
    Launching facilities
    Moorage
    Sail repair
    Rigging
Maintenance
    Number of boats maintained per year: 10
    Percentage of wooden boats: 90
    Owner maintenance allowed above and below rail.
Retail supplies:
    General inventory of supplies.

■ BILL'S BUSINESS

William Paine
22960 S.E. 288th St.
Kent, WA 98042
206-432-6181

Builder Information
Years in business: 4
Carpenters employed: 1
Shop capacity: 20′
Willing to travel for on-the-site building projects.

Recent New Construction
17′6″ wood/canvas Atkinson Traveler canoe. Rollin Thurlow design. 3 built 1990 amd 1993.

Recent Repair Projects
18′ Old Town canoe. Replaced 30% of ribs and completed other restoration work. 1992.
15′ Peterborough canoe. Repaired ribs and planking. 1990.

■ THE BOATWRIGHT

Brad Rice
1150½ N.W. 46 St.
Seattle, WA 98107
206-784-5077

Builder Information
Years in business: 8
Carpenters employed: 1-3
Shop capacity: 36′
Willing to travel for on-the-site building projects.

Recent New Construction
Boats designed by Brad Rice:
17′ lapstrake plywood touring kayak. Built 1993.
18′ wood/epoxy electric-powered raceboat. Built 1993.
36′ plywood/epoxy liveaboard houseboat. Built 1992–'93.
7′8″ plywood Portage Bay skiff. 40 kit boats supplied 1992–'93.
(continues)

(The Boatwright, continued)
Other new construction:
17' wood/canvas North Alaskan kayak. Eskimo reproduction. 3 built for film props, 1993.

Recent Repair Projects
20' Reinell power cruiser (1958). Renewed structural members, replaced transom. 1993.
16' Old Town canoe. Totally restored. Renewed structural members, recanvased and refinished. 1993.
35' Chris-Craft power cruiser. Replaced chine logs, renewed structural members. 1992.
25' Blanchard sloop. Repaired broken mast with scarfed 5' length. 1992.
12' North Shore dinghy. Repaired centerboard. Refinished. 1992.
15' Finn class. Restored and refinished. 1992.
14' Wolverine Wagemaker (1949). Repaired topside damage, replaced rubrails, and refinished. 1991.

■ CABIN BOAT SHOP

Don Nyman
P.O. Box 148
Cle Elum, WA 98922
509-674-5597

Builder Information
Years in business: 2
Carpenters employed: 1
Shop capacity: 24'

Recent New Construction
Business is just starting. Will build and repair all types of wooden boats.

Yard Information
Retail supplies:
Inboard and outboard motors. Trailers.

■ CANOES & KAYAKS/KAYAK WAY

Skip Snaith
P.O. Box 451
Eastsound, WA 98245
206-376-4754

Builder Information
Years in business: 15
Carpenters employed: 1
Shop capacity: 30'

Recent New Construction
11' and 17' kayaks. Wood-framed, skin-covered construction. Skip Snaith designs. 2 built 1993–'94.
10'6" lapstrake plywood Wee Lassie canoe. J.H. Rushton design. 6 built 1984–'90.

■ CANVASBACK CANOE SHOP

Terry Cornelius
31320 N.W. 41st Ave.
Ridgefield, WA 98642
206-695-0707 Fax: 206-695-9782

Builder Information
Years in business: 5
Carpenters employed: 1
Shop capacity: 20'

Recent Repair Projects
Repair, recanvasing, and refinishing of the following canoes:
14' Peterborough canoe. 1993.
18' Old Town Otca canoe. 1993.
18' Old Town Guide canoe. 1993.
17' Old Town Otca canoe. 1992.
17' Old Town Molitor canoe. 1992.
17' Chestnut canoe. 1991. Won "Best Restored Boat" award at 1991 Seattle Wooden Boat Show.

■ CENTER FOR WOOD CONSTRUCTION S.C.C.C.

David Mullens and Gordon Sanstad
Seattle Central Community College
2310 South Lane
Seattle, WA 98144
206-587-5460 Fax: 206-587-5461

Builder Information
Years in business: 58
Carpenters employed: 2 instructors, 36 students
Shop capacity: 30'

Recent New Construction
24' plywood/planked steam tug. Faust design. Current project.
10' stitch-and-glue sailing dinghy. Flounder Bay design. 4 built 1993–'94.
9' strip-planked sailing dinghy. Built 1993.
15'6" yard tug. R.D. Culler design. Built 1993.
17'6" strip-planked sea kayak. Lynn Senour design. Built 1992.
9'6" lapstrake semi-dory. John Gardner design. Built 1991.

Recent Repair Projects
17' Chris-Craft. Completely restoring. Current project.
21' Lowell dory. Renewed planking, frames, and motorwell. 1993.
18' lifeboat. Renewed frames, planking, stems, and deck. 1992.

■ CUNNINGHAM WOODWORKS

Christopher Cunningham
822 N.W. 70th St.
Seattle, WA 98117
206-784-6573

Builder Information

Years in business: 15
Carpenters employed: 1
Shop capacity: 20'

Recent New Construction

18' Greenland kayak. Plywood stitch-and-glue construction. Traditional design modified by Cunningham. Built 1993.

18' wood/canvas Greenland kayak. Modified H.C. Petersen design. 2 built 1992.

10' flat-bottomed skiff. Plans from *The American Boy's Handy Book*. Built 1991.

■ GEOFF CUSTER, BOATBUILDER

Geoff Custer
2525 N.E. Helm St.
Bremerton, WA 98310
206-479-2833

Builder Information

Years in business: 4
Carpenters employed: 1
Shop capacity: 30'
Willing to travel for on-the-site building projects.

Recent New Construction

15'6" daysailer. Ed Monk design. Current project.
12' plywood McKenzie River drift boat. Don Hill design. Built 1991.

Recent Repair Projects

85' schooner. Ongoing maintenance. 1993.
16' Poulsbo launch. Completely restorated. 1993.
65' motoryacht. Renewed wiring. 1991–'92.
100' schooner. Renewed interior joinery and pinrails. 1990.
12'6" semi-dory. Completely restored. 1990.

Yard Information

Maintenance
    Number of boats maintained per year: 6
    Percentage of wooden boats: 95
    Owner maintenance allowed above and below rail.

■ DEVLIN DESIGNING BOATBUILDERS

Sam Devlin
2424 Gravelly Beach Loop NW
Olympia, WA 98502
206-866-0164 Fax: 206-866-4548

Builder Information

Years in business: 16
Carpenters employed: 8
Shop capacity: 60'
Willing to travel for on-the-site building projects.

Recent New Construction

Boats designed by Sam Devlin for stitch-and-glue plywood construction:
20' Lichen-class scow sloop. 3 built 1990–'93.
14'4" Cackler power skiff. 6 built 1990–'93.

22' Surf Scoter power cruiser. 8 built 1990–'93.
35' Czarinna 35 power cruiser. Built 1993.
27'4" Black Crown E.C. power cruiser. Built 1993.
14'4" Cackler power skiff. 6 built 1990–'93.

Recent Repair Projects

30' motorsailer Oysta 30. Repowered and refinished. 1993.
Major restorations of approximately 5 vessels during 1990–'93, as well as numerous jobs involving minor repairs and refinishing.

Yard Information

Services
    Launching facilities
    Moorage
Storage
    Number of boats stored per year: 4
    Percentage of wooden boats: 100
    Inside storage facilities
    Maximum size for hauling and storing: 40' LOA, 6' draft, 15 tons

■ DUNBAR MARINE SERVICE

Roy Dunbar and Marshall Johnson
3030 West Commodore Way
Seattle, WA 98199
206-283-6260

Builder Information

Years in business: 35
Carpenters employed: 2
Shop capacity: 75'
Willing to travel for on-the-site building projects.

Recent New Construction

14' cold-molded rowing wherry. Built 1993.
10' plywood skiff. Built 1992.

Recent Repair Projects

71' motoryacht (1971). Repairing extensive dry rot damage. Renewing stem and cabin sides. Current project.
43' Monk tri-cabin power cruiser (1947). Completely restoring. Rebuilding interior, replacing tanks, engines, and wiring. Ongoing project. 1991–current.
32' custom power cruiser (1914). Restoring, ongoing project. 1990–current.
57' Rhodes yawl CARRIBBEE. Completely rebuilding. Replacing planking, 57 frames, decks, interior, and rig. 1991–current.
60' motorsailer (1932). Renewed planking, frames, and transom. Refinished. 1993.
55' power cruiser (1965). Replaced 300' of planking, 35 frames, and teak decks. Repaired dry rot damage. 1993.
36' Lake Union Dreamboat (1926). Renewed planking, frames, interior, wiring, and plumbing. 1992.
(continues)

(Dunbar Marine Service, continued)

Yard Information

Services
Marina facilities
Launching facilities
Moorage
Rigging
Maintenance
Number of boats maintained per year: 6
Percentage of wooden boats: 100
Owner maintenance allowed above and below rail.

■ EAGLE HARBOR BOATYARD, INC.

Mark Julian
405 Harborview
Bainbridge Island, WA 98110
206-842-9930 Fax: 206-842-0854

Builder Information
Years in business: 20
Carpenters employed: 3
Shop capacity: 70'

Recent Repair Projects
45' ketch. Replaced cabintop and part of deck. 1993.
36' sloop PIPE DREAM. Repaired keel, refastened garboard, recaulked. 1993.
30' sloop. Renewed keel and planking. 1992.
36' cutter. Renewed planking. Recaulked and refinished hull. 1992.
42' Monk/Franck power cruiser. Renewed planking and transom. Refinished hull. 1991.
45' Romsdal trawler. Replaced planking. Recaulked and refinished hull. 1991.

Yard Information
Services
Launching facilities
Engine repair
Rigging
Storage
Number of boats stored per year: var
Percentage of wooden boats: 20
Maximum size for hauling and storing: 70' LOA, 60 tons
Maintenance
Number of boats maintained per year: 300
Percentage of wooden boats: 20
Owner maintenance allowed above and below rail.
Retail supplies:
Wood, fastenings, paint. Most materials for boat repair and maintenance.

■ FAR NORTH DESIGNS

Marc Daniels
2604 Lummi View Dr.
Bellingham, WA 98226
206-758-2423

Builder Information
Years in business: 8
Carpenters employed: 1
Shop capacity: 25'
Willing to travel for on-the-site building projects.

Recent New Construction
Frame-and-fabric "skin boat" kayaks — designs modified by Marc Daniels:
18' umiak (open skin boat). St. Lawrence Island Eskimo design. Current project.
16' and 16'6" King Island kayaks. Bering Strait Inuit designs. One of each size built 1993.
17' and 17'6" Aleut kayak. 3 built 1993.
17' Greenland kayak. Greenland Inuit design. Built 1992.

Yard Information
Retail supplies:
Umiak and kayak kits also available.

■ FLEET MARINE INC.

Nadine Jonientz
419 Jackson
Port Townsend, WA 98368
206-385-4000

Builder Information
Years in business: 18
Carpenters employed: 2
Shop capacity: 50'
Willing to travel for on-the-site building projects.

Recent Repair Projects
43' sailboat. Renewed caulking. 1992.
48' power cruiser. Completed extensive repairs to bow. 1992.
50' power cruiser. Renewed cabinetry and deck. 1992.
Over last several years, company has done maintenance work (painting, rigging, electrical, etc.) on numerous vessels in the 20' to 50' range.

Yard Information
Services
Marina facilities
Launching facilities
Overland transport
Rigging
Storage
Number of boats stored per year: 100
Percentage of wooden boats: 15
Inside storage facilities
Maximum size for hauling and storing: 50' LOA, 30 tons
Maintenance
Number of boats maintained per year: 624
Percentage of wooden boats: 30
Owner maintenance allowed above and below rail.
Retail supplies:
Complete inventory of supplies.

■ FLETCHER BOATS

Simon Fletcher
292 Wellman Rd.
Port Angeles, WA 98362
206-452-8430

Builder Information
Years in business: 8
Carpenters employed: 1
Shop capacity: 20'

Recent New Construction
18' cold-molded/composite runabout. Simon Fletcher/Speedliner design. 9 built 1990–'93.
10' plywood skiffs. Various designs. 9 built 1990–'93.

Recent Repair Projects
18' Chris-Craft. Replaced deck and frames, refinished. 1992.
18' Chris-Craft. Stripped and varnished. 1992.
18' Thompson. Repaired leak problems. 1992.
14' skiff. Strengthened hull. 1991.

Yard Information
Maintenance
    Number of boats maintained per year: 2
    Percentage of wooden boats: 100
Retail supplies:
    Inquire.

■ GEORGE'S LIL SHIPYARD

George Calkins
1441 Griffiths Point Rd.
P.O. Box 222
Nordland, WA 98358
206-385-3649

Builder Information
Years in business: 60
Carpenters employed: 1-2
Shop capacity: 40'
19' plywood Bartender. George Calkins design. 5 built 1990–'93.
26' plywood Bartender. Built 1990.

Recent Repair Projects
26' Bartender. Refinished. 1990.

■ GUZZWELL YACHTS

John Guzzwell
914 N.W. 50th St.
Seattle, WA 98102
206-781-8668

Builder Information
Years in business: 35
Carpenters employed: 1
Shop capacity: Any size
Willing to travel for on-the-site building projects.

Recent New Construction
23' cold-molded cutter. John Guzzwell design. Built 1993.

Recent Repair Projects
140' tugboat. Reworking interior. Current project.
108' tugboat. Laid teak deck. Renewed interior. 1993.
106' ketch. Laid teak pilothouse sole. 1993.
108' motoryacht. Rebuilt crew quarters forward. Laid teak foredeck. 1992–'93.
65' cutter. Renewed companionway doors. 1992.
72' ketch. Rebuilt interior. 1991–'92.
98' motoryacht. Laid teak decks. 1990.

■ HAVORN MARINE SERVICES

Lee H. Ehrheart
3530 Interlake Ave. North
Seattle, WA 98103
206-789-7043

Builder Information
Years in business: 15
Carpenters employed: 1
Shop capacity: 110'
Willing to travel for on-the-site building projects.

Recent Repair Projects
28' log pusher. Rebuilding hull. Current project.
38' cutter. Replaced horn timber and some framing. Refastened. 1994.
67' motoryacht. Rebuilt hull. Renewed planking and frames, refastened. 1993.
36' Tahiti ketch. Refastened hull below waterline. 1993.
36' Bermudian sloop. Replaced keelson and keelbolts. Renewed planking. 1993.
50' gaff ketch. Refastened and recaulked hull below waterline. 1992.
38' Bermudian ketch. Renewed hull planking. Replaced bulwarks. 1992.

■ ART HOBAN, BOATBUILDER

Art Hoban
2121 King St.
Bellingham, WA 98225
206-671-7719

Builder Information
Years in business: 15
Carpenters employed: 1
Shop capacity: Any size
Willing to travel for on-the-site building projects.

Recent New Construction
Boats of cold-molded construction:
14' Puffin wherry. Art Hoban design. 4 built 1992–'93.
20' wherry. Art Hoban design. Built 1990.
15' Delaware River tuckup. Built 1991.
(continues)

(Art Hoban, Boatbuilder, continued)

Recent Repair Projects

50' fishboat. Renewed planking. 1993.

127' Gloucester schooner. Replaced 800' of planking, renewed framing and stanchions. 1993.

32' Atkin Tally Ho cutter. Replaced keelbolts and floor timbers. Recaulked decks. 1993.

30' Tahiti ketch. Recaulked decks. 1992.

60' tugboat. Built master stateroom. 1992.

Yard Information

Services
  Overland transport
  Engine repair
  Sail repair
  Rigging
Storage
  Number of boats stored per year: 4
  Percentage of wooden boats: 100
  Inside storage facilities
  Maximum size for hauling and storing: 40' LOA
Maintenance
  Number of boats maintained per year: 20
  Percentage of wooden boats: 100
  Owner maintenance allowed.
Retail supplies:
  Marine supplies, oars, rowing parts.

■ HVALSOE BOATS

Eric D. Hvalsoe
7356 13th Ave. NW
Seattle, WA 98117
206-622-2566

Builder Information

Years in business: 12
Carpenters employed: 1-2
Shop capacity: 30'
Willing to travel for on-the-site building projects.

Recent New Construction

13' lapstrake Hvalsoe 13 dinghy for oar and sail. Eric Hvalsoe design. 5 built 1990–'93.

10'6" lapstrake tender. Modified Lawley design. 4 built 1990–'93.

14' lapstrake Acme Skiff. 2 built 1991–'92.

12' lapstrake North Shore dinghy. Bob Baker design. Built 1992.

15' lapstrake Lake Oswego pulling boat. 5 built 1990–'92.

22' cold-molded Aurora speedboat. Eric Hvalsoe design. Completed 1990.

17'6" strip-planked sea kayak. Moyer design. 2 built 1990 and 1993.

Recent Repair Projects

25' Bear-class sloop. Installed sister framing. 1993.

25' Cheoy Lee sloop. Renewed main bulkhead and cockpit, repaired mast. Refinished. 1992–'93.

35' Seaborn/Blanchard sloop NAUTILUS. Renewed planking and framing. 1992.

18' Dispro. Rebuilt 90% of boat. Renewed planking, decks, stem, framing, and interior. 1991–'92.

20' Kutter sloop (Norwegian). Renewed framing and planking. 1992.

16' Poulsbo launch. Renewed interior, decks, seats, and engine box console. Faired hull. 1990–'92.

17' Century Resorter. Replaced keel, bottom, and decks. Refinished. 1990–'92.

■ KOLIN BOAT WORKS

Richard S. Kolin
4107 77th Place NW
Marysville, WA 98271
206-659-5591

Builder Information

Years in business: 25
Carpenters employed: 1
Shop capacity: 20'

Recent New Construction

Boats designed by Richard Kolin:

12' lapstrake skiff. 2 currently under construction.

8' plywood pram. Built 1993.

8' lapstrake plywood pram. Built 1992.

Other new construction:

14' lapstrake plywood Swampscott dory for oar and sail. John Gardner design. Built 1990.

■ LOPEZ MARINE INC./UPRIGHT BOAT WORKS

Geremy Snapp
Rte. 2, Box 3078
Lopez Island, WA 98261
206-468-2052

Builder Information

Years in business: 20
Carpenters employed: 1
Shop capacity: 100'

Recent New Construction

12'6" lapstrake skiff. Built 1993.

Recent Repair Projects

Current projects involve the restoration of 4 schooner/fishing tenders to working condition. Boats were built prior to 1930 and range in size from 60' to 86'.

■ LOVRIC'S SEA CRAFT

Tony and Florence Lovric
3022 Oakes Ave.
Anacortes, WA 98221
206-293-2042 Fax: 206-293-2042

Builder Information

Years in business: 25
Carpenters employed: 7-15
Shop capacity: 150'

Recent Repair Projects

115' power scow/fish tender. Repaired and refastened skegs; installed steel shoes. Replaced some wood, renewed caulking. 1993.

135' converted tug/yacht. Repaired keel and worm shoe. Renewed caulking, refinished. 1993.

58' limit seiner. Repaired bulwarks, refastened some planking, recaulked. 1993.

90' passenger vessel. Replaced frames from bow to stern at turn of bilge. Renewed planking and caulking. 1992.

85' power scow/fish tender. Replaced wood in bow section, installed steel plating. 1991.

55' yacht. Replaced transom, numerous frames, and some planking. Renewed stem, refinished. 1991.

65' single-truck ferry. Removed old wooden cabin, and replaced with aluminum pilothouse/cabin. 1991.

Yard Information

Services
   Marina facilities
   Launching facilities
   Moorage
   Engine repair
Maintenance
   Number of boats maintained per year: 40
   Percentage of wooden boats: 70
   Owner maintenance allowed above rail.

JOHN MARPLES MARINE SERVICES

John R. Marples
4530 S.E. Firmont Dr.
Port Orchard, WA 98366
206-871-5634 Fax: same

Builder Information

Years in business: 15
Carpenters employed: 3
Shop capacity: 64'
Willing to travel for on-the-site building projects.

Recent New Construction

50' plywood/epoxy Harbor Tour catamaran, high-speed ferryboat. Dana/Marples design. Built 1993.

40' plywood/epoxy Harbor Tour catamaran. Marples/Devlin design. Built 1992.

CARL MEINZINGER SHIPWRIGHT

Carl Meinzinger
355 No Name Rd.
Guemes Island, WA 98221
206-293-3634

Builder Information

Years in business: 18
Carpenters employed: 1
Shop capacity: 50'
Willing to travel for on-the-site building projects.

Recent Repair Projects

65' Hodgdon motorsailer. Repaired cornerpost, renewed house. 1993.

55' Alaskan longliner. Rebuilt interior. 1993.

65' motoryacht. Laid new teak decks. Redesigned and built new galley and saloon. 1992.

45' New York 32-class sloop. Renewed frames, floors, maststep, and interior. 1990–'92.

Yard Information

Services
   Rigging

NACHES BOATS

Eric Harman
16920 122nd Ave. NE
Arlington, WA 98223
206-435-9311

Builder Information

Years in business: 19
Carpenters employed: 1
Shop capacity: 30'

Recent New Construction

Boats designed by Eric Harman for taped-seam plywood construction:

24' sportfisherman. Current project.

14' and 15'6" duckboats. Built 1991 and 1993.

Other new cedar strip/epoxy construction:

13'6" and 17' canoes. Bob Brown designs. Built 1990 and 1991.

15' canoe. Eric Harman design. Built 1990.

Recent Repair Projects

16' Old Town canoe. Refinished hull. 1993.

17' strip-planked canoe. Replaced outwale and revarnished hull. 1992.

13'6" and 14'6" Tremblay wood/canvas canoes. Renewed decks, gunwales, and thwarts. Stripped and refinished interiors, recanvased hulls. 1992.

23' Clipper-Craft power dory. Replaced cabin, deck, cabinetry, and chine guard. Refastened and repainted hull. 1990–'91.

NEXUS MARINE CORPORATION

David Roberts and Nancy Sosnove
3816 Railway Ave.
Everett, WA 98201
206-252-8330

Builder Information

Years in business: 20
Carpenters employed: 4
Shop capacity: 45'
Willing to travel for on-the-site building projects.
(continues)

(Nexus Marine Corporation, continued)
Recent New Construction
Boats designed by David Roberts for plywood/epoxy construction:
24' power cruiser. Built 1993.
23' planing dory. Built 1991.
21' planing dory. Built 1991.
23' power cruiser. 2 built 1990 and 1993.

Recent Repair Projects
25' Thunderbird-class sloop. Renewed garboards and floors, faired keel and bottom. 1993.
18' runabout. Renewed planking and guardrail. 1993.
14' drift boat. Repaired side planking, varnished. 1993.
15' sailing dory. Repaired delaminated plywood. 1993.
21' ski boat. Renewed frames and planking. 1992.
18' skiff. Installed wedges on bottom. 1993.
26' sloop. Installed double berth and washboards. 1992.

Yard Information
Maintenance
    Number of boats maintained per year: 1-2
    Percentage of wooden boats: 100
    Owner maintenance allowed above and below rail.
Retail supplies:
    Will order materials on request.

■ NORTHWEST SCHOOL OF WOODEN BOAT BUILDING

Jeff Hammond/Chief Instructor
251 Otto St.
Port Townsend, WA 98368
206-385-4948 Fax: 206-385-5089

Builder Information
Years in business: 12
Carpenters employed: 4 instructors, 35 students
Shop capacity: 30'

Recent New Construction
27' lobsterboat. Arno Day design. Current project.
28' Gary Thomas 25 gaff sloop. William Atkin design. 1 built 1992–'93, 1 under construction.
29' and 30' cutters. Lyle Hess designs. 1 built 1991, 1 built 1993.
21' lapstrake skipjack. William Atkin design. Built 1993.
15' lapstrake Bluefish skiff. Ted Ardito design. Built 1993.
28' Eric Jr. sloop. William Atkin design. Built 1992.
37' schooner. John Alden design. Built 1991.

Yard Information
Services
    Rigging

■ PENNY BOATWORKS

Andy Erickson
2144 Westlake Ave. N., #4
Seattle, WA 98109

Builder Information
Years in business: 11
Carpenters employed: 1
Shop capacity: 38'
Willing to travel for on-the-site building projects.

Recent New Construction
10' skiff. Andy Erickson design. 8 built 1990–'93.
13' lapstrake plywood Butternut double-paddle canoe. R.D. Culler design. Built 1991.
6' lapstrake plywood tender. Andy Erickson design. Built 1991.
10' plywood skiff. Andy Erickson design. 2 built 1990.

Recent Repair Projects
12' Beetle Cat. Replaced deck and recanvased. 1993.
36' Monk cabin cruiser (1952). Renewed forward stateroom and refinished interior and exterior. 1993.
20'6" Danish Mermaid-class sloop. Renewed frames, decks, cabin interior, and rigging. 1992.
26' Monk cabin cruiser (1950). Rebuilt interior, recanvased cabin and decks. 1991.
25' Picaroon sloop. Replaced keel and restored mast. 1990.

■ POINT HUDSON BOAT SHOP

Ed Louchard and Steve Chapin
311 Jackson St., Point Hudson Hbr.
Port Townsend, WA 98368
206-385-2793 Fax: 206-385-1640

Builder Information
Years in business: 12
Carpenters employed: 3-5
Shop capacity: 40'
Willing to travel for on-the-site building projects.

Recent Repair Projects
30' 5.5-Meter class CHANCE (1960). Replacing deck and transom. Sheathing hull in fiberglass and epoxy. Totally refitting. Current project.
26' lifeboat DORJUN (1905). Converted to cruiser. Restored and modified to include house, half decks, folding mast, and interior. 1991–'92.
65' Alden schooner CURLEW (1929). Renewed 60% of framing and planking. Replaced bulwarks and waterways, and transom. Extensive refit. 1990–'91.
37' Aas Six-Meter-class SAGA (1935). Modified cockpit, added small house. 1991.
26' spidsgatter (1937). Replaced decks, covering boards, bulwarks, and cockpit. General refit. 1990.

Yard Information
Services
    Marina facilities
    Launching facilities
    Engine repair
    Sail repair
    Rigging

■ PORT TOWNSEND SHIPWRIGHTS CO-OP

P.O. Box 1163
Port Townsend, WA 98368
206-385-6138 Fax: 206-385-5710

Builder Information
Years in business: 12
Carpenters employed: 8
Shop capacity: 65'
Willing to travel for on-the-site building projects.

Recent Repair Projects
42' Lake Union Dreamboat VAGABOND (1927). Repaired keel, renewed planking and frames, refastened and recaulked. Refinished. 1993.
32' Blanchard Dreamboat RESOLUTE (1929). Refastened and recaulked. Renewed topside finish. 1993.
32' Egg Harbor power cruiser HAGAN (1969). Repaired transom. 1993.
62' Alden ketch (1927). Renewed frames, planking, and chainplates. 1993.
26' Danish Folkboat (1948). Rebuilt cockpit, recanvased decks, and refinished. 1993.
72' Blanchard staysail schooner RED JACKET (1927). Renewed horn timber, sawn frames, transom, and planking. 1992.
28' Warner cutter. Renewed finish and rigging. 1991.

Yard Information
Services
　Marina facilities
　Launching facilities
　Engine repair
　Rigging
Storage
　Number of boats stored per year: 30
　Percentage of wooden boats: 95
　Inside storage facilities
　Maximum size for hauling and storing: 65' LOA, 8' draft, 70 tons
Maintenance
　Number of boats maintained per year: 5
　Percentage of wooden boats: 100
　Owner maintenance allowed above and below rail.
Retail supplies:
　Wood, fastenings, paint, adhesives, and abrasives.

■ PROCTOR BOAT CO.

Peter W. Proctor
15715 76th Place NE
Bothell, WA 98011
206-488-7730

Builder Information
Years in business: 20
Carpenters employed: 1-5
Shop capacity: 60'
Willing to travel for on-the-site building projects.

Recent Repair Projects
34' Monk power cruiser. Renewed transom, planking, chine, anchor guard. 1993.
30' Evergreen sloop. Renewed stem, planking, and deck. 1993.
60' power cruiser. Replaced aft planking, port side. 1993.
50' Monk/McQueen cruiser. Laid new teak deck. 1992-'93.
36' Blanchard Standard Cruiser. Replaced 95% of decks and cabintop. 1990-'92.
45' Alaskan cruiser. Replaced bottom planking, half of transom. 1990.
85' Monk/McQueen cruiser. Remodeled main saloon, renewed after deck area. 1989-'90.

Yard Information
Services
　Launching facilities
　Overland transport
　Engine repair
　Rigging
Maintenance
　Number of boats maintained per year: 20-30
　Percentage of wooden boats: 90
　Owner maintenance allowed above and below rail.

■ PYGMY BOAT CO.

John Lockwood
P.O. Box 1529
Port Townsend, WA 98368
206-385-6143

Builder Information
Years in business: 8
Carpenters employed: 1

Recent New Construction
Boats designed by John Lockwood and available as stitch-and-glue kits:
10' and 13' Golden Eye children's kayaks.
15'8" Golden Eye kayak.
17', 17'6", and 19' Queen Charlotte touring and expedition kayaks.
14' dory.

Yard Information
Retail supplies:
　Kayak and dory kits. Kayak accessories including sprayskirts, sea socks, wooden paddles, back pads, and paddling mitts.

■ RAGGED ASS BOAT SHOP

Pete Hurd
4023-188th St. NW
Stanwood, WA 98292
206-652-6922

Builder Information
Years in business: 15
(continues)

(Ragged Ass Boat Shop, continued)
Carpenters employed: 1
Shop capacity: 24'

Recent New Construction
23' fantail launch. Phil Bolger design. Built 1993.
9'6" lapstrake tender. Lawley design. Built 1992.
10' lapstrake tender. Ed Monk design. Built 1992.
12' lapstrake tender. Built 1992.
Company specializes in construction of yacht tenders varying in size to 12', as well as 14' Whitehalls and 12' Catspaw dinghies.

■ RAINSHADOW MARINE INC.

Patrick J. Mahon and A. Franz Witte III
2900 Washington St., Suite E
Port Townsend, WA 98368
206-385-9476

Builder Information
Years in business: 20
Carpenters employed: 3
Shop capacity: 80'
Willing to travel for on-the-site building projects.

Recent New Construction
20' lapstrake outboard dory-skiff. Franz Witte design. Built 1993.
23' electric-powered endurance raceboat. Tortured-plywood construction. Tim Nolan design. Built 1992.
8' lapstrake pram. L.F. Herreshoff design. Built 1991.

Recent Repair Projects
33' William Garden power cruiser. Reframing 50% of boat, renewing canvas decks, and refinishing. Current project.
50' Frers Sr. ocean racer/cruiser. Replacing interior and repowering. Current project.
40' Monk Sr. power cruiser. Replaced transom. 1993.
8' dinghy/lifeboat. Completely restored. 1993.
14' lapstrake Whitehall. Renewed frames and planking. Refinished. 1992.
32' Bristol Bay conversion. Laid new wooden deck. Refinished. 1992.
60' schooner. Reframed deck and replaced forward hatch. 1992.

Yard Information
Services
  Engine repair
  Rigging
Storage
  Inside storage facilities
  Maximum size for hauling and storing: 80' LOA, 70 tons
Maintenance
  Number of boats maintained per year: 8-10
  Percentage of wooden boats: 100
  Owner maintenance allowed above and below rail.

■ RIGHTS O'MAN BOAT WORKS

Carl Brownstein
S.E. 361 McComb Way
Shelton, WA 98584
206-426-7307

Builder Information
Years in business: 17
Carpenters employed: 5
Shop capacity: 40'
Willing to travel for on-the-site building projects.

Recent New Construction
26' longboat with 10 rowing stations. Hogland/Jackson design, based on historic longboat. 2 built 1993.
30' cutter. Lyle Hess design. Built 1991.
30' leeboard yawl. Phil Bolger design. Built 1990.
40' 11-ton cutter. Built 1990.

Recent Repair Projects
80' schooner. Renewed planking, cockpit, and house. Ongoing project. 1985-current.
90' motoryacht LOTUS. Renewed planking, deckbeams, carlins, rubrails, sponsons. Ongoing project. 1988–'92.

■ SCHOONER CREEK BOAT WORKS

Steve Rander
P.O. Box 307
Vancouver, WA 98666
503-735-0569 Fax: 503-289-7444

Builder Information
Years in business: 14
Carpenters employed: 8-10
Shop capacity: 80'
Willing to travel for on-the-site building projects.

Recent New Construction
70' cold-molded/composite sloop. Tom Wylie design. Built 1993.

Recent Repair Projects
37' sloop. Refastened and recaulked hull. Renewed deck and hardware. Refinished both interior and exterior. 1992–'93.
45' motorsailer. Replaced deck and engine, rebuilt interior. Recaulked and refinished hull. 1991–'92.
42' Lake Union Dreamboat. Renewed decks and planking. Recaulked hull. 1990–'92.
65' motorsailer. Converted fishboat to yacht. Completely restored interior. 1989–'91.

Yard Information
Services
  Marina facilities
  Launching facilities
  Moorage
  Engine repair
  Rigging
  Maximum size for hauling and storing: 25 tons

■ SEATTLE SHIPWRIGHTS

Stewart McDougall
4300 Eleventh Ave. NW
Seattle, WA 98107
206-782-1724

Builder Information
Years in business: 14
Carpenters employed: 7
Shop capacity: 80'
Willing to travel for on-the-site building projects.

Recent Repair Projects
32' ketch. Renewed mainmast and boom. 1993.
39' Concordia yawl. Repaired 3 floors, replaced keelbolts. 1993.
32' Alden Malabar sloop. Renewed stem and foredeck. 1993.
45' Monk power cruiser. Remodeled cabin interior, replaced 12 bottom planks, and refastened. 1993.
55' Alaskan trawler-yacht. Replaced transom and forward bulwarks. Remodeled cabin interior. 1993.
42' Rhodes cutter. Renewed cockpit. Replaced exhaust and bilge-pump systems. 1993.
41' Concordia yawl. Lengthened mainmast 6', replaced rigging, bow roller, and anchor windlass. 1992.

■ SHAW BOATS INC.

Steve Jones
P.O. Box 367
Aberdeen, WA 98520
206-532-9338 Fax: 206-533-1009 .

Builder Information
Years in business: 3
Carpenters employed: 25
Shop capacity: 90'+

Recent New Construction
64' SR-64 catamaran. Constant Camber construction. Marples/Brown design. 1 under construction, 1 built 1992–'93.
45' strip-planked catamaran VOYAGER. Chris White design. Current project.
57' sportfisherman. Stitch-and-glue panel construction. Steve Jones & Shaw Design Team design. Current project.
54' strip-planked sportfisherman ANGEL AMERICA. Howard Apollonio design. Current project.
42' strip-planked sportfisherman. Mike Kaufman design. Current project.
31' strip-planked trimarans. Ian Farrier's F-9A and F-9AX designs. Built 1993.

■ SKAGIT BAY BOATYARD

Bob Coe
1870 McGlinn Island Rd.
P.O. Box 871
LaConner, WA 98257
206-466-4905

Builder Information
Years in business: 20
Carpenters employed: 2
Shop capacity: 70'
Willing to travel for on-the-site building projects.

Recent Repair Projects
50' Blanchard sloop. Renewing frames, cabin, decks, and rails. Current project.
50' Chris-Craft power cruiser. Replaced transom and planking. 1993.
58' limit seiner. Renewed planking and bulwarks. 1993.
51' Viking power cruiser. Repaired plank and frame collision damage. 1993.
36' gillnetter. Repaired planking. Refastened and recaulked hull. 1992.
36' military boat. Converted to pleasure tug. Replaced frames, planking, stem, deck, wheelhouse, and cabin. Repowered. 1991–'92.
45' Monk power cruiser. Repaired planking, refastened and refinished hull. 1992.

Yard Information
Services
 Launching facilities
 Moorage
 Engine repair
 Rigging
Storage
 Number of boats stored per year: 50
 Percentage of wooden boats: 20
 Inside storage facilities
 Maximum size for hauling and storing: 70' LOA, 9' draft, 100 tons
Maintenance
 Number of boats maintained per year: 30
 Percentage of wooden boats: 20
 Owner maintenance allowed above and below rail.
Retail supplies:
 Paint, wood, bedding compounds, fastenings.

■ SMALL ISLAND BUILDERS

Paul Jeffery Heyse
5046 19th St. NE
Seattle, WA 98105
206-522-2256

Builder Information
Years in business: 2
Carpenters employed: 1
Shop capacity: 20'
(continues)

(Small Island Builders, continued)

Recent New Construction

18'4" strip-planked racing sloop. Paul Heyse design. Built 1993.

Recent Repair Projects

15'3" Chippewa canoe. Renewed sheer, thwarts, and floorboards. Completely refinished. 1992.

17' inboard runabout. Repaired hull, renewed deck frames, transom, and interior. Refinished. 1991.

■ RAY SPECK BOATBUILDING, INC.

Ray Speck
228 37th St.
Port Townsend, WA 98368
206-385-4519

Builder Information

Years in business: 23
Carpenters employed: 1
Shop capacity: 40'
Willing to travel for on-the-site building projects.

Recent New Construction

17' lapstrake Jolly Boat. Greg Foster design. Built 1993.
26' cutter. Lyle Hess design. Built 1993.
9'8" lapstrake tender. Lawton design. Built 1993.
17' lapstrake Whitehall. Ray Speck design. Built 1992.
26' lapstrake longboat. Foster/Speck design. Built 1992.
17' lapstrake Washington County peapod. Built 1991.
36' cutter. Howard Cox design. Built 1990.

■ TRADITIONAL BOAT CAULKING

Tim Reagan
P.O. Box 70125
Seattle, WA 98107
206-781-5128

Builder Information

Years in business: 17
Carpenters employed: 1
Shop capacity: Any size
Willing to travel for on-the-site building projects.

Recent Repair Projects

70' tug WALLACE FOSS. Recaulked from sheer to garboard. 1994.
52' purse seiner SCANDI. Recaulked. 1994.
204' ship U.S.S. CONSTITUTION. Recaulked garboards and first 10 strakes. 1993.
50' yawl TIOGA. Restored and recaulked deck. 1993.
65' yawl ADIOS. Refastened and recaulked deck. 1993.
42' Matthews power cruiser. Recaulked waterline to garboard. 1993.
54' purse seiner JOANN. Recaulked. 1993.

Maintenance
Number of boats maintained per year: 10-25
Percentage of wooden boats: 85
Owner maintenance allowed above and below rail.
Retail supplies:
Cotton, oakum, pitch, caulking compounds.

■ TUCKER YACHT DESIGN

Tom Tucker
P.O. Box 328
Port Townsend, WA 98368
206-385-7346

Builder Information

Years in business: 26
Carpenters employed: 1
Shop capacity: 40'
Willing to travel for on-the-site building projects.

Recent New Construction

39' ketch ALAGRIA. Strip-plank/cold-molded construction. Tom Tucker design. Hull built 1990; currently being completed.

Recent Repair Projects

38' Alaskan troller. Renewed aft deck and hold. 1993.

■ VLAHOVICH BOAT CORP.

A. Michael Vlahovich
301 E. 11th St., P.O. Box 1133
Tacoma, WA 98401-1133
206-272-2563 Fax: 206-383-2374

Builder Information

Years in business: 20
Carpenters employed: 1-12
Shop capacity: 100+
Willing to travel for on-the-site building projects.

Recent New Construction

13'6" lapstrake rowing/sailing skiff. R.D. Culler design. 3 built 1993.
16'8" lapstrake surf boat. R.D. Culler design. Built 1993.
48' strip-planked deadrise crab boat. Vlahovich/Trumbly design. Built 1992–'93.
30' lapstrake outboard launch. R.D. Culler design. Built 1992.

Recent Repair Projects

30' double-ended troller (c. 1926). Completely rebuilt hull, converted to motor launch. 1992.
Numerous hull repairs on purse seine vessels, up to 70' in length.

Yard Information

Retail supplies:
Boat lumber.

■ BARABOO RIVER CANOE CO.

Bill Hicklin
523 2nd Ave.
Baraboo, WI 53915
608-356-3766

Builder Information
Years in business: 7
Carpenters employed: 1
Shop capacity: 20'
Willing to travel for on-the-site building projects.

Recent New Construction
Strip-planked canoes. Bill Hicklin design. 5 built 1991–'93.

Recent Repair Projects
16' Peterborough canoe. Rebuilt and recanvased. 1992.

Yard Information
Services
  Launching facilities
  Overland transport
Storage
  Number of boats stored per year: 10
  Percentage of wooden boats: 90
  Inside storage facilities
  Maximum size for hauling and storing: Canoes to 20'
Maintenance
  Number of boats maintained per year: 10
  Percentage of wooden boats: 90
Retail supplies:
  Wood-strip planking and gunwale material. Thwarts,
    seats, stembands.

■ BAY BOATS

Jim Van Den Berg
3233 Nicolet Dr.
Green Bay, WI 54311
414-336-6338 Fax: 414-336-9141

Builder Information
Years in business: 5
Carpenters employed: 1
Shop capacity: 36'

Recent New Construction
33' cold-molded E-Skeeter-class iceboat. F. Yaeso design.
  Built 1994.
18' strip-planked kayak. Rob Macks design. Built 1993.
32' cold-molded E-Skeeter-class iceboat. Jim Van Den Berg
  design. 2 built 1992.
18' strip-planked canoe. Jim Van Den Berg design. Built 1990.
12' DN-class iceboat. 13 built 1990–'93.

Recent Repair Projects
Complete restoration of the following runabouts/power
  cruisers:
16' Century (1958). 1994.
32' Johnson stern-steerer (1930). 1993.
21' Chris-Craft (1957). 1992.
Maintenance
  Number of boats maintained per year: 5
  Percentage of wooden boats: 100

■ BOAT WORKS, INC.

Fred Oskar
Neenah, WI 54957-0407
414-725-4204 Fax: 414-725-8278

Builder Information
Years in business: 20
Carpenters employed: 2
Shop capacity: 44'

Recent Repair Projects
Rebuilt 5 wooden boats in the 22'–37' range during 1993.

Yard Information
Services
  Marina facilities
  Launching facilities
  Moorage
  Engine repair
  Rigging
Storage
  Number of boats stored per year: 75
  Percentage of wooden boats: 50
  Inside storage facilities
  Maximum size for hauling and storing: 44' LOA, 4'
    draft, 20 tons
Maintenance
  Number of boats maintained per year: 60
  Percentage of wooden boats: 50
  Owner maintenance allowed above and below rail.

■ BRIGHTWORK BOAT & LEYDA
LUMBER CO., INC.

Joe Daniels
5380 Farmco Dr.
Madison, WI 53718
608-244-8200

Builder Information
Years in business: 6
(continues)

(Brightwork Boat & Leyda Lumber Co., Inc, continued)
Carpenters employed: 2
Shop capacity: 36'

Recent Repair Projects

26'4" Riva Tritone runabout. Partially refastened hull, renewed sole and upholstery, rechromed hardware. Completely refinished. 1993.

19' Fitzgerald & Lee runabout. Replaced engine, completely refinished. 1993.

19' Century Sea Maid runabout. Replaced 70% of wood, including bottom. Completely refinished. 1993.

18' Chris-Craft Continental utility cruiser. Completely refinished. 1993.

17' Century Sea Maid runabout. Replaced deck, refinished. 1993.

20' Chris-Craft Holiday utility cruiser. Replaced engine, refinished. 1993.

From 1990–'93, company has averaged 3-4 major restorations and 6-8 minor restorations per year, as well as 10-15 maintenance projects.

Yard Information

Services
   Engine repair
Storage
   Number of boats stored per year: 25
   Percentage of wooden boats: 95
   Inside storage facilities
   Maximum size for hauling and storing: 28' LOA
Maintenance
   Number of boats maintained per year: 40
   Percentage of wooden boats: 95
Retail supplies:
   Marine lumber and plywood, paint, varnish, caulk, fastenings, and epoxy.

■ EAU GALLE BOAT SHOP

Martin A. Van
Rte. 2, Box 125B
Elmwood, WI 54740
715-283-4302

Builder Information

Years in business: 8
Carpenters employed: 1
Shop capacity: 24'

Recent New Construction

18' lapstrake pulling boat LIZ. Ken Bassett design. Current project.

15'–18'6" strip-planked canoes. Various designs. 15 built 1990–'93.

15'10" lapstrake sailing dory. Iain Oughtred design. 4 built 1990–'93.

16' strip-planked Arkansas Traveler canoe. J.H. Rushton design. 14 built 1990–'93.

16'4" strip-planked Prospector canoe. Chestnut Canoe Co. design. 15 built 1990–'93.

17' lapstrake Rangeley Lake boat. Ellis design. Built 1992.

16' strip-planked guideboat. J.H. Rushton design. Built 1990.

Recent Repair Projects

15'–18'6" strip-planked canoes. Major structural repairs to refinishing. 25 boats worked on from 1990–'93.

Yard Information

Maintenance
   Number of boats maintained per year: 6
   Percentage of wooden boats: 100

■ FERDY GOODE

Ferdy Goode
9241 Highway J
Minocqua, WI 54548
715-356-1991

Builder Information

Years in business: 15
Carpenters employed: 1
Shop capacity: 18'
Willing to travel for on-the-site building projects.

Recent New Construction

Specializes in the construction of 10' to 18' birchbark canoes. Designs by Ferdy Goode. 4 canoes built each year.

■ JECHORTS' WOOD BOAT WORKS

Dwight Jechort
P.O. Box 429
Winneconne, WI 54986
414-582-7557

Builder Information

Years in business: 12
Carpenters employed: 3
Shop capacity: 57'
Willing to travel for on-the-site building projects.

Recent New Construction

16' Chris-Craft DeLuxe Runabout. Replica of 1935 model. Current project.

Recent Repair Projects

Over the last few years, company has completely restored several Chris-Crafts, Centurys, Lymans, and Hacker-Crafts, including the following:

16' Chris-Craft Utility (1947). Customizing to single-cockpit speedster. Current project.

17' Chris-Craft DeLuxe Runabout (1948). Customizing to triple cockpit. Current project.

15' Milo-Craft outboard (1958). 1993.

21' Chris-Craft. 1992.

17' Chris-Craft. 1992.

23' Hacker-Craft. 1991.

Yard Information

Services
   Engine repair
   Rigging

Storage
Number of boats stored per year: 10
Percentage of wooden boats: 100
Inside storage facilities
Maximum size for hauling and storing: 30' LOA
Maintenance
Number of boats maintained per year: 10
Percentage of wooden boats: 100
Retail supplies:
Wood, fastenings, paint.

■ NIMPHIUS BOATS INC.

F.M. Nimphius
1602 Highway 22
Neshkoro, WI 54960
414-293-4465

Builder Information
Years in business: 65
Carpenters employed: 3
Shop capacity: 60'

Recent New Construction
20' sloop. F.M. Nimphius design. Current project.
23' power launch. Nelson Zimmer design. Current project.
40' cutter-rigged double-ender. F.M. Nimphius design. Current project.

Recent Repair Projects
35' Sparkman & Stephens Weekender sloop (1938). Renewing planking, cockpit, and electrial system. Recanvasing deck. Current project.
28' Owens cabin cruiser. Replacing bottom. Current project.
18' Chris-Craft Continental runabout. Replacing transom and various structural members. Current project.
18' Nimphius Arrow daysailer. Major rebuilding. Current project.
40' Sparkman & Stephens Mackinac class. Major rebuilding including new floors, lower stem, and decks. Replaced hollow spar. 1993.
26' power launch (1920). Renewed planking, chine, stem, keel, and skeg. 1993.
18'–25' Chris-Craft and Century runabouts. Replaced bottom planking as original. 5 boats completed 1990–'93.

Yard Information
Services
Overland transport
Engine repair
Rigging
Storage
Number of boats stored per year: 7
Percentage of wooden boats: 100
Inside storage facilities
Maximum size for hauling and storing: 30' LOA, 5' draft, 6 tons
Maintenance
Number of boats maintained per year: 7
Percentage of wooden boats: 100

■ NORTON BOAT WORKS

Joe Norton
535 Commercial Ave., P.O. Box 464
Green Lake, WI 54941
414-294-6813 Fax: same

Builder Information
Years in business: 23
Carpenters employed: 3
Shop capacity: 50'
Willing to travel for on-the-site building projects.

Recent New Construction
13' plywood center-console outboard skiff. Joel White design. Current project.
23' strip-planked/cold-molded sloop. Joel White design. Built 1993.
12' DN-60-class iceboat. DN class/Joe Norton design. 28 built 1990–'93.
25'6" Dodge Watercar replica. Batten-seam/epoxy construction. Dodge Boat Co. design. Current project.

Recent Repair Projects
20' Italian gondola. Completely restored. 1993.
18' Chris-Craft Cobra. Completely restored, including WEST System bottom. 1992.
17'–25' Chris-Craft and Century power cruisers/runabouts. 18 boats renewed with WEST System bottoms. 1990–'93.
17'–25' runabouts. Restored or refinished. 32 boats worked on 1990–'93.

Yard Information
Rigging
Storage
Number of boats stored per year: 8
Percentage of wooden boats: 100
Inside storage facilities
Maximum size for hauling and storing: 25' LOA
Maintenance
Number of boats maintained per year: 10-15
Percentage of wooden boats: 100
Retail supplies:
All materials necessary for new construction, maintenance, and repair.

■ OLD SQUAW CANOE CO.

N11543 Squaw Lake Rd.
Rhinelander, WI 54501
715-362-5971

Builder Information
Years in business: 5
Carpenters employed: 2
Shop capacity: 35'

Recent New Construction
Designs by J.C. Tilley for wood/canvas construction:
20' and 26' canoes (from fur-trading era). 6 built 1990–'93.
17' canoe (Algonquin hunting type). 6 built 1991–'93.
(continues)

(Old Squaw Canoe Co., continued)
Recent Repair Projects
12'–35' canoes, dinghies, and runabouts. Chestnut, Old
    Town, Penn Yan, Thompson, Rhinelander designs. All
    types of repairs including rib, gunwale, planking, and
    stem renewal, recanvasing and refinishing.

Yard Information
Storage
    Number of boats stored per year: 32
    Percentage of wooden boats: 100
    Inside storage facilities
    Maximum size for hauling and storing: Storage for
        canoes
Retail supplies:
    Materials for canoe repair. Cedar, ash, maple, canoe
        tacks, fastenings, canvas.

■ PETENWELL BOATWORKS

Mike Alekna
P.O. Box 70
Arkdale, WI 54613
608-564-7405

Builder Information
Years in business: 9
Carpenters employed: 1-2
Shop capacity: 36'
Willing to travel for on-the-site building projects.

Recent New Construction
Boats designed by Petenwell Boatworks:
18' catamaran. Composite construction. Current project.
19' Viking longboat. Lapstrake plywood construction.
    Current project.
10' plywood catboat. Built 1992.
8' plywood Cat's Eye catboat. Built 1992.
Other new construction:
8' plywood Nymph pram. Phil Bolger design. Built 1991.

Recent Repair Projects
14' Berglund runabout. Renewed plywood, refinished.
    1993.
15' Correct Craft runabout. Completely restored. 1993.
17' Old Town canoe (1923). Replaced 7 ribs, deck, and gun-
    wales. Recanvased and refinished. 1992.
26' Norwalk Islands sharpie. Renewed deck and moldings.
    1992.
18' Chris-Craft runabout. Completely restored. 1991.
17' Thompson runabout. Replaced frames. Refinished.
    1991.
16' Century runabout. Completely restored. 1990.

■ SPRING HARBOR KAYAK CO.

John Prazak
5156 Spring Court
Madison, WI 53705
608-231-3267

Builder Information
Years in business: 4
Carpenters employed: 1
Shop capacity: 20'
Willing to travel for on-the-site building projects.

Recent New Construction
Boats designed by John Prazak for stitch-and-glue ply-
    wood construction. Available as kit boats or as com-
    pleted kayaks.
17'3" West Greenland touring kayak. Ganymede design. 8
    boats completed by Prazak or as kits, 1990–'93.
20' West Greenland expedition tandem kayak. Gemini
    design. 5 boats completed, 1993.
20' West Greenland expedition kayak. Orion design. 2
    boats completed, 1993.

Yard Information
Maintenance
    Number of boats maintained per year: 4
    Percentage of wooden boats: 100
Retail supplies:
    Plywood, epoxy, and other supplies for boatbuilding.

■ STREBLOW CUSTOM BOATS INC.

Randal Streblow
2672 County Rd. "F" S.
Walworth, WI 53184
414-728-6898

Builder Information
Years in business: 40
Carpenters employed: 5
Shop capacity: 30'

Recent New Construction
Boats designed by L.A. Streblow and built with plywood
    inner skin sheathed in treated canvas, then planked
    with mahogany:
23' custom sport utility. 19 built 1990–'93.
26' custom sport utility. 3 built 1990–'93.
28' custom sport utility with cuddy and twin engines. Built
    1990.

Yard Information
Services
    Marina facilities
    Launching facilities
    Engine repair
Storage
    Number of boats stored per year: 73
    Percentage of wooden boats: 100
    Inside storage facilities
    Maximum size for hauling and storing: 30' LOA, 2'6"
        draft
Maintenance
    Number of boats maintained per year: 12-15
    Percentage of wooden boats: 100
Retail supplies:
    Anything for wooden sport utility boats.

◼ SUPERIOR KAYAKS, INC.

Mark A. Rogers
108 Menasha Ave., P.O. Box 355
Whitelaw, WI 54247
414-732-3784

Builder Information
Years in business: 4
Carpenters employed: 1
Shop capacity: 22'
Willing to travel for on-the-site building projects.

Recent New Construction
Sea touring kayaks designed by Mark Rogers for cold-molded or skin-on-frame construction. Available in a variety of lengths from 16'6" to 22'. Nearly 100 kayaks built between 1990 and 1993.

Yard Information
Services
    Overland transport
Storage
    Number of boats stored per year: 2
    Percentage of wooden boats: 100
    Inside storage facilities
    Maximum size for hauling and storing: 22' LOA, 6" draft, 75 lbs
Maintenance
    Number of boats maintained per year: 2
    Percentage of wooden boats: 100
Retail supplies:
    Kayaking supplies.

◼ VELATURA WERK

Davide Gaworek
4879 Edgewater Beach Rd.
Green Bay, WI 54311
414-866-9888 Fax: 414-437-1418

Builder Information
Years in business: 5
Carpenters employed: 1
Shop capacity: 40'
Willing to travel for on-the-site building projects.

Recent Repair Projects
30' sloop. Renewing hull and mast. Current project.
26' sloop. Replacing frames and planking. Current project.

Yard Information
Services
    Launching facilities
    Overland transport
    Moorage
    Engine repair
    Rigging
Storage
    Number of boats stored per year: 4
    Percentage of wooden boats: 100
    Maximum size for hauling and storing: 30' LOA, 6' draft, 6 tons

Maintenance
    Number of boats maintained per year: 4
    Percentage of wooden boats: 100
    Owner maintenance allowed.

◼ WOODS HOLE WOODWORKS

Mike Pieklo
N1352 Lake Dr.
Fontana, WI 53125
414-275-8080

Builder Information
Years in business: 2
Carpenters employed: 1
Shop capacity: 20'
Willing to travel for on-the-site building projects.

Recent New Construction
13'6" plywood outboard skiff. Ken Swan design. Built 1993.
10'6" lapstrake sailing dinghy. Built 1993.

Recent Repair Projects
16' lake scow. Repaired bow. 1993.

CANADA

◼ HAROLD KAMITAKAHARA

Harold Kamitakahara
10 Woodlark Dr. SW
Calgary, AB Canada T3C 3H5
403-242-3732

Builder Information
Years in business: 10
Carpenters employed: 1
Shop capacity: 16'
Willing to travel for on-the-site building projects.

Recent New Construction
13'8" lapstrake plywood daysailer. Harold Kamitakahara design. Built 1993.
13' lapstrake plywood sailing skiff. Harold Kamitakahara design. Built 1990.

Recent Repair Projects
16' wood/canvas canoe. Repaired ribs, recanvased hull, and replaced outwales. 1992.
10' rowing boat. Refinished. 1992.

■ VIRGIN FOREST BOATWORKS

Martin Herbert
42 6th St. NE
Calgary, AB Canada T2E 3X9
403-266-6569

Builder Information
Years in business: 13
Carpenters employed: 3
Shop capacity: 22'

Recent New Construction
17' cold-molded International canoe. Nethercot design. Built 1993.
8' plywood Optimist pram. Clark Mills design. 6 built 1992.
15' lapstrake plywood Delaware Ducker. Traditional design. Built 1991.
20'6" lapstrake plywood St. Lawrence River skiff. Traditional design. Built 1990.

Recent Repair Projects
17' International Canoe. Remolded delaminated sections. 1992.
16'3" International Fireball class. Refitted. 1992.

Yard Information
Services
    Sail repair
    Rigging
Storage
    Number of boats stored per year: 12
    Percentage of wooden boats: 100
    Inside storage facilities
    Maximum size for hauling and storing: 22' LOA, 200 lbs.
Maintenance
    Number of boats maintained per year: 6
    Percentage of wooden boats: 100

■ ALDER BAY BOAT CO.

1247 Cartwright St.
Vancouver, BC Canada V6H 3R8
604-685-1730

Builder Information
Years in business: 5
Carpenters employed: 4
Shop capacity: 25'
Willing to travel for on-the-site building projects.

Recent New Construction
12' lapstrake Jebb fishing skiff. William and John Atkin design. Current project.
20' lapstrake, cat-rigged Newport Point boat. R.D. Culler design. Current project.
17' lapstrake Butternut double-paddle canoe. R.D. Culler design. 1 built 1993, 1 under construction.
12' lapstrake Acorn skiff. Iain Oughtred design. Built 1993.
22'6" plywood Kingfisher recreational rowing shell. Graeme King design. 2 built 1992–'93, 1 under construction.
8'6" lapstrake tender. Traditional design from *Small Yachts* by C.P. Kunhardt. 2 built 1992–'93.
8' lapstrake Wren tender. Iain Oughtred design. 14 built 1992–'93.

Recent Repair Projects
13' Enterprise-class sloop. Replaced transom. Refinished. 1993.
13' double-ended Georgia Strait hand-troller. Replaced frames and refinished. 1992.
Numerous large vessels involving interior repair and refinishing. Rowing shell repairs.

■ GAR & WOOD YACHT RESTORATIONS

Gar. and Jean Fuller
415 W. Esplanade
Mosquito Creek Marina
North Vancouver, BC Canada V7M 1A6
604-980-9172

Builder Information
Years in business: 15
Carpenters employed: 4-6
Shop capacity: 50'

Recent Repair Projects
36' power cruiser TUYA (1943). Restoring. Current project.
42' Grand Banks 42 trawler-yacht. Completely restored interior, repaired house, and refinished. 1993–'94.
36' ketch STROMA. Completely restored. 1992.
36' Trojan power cruiser RUNNING BEAR. Renewed planking and house. Refinished. 1992.
28' sloop CHRISTIE. Renewed interior and cockpit. Installed engine. 1992.
36' Tahiti ketch VAILIMA. Renewed topside planking, frames, and deck. Refinished hull. 1991–'93.
30' Columbia River Bar Boat. Completely restored. Repaired planking. Refinished. 1990–'91. Award winner at Victoria Wooden Boat Show 1992.

Yard Information
Services
    Engine repair
    Rigging
Maintenance
    Number of boats maintained per year: 20
    Percentage of wooden boats: 95
    Owner maintenance allowed above and below rail.

■ BENT JESPERSEN BOATBUILDERS LTD.

Bent Jespersen
10995 Madrona Dr., RR #2
Sidney, BC Canada V8L 3R9
604-656-2581 Fax: same

Builder Information
Years in business: 42
Carpenters employed: 5
Shop capacity: 60'

Recent New Construction
44' cold-molded ketch. Cherubini Boat Co. design. Built 1993.
40' cold-molded schooner MAGIC. Craig Johnsen design. Built 1992.

■ TED KNOWLES SHIPWRIGHT SERVICES

Ted Knowles
3355 Maplewood Rd.
Victoria, BC Canada V8P 3M9
604-598-0330

Builder Information
Years in business: 35
Carpenters employed: 1
Shop capacity: 150'
Willing to travel for on-the-site building projects.

Recent New Construction
50' sloop-rigged motorsailer. E.L. Knowles design. Built 1993.

Recent Repair Projects
42' trawler-yacht. General hull repairs and maintenance. 1993.
42' West Coast salmon troller. Made on-site repairs to garboard planks and other sections of hull. 1993.
39' West Coast prawner. Replaced bow planking, continued ongoing maintenance and upgrading. 1993.
50' West Coast salmon troller. Repaired forefoot, stem, keel, and horn timber. Renewed planking, completely refastened, and recaulked. Faired and refinished hull. 1993.
50' coastal pleasure boat. Renewed forward and after decks, replaced beam ends, recaulked and refinished hull. 1993.
40' West Coast salmon troller. Renewed 4-5 planks and keel shoe. Refastened, recaulked, and refinished hull. 1993.
26' steam launch. Replaced most structural members, including keel. Renewed planking and completely refastened. 1991–'93.

Yard Information
Services
    Overland transport
    Engine repair
    Rigging

Maintenance
    Number of boats maintained per year: 10
    Percentage of wooden boats: 100
    Owner maintenance allowed above and below rail.

■ KOOTENAY JOINERY

David Kayle
P.O. Box 95
Gray Creek, BC Canada V0B 1S0
604-227-9502

Builder Information
Years in business: 15
Carpenters employed: 1-2
Shop capacity: 24'
Willing to travel for on-the-site building projects.

Recent New Construction
14'–17' lapstrake plywood sailing canoes. David Kayle designs. Several built to date.

Recent Repair Projects
17' Gullwing Beach Skiff. Renewed rigging and finish. 1993.
20' St. Lawrence River skiff. Renewed floors, thwarts, and topsides. 1992.
15' Peterborough canoe. Renewed ribs, stem, and gunwales. Recanvased. 1991.

Yard Information
Services
    Engine repair
    Sail repair
    Rigging
Storage
    Number of boats stored per year: 5
    Percentage of wooden boats: 90
    Maximum size for hauling and storing: Inquire
Maintenance
    Number of boats maintained per year: 7
    Percentage of wooden boats: 70

■ K SQUARED AEROMARINE WOODWORKS

Kevin Maher
4851 Elgin St.
Vancouver, BC Canada V5V 4S2
604-873-5421

Builder Information
Years in business: 9
Carpenters employed: 1
Shop capacity: 26'
Willing to travel for on-the-site building projects.

Recent New Construction
15'6" kayak. Tortured-plywood construction. Chesapeake Light Craft design. 5 built 1993.
(continues)

(K Squared Aeromarine Woodworks, continued)

16'6" cold-molded canoe. Chestnut Prospector model. Built 1992.

19' racing catamaran. Tortured-plywood construction. Built 1992.

8' plywood sailing dinghy. Joel White design. Built 1991.

Recent Repair Projects

18' Lightning-class sloop. Replaced deck. 1993.

16' Mirror-class sloop. Completely restored. 1992.

16' strip-planked canoe. Renewed seats, thwart, and gunwales. 1991.

Company averages about 8 repair projects a year. Boats worked on are usually canoes, kayaks, or daysailers.

Yard Information

Services

Overland transport

Rigging

Maximum size for hauling and storing: 26' LOA, 7' draft, 1½ tons

Maintenance

Number of boats maintained per year: 5

Percentage of wooden boats: 100

Owner maintenance allowed above and below rail.

Retail supplies:

Lumber, plywood, glue, and paint.

■ LATIMER MARINE

Anthony R. Latimer
Unit #9, 2064 Henry Ave.
Sidney, BC Canada V8L 3S1
604-656-9539

Builder Information

Years in business: 23

Carpenters employed: 1-3

Shop capacity: 80'

Recent New Construction

58' cold-molded pinky schooner. Anthony Latimer design. Launched 1993.

10'6" cold-molded dinghy for oar and sail. Modified H.I. Chapelle design. Built 1993.

Recent Repair Projects

45' trawler-yacht SUMMER STAR. Replaced stem knee and 14 planks. Sister several frames. 1993.

40' lobsterboat. Replaced horn timber. 1993.

30' cold-molded yacht. Repaired collision damage — renewed 60 sq. ft. of planking. 1993.

37' cold-molded yacht. Replaced keel, floors, and sole. Laid new teak decks. 1990.

Yard Information

Rigging

Retail supplies:

Specializes in wooden mast construction and rigging.

■ LINDSTROM BOAT BUILDING

Stephen Lindstrom
P.O. Box 591
Duncan, BC Canada V9L 3X9
604-748-4149 Fax: 604-748-7749

Builder Information

Years in business: 15

Carpenters employed: 1

Shop capacity: 40'

Recent New Construction

Boats designed by Stephen Lindstrom:

32' plywood/epoxy cruising dory. Current project.

38' composite salmon/crab trawler type. Built 1993.

12' plywood/epoxy solo drifter. 12 built 1993.

15' plywood/epoxy drift boat. Built 1992.

Recent Repair Projects

28' H-28 ketch. Restoring. Current project.

28' Navy cutter. Restored. 1990.

Hundreds of small repairs on various boats also completed over last several years.

■ PETER LONDON, BOATBUILDER

Peter London
2220 Harbour Rd.
Sidney, BC Canada V8L 2P6
604-656-1196

Builder Information

Years in business: 40

Carpenters employed: 1

Shop capacity: 70'

Willing to travel for on-the-site building projects.

Recent New Construction

14' plywood workboat. Built 1992.

18' workboat. Paul Gartside design. Built 1992.

23' H.M.S. BOUNTY longboat replica. Built 1992.

8' lapstrake pram. Paul Gartside design. Built 1991.

Recent Repair Projects

45' power cruiser. Renewed keelbolts and floors. Refastened and recaulked. 1993.

38' sailboat. Rebuilt interior in teak. 1993.

58' tugboat GILLCREST. Renewed decks, bulwarks, and steering. 1992–'93.

42' fishing vessel. Renewed wheelhouse, tanks, main engine. Rerigged. 1992–'93.

38' launch. Completely rebuilt. 1992.

42' fishing vessel. Renewed forefoot and shoe. Recaulked and refastened. 1991.

42' fishing vessel. Renewed decks and bulwarks. 1991.

Yard Information

Services

Marina facilities

Launching facilities

Moorage

Rigging

Maintenance
    Number of boats maintained per year: 30
    Percentage of wooden boats: 100
    Owner maintenance allowed above and below rail.

◼ McQUEEN BOATWORKS LTD.

Tim Bell, General Manager
11571 Twigg Place
Richmond, BC Canada V6V 2K7
604-325-4544 Fax: 604-325-4516

Builder Information
Years in business: 40
Carpenters employed: 6
Shop capacity: 132′

Recent New Construction
95′ cold-molded express cruiser. William Garden design. Built 1992.
Over 100 custom wooden boats from 28′ to 95′ built since 1952.

Recent Repair Projects
43′ lapstrake power cruiser. Replaced planking. 1993.
80′ power cruiser. Replaced planking and associated interior joinerwork. 1993.
75′ power cruiser. Repaired damaged propulsion gear, frames, sawn floors, and transom. 1993.
72′ power cruiser. Repaired damage from sinking. Recaulked hull. 1992.
80′ power cruiser. Installed bow thruster. 1991.

Yard Information
Services
    Launching facilities
    Overland transport
    Engine repair

◼ NW HISTORIC WATERCRAFT

Gregory Foster
Whaler Bay
Galiano Island, BC Canada V0N 1P0

Builder Information
Years in business: 23
Carpenters employed: 1-3
Shop capacity: 80′
Willing to travel for on-the-site building projects.

Recent New Construction
40′ early Spanish exploring schooner. 1790s design. Current project.
21′ lapstrake sharpie. Howard Chapelle design. Built 1993.
14′ lapstrake ancient Norse faering. Traditional design. Built 1993.
14′6″, 16′, and 16′6″ 18th-century Jolly Boats. Lapstrake construction, traditional British and American designs. 5 built 1991–′92.
18′ lapstrake ship's cutter. Built 1990.
18′ lapstrake Shetland sixern. 2 built 1990.
23′ 18th-century Spanish lancha. Lapstrake construction. Traditional design. Built 1990.

Yard Information
Services
    Launching facilities
    Sail repair
    Rigging
Retail supplies:
    Sails of natural fiber. Lug, sprit, and gaff rig are specialties.

◼ ROCKY MOUNTAIN CANOE WORKS

Jackson Wood
P.O. Box 167
Aldergrove, BC Canada V0X 1A0
604-576-5388 Fax: 604-576-8575

Builder Information
Years in business: 10
Carpenters employed: 2
Shop capacity: 19′

Recent Repair Projects
Restoration, repair, and refinishing of wood/canvas canoes. Chestnut, Peterborough, Greenwood, Temagami, Tremblay, and Plycraft models. Numerous projects during 1990–′93.

Yard Information
Services
    Overland transport
Maintenance
    Number of boats maintained per year: 10-15
    Percentage of wooden boats: 80
Retail supplies:
    Materials and advice for restoration of wood/canvas canoes.

◼ WEST COAST CANOE COMPANY

Larry B. Bowers
P.O. Box 143
Campbell River, BC Canada V9W 5A7
604-287-7348

Builder Information
Years in business: 10
Carpenters employed: 3
Shop capacity: 26′
Willing to travel for on-the-site building projects.

Recent New Construction
Boats designed by Larry Bowers:
14′ lapstrake rowboat. Built 1993.
16′ wood/canvas Prospector canoe. 3 built 1993.
18′ wood/canvas Prospector Tripper canoe. 3 built 1993.
(continues)

(West Coast Canoe Company, continued)

Recent Repair Projects

15' wood/canvas canoe. Completely restored. 1992.

12' wood/canvas canoe. Renewed decks, outer gunwales. 1990.

Yard Information

Storage

Number of boats stored per year: 10

Percentage of wooden boats: 100

Retail supplies:

Lumber, hardware, paint, filler.

■ WINARD WOOD LTD.

Hugh Campbell
10563 McDonald Park Rd.
Sidney, BC Canada V8L 3J3
604-656-5466 Fax: same

Builder Information

Years in business: 16

Carpenters employed: 1

Shop capacity: 50'

Willing to travel for on-the-site building projects.

Recent New Construction

12' lapstrake Whitehall. Traditional design. 3 built 1993.

17' lapstrake sailing Whitehall. John Gardner design. Built 1992.

9'6" lapstrake pulling boat. Built 1991.

18' lapstrake St. Lawrence River skiff. Built 1990.

26' plywood houseboat. Paul Gartside design. Built 1990.

Recent Repair Projects

32' Monk power cruiser. Renewed decks and planking. 1993.

26' Hess cutter. Renewed horn timber. 1993.

32' Vogel sailboat. Replaced decks. 1992.

28' Bristol Channel cutter. Rebuilt interior. 1992.

18' Dispro launch. Replaced planking, frames, and seats. 1992.

12' lapstrake rowing boat. Completely rebuilt. 1991.

28' Columbia River boat. Completely restored. 1990.

Yard Information

Maintenance

Number of boats maintained per year: 20

Percentage of wooden boats: 80

Owner maintenance allowed above rail.

Retail supplies:

Materials for boat construction and repair.

■ WOOD CANVAS CANOES

Boudi van Oldenborgh
1701 London St.
New Westminster, BC Canada V3M 3C9
604-522-1434

Builder Information

Years in business: 10

Carpenters employed: 1

Shop capacity: 18'

Recent New Construction

17' wood/canvas canoe. Boudi van Oldenborgh design. 3 built 1990–'93.

Recent Repair Projects

14' to 17' wood/canvas canoes. Restored and recanvased 4 canoes 1990–'93.

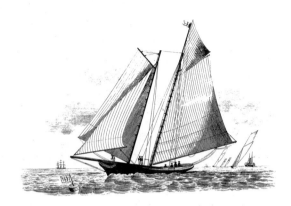

■ WATSON MARINE LTD.

Tom Watson
871 Grassmere Rd.
RR #1B, Box 34, Group 31
Winnipeg, MB Canada R3C 4A3
204-334-5161

Builder Information

Years in business: 50

Carpenters employed: 3

Shop capacity: Any size

Willing to travel for on-the-site building projects.

Recent New Construction

15'8" plywood Tursiops sea kayak. Mike Alford design. Built 1993.

16' strip-planked canoes. Various designs. 4 built 1990–'93.

8' plywood prams. Tom Watson design. 5 built 1990–'92.

16' plywood rowing skiff. Tom Watson design. Built 1991.

10' plywood Wetback hydroplane. Clark-Craft design. Built 1991.

15'4" plywood Bluegill skiff. Steve Redmond design. Built 1991.

Recent Repair Projects

20' Greavette Sedan cruiser. Replacing keel and damaged planking. Renewing cabin and interior. Current project.

22' Shepherd runabout (1949). Replacing damaged and rotten framing, bottom planking, and some topside and deck planking. Renewing interior. Current project.

16' Peterborough Muskoka rowboat. Renewing frames, refinishing. Current project.

20' lapstrake sedan cruiser. Repairing bottom and deck, rebuilding cabin. Current project.

29' Hacker-Craft runabout (1920s). Replaced keel, bottom frames and planking. Completely refinished, installed new engine. 1993.

55' Chris-Craft (1953). Repaired frames and bottom planking. 1990–'93.

20' Century Resorter. Renewed bottom, transom, deck, and interior. Replaced dashboard and deck behind front seat. 1991–'92.

Yard Information

Engine repair

Maintenance

Number of boats maintained per year: 75-100

Percentage of wooden boats: 90

Owner maintenance allowed.

Retail supplies:

Complete inventory of boatbuilding supplies.

ARBOR VITAE CANOES

Mark Connell, Lin Tremblay, Ed Eustace, and Gart Bishop
P.O. Box 1916
Sussex, NB Canada E0E 1P0
506-433-4994

Builder Information

Years in business: 4

Carpenters employed: 4

Shop capacity: 24'

Recent New Construction

16'–17' wood/canvas canoes for sail or paddle. Connell/Bishop designs. 30 built 1990–'93.

Recent Repair Projects

Numerous repairs to wood/canvas canoes. Recanvasing and complete restorations.

Yard Information

Retail supplies:

Wanigans, lateen sailing rigs, rudder and leeboard assemblies.

BRYAN BOATBUILDING

Harold B. Bryan
RR #4
St. George, NB Canada E0G 2Y0
506-755-2486

Builder Information

Years in business: 20

Carpenters employed: 2-3

Shop capacity: 40'

Recent New Construction

Boats designed by Harry Bryan:

30' motorsailer. Built 1993.

10'6" lapstrake, decked, double-paddle canoe. 3 built 1992–'93.

12'6" lapstrake skiff for oar and sail. 2 built 1992–'93.

12'6" lapstrake fin-powered, decked canoe. Built 1992.

15' lapstrake skiff for oar, sail, and outboard. 3 built 1992–'93.

2' child's toy dory. 95 built 1992–'93.

Yard Information

Services

Sail repair

Rigging

CHAMCOOK BOAT & CANOE

David Needler
Glebe Rd., RR #2
St. Andrews, NB Canada E0G 2X0
506-529-4776

Builder Information

Years in business: 3

Carpenters employed: 1

Shop capacity: 40'

Recent New Construction

Boats of wood/canvas construction designed by Lewis:

16' double-ended canoe. 8 built 1991–'93.

14' double-ended canoe. Built 1993.

14' square-sterned runabout. Built 1993.

20' log-end canoe. Built 1993.

Recent Repair Projects

Restoration of the following wood/canvas canoes:

20' E.M. White inboard-powered canoe with invisible sponsons (1902). Repaired and recanvased hull, modified interior, and refinished. 1993.

18' B.N. Morris canoe (1945). Repaired, recanvased, and refinished hull. 1993.

15' Chestnut canoe. Completely restored and refinished. 1993.

17' Chestnut Prospector canoe. Converted to square stern. 1992.

16' Chestnut Prospector canoe. Renewed ribs and planking. Repaired stem. Recanvased and refinished hull. 1991.

WAYNE EDDY

Wayne Eddy
RR #2
St. Andrews, NB Canada E0G 2X0
506-529-8723

Builder Information

Years in business: 5

Carpenters employed: 1

(continues)

(Wayne Eddy, continued)
Shop capacity: 28'
Willing to travel for on-the-site building projects.

Recent New Construction

16' Haven 12½. Joel White design. Current project.
12' lapstrake skiff. Joel White design. 2 built 1990–'91.
9' lapstrake pram. Wayne Eddy design. Built 1991.

Recent Repair Projects

12' Mirror dinghy. Completed numerous repairs, sheathed
hull in fiberglass and epoxy. 1993.
21' Mic Mac sloop. Completely restored. 1990.

DONALD FRASER CANOES

Donald Fraser
176 Woodstock Rd.
Fredericton, NB Canada E3B 2H5
506-454-2127

Builder Information

Years in business: 14
Carpenters employed: 1
Shop capacity: 22'

Recent New Construction

17' wood/canvas canoes. Chestnut Canoe Co. design. 20
built to date.

MILLER CANOES

William V. Miller
RR #1, Nictau
Plaster Rock, NB Canada E0J 1W0
506-356-2409

Builder Information

Years in business: 69
Carpenters employed: 1
Shop capacity: 26'
Willing to travel for on-the-site building projects.

Recent New Construction

Wood/canvas or wood/fiberglass canoes custom-built by
Miller Canoes during 1990–'93:
11' children's duckboat. B.S. Moore design (originated in
1934). 6 built.
16' rough-water solo canoe. W.V. Miller III design (1987). 7
built.
17' pleasure canoe. W.V. Miller III design (1983). 30 built.
18' guide/wilderness tripping canoe. W.V. Miller I design
(1925). 15 built.
20' guide/wilderness tripping canoe. B.S. Moore design
(1930 and 1938 models). 16 built.
15' kayak. W.V. Miller III design (1991). 10 built.

Recent Repair Projects

18' Chestnut canoe (1925). Replaced 27 ribs, recanvased.
1993.
12' B.N. Morris canoe (1916). Replaced 5 ribs and gunwales. 1993.

19' Miller canoe (1943). Replaced 7 ribs, renewed gunwales,
and sheathed in fiberglass. 1993.
20' Gallop canoe (1950). Replaced 9 ribs, sheathed in fiberglass. 1993.
16' Chestnut canoe (1947). Recanvased. Varnished interior.
1993.

Yard Information

Services
    Overland transport
    Rigging
Storage
    Number of boats stored per year: 5
    Percentage of wooden boats: 100
Maintenance
    Number of boats maintained per year: 15
    Percentage of wooden boats: 100
Retail supplies:
    Cedar ribs and planking stock. White spruce for gun-
    wales, brass fastenings.

CHETICAMP BOATBUILDERS LTD.

P.O. Box 39
Cheticamp, NS Canada B0E 1H0
902-224-2600 Fax: 902-224-3443

Builder Information

Years in business: 14
Carpenters employed: 5-10
Shop capacity: 65'
Willing to travel for on-the-site building projects.

Recent New Construction

19' lapstrake canoe for oar and paddle. John Gardner
design. Built 1993.

Recent Repair Projects

55' Danish seiner. Renewed wheelhouse, rails, deck, and
mast. 1993.
36' lobsterboat. Completely overhauled. 1993.
85' fishing boat. Renewed deck, rails, and fo'c's'le. Built
new fishhold. 1992.
60' converted fishing boat. Completely refurbished. 1990.

Yard Information

Services
    Marina facilities
    Launching facilities
    Overland transport
    Moorage
    Engine repair
Storage
    Number of boats stored per year: 4
    Percentage of wooden boats: 50

Maintenance
 Number of boats maintained per year: 20
 Percentage of wooden boats: 75
 Owner maintenance allowed above and below rail.
Retail supplies:
 Oak, spruce, fastenings, epoxy, fiberglass.

■ CORMORANT CANOE AND BOAT WORKS

Matt Durnford
P.O. Box 71
Riverport, NS Canada B0J 2W0
902-766-4104

Builder Information
Years in business: 8
Carpenters employed: 1
Shop capacity: 20'

Recent Repair Projects
16' Harold Gates canoe. Replacing planks and gunwales. Recanvasing and refinishing. Current project.
17' Peterborough canoe (ca. 1900). Replaced deck, floorboards, and seats. Repaired outwales, completed general restoration. 1992.
18' Chestnut canoe. Renewed ribs, decks, and planking. Recanvased and refinished. 1991.
15'10" Peterborough canoe. Recaned and replaced seats. Renewed outwales and partial stems. Refinished interior. 1990.

■ COVEY ISLAND BOATWORKS LTD.

Petite Riviere, NS Canada B0J 2P0
902-688-2843 Fax: 902-688-2591

Builder Information
Years in business: 17
Carpenters employed: 8
Shop capacity: 80'
Willing to travel for on-the-site building projects.

Recent New Construction
Boats of wood/epoxy construction:
49' Bristol Channel Pilot cutter. Nigel Irnes design. Under construction.
65' Tioga ketch. L.F. Herreshoff design. Built 1993.
43' sportfisherman. Spencer Lincoln design. Built 1993.
25' recreational fishing boat. Iain Tulloch design. Built 1993.
35' lobsteryacht. Spencer Lincoln design. Built 1993.
93' schooner. Ted Brewer design. Built 1992.

Recent Repair Projects
46' ketch TAMARUGO. Repowering and altering rig. Refinishing. Current project.
46' ketch ANNIE J. Refinished. 1993.
32' sloop ANDRILLOT II. Renewed interior, cockpit, and decks. Sheathed hull in epoxy/'glass. 1993.

35' sloop AKARI. Replaced deadwood. Sheathed hull in epoxy/'glass. 1992.
45' trimaran FIERY CROSS. Replaced outriggers, completely refit. 1991.

Yard Information
Services
 Launching facilities
 Overland transport
 Moorage
 Engine repair
 Sail repair
 Rigging
Storage
 Number of boats stored per year: 4
 Percentage of wooden boats: 100
 Maximum size for hauling and storing: 70' LOA, 8' draft, 60 tons
Maintenance
 Number of boats maintained per year: 4
 Percentage of wooden boats: 100
 Owner maintenance allowed above and below rail.
Retail supplies:
 Complete inventory of supplies.

■ THE DORY SHOP

Kim Smith
Box 1678
Lunenburg, NS Canada B0J 2C0
902-634-9196 Fax: 902-634-8463

Builder Information
Years in business: 75
Carpenters employed: 1-5
Shop capacity: 65'
Willing to travel for on-the-site building projects.

Recent New Construction
Company has built 36 traditional lapstrake dories with gaff, junk, lug, and marconi rigs. Two round-sided and two cabin versions. 1990–'93.

Recent Repair Projects
52' Bristol Channel Pilot cutter MARGUERITE T (1893). Replaced some planking, renewed caulking. Repaired mast, rigging, and engine. 1992–'93.
37' Cape boat. Refastened and recaulked hull. 1990.

Yard Information
Services
 Launching facilities
 Overland transport
 Moorage
 Engine repair
 Sail repair
 Rigging
Storage
 Number of boats stored per year: 5
 Percentage of wooden boats: 100
(continues)

(The Dory Shop, continued)
  Maximum size for hauling and storing: 50′ LOA, 7′6″
    draft, 50 tons
Maintenance
  Number of boats maintained per year: 3
  Percentage of wooden boats: 100
  Owner maintenance allowed above and below rail.
Retail supplies:
  Assorted marine hardware.

■ CLARENCE R. HEISLER & SON LTD.

Cecil R. Heisler
Indian Point, RR #2
Mahone Bay, NS Canada B0J 2E0
902-624-9134

Builder Information
Years in business: 75
Carpenters employed: 5-6
Shop capacity: 60′
Willing to travel for on-the-site building projects.

Recent New Construction
14′ and 16′ lapstrake rowing boats. 3 built 1991–'92.
14′ plywood outboard boat. Built 1991–'92.
33′ Cape Islander. Built 1991–'92.
17′ dory. Traditional design. Built 1991–'92.
46′ ketch. William Garden design. Built 1991.
9′6″ plywood tender. Built 1990.
27′ whalers. 2 built 1990.

Recent Repair Projects
28′ Stevens sloop. Renewed frames, planking, keelbolts,
  floors. 1992.
42′ Cape Island style dragger. General repairs. 1992.
139′ Banks schooner THERESA E. CONNOR. Recaulked.
  1991.
36′ schooner. Renewed cabin, deckbeams, and deck. 1991.
38′ Cape Islander. Renewed frames, gunwales, and deck.
  1990–'91.

Yard Information
Services
  Launching facilities
  Moorage
  Rigging
Storage
  Number of boats stored per year: 40
  Percentage of wooden boats: 75
  Inside storage facilities
  Maximum size for hauling and storing: 50′ LOA, 6′6″
    draft
Maintenance
  Number of boats maintained per year: 50
  Percentage of wooden boats: 75
  Owner maintenance allowed above and below rail.

■ HERRING COVE MARINE

Charles H. Brown
Government Wharf Rd.
Herring Cove, NS Canada B0J 1S0
902-477-4069

Builder Information
Years in business: 20
Carpenters employed: 1-3
Shop capacity: 50′
Willing to travel for on-the-site building projects.

Recent New Construction
8′ plywood/epoxy pram. Herreshoff design. 2 built 1993.
14′ Geodesic Airolite Snowshoe canoe. Platt Monfort
  design. Built 1991.

Recent Repair Projects
35′ Jim Smith schooner (1972). Moved ballast keel aft 32″,
  replaced floors, keelbolts, and deadwood. 1993.
26′ Thames bawley. Replaced garboards and first plank.
  1993.
36′ Crocker ketch. Sheathed hull, deck, and cabin in epoxy
  and fiberglass, renewed through-hull fittings and keelbolts. 1992–'93.
Other repair work has involved recanvasing a canoe and a
  powerboat deck, as well as building tillers and
  bowsprits. Structural and woodworking repairs are
  most typical.

Yard Information
Services
  Engine repair
  Rigging
Maintenance
  Number of boats maintained per year: 10-12
  Percentage of wooden boats: 100
  Owner maintenance allowed above and below rail.

■ LAHAVE MARINE WOODWORKING

Kevin Wambach
P.O. Box 144
LaHave, NS Canada B0R 1C0
902-688-2998

Builder Information
Years in business: 9
Carpenters employed: 1-3
Shop capacity: 20′
Willing to travel for on-the-site building projects.

Recent New Construction
16′ lapstrake gunning dory. William Chamberlain design.
  Current project.
14′9″ lapstrake Lunenburg sailing dory. Traditional design.
  5 built 1993–'94.
7′6″ lapstrake plywood Nutshell pram. Joel White design.
  Built 1993.
7′6″ Nymph sailing pram. Stitch-and-glue construction.
  Phil Bolger design. Built 1992.

14' plywood Chamberlain skiff. William Chamberlain design. Built 1992.

10' lapstrake pram. L.F. Herreshoff design. Built 1991.

12' lapstrake plywood cartop semi-dory. John Gardner design. 2 built 1991.

Recent Repair Projects

19' Lightning-class sloop. Restoration just beginning.

13'9" Shelburne skiff. Renewed frames, keel, and transom. Added lug rig. 1993.

12' Morse catboat. Replaced frames, transom, deckbeams, deck, and coaming. 1992.

35' lobsterboat. Sheathed hull in fiberglass, replaced wheel-house and deck. 1990.

Yard Information

Services
  Marina facilities
  Moorage
Maintenance
  Number of boats maintained per year: 4
  Percentage of wooden boats: 100
Retail supplies:
  Materials for building and repair. Hardware and other supplies can be ordered on request.

■ LANGILLE BOAT BUILDING

Ernest J. Langille
RR #2, Oakland
Mahone Bay, NS Canada B0J 2E0
902-624-8462

Builder Information

Years in business: 40
Carpenters employed: 2-4
Shop capacity: 42'

Recent New Construction

25' sloop. Ernest Langille design. Built 1990.

Recent Repair Projects

28' Cape-style lobsterboat. Completed major refit. 1992.

Yard Information

Services
  Marina facilities
  Launching facilities
  Moorage
  Engine repair
  Rigging
Storage
  Number of boats stored per year: 10
  Percentage of wooden boats: 50
  Maximum size for hauling and storing: 35' LOA, 5' draft
Maintenance
  Number of boats maintained per year: 10
  Percentage of wooden boats: 50
  Owner maintenance allowed above and below rail.

■ McCURDY & REED CANOES

J. Kip McCurdy
RR#2, Hampton
Annapolis County, NS Canada B0S 1L0
902-665-2435

Builder Information

Years in business: 10
Carpenters employed: 1
Shop capacity: 25'

Recent New Construction

12'–25' wood/canvas canoes. Various models by B.N. Morris, Stewart, Gates, and McCurdy & Reed.

Recent Repair Projects

Restoration, repair, and recanvasing of wood/canvas canoes.

Yard Information

Retail supplies:
  White cedar, paint, brass hardware, stembands, canvas and filler, and paddles.

■ NEW DUBLIN WATERCRAFT

Wayne D. Mosher
RR #1, LaHave (Dublin Shore)
Lunenburg County, NS Canada B0R 1C0
902-688-2903

Builder Information

Years in business: 9
Carpenters employed: 1
Shop capacity: 35'
Willing to travel for on-the-site building projects.

Recent New Construction

Plywood/epoxy New Dublin skiffs. Wayne Mosher designs. Three 12½-footers built 1990–'93; four 10-footers built 1991–'92.

16' wood/canvas Chestnut Prospector canoe. 4 built 1990–'93.

16' Bush Island peapod for sail and oar. Mike Bush design. 4 built 1990–'92.

14' lapstrake skiff. Wayne Mosher design. Built 1991.

15'4" lapstrake Banks dory. Jim Smith design. Built 1990.

Recent Repair Projects

16' Banks dory. Renewed caprails and gunwales. 1992.

26' Bush Island double-ender. Renewed cabin and interior. 1992.

27' Cape Islander. Renewed cabin. 1992.

25' Friendship sloop. Renewed cabin interior. 1991.

27' Cape Islander. Replaced section of keel and timbers. 1990.

Yard Information

Launching facilities

■ NOVA SCOTIA COMMUNITY COLLEGE

Nelson Cutler
Lunenburg Campus, 75 High St.
Bridgewater, NS Canada B4V 1V8
902-543-4608

Builder Information
Years in business: 24
Carpenters employed: 1 instructor, 6–10 students
Shop capacity: 30'

Recent New Construction
20' Sallee Rover yawl. S.S. Crocker design. Current project.
21' and 26' Cape Island boats. Steve Slaunwhite designs. 26-footer built 1991–'92; 21-footer under construction.
12'9" Catspaw dinghy. Herreshoff/White design. Current project.
14' dayboat. O'Brien/Kennedy design for *Yachting World*. Built cold-molded version 1992–'93; lapstrake plywood version under construction.
9' lapstrake tender. George Lawley design. 3 built 1991–'94.
6'6" lapstrake Lilliput pram. Alan Buchanan design. 3 built 1990–'94.
8' and 10' Acorn dinghies. Lapstrake plywood construction. Iain Oughtred designs. 8-footer built 1991–'92; 10-footer built 1992–'93.

Recent Repair Projects
Various repairs on canoes and small craft. 2-3 boats worked on each year.

Yard Information
Maintenance
    Number of boats maintained per year: 2-3
    Percentage of wooden boats: 50

■ PATTERSON'S MOBILE MARINE SERVICES

Peter Patterson
168 Queen St., P.O. Box 402
Baddeck, NS Canada B0E 1B0
902-295-1455 Fax: 902-295-2795

Builder Information
Years in business:
Carpenters employed: 2
Shop capacity: 55'
Willing to travel for on-the-site building projects.

Recent Repair Projects
55' power cruiser. Replaced transom. 1993.
32' St. Mackay power cruiser. Renewed interior. 1993.
38' lobster yacht. Sheathed hull and deck in fiberglass. 1992.
32' lobsterboat. Epoxy-sheathed bottom. 1992.
38' lobster yacht. Replaced flying bridge, renewed interior joinerwork. 1991.
32' lapstrake cruiser. Renewed decks and transom. 1991.
55' former RCMP cutter. Renewed 50% of bottom, replaced transom. 1990.

Yard Information
Services
    Launching facilities
Storage
    Number of boats stored per year: 10
    Percentage of wooden boats: 50
    Maximum size for hauling and storing: 40' LOA, 7' draft, 20 tons
Maintenance
    Number of boats maintained per year: 10
    Percentage of wooden boats: 50
    Owner maintenance allowed.
Retail supplies:
    Boatbuilding supplies — will order on request.

■ WAYNE C. SHIBLEY WOODEN BOATS

Wayne C. Shibley
RR #1
Rose Bay, NS Canada B0J 2X0
902-766-4516

Builder Information
Years in business: 10
Carpenters employed: 1
Shop capacity: 45'
Willing to travel for on-the-site building projects.

Recent New Construction
12' catboat. Wayne Shibley design. 2 built 1992–'93.
8' lapstrake pram. H.I. Chapelle design. 2 built 1992.
13'6" lapstrake sailing skiff. Local type. 3 built 1991–'92.
26' Bush Island double-ended sloop. Local type. Built 1990–'91.
26' lapstrake sailing dory. Wayne Shibley design. Built 1990.

Recent Repair Projects
40' sailboat. Renewing frames, planking, and interior. Refastening. 1993–'94.

■ SLAUNWHITE'S BOAT & JOINERY SHOP

Stephen H. Slaunwhite
RR #1, Mader's Cove
Mahone Bay, NS Canada B0J 2E0
902-624-8861

Builder Information
Years in business: 38
Carpenters employed: 1
Shop capacity: 42'

Recent New Construction
Boats designed by Stephen Slaunwhite:
33' schooner. Current project.
12' plywood tender. 6 built 1990–'93.
8' plywood tender. 7 built 1990–'93.
Other new construction:
41'6" Malabar II schooner. John Alden design. Built 1993.
16' plywood skiff Whisp. Steve Redmond design. Built 1990.

Recent Repair Projects

30' Herreshoff Wagonbox ketch. Installed diesel engine, added bulwarks. 1993.

■ SNYDER'S SHIPYARD LTD.

Philip R. Snyder
RR #3
Bridgewater, NS Canada B4V 2W2
902-543-8326 Fax: 902-543-1951

Builder Information
Years in business: 50
Carpenters employed: 14
Shop capacity: 100'
Willing to travel for on-the-site building projects.

Recent New Construction
65', 70', and 78' commercial fishing boats. Philip Snyder designs. 4 built 1990–'91.

Recent Repair Projects
Mostly fishing vessels.

Yard Information
Services
Engine repair

■ STEVEN'S BOATWORKS

Steven Swinamer
P.O. Box 2, Western Shore
Lunenburg, NS Canada B0J 3M0
902-627-2951

Builder Information
Years in business: 50
Carpenters employed: 3
Shop capacity: 50'
Willing to travel for on-the-site building projects.

Recent New Construction
Boats designed by Steven Swinamer:
42' schooner. Built 1993.
31' schooner. Built 1992.
44' motorsailer. Built 1991.
32' lobsterboat. Built 1990.

Recent Repair Projects
30' Roué 20 class. Built new hollow mast and rerigged. 1993.
23' Bluenose sloop. Renewed deck, stem, and frames. 1993.
42' motorsailer. Renewed rudder and bottom planking. 1992.
36' lobsterboat. Replaced deck, renewed bottom planking. 1991.
40' power cruiser. Renewed deck, cabin, and frames. 1990.
23' Bluenose sloop. Renewed deck and frames. 2 boats repaired. 1990.

Yard Information
Services
Marina facilities

Launching facilities
Moorage
Engine repair
Rigging
Storage
Number of boats stored per year: 15
Percentage of wooden boats: 90
Inside storage facilities
Maximum size for hauling and storing: 40' LOA, 6' draft
Maintenance
Number of boats maintained per year: 12
Percentage of wooden boats: 90
Owner maintenance allowed above rail.

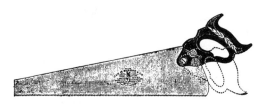

■ ROY ALLMAN

Roy Allman
RR #1
Huntsville, ON Canada P0A 1K0
705-789-4005

Builder Information
Years in business: 10
Carpenters employed: 1
Shop capacity: 30'

Recent New Construction
10', 14' and 16' wood/canvas canoes. Roy Allman designs. 16 built 1990–'92.

Recent Repair Projects
14'–16' wood/canvas canoes and 24'–34' war canoes. Rib, gunwale, keel, seat, and thwart repairs. Recanvasing and refinishing. 183 canoes restored during last 10 years.

Yard Information
Services
Overland transport
Storage
Number of boats stored per year: 30
Percentage of wooden boats: 100
Inside storage facilities
Maximum size for hauling and storing: 30' LOA; storage for canoes only
Retail supplies:
Rib stock and cedar planking stock, ash and cherry, canvas, and hardware for canoes.

◼ BAYCREST LODGE, MARINA & YARD

Big Island
Demorestville, ON Canada K0K 1W0
613-476-5357

Builder Information
Years in business: 37
Carpenters employed: 1-3
Shop capacity: 40'

Recent Repair Projects
14' outboard runabout. Refinished. 1992.
14' outboard fishing boat. Renewed planking, frames, and transom. 1990–'91.
12'–26' lapstrake runabouts and skiffs. Planking and decks repairs, refinishing. 1992–'93.

Yard Information
Services
    Marina facilities
    Launching facilities
    Overland transport
    Moorage
    Engine repair
    Rigging
Storage
    Number of boats stored per year: 100
    Percentage of wooden boats: 15
    Maximum size for hauling and storing: 46' LOA, 6' draft, 18 tons
Maintenance
    Number of boats maintained per year: 150
    Percentage of wooden boats: 20
    Owner maintenance allowed above and below rail.
Retail supplies:
    Inquire.

◼ BEAR MOUNTAIN BOAT SHOP

Ted Moores
P.O. Box 1041
Bancroft, ON Canada K0L 1C0
613-332-4456 Fax: 613-332-5654

Builder Information
Years in business: 20
Carpenters employed: 1
Shop capacity: 30'
Willing to travel for on-the-site building projects.

Recent New Construction
Boats designed by Ted Moores for strip-plank/epoxy construction:
30' C-15 sprint racing canoe. 3 built 1991–'93.
20' C-4 sprint racing canoe. 4 built 1991–'93.
13' double-paddle solo canoe. Built 1992.
16' recreational canoe. Several built 1990–'93.
Other new construction:
13'9" plywood/epoxy punt. Ted Moores design. Built 1992.

Recent Repair Projects
19' Greavette runabout (1960). Replaced bottom, keel, framing, transom, and stem.

Yard Information
Retail supplies:
    Canoe plans, books, videos, and building materials.

◼ GILL BIBBY, BOATBUILDER

Gill Bibby
151 Hendershott Rd.
Hannon, ON Canada L0R 1P0
905-692-3244 Fax: 905-561-4787

Builder Information
Years in business: 16
Carpenters employed: 3
Shop capacity: 40'
Willing to travel for on-the-site building projects.

Recent New Construction
20' and 23' longboats. Replicas of 17th- and 18th-century British designs. Built 1993.
18' lapstrake plywood St. Lawrence River skiff. Traditional design. 3 built 1992–'93.
8' lapstrake plywood dinghy. Traditional design. 2 built 1992.

Recent Repair Projects
170' Canadian government research vessel. Renewed wheelhouse, refitted cabin. 1993.
65' passenger motor vessel. Rebuilt wheelhouse, renewed cabin and handrails. 1993.
20' St. Lawrence River skiff. Renewed planking and frames. 1992.
60' passenger ferry vessel. Renewed cabin area, heads, captain's quarters. 1992.
16' Chestnut canoe. Recanvased, renewed woodwork. 1991.
33' motor vessel (1933). Renewed bottom and topside planking. 1991.
20' and 23' runabouts. Renewed planking and finish, repowered. Both completed in 1991.

Yard Information
Services
    Rigging
Retail supplies:
    Complete inventory of supplies.

◼ BREPET HOLDINGS INC.

Peter Breen
RR #2
Rockwood, ON Canada N0B 2K0
519-856-9113

Builder Information
Years in business: 12
Carpenters employed: 4
Shop capacity: 55'

Recent Repair Projects
Complete rebuilding of the following Muskoka Lake boats:
20' Greavette raceboat. 1993.
24' Ditchburn launch (1921). 1993.
31' Minett launch (#105). 1993.
22' Ditchburn launch (1924). 1992.
26' Croswell launch. 1991.
19' Chris-Craft racing runabout. 1991.

■ CANOE CRAFT

Cecil Toombs
151 Clarendon Ave.
Ottawa, ON Canada K1Y 0R6
613-722-6277

Builder Information
Years in business: 40
Carpenters employed: 1
Shop capacity: 20'

Recent Repair Projects
Toombs specializes in the repair and restoration of wood/canvas canoes and other small craft. Several boats worked on each year.

Yard Information
Retail supplies:
Wood for gunwales and keels, canoe tacks, copper nails, canvas and canvas filler.

■ CARRYING PLACE CANOE & BOAT WORKS

Joe Ziemba
11611 Hwy. 27
Kleinburg, ON Canada L0J 1C0
905-893-1350

Builder Information
Years in business: 20
Carpenters employed: 1
Shop capacity: 18'

Recent New Construction
14' lapstrake rowing boat. Joe Ziemba design. 14 built over last several years.
12'–18' wood/canvas canoes (flush-lap or strip-plank construction). 11 strip-planked models have been built to date; numerous flush-lap canoes also built.

Yard Information
Maintenance
Number of boats maintained per year: 30
Percentage of wooden boats: 100
Retail supplies:
Wood, fastenings, paint, canvas, filler.

■ CEDAR CREEK CANOE

Bob, Ron, and Greg Salton
Port Stanley, ON Canada N5L 1C7
519-782-4682 Fax: 519-782-4747

Builder Information
Years in business: 4
Carpenters employed: 3
Shop capacity: 18'

Recent New Construction
16' and 17' strip-planked Prospector canoes. Chestnut Canoe Co. designs. Six 16-footers built 1991–'93, two 17-footers built 1993–'94.
17' strip-planked Micmac canoe. Built 1990.
Canoe kits are also available and can be shipped worldwide.

Recent Repair Projects
A multitude of repairs on various wood/canvas canoes. Most recent project involved the complete restoration of an 18' wood/canvas freighter canoe.

Yard Information
Maintenance
Number of boats maintained per year: 10
Percentage of wooden boats: 100
Retail supplies:
Canoe kits. Materials for canoe construction and repair.

■ CLARION BOATS

Robert Harvey
1155 N. Service Rd. West
Suite 11
Oakville, ON Canada L6M 3E3
905-847-5504 Fax: 905-847-8840

Builder Information
Years in business: 9
Carpenters employed: 6
Shop capacity: 68'
Willing to travel for on-the-site building projects.

Recent New Construction
Boats designed by Steve Killing for cold-molded construction:
25' Gentleman's raceboat. 4 built 1990–'92.
19' Speedster. 2 built 1992–'93.

Recent Repair Projects
Complete rebuilding of the following boats during 1990 and 1991:
33' Ditchburn launch (1940).
24' Borneman launch (1918).
21' Ditchburn launch (1924).
35' Gilbert launch (1914).

■ GARY CLARK WOODEN BOATS

Gary Clark
RR #1
Severn Bridge, ON Canada P0E 1N0
705-689-5758

Builder Information
Years in business: 6
Carpenters employed: 2
Shop capacity: 36'

Recent Repair Projects
Complete restoration of the following boats:
32' Minett (1920s). Current project.
27' Ditchburn Viking. (1929). Current project.
30' Minett (1923).
26' Greavette Streamliner (1930s and 1950s models).
Other repairwork:
29' Shwartzman (1900s). Repairing bow after accident.
    Current project.

■ CLIFTS MARINE SALES, LTD.

P.O. Box 45009, 81 Lakeshore Rd. East
Mississauga, ON Canada L5G 4S7
905-278-2628 Fax: 905-278-5708

Builder Information
Years in business: 18
Carpenters employed: 4
Shop capacity: 50'
Willing to travel for on-the-site building projects.

Recent Repair Projects
Restoration, repair, and refinishing of antique and classic
    runabouts and larger wooden cabin cruisers.
    Numerous projects over last 4 years.

Yard Information
Services
    Launching facilities
    Overland transport
Storage
    Number of boats stored per year: 30
    Percentage of wooden boats: 60
    Inside storage facilities
    Maximum size for hauling and storing: 50' LOA, 4' draft
Maintenance
    Number of boats maintained per year: 20
    Percentage of wooden boats: 50
    Owner maintenance allowed above and below rail.
Retail supplies:
    Wood, fastenings, and paint.

■ DISAPPEARING PROPELLER BOAT CO. LTD.

Paul Dodington
Box 152
Port Carling, ON Canada P0B 1J0
705-765-5037

Builder Information
Years in business: 35
Carpenters employed: 3
Shop capacity: 20'

Recent Repair Projects
Company specializes in the mechanical restoration of
    Dispros, but also offers hull restoration on a subcontract
    basis. Approximately 10 to 15 Dispros (built from 1916
    to 1956) are restored annually; boats come from as far
    away as California and Washington state. Company
    maintains about 50 locally owned boats each year; also
    restores antique one- and two-cylinder marine engines.

Yard Information
Services
    Launching facilities
    Overland transport
    Engine repair
Maintenance
    Number of boats maintained per year: 50
    Percentage of wooden boats: 100
Retail supplies:
    Engine parts, reproduction/replica fittings, and other
        materials pertaining to Dispro boats.

■ DUKE MARINE SERVICES LTD.

Ed Skinner
Box 355
Port Carling, ON Canada P0B 1J0
705-765-3141

Builder Information
Years in business: 69
Carpenters employed: 3
Shop capacity: 37'
Willing to travel for on-the-site building projects.

Recent Repair Projects
22' Greavette Streamliner (1951). Epoxy-saturated hull and
    refinished. 1993.
18' Duke Playmate (1938). Replaced frames, keel, bottom
    and side planking, and transom. 1993.

Yard Information
Services
    Marina facilities
    Overland transport
    Engine repair
Storage
    Number of boats stored per year: 32
    Percentage of wooden boats: 95
    Inside storage facilities
    Maximum size for hauling and storing: 37' LOA, 3'
        draft, 3 tons
Maintenance
    Number of boats maintained per year: 150
    Percentage of wooden boats: 90
    Owner maintenance allowed above and below rail.
Retail supplies:
    Paint, fastenings, wood, caulking materials.

■ GIBSON CANOE

Dan Gibson
P.O. Box 43001
Sheppard Center Post Office
Toronto, ON Canada M2N 6N1
416-284-4689

Builder Information
Years in business: 1
Carpenters employed: 1
Shop capacity: 16'

Recent New Construction
15'6" lapstrake skiff for oar and outboard. 4 built 1993.

Recent Repair Projects
15'6" skiff. Replaced planking, transom, frames, deck, and
    rails. 1992.

■ B. GIESLER & SONS LIMITED

Box 226
Powassan, ON Canada P0H 1Z0
705-724-2648

Builder Information
Years in business: 65
Carpenters employed: 8
Shop capacity: 30'

Recent New Construction
Boats designed by Giesler for strip-plank construction:
15' rowing wherry. 6 built 1993.
16' canoes (3 different models). 20 built 1993.
16' double-ended rowing boat. 20 built 1993.
11' sailing dinghy. 7 built 1993.
30' war canoe. 4 built 1993.
14'–18' runabouts and fishing boats in 6 different models.
    150 boats built 1993.

Recent Repair Projects
22' Grew power cruiser (1936). Replaced keel, stem, tran-
    som, and planking. 1993.
16' Peterborough Speedster (1947). Completely restored.
    1993.

Yard Information
Storage
    Number of boats stored per year: 20
    Percentage of wooden boats: 100
    Maximum size for hauling and storing: 18' LOA, 7'
        draft, 1000 lbs.
Maintenance
    Number of boats maintained per year: 25
    Percentage of wooden boats: 100
Retail supplies:
    Paint, varnish, wood.

■ PHILIP GILLESSE, BOATBUILDER

Philip Gillesse
Amherst Island, ON Canada K0H 2S0
613-384-7772 Fax: 613-389-0040

Builder Information
Years in business: 12
Carpenters employed: 1
Shop capacity: 20'

Recent New Construction
17' lapstrake St. Lawrence River skiff. Replica of Dowset
    skiff. 3 built 1990–'93.
14' lapstrake St. Lawrence River skiff. Replica of Tisdale
    skiff. 2 built 1987 and 1991.
15' plywood Amherst Island punt. Traditional design. Built
    1991.
16' Rice Lake canoe. Replica of D. Herald design. 2 built
    1990.

Recent Repair Projects
13', 14', 16', and 17' St. Lawrence River skiffs. Johnson,
    Tisdale, Dowset, and Nichol designs. 7 skiffs complete-
    ly restored 1991–'93.
15' Peterborough canoe. Completely restored. 1993.
15' Peterborough skiff. 2 boats restored 1991–'92.

■ PAUL W. GOCKEL, BOATBUILDER

Paul W. Gockel III
RR #2
Port Carling, ON Canada P0B 1J0
705-765-3576

Builder Information
Years in business: 17
Carpenters employed: 1
Shop capacity: 20'

Recent New Construction
16' lapstrake double-ended rowing skiff. Traditional
    design. 3 built 1990–'93.

Recent Repair Projects
15' Richardson "Special" (1920). Restoring. Current project.
16' Dispro (1980). Replaced keel, garboards, some planking
    aft, and 2 frames. 1993.
16' Dispro (1925). Renewed keel, stem, sternpost, bottom,
    sheerstrake, frames, floorboards, and splashboards.
    1992.
19' Dispro (1927). Replaced keel, stem, sternpost, bottom,
    frames, splashboards, and floorboards. 1991.
16' Ackroyd sloop (1924). Renewed keel, garboards,
    frames, and maststep. 1990.
16' Matheson skiff (1921). Replaced frames and sheer-
    strake. Refinished. 1990.
16' Ackroyd catboat. Replaced frames. Recanvased deck
    and refinished. 1990.
(continues)

(Paul W. Gockel, Boatbuilder, continued)

Yard Information

Services
    Engine repair
Storage
    Number of boats stored per year: 2
    Maximum size for hauling and storing: 18' LOA, 6' draft
Maintenance
    Number of boats maintained per year: 5
    Percentage of wooden boats: 100

THE KIJIK CANOE COMPANY

Jim Chatsick and Mike Dearborn
51 Centennial Dr.
Port Hope, ON Canada L1A 3S9
905-885-6201

Builder Information

Years in business: 12
Carpenters employed: 2
Shop capacity: 17'

Recent New Construction

16' wood/canvas canoe. Omer Stringer design. 24 built 1990–'93.
15' and 17' wood/canvas canoes. Jim Chatsick and Mike Dearborn designs. Four 15-footers built 1992–'93, one 17-footer built 1993.

Recent Repair Projects

Wood/canvas canoe. Replaced poor wood, recanvased, revarnished interior. 1992.
Repairs approximately 8 wooden canoes each year.

Yard Information

Services
    Launching facilities
    Overland transport
Maintenance
    Number of boats maintained per year: 10
    Percentage of wooden boats: 80
Retail supplies:
    Pre-cut wood, tacks, screws, canoe accessories (seats, thwarts). Canvas, filler, stembands, gunwales, and paddles. Hardwood and cedar.

LEGACY WOODEN BOATS

Patrick J. Wren
1 Donmac Dr.
Don Mills, ON Canada M3B 1N4
416-444-9325 (winter)
705-656-9308 (May–Sept.)

Builder Information

Years in business: 3
Carpenters employed: 1
Shop capacity: 18'

Recent New Construction

12' hydroplane. Reproduction of 1929 Eckfield Boat Co. single-step racing hydroplane. Current project.

Recent Repair Projects

10' Speedliner Utility (1950). Refinishing. Current project.
16' Brown Canoe Co. canoe (1900). Replacing decks and refinishing. Current project.
16' Peterborough cedar-strip runabout (1954). Repaired and refinished. 1993.
13' Aristo-Craft mahogany-plywood runabout (1957). Completely rebuilt and refinished. 1993.
16' Grenell runabout (1957). Renewed structural members and deck. Refastened and refinished. 1993.
13'6" Lakefield cedar-strip runabout. Completely rebuilt and refinished. 1992.

Yard Information

Services
    Launching facilities
    Overland transport
Storage
    Number of boats stored per year: 5
    Percentage of wooden boats: 100
    Inside storage facilities
    Maximum size for hauling and storing: 18' LOA, 7' draft
Maintenance
    Number of boats maintained per year: 5
    Percentage of wooden boats: 100
    Owner maintenance allowed above rail.
Retail supplies:
    Paint, varnish, and fastenings in limited amounts.

LUDLOW BOATWORKS

Philip C. Ludlow
RR #4
Kemptville, ON Canada K0G 1J0
613-258-4270 Fax: 613-258-7734

Builder Information

Years in business: 17
Carpenters employed: 1-7
Shop capacity: 60'

Recent New Construction

16' Haven 12½. Joel White design. Current project.
11'6" Columbia dinghy. N.G. Herreshoff design. 2 built in carvel and lapstrake construction 1991–'92.

Recent Repair Projects

42' racing sloop CANADA (1898). Completely restoring. Upcoming project.
48'8" New York Yacht, Launch & Engine commuter launch (1909). Renewing deck, floors, sternpost, planking, and engine. Ongoing project.
36' Grand Banks 36. Replaced electrical system. 1993.
15' Wayfarer-class sloops. Renewed centerboard trunks, floors, and decks. Two boats restored 1993.
52' Elco Flattop 50 power cruiser (1928). Replaced transom, wheelhouse side, deck, and several planks. 1992.

Yard Information
Services
  Launching facilities
  Moorage
Storage
  Number of boats stored per year: 20
  Percentage of wooden boats: 85
  Inside storage facilities
  Maximum size for hauling and storing: 55' LOA, 5'
    draft, 45 tons
Maintenance
  Number of boats maintained per year: Varies
  Percentage of wooden boats: 100
  Owner maintenance allowed above and below rail.
Retail supplies:
  Wood, fastenings, paint, sealant, books, and other sup-
    plies.

■ MILLAR-POTTER BOAT RESTORATION

Jim Potter
P.O. Box 56
Manotick, ON Canada K4M 1A2
613-692-3455

Builder Information
Years in business: 15
Carpenters employed: 3
Shop capacity: 36'

Recent New Construction
7' wood/canvas dinghy. Penn Yan design. 4 built 1991–'92.

Recent Repair Projects
24' Seabird triple-cockpit runabout (1930). Replaced decks
  and transom. 1993.
23' Grew Jolly Giant launch (1955). Replaced frames, stem,
  and some bottom planking. 1993.
22'6" Dowset runabout (1937). Replaced bottom and
  transom. 1993.
18' Chris-Craft Utility. (1952). Renewed topside planking.
  1993.
17' Jeffrey Utility. (1941). Completely restored. 1993.
20' Chris-Craft Deluxe Runabout (1940). Replaced transom
  and topsides. 1993.
22'6" Dodge Watercar (1925). Completely restored.
  1992–'93.

Yard Information
Services
  Overland transport
  Engine repair
Storage
  Percentage of wooden boats: 100
  Inside storage facilities
  Maximum size for hauling and storing: 30' LOA
Maintenance
  Number of boats maintained per year: 25
  Percentage of wooden boats: 100
Retail supplies:
  Wood, fastenings, paint, and other supplies.

■ NORTH BAY CANOE COMPANY

William Schorse
RR #2
Corbeil, ON Canada P0H 1K0
705-752-1770 Fax: same

Builder Information
Years in business: 15
Carpenters employed: 2
Shop capacity: 24'
Willing to travel for on-the-site building projects.

Recent New Construction
Canoes designed by William Schorse for wood/canvas
    construction:
18' Freighter canoe. Built 1993.
17' cruising canoe. 4 built 1992–'93.
17' Guide Special canoe. Built 1993.
16' Tripper canoe. 6 built 1992–'93.

Recent Repair Projects
Specializes in the repair and restoration of canoes.
    Approximately 40 boats restored each year.

Yard Information
Retail supplies:
  Supplies related to canoe repair and use. Paint, varnish,
    filler, canvas, fiberglass cloth, epoxy. Brass and bronze
    hardware, paddles.

■ OLD DELTA CANOEWORKS

Dave Alguire
Box 69
Delta, ON Canada K0E 1G0
613-928-2850

Builder Information
Years in business: 5
Carpenters employed: 1
Shop capacity: 17'

Recent Repair Projects
Specializes in the repair and restoration of any type of
    wood/canvas canoe.

Yard Information
Retail supplies:
  Wood, stembands, fastenings. Custom-made parts for
    canoes including caned seats, thwarts, gunwales, and
    paddles.

■ PHOENIX WOODWORK

Jim Stanton
RR #1
Janetville, ON Canada L0B 1K0
705-328-1175

Builder Information
Years in business: 30
(continues)

(Phoenix Woodwork, continued)
Carpenters employed: 1
Shop capacity: 40'
Willing to travel for on-the-site building projects.

Recent New Construction
32' cold-molded, twin-keel, Noon-Tide 32 cutter. Maurice Griffiths design. Built 1992.
8' plywood dinghy for oar and sail. Jim Stanton design. 2 built 1991.
Company specializes in construction of twin-keeled, shallow-draft, sailing boats.

Recent Repair Projects
30' Trojan power cruiser. Renewed transom, made general repairs. 1993.
30' Griffiths Waterwitch sloop. Rebedded and overhauled engine, renewed interior. Refinished exterior, mast, and boom. 1992.
14'–20' canoes. Repairs including rib and gunwale replacement, stem and stern replacement, recanvasing and refinishing. 1993.

Yard Information
Services
  Rigging
Storage
  Number of boats stored per year: 3
  Percentage of wooden boats: 100
  Inside storage facilities
  Maximum size for hauling and storing: Inquire

■ PORT DOVER BOAT WORKS

River Dr.
Port Dover, ON Canada N0A 1N0
613-583-2442

Builder Information
Years in business: 16
Carpenters employed: 1-2
Shop capacity: 40'

Recent New Construction
17' skiff. Built 1993.
18' camp-skiff. H.I. Chapelle design. Built 1992.
18' tugboat. Built 1991.
13' skiff. Built 1990.

Recent Repair Projects
34' Richardson sedan cruiser (1956). Rebuilt and recanvased cabintop. 1993.
25' Chris-Craft sedan cruiser (1956). Replaced deck, installed hardtop and trimmed out. 1993.
15' Wayfarer-class sloop (1955). Renewed bottom and decks. 1993.
20' Century runabout (1951). Renewed frames, rebuilt. 1993.
34' Century power cruiser (1961). Replaced transom. 1992.
26' Chris-Craft Sea Skiff (1957). Refinished woodwork, installed new engine. 1991.
26' Sea Bird yawl (1936). Replaced chines, installed new engine. 1990.

Yard Information
Services
  Marina facilities
  Launching facilities
  Moorage
Storage
  Number of boats stored per year: 30
  Percentage of wooden boats: 90
  Inside storage facilities
  Maximum size for hauling and storing: 50' LOA, 12' draft, 16 tons
Maintenance
  Number of boats maintained per year: 10
  Percentage of wooden boats: 90
  Owner maintenance allowed above and below rail.

■ RUCH CANOES

Will Ruch
Minett Post Office
Muskoka, ON Canada P0B 1G0
705-765-5390

Builder Information
Years in business: 6
Carpenters employed: 1
Shop capacity: 18'

Recent New Construction
15' and 16' wood/canvas canoes. Peterborough designs. 14 built 1990–'93.

Recent Repair Projects
16' Walter Dean canoe (early 1900s). Renewed deck, refinished. 2 canoes restored 1992.
17' Peterborough skiff (1920). Renewed ribs and gunwales, refinished. 1992.
16' Peterborough canoe (1900). Renewed planking, ribs, and floorboards. Refinished. 1992.
16' Peterborough sponson canoe (1920). Repaired planking, ribs, seats, and gunwales. Recanvased and refinished. 1992.
16' Lakefield canoe (1930). Renewed ribs and floorboards. Refinished. 1992.
18' Old Town sailing canoe (1930). Renewed ribs and planking. Recanvased and refinished. 1991.
16' Canadian Canoe Co. canoe (1910). Repaired stems, revarnished. 1991.

■ RUDY'S WATERCRAFT

James Rudy
RR #1
Essex, ON Canada N8M 2X5
519-839-4506 Fax: same

Builder Information
Years in business: 3
Carpenters employed: 1-3
Shop capacity: 40'
Willing to travel for on-the-site building projects.

Recent Repair Projects

22' Chris-Craft Sportsman (1941). Completely rebuilding to showroom condition. Current project.

37' Pacemaker double-cabin power cruiser. Reframing 90% of boat, renewing 20' of keelson, stem and knee, shaft-logs, and cabin sides. Raising foredeck 4", installing bulwarks, and remodeling interior. Completely refinishing. 1992 to current.

42' 30-Square-Meter sloop (1929). Renewed framing, planking, and deadwood. Replaced deck. 1990.

Yard Information

Services

Engine repair

Maintenance

Number of boats maintained per year: 3-4

Percentage of wooden boats: 100

Owner maintenance allowed above rail.

Retail supplies:

Lumber and fastenings. Other material and equipment can be ordered.

■ SPENCER & HURLEY CANOE CO.

Jim Spencer and Jack Hurley
Box 42
Dwight, ON Canada P0A 1H0
705-635-1565

Builder Information

Years in business: 18

Carpenters employed: 2

Shop capacity: 20'

Recent New Construction

Wood/canvas canoes:

16' Peterborough canoes. 2 different designs. 10 built 1993.

15' Chestnut canoes. 2 designs. 6 built 1993.

9' trapper canoe. Clarence Bouges design. 2 built 1993.

Recent Repair Projects

15' Peterborough canoe (1917). Replaced 26 ribs, 80% of planking. Renewed decks, stems, inwales, and canvas. 1994.

16' Chestnut canoe (1950s). Replaced ribs and planking, recanvased hull. 1994.

16' and 18' Peterborough outboard boats. Completely refinished. 1993.

18' Atlantic rowing dory. Refinished. 1991.

Restored or repaired about 20 other wood/canvas canoes from 1990–'93 for individuals and nearby children's camps.

Yard Information

Retail supplies:

Varnish, stembands, hardware, fastenings, canvas and filler, white cedar and ash. Custom-made paddles and wanigans.

■ TEMAGAMI CANOE COMPANY

John C. Kilbridge
P.O. Box 520-W
Temagami, ON Canada P0H 2H0
705-569-3777

Builder Information

Years in business: 65

Carpenters employed: 1

Shop capacity: 18'

Recent New Construction

Wood/canvas canoes available on order basis:

14' Temagami Trapper day-tripping canoe. 1929 William Smith design

16' Temagami Special wilderness-tripping canoe. 1929 William Smith design.

12' wilderness-tripping solo canoe.

16' Chestnut Prospector reproduction.

17' wilderness-tripping canoe.

16' and 17' Chestnut Cruiser reproductions.

Recent Repair Projects

Wood/canvas canoes to 18'. Minor to major repairs, including recanvasing and replacement of ribs, planking, decks, and gunwales. Seat caning a specialty.

Yard Information

Retail supplies:

Cedar, ash, paint, fastenings, stembands, canvas, filler, and milled parts.

■ THE TENDER CRAFT BOAT SHOP INC.

Barb Williams and Bill Steiss
284 Brock Ave.
Toronto, ON Canada M6K 2M4
416-531-2941 Fax: 416-323-0992

Builder Information

Years in business: 15

Carpenters employed: 2

Shop capacity: 25'

Recent New Construction

Boats of strip-plank construction:

16' and 18' outboard runabouts. Peterborough Co. designs. Eight 16-footers built 1990–'93, one 18-footer built 1992–'93.

12' electric launch. Tom Williams design. Built 1993.

10'9" sailing dinghy. 12 built 1990–'93.

16' double-ended pulling boat. 9 built 1990–'93.

15'10" canoe. Peterborough Co. design. 9 built 1990–'93.

9'6" tender. Tom Williams design. 6 built 1992–'93.

Recent Repair Projects

16' Albacore daysailer. Repaired and refinished. 1993.

14'–17' canoes. Replaced ribs, planking, decks, stems, gunwales. Recanvased. Several projects 1990–'93.

11' Richardson dinghy. Renewed frames and planking. Refinished. 1993.

(continues)

(The Tender Craft Boat Shop Inc., continued)

12'–16' skiffs and runabouts. Various repairs and refinishing. Several projects 1990–'93.

Yard Information

Storage

Maximum size for hauling and storing: Inquire

Retail supplies:

Canoe, skiff, and dinghy kits and supplies. Small boat plans. Custom bronze and chrome-plated fittings and hardware. Spars, oars, and paddles. Custom milling and joinerwork. Rope fenders.

■ TRAILHEAD

Reid McLachlan and Geoff Tomlinson
1960 Scott St.
Ottawa, ON Canada K1Z 8L8
613-722-4229 Fax: 613-722-0245

Builder Information

Years in business: 8
Carpenters employed: 2-3
Shop capacity: 21'

Recent New Construction

16' Prospector wood/canvas canoes. 20-30 built each year since 1991.

Recent Repair Projects

16' Old Town H.W. Model canoe (1937). Replaced stem, 3 ribs, 40' of planking. Recanvased hull, replaced outwales, and revarnished. 1993.

15' Chestnut canoe (ca. 1960). Replaced stem, 12 ribs, 60' of planking. Renewed inwale and outwales, and stemband. Recanvased hull. 1993.

16' Peterborough canoe (ca. 1910). Replaced decks, coaming, and outwales. Reconditioned and varnished hull. 1992.

Approximately 20-25 canoes recanvased and/or restored each year.

Yard Information

Services

Overland transport

Storage

Inside storage facilities

Maximum size for hauling and storing: Storage for canoes and kayaks to 21'.

Retail supplies:

Rough or milled Eastern white cedar and white ash. Canvas, filler, canoe hardware.

■ WESTPORT CANOE

Jack LaPointe
26 Spring St.
Westport, ON Canada K0G 1X0
613-273-3530

Builder Information

Years in business: 7

Carpenters employed: 1
Shop capacity: 20'
Willing to travel for on-the-site building projects.

Recent New Construction

Wood/canvas canoes:

16' Peterborough design. Built 1993.

15' Chestnut Prospector. 2 built 1993.

17' square-sterned freight canoe for sail and oar. Dean Paine design for Mistassini River. 2 built 1992–'93.

14' modified Peterborough design. 8 built since 1991.

Recent Repair Projects

12'–20' wood/canvas canoes. Peterborough, Chestnut, Old Town, Carleton, Penn Yan, Lakefield, and Tremblay models. Repairs or restores approximately 20 canoes each year.

Yard Information

Services

Overland transport

Sail repair

Rigging

Retail supplies:

Wood, canvas, filler, hardware, parts, paint, and varnish. Stripper canoe kits.

■ WOOD BOATWORKS

Patrick Doherty
RR #3
Penetanguishene, ON Canada L0K 1P0
705-533-4550

Builder Information

Years in business: 15
Carpenters employed: 3-8
Shop capacity: 50'
Willing to travel for on-the-site building projects.

Recent New Construction

14', 16', 18', and 20' wood/canvas canoes. Bolan designs. 43 canoes built 1990–'93.

Recent Repair Projects

29'6" Dragon-class sloop. Renewed 50% of planking and frames. 1993.

Peterborough Handyboy. Replaced frames and planking. Refinished. 1993.

36' Nourse powerboat. Replaced frames, renewed finish. 1992.

26' Rainbow-class sloop. Renewed frames, planking, and deck. 1992.

16' Greavette power launch. Renewed planking and refinished. 1990.

12'–20' canoes. Rib and planking repairs, and recanvasing. Several canoes restored 1990–'93.

Yard Information

Services

Marina facilities

Launching facilities

Moorage
Engine repair
Rigging
Storage
Number of boats stored per year: 60
Percentage of wooden boats: 50
Inside storage facilities
Maximum size for hauling and storing: 50' LOA, 6'
draft, 40 tons
Maintenance
Number of boats maintained per year: 100
Percentage of wooden boats: 50
Retail supplies:
Paint, varnish, WEST System supplies, wood, and fastenings. Everything needed for new construction or repair.

◼ WOODWIND YACHTS

Ken Lavalette
3986 Highway 7A
Nestleton, ON Canada L0B 1L0
905-986-9663 Fax: 905-986-5512

Builder Information
Years in business: 15
Carpenters employed: 4
Shop capacity: 45'
Willing to travel for on-the-site building projects.

Recent Repair Projects
30' Dragon-class sloop. Completely restoring. Only six
pieces of original hull saved. Current project.
34' 5.5-Meter-class sloop. Extensive restoration.
Approximately half of the vessel is being replaced.
Current project.
23' Rainbow sloop. Extensive restoration. Approximately
60% of the vessel is being replaced. Current project.
25' Folkboat. Replacing 9 planks, 14 frames, bulkheads,
and floor timbers. Completely refinishing. Current
project.
22' Greavette runabout. Replacing bottom. Renewing
frames, planking, and transom. Completely refinishing.
Current project.
14' International-class sloop. Renewing planking and
frames. Repairing deck and centerboard. Completely
refinishing. Current project.
16' Century Resorter runabout. Renewing planking, keel,
transom, and deck. Completely refinishing. Current
project.

Yard Information
Services
Overland transport
Storage
Number of boats stored per year: 30
Percentage of wooden boats: 100
Inside storage facilities
Maximum size for hauling and storing: 40' LOA, 8'
draft, 10 tons

Maintenance
Number of boats maintained per year: 10
Percentage of wooden boats: 100
Owner maintenance allowed.
Retail supplies:
Wood, epoxy, paint, varnish, fastenings, caulking supplies.

◼ CAMP NOMININGUE INC.

Peter Van Wagner
119 rue Guy
Vaudreuil, PQ Canada H9R 3K7
514-455-4447 Fax: 514-455-7062

Builder Information
Years in business: 26
Carpenters employed: 2
Shop capacity: 16'

Recent New Construction
16' wood/canvas canoe. Peter Van Wagner design. 30 built
1990–'93.

Recent Repair Projects
12' to 25' wood/canvas canoes. Repair, restoration, and
refinishing. Approximately 30 canoes worked on each
year.

Yard Information
Maintenance
Number of boats maintained per year: 30
Percentage of wooden boats: 100
Retail supplies:
White cedar ribs and planking, brass canoe tacks, and
brass stembands.

■ SERVICE MARITIME INDEPENDANT

Jean-Pierre Fournel
2145 Du Tremblay
Longueuil, PQ Canada J4N 1A9
514-468-2806

Builder Information
Years in business: 12
Carpenters employed: 1
Shop capacity: Any size
Willing to travel for on-the-site building projects.

Recent New Construction
18'8" Buzzards Bay sloop. R.D. Culler design. Built 1992–'93.
24' Kingston lobsterboat sloop. H.I. Chapelle design. Built 1989–'91.

Recent Repair Projects
23' Chris-Craft Constellation. Renewed hull and transom. 1993.

45' La Chance cruiser. Replaced floor timbers and bottom planking. 1993.
35' La Voie cruiser. Renewed stem and forefoot. 1992.
42' lobsterboat. Renewed strip planking above waterline. 1992.
32' DesGane sloop. Renewed sternpost and deadwood. 1991.
38' Glen-L trawler. Renewed cabintop and flying bridge. 1991.
36' Chinese junk. Renewed teak deck. 1991.

Yard Information
Services
Engine repair
Rigging
Maintenance
Number of boats maintained per year: 20
Percentage of wooden boats: 80
Retail supplies:
Epoxy and other materials for boatbuilding.

DESIGNERS

Please note that the following descriptions were provided by the designers or their agents.

Accumar Corporation

Scott Sprague
1180 N.W. Finn Hill Rd.
Poulsbo, WA 98370
206-779-7795 Fax: 206-697-6779

Design catalog available.

Yacht design, boatbuilding, and custom yacht hardware are specialties at Accumar. Scott Sprague, Nathan Smith, and Will Carter run the company. Accomplishments include successful designs in sail and power from an 8' lapstrake pram to a 64' world cruiser. The shop has built and renovated vessels to 50'.

John G. Alden, Inc.

Donald G. Parrot
89 Commercial Wharf
Boston, MA 02110
617-227-9480 Fax: 617-523-5465

The Alden company designs custom and production sail or motor yachts for construction in any suitable material. Existing designs are available for sale, as are plans for more than 1,000 original wooden boat designs going back to the turn of the century. All designs require manual lofting.

Atkin & Co.

Pat or John Atkin
P.O. Box 3005
Noroton, CT 06820
203-655-0886

Design catalog available.

The Atkin office has been designing practical wood, steel, and aluminum power and sailing boats since 1906. They specialize in wholesome, safe, and well-conceived designs of proven ability. Since the magazine's inception, *WoodenBoat* has continually published Atkin designs in its Design Section.

R.H. Baker Boats

Anne Baker
29 Drift Rd.
Westport, MA 02790
508-636-3272

Design catalog available for $8.00.

Plans for traditional sailing and rowing boats, 8' to 30'.

W.A. Baker

Write for price and availability of plans.

Hart Nautical Collections, MIT Museum
265 Massachusetts Ave.
Cambridge, MA 02139
617-253-5942 Fax: 617-258-9107

B & B Yacht Designs

Graham S. Byrnes, N.A.
P.O. Box 206, 202 Elm St.
Vandemere, NC 28587-0206
919-745-4793 Fax: same

Design catalog available.

Stock and custom designs in traditional and modern construction. Sail, power, monohulls, multihulls, in lengths from 6' to 100'. Modifications and additions. Thirty years and over 100,000 ocean miles experience. Designer of 1993 WOOD Regatta winner. Very personal, in-depth service with attention paid to client's exact needs from concept to launching.

Morgan Barney

Inquire for price and availability of plans.

Mystic Seaport Museum
Ships Plans Division
Mystic, CT 06355
203-572-5360

Ken Bassett

Onion River Boatworks
55 River St.
Franklin, NH 03235
603-934-3034 Fax: same

Designs specialized boats to 30' for one or two people.

Grant W. Bauer & Co.

Grant W. Bauer, N.A.
3 Bayberry Lane
Bay Head, NJ 08742
908-892-2507

Grant Bauer has more than 40 years' experience in designing and supervising the construction of high-performance, seakindly wooden boats, especially offshore sportfishermen. He is a member of the Hull Technical Project Committee of the American Boat and Yacht Council, former chair-man of the ABYC's Technical Board, former treasurer of the Yacht Architects & Brokers Association, and a member since 1958 of the Society of Naval Architects & Marine Engineers.

Beach Naval Architecture

David D. Beach, N.A.
405 North Wabash
River Plaza Building, Suite 5008
Chicago, IL 60611
312-836-4747

Having recently retired after 25 years as Staff Naval Architect for the National Marine Manufacturers Association, David Beach is returning to wooden boat design, specializing in nostalgic and classic models of performance and cruising powerboats. Custom designs available for cold-molded, batten-seam plywood hulls to 35'. Member SNAME, Fellow RINA, P.E.

Benford Design Group

Jay R. Benford
P.O. Box 447, 605 Talbot St.
St. Michaels, MD 21663-0447
410-745-3235 Fax: 410-745-9743

Cruising Designs, 3rd Edition ($13.00 U.S. & CDN; $20.00 Air overseas)

BDG's specialty is traditional cruising yachts, power and sail, in all materials. "Benford is a widely known yacht designer with a far-ranging imagination and great versatility...."—*WoodenBoat*

"Benford's boats all seem to have some sort of magical quality, a unique character all their own that defies definition." —*Cruising Sailboat Kinetics*

Jeffrey L. Blume, P.E., Naval Architects

Jeffrey L. Blume
9923 Halifax St.
San Buenaventura, CA 93004
805-659-3716 Fax: same

Mr. Blume is a licensed naval architect, specializing in sail/power yachts and power/sail commercial fishing boats. Mr. Blume has the experience of over wooden construction in its many forms. Mr. Blume's vessels have been built on several continents, and his custom vessels have been featured in prominent publications.

Boat Plans International Ltd.

Scott Wurtele
Box 18000—WBD
Boulder, CO 80308
800-782-7218 Fax: 604-938-1186

Thirty design catalogs available. Over 4,000 designs by more than 80 yacht designers and naval architects.

Phil Bolger and Friends

Susanne Altenburger
29 Ferry St.
Gloucester, MA 01930
Fax: 508-282-1349

Design catalog available.

Forty years devotion to exploiting overlooked options and to developing cost-effective designs. Realized concepts in straight sail, auxiliary, motorsailer, displacement, and planing power craft, monohull and multihull, from 5½' and 35 pounds to 125' and 450 tons. Traditional and contemporary construction, form, and style. Minimum rule and trend influence. Zest!

Ted Brewer Yacht Designs Ltd.

Ted Brewer
P.O. Box 187
Lyman, WA 98263
206-826-1140 Fax: same

Free detailed listing of designs available.

Ted Brewer has over 33 years' experience in the design of wooden yachts, working on all types from AMERICA's Cup 12-Metre racers to the 70' gaff-rigged schooner TREE OF LIFE, named one of America's 100 Greatest Yachts by *Sail* magazine in 1993. Stock and custom designs are available.

George Buehler Yacht Design

George Buehler
Box 966
Freeland, WA 98249
206-331-5866 Fax: same

Design catalog available for $8.00.

Sail and power vessels. Buehler is especially interested in traditional construction but designs for cold-molded and plywood construction as well. Custom design service a specialty. Plans furnished on paper and AutoCad disc. Recent designs: 80' traditional schooner; 42' ultralight sloop; 60' long-range powerboat.

Burgess & Paine

Write for price and availability of plans.

Hart Nautical Collections, MIT Museum
265 Massachusetts Ave.
Cambridge, MA 02139
617-253-5942 Fax: 617-258-9107

Burgess, Swasey and Paine

Write for price and availability of plans.

Hart Nautical Collections, MIT Museum
265 Massachusetts Ave.
Cambridge, MA 02139
617-253-5942 Fax: 617-258-9107

W. Starling Burgess

Inquire for price and availability of plans.

Mystic Seaport Museum
Ships Plans Division
Mystic, CT 06355
203-572-5360

Chuck Burns, Naval Architect

Chuck Burns
89 Rogers Lane
Little Compton, RI 02837-2132
401-635-2592 Fax: 401-635-2592

Many designs for cold-molded racing and cruising boats in lengths from 24' to 60'. See *WoodenBoat* No. 51 for feature on ULDB SKIDOO and No. 26 for cutters TOPAZ and PETRIFIED. Burns will also re-engineer other designs for strip-plank and cold-molded construction if hull shape is suitable.

George Calkins

George Calkins
P.O. Box 222
Nordland, WA 98358
206-385-3649

Brochure available.

George Calkins has plans available only for his Bartender design (19', 22', 26', and 29' lengths). His design experience includes boats in the 10' to 60' range, which he built for racing, pleasure, commercial fishing, cruising, and sailing. Basically retired, he is knowledgable about boat design and is available for consultation.

Chance & Company, Inc.

Britton Chance, Jr.
37 Pratt St.
Essex, CT 06426
203-767-2161 Fax: 203-767-2162

Britt Chance's portfolio ranges from shells to powerboats, dinghies to multihulls, cruisers to racers, and to AMERICA's Cup boats. Chance is closely identified with Cup design and recently worked with Boeing's CFD staff developing appendages for the new IACC class. Chance has designed numerous wooden boats and is responsible for several advances in wooden construction. Call to discuss your project.

Howard I. Chapelle

Smithsonian Institution
Div. of Trans./NMAH 5010/MRC 628
Washington, DC 20560

The Ship Plan List of the Maritime Collection is available from the Smithsonian Institution for $10.00, and is a complete listing of all the plans published in reduced form in Howard Chapelle's books. Full-scale drawings for any of these designs can be ordered through the catalog. Other Chapelle drawings are also in the Smithsonian collection; inquire for price and availability.

Howard I. Chapelle

Inquire for price and availability of plans.

Chesapeake Bay Maritime Museum
P.O. Box 636
St. Michaels, MD 21633
410-745-2916

Chris-Craft Corp.

Inquire for price and availability of plans.

Mariners' Museum
100 Museum Drive
Newport News, VA 23606
804-595-0368

Clark Craft

Gary Brown
16 Aqua Lane
Tonawanda, NY 14150
716-873-2640 Fax: 716-873-2651

Design catalog available.

Stock designs for oar, power, sail, or paddle. All types and sizes of boats from 6' to 70', including international designs.

Louis T. Codega, P.E., Naval Architect

Lou Codega
Box 15610
Alexandria, VA 22309
703-799-6588 Fax: same

A degreed naval architect and professional engineer with 15 years' experience, Lou designs and consults on high-performance custom and production power craft. He works primarily for boatbuilders, with emphasis on large sportfishermen built using epoxy/cold-molded construction. His services combine innovative designs, money-saving processes, and flawless engineering.

Thomas E. Colvin., Naval Architect

Thomas E. Colvin
2140 Gardner Rd.
Alva, FL 33920
813-728-2196   Fax: same

Designs available for sailing vessels from 26' to 50' in length—mostly ketch and schooner-rigged. A few powerboat designs are also available.

Common Sense Designs

Bernie Wolfard
11765 S.W. Ebberts Ct.
Beaverton, OR 97005
503-524-8264   Fax: same

Design catalog available.

Common Sense Designs specializes in designs by Phil Bolger for inexperienced and first-time builders who would like to build a boat they can complete without going to school, without having to equip a shop, without having to take out a loan, and without sacrificing performance for ease of building.

CompuMarine

John R. Clark
P.O. Box 7565 - WBC
Everett, WA 98201-0565
206-259-6020

CompuMarine specializes in cedar strip/epoxy small craft designs for amateur boatbuilders. Designs available for strong, lightweight, and beautiful rowing, paddling, sailing, and planing hulls from 7' to 21'. Plans include full-sized patterns and a comprehensive instruction manual with a complete pictorial. Info-Pak available for $5.00.

Albert E. Condon

Inquire for price and availability of plans.

Mystic Seaport Museum
Ships Plans Division
Mystic, CT 06355
203-572-5360

Consolidated Shipbuilding Corp.

Inquire for price and availability of plans.

Mystic Seaport Museum
Ships Plans Division
Mystic, CT 06355
203-572-5360

Cook Yacht Design

Bill Cook
832 Main St.
Osterville, MA 02655
508-420-1180   Fax: 508-420-1181

Primary focus in the design of wooden boats is in sailing yachts of classic lines, such as the 58' yawl CAROLER.

Leigh Coolidge

Inquire for price and availability of plans.

Seattle Museum of History and Industry
2161 E. Hamlin St.
Seattle, WA 98102

Cosine Boats

John Hartsock
619 Sater Lane
Edmonds, WA 98020
206-774-5846   Fax: 206-670-6736

Design catalog available.

Plans and instructions for 8' to 21' strip-planked rowing boats from the designer of the Cosine Wherry. Seaworthy boats that row with ease. Traditional lines, yet can be built by amateurs with little experience and few special tools. Plans include full-sized patterns. No lofting required. Study set, $5.00.

Cox & Stevens

Inquire for price and availability of plans.

Mystic Seaport Museum
Ships Plans Division
Mystic, CT 06355
203-572-5360

S.S. Crocker

S. Sturgis Crocker's Boat Yard, Inc.
P.O. Box 268, 15 Ashland Ave.
Manchester, MA 01944
508-526-1971   Fax: 508-526-7625

Design list available.

S. Sturgis Crocker has all of his father's designs available. Some modifications to the plans have been made by Sturgis, though basic designs remain the same.

William F. Crosby

Inquire for price and availability of plans.

Mystic Seaport Museum
Ships Plans Division
Mystic, CT 06355
203-572-5360

B.B. Crowninshield

Inquire for price and availability of plans.

Peabody & Essex Museum
East India Square
Salem, MA 01970
617-745-1876

Capt. Pete Culler's Plans

c/o George B. Kelley
20 Lookout Lane
Hyannis, MA 02601
508-775-2679

For a guide to Culler's designs, refer to *Pete Culler's Boats* by John Burke. Plans are available for 101 traditionally designed boats and vessels, ranging from a 10'6" wherry yawl to a 125' three-masted schooner.

Custom Boat Designs

Ernie Pfannenschmidt
1734 Fairfield Rd.
Victoria, BC, V8S 1G3 Canada
604-598-6197

Designs for small, traditional cruising boats of classic appearance. Gaff rig and diesel power a specialty. Fifty years' experience.

Arch Davis Design

Arch Davis
c/o Snug Harbor, 18970 Azure Rd.
Wayzata, MN 55391
612-473-2360

Inquire for price and availability of plans.

Arch Davis uses modern materials and techniques in his designs to make the most of the unique aesthetic and engineering qualities of wood. He has plans for small plywood craft for the home builder, and designs practical, economical, offshore cruising sailboats.

DESIGNERS

R.O. Davis

Write for price and availability of plans.

Hart Nautical Collections, MIT Museum
265 Massachusetts Ave.
Cambridge, MA 02139
617-253-5942 Fax: 617-258-9107

Arno N. Day

Arno N. Day
P.O. Box 23
Sedgwick, ME 04676
207-359-8353

Arno has designed and built Maine
Coast lobsterboats from 24' to 50'. Many
have been converted to pleasure boats.
These designs are all available upon
request; dinghy and skiff plans are also
available. Arno will design as well, to
individual owners' requirements.

William J. Deed

Inquire for price and availability of plans.

Mystic Seaport Museum
Ships Plans Division
Mystic, CT 06355
203-572-5360

Designautics

Jay E. Paris, Jr.
P.O. Box 459
Brunswick, ME 04011-0459
207-443-9146 Fax: 207-443-9541

Diversified services in naval architecture, engineering, and technical writing.
Design details are generally developed
by working closely with the building
yard and utilizing models/mock-ups.
Notable designs: 61½' ketch LONE STAR,
teak on iroko with bronze floors and
strapping; Freedom 33 cat-ketch prototype, cold-molded mahogany; Petrel 32
sloop, wood/foam/wood composite.

Henry Devereaux

Inquire for price and availability of plans.

Mystic Seaport Museum
Ships Plans Division
Mystic, CT 06355
203-572-5360

Devlin Designing

Sam Devlin
2424 Gravelly Beach Loop NW
Olympia, WA 98502
206-866-0164 Fax: 206-866-4548

Design catalog available for $7.00.

Devlin has been specializing in distinc-
tive wooden stitch-and-glue designs
since 1977. Working with sheet marine
plywood, he's designed and built boats
from 7'6" dinghies to sailboats and
powerboats up to 50'. His number one
objective is to conceive and create boats
that look good and perform their mission
successfully. Stock plans are available
for amateur construction.

Antonio Dias/Marine Design & Construction

Tony Dias
193 Tillson Lake Rd.
Wallkill, NY 12589-3214
914-895-9165

Design catalog available.

Boats should meet their owners' needs,
and fulfill their dreams as well. To this
end, the company has developed
unique craft in a traditional spirit, with
adaptation for contemporary circum-
stances. Focus is on smaller craft, under
30'. Most boats are trailerable.

Dickes Yacht Design

Geoffrey Dickes
P.O. Box 1746
Edgartown, MA 02539
508-627-3013 Fax: same

Relevant portions of design portfolio
available to prospective clients.

Specialists in the architecture and engineering of powerboats of extraordinary
efficiency and performance. Present focus
is custom-built, high-speed sportfishermen and motor cruisers, 30' to 70'
in length, of wood/epoxy/fiber composite construction. Design services are
also available for series production,
refits, and interiors.

Joseph C. Dobler, N.A.

Joseph C. Dobler
4 Park Place
Manhattan Beach, CA 90266-7213
310-545-5122

Design catalog available for $7.00.

Plans for oar-, sail-, and outboard-
powered boats. Plywood taped-seam,
cold-molded, and glued-lapstrake construction. Camp-cruisers, open-water
fixed- seat, multi-oar rowing boats.

Gilbert Dunham

Inquire for price and availability of plans.

Mystic Seaport Museum
Ships Plans Division
Mystic, CT 06355
203-572-5360

Elco Works

Inquire for price and availability of plans.

Mystic Seaport Museum
Ships Plans Division
Mystic, CT 06355
203-572-5360

Eldredge & Matteson Co.

Craig E. Matteson, N.A.
Box 262, Rte. 196
Topsham, ME 04086
207-729-5300

Design catalog available.

Naval architects and marine engineers.
Traditional and custom design of yachts
and commercial vessels to 120'. Marine and
mechanical engineering, renovation and
new design. Consultants—surveying
and boatbuilding experience. Free con-
sultations; stability testing. Schooners
are a specialty. Member: SNAME.

Eldredge-McInnis, Inc.

Alan J. McInnis
P.O. Box F
Hingham, MA 02043
617-749-5570 Fax: call first

Existing plans are largely for powerboats from 23' to 85', motorsailers 30' to
60', and fishing vessels up to 110'. Some
sailboat designs from 24' to 50', sloops,
ketches, and schooners. Currently in
semi-retirement, Alan is not accepting
any new work, but can do design
changes on existing designs.

Weston Farmer Associates

Mary Farmer
18970 Azure Rd.
Wayzata, MN 55391
612-473-2360

Design catalog available for $2.00.

Weston Farmer, N.A., now deceased,
had a long and illustrious career in
naval architecture. With great versatility,
he designed boats from an 8' dinghy to
large pleasure yachts in wood, aluminum, and steel. The catalog of plans

168

defines 23 boats in sail and power that Weston designed specifically for the amateur builder.

Farrier Marine

Ian Farrier
P.O. Box 40675
Bellevue, WA 98015
206-957-1903 Fax: 206-957-1915

Design catalog available.

Multihull designs from 18' to 36' for amateur builders. Light, easy-to-build designs with roomy interiors. Fun to sail, with exhilarating performance combined with level sailing. Well proven, with over 1,000 sailing worldwide. All trailerable designs feature the patented Farrier Folding System™ for singlehanded trailering in minutes.

Frederick A. Fenger

Inquire for price and availability of plans.

Mystic Seaport Museum
Ships Plans Division
Mystic, CT 06355
203-572-5360

Jules Fleder, Naval Architect

Jules G. Fleder
165 Wellington Dr.
Stamford, CT 06903
203-322-3023

Yacht design and marine consulting.

Glenn Furness

Inquire for price and availability of plans.

Mystic Seaport Museum
Ships Plans Division
Mystic, CT 06355
203-572-5360

William Garden

Mystic Seaport Museum
Ships Plans Division
Mystic, CT 06355
203-572-5360

Plans cover 1937-1968 work from Garden's Seattle, WA, office. Inquire for price and availability of plans; some restrictions may apply.

Paul Gartside Ltd.

Paul Gartside
10305 West Saanich Rd., RR #1
Sidney, BC, V8L 3R9 Canada
604-656-2048

Gartside designs sail and power boats, for pleasure and commercial use. Wooden boats form the majority of his work, due to his background and inclination. He does a limited business in stock plans but prefers working on new ideas. Inquiries from potential builders are welcome.

L.E. Geary

Inquire for price and availability of plans.

Smithsonian Institution
Div. of Trans./NMAH 5010/MRC 628
Washington, DC 20560

Frederick C. Geiger

Inquire for price and availability of plans.

Mystic Seaport Museum
Ships Plans Division
Mystic, CT 06355
203-572-5360

Henry Gielow

Inquire for price and availability of plans.

Maine Maritime Museum
963 Washington Ave.
Bath, ME 04333
207-443-1316

Mystic Seaport Museum
Ships Plans Division
Mystic, CT 06355
203-572-5360

Thomas C. Gillmer, Naval Architect, Inc.

Thomas C. Gillmer
300 State St.
Annapolis, MD 21403
410-268-2105

Tom Gillmer began to offer wooden boat designs professionally in 1946. His primary employment until 1968 was teaching naval architecture at the U.S. Naval Academy. The Gillmer firm currently has a file of designs for conventionally built wooden boats from 23' to 120'. Proposals for custom design and consultation are welcome.

Glen-L Marine Designs

Barry Witt
9152 Rosecrans/WBD
Bellflower, CA 90706-2138
310-630-6258 Fax: 310-630-6280

Design catalog available for $4.00.

Glen-L specializes in plans, full-sized patterns, and frame kits especially for

amateur boatbuilders. The 168-page catalog features over 200 designs, 7' to 55' for sail, power, and oar, and also includes a free boatbuilding supplies catalog. Designs are available for plywood, stitch-and-glue, fiberglass, steel, and aluminum construction.

Gougeon Brothers, Inc.

J.R. Watson
100 Patterson Ave.
Bay City, MI 48706
517-684-7286 Fax: 517-684-1287

Design catalog available.

Designs for cold-molded construction. Two catamarans, two prams, a daysailer, and a dory. Wing mast designs.

J.F. Gregory, Yacht Designer & Marine Surveyor

J.F. (Joe) Gregory
301 Janis Dr.
Yorktown, VA 23692
804-898-5329

Gregory is no longer actively designing boats, but his earlier plans for Chesapeake Bay-type deadrise sailing craft may be available. Inquire for details. Boats are designed for wood construction, centerboard or keel, self-bailing cockpits, and accommodations to suit hull length. Specializes in skipjack and bugeye rigs.

John L. Hacker

Inquire for price and availability of plans.

Mariners' Museum
100 Museum Drive
Newport News, VA 23606
804-595-0368

Cyrus Hamlin, N.A.

Cyrus Hamlin
Box 67
Kennebunk, ME 04043
207-985-4520 Fax: same

Some design data sheets available, mostly for sailing yachts.

Pleasure craft: Specializing in sail, but will also do power craft. Glued-strip is preferred method of construction—particularly for amateurs.

Fishing vessels: Computer program developed for determining best size and configurations for maximum efficiency of fishing vessels. Wood, steel, or aluminum construction.

William H. Hand, Jr.

Write for price and availability of plans.

Hart Nautical Collections, MIT Museum
265 Massachusetts Ave.
Cambridge, MA 02139
617-253-5942 Fax: 617-258-9107

Ken Hankinson Associates

Ken Hankinson
P.O. Box 2551WX
La Habra, CA 90631
310-947-1241

Design catalog available for $5.00.

Boat plans, patterns, and kits especially for amateur builders. Sailboats, power-boats, and rowboats from 8' to 67'. All wood methods including sheet-plywood, stitch-and-glue, cold-molded, strip-plank, carvel, and lapstrake, as well as aluminum, steel, and one-off fiberglass. Catalog includes new classic replica mahogany runabouts featuring modern construction methods.

John G. Hanna Designs

Helen Hanna Brown
30 Winchester Rd. #83
Goleta, CA 93117
805-968-5945

John Hanna designed the well-known 30' double-ended Tahiti ketch and the 36' Carol. Plans for these and other designs are available.

Robert G. Henry

Inquire for price and availability of plans.

Chesapeake Bay Maritime Museum
P.O. Box 636
St. Michaels, MD 21633
410-745-2916

Herreshoff Designs

Halsey C. Herreshoff
18 Burnside St., P.O. Box 450
Bristol, RI 02809
401-253-5000 Fax: 401-253-6222

Designers of custom and production yachts, from which 10,000 boats have built built. Herreshoff Designs special-izes in high-performance sail and diesel-powered yachts. Halsey C. Herreshoff brings a remarkable heritage, educa-tion, and experience to the process of original design for racing or cruising.

L. Francis Herreshoff

LFH Plans — Elizabeth Vaughn
P.O. Box 613
Santa Rosa, CA 95402

Inquire for price list or information on specific designs.

Many of L. Francis Herreshoff's classic designs are available. In lieu of a catalog, please refer to Herreshoff's book, *Sensible Cruising Designs*, published by International Marine Publishing Co. Plans may be viewed at Mystic Seaport Museum. All inquiries and purchases are mail order from LFH Plans.

N.G. Herreshoff and Herreshoff Mfg. Co.

Write for price and availability of plans.

Hart Nautical Collections, MIT Museum
265 Massachusetts Ave.
Cambridge, MA 02139
617-253-5942 Fax: 617-258-9107

Lyle C. Hess Designs

5911 E. Spring St. #360
Long Beach, CA 90808

Though Lyle Hess is retired and no longer doing custom-design work, plans are available for his earlier-designed cut-ters in lengths of 24'7", 26', 30', 32', and 40'. Study plans are $10.00 per design.

Don Hill River Boats

Don Hill
6690 Main St.
Springfield, OR 97478
503-747-7430

Design catalog available.

Main business is the sale of plans and kits for the McKenzie River Boat. The McKenzie is a dory that has been modi-fied for white-water rivers. It also will except a 7 ½-hp long shaft outboard for use on lakes.

Hill Family Boatbuilding Co.

Tom Hill
RR #1, Box 2310
Huntington, VT 05462
802-434-2532

Design catalog available.

Designer and builder of small craft to 30', and author of *Ultralight Boatbuilding*. Specializes in the design of small boats for the glued-lapstrake-plywood method of construction.

Henry R. Hinckley & Co.

Mystic Seaport Museum
Ships Plans Division
Mystic, CT 06355
203-572-5360

Inquire for plans availability; some restrictions may apply.

Designs for wooden boats and fiberglass hulls not in production are at Mystic Sea-port. For all other plans, contact: Henry R. Hinckley & Co., Shore Rd., Southwest Harbor, ME 04679. Phone 207-244-5531.

Russell D. Hohmann, Boatbuilder & Designer

Russ Hohmann
RR #1, Beaver Point Rd.
Fulford Harbour, BC, V0S 1C0 Canada
604-653-9419 Fax: 604-656-2581

Practice has encompassed both power and sailing yachts, ranging in size from tenders and pulling boats to ocean-going vessels. Designs for commercial fishing vessels as well. Although spe-cializing in wood construction tech-niques, Hohmann is also experienced in design for GRP, aluminum, and steel.

H.S. Boats/Boat & Sport Boat Plans

Jerome MacDermott
1022 Farmersville Rd.
Mount Vernon, IN 47620
812-838-6855

Plans for three sport boats: a 14' utility-type inboard; a 14', 16', or 18' flat-bot-tomed ski boat; a 21' V-bottomed sport boat. Construction is fiberglass over wood.

Kurt Hughes Sailing Designs

Kurt Hughes
612-1/2 West McGraw St.
Seattle, WA 98119
206-284-6346 Fax: 206-283-4106

Design catalog available.

Catamarans and trimarans for cruising, racing, and charter. A multihull design office featuring catamaran and trimaran designs using wood-epoxy as an engi-neering material. The latest wood-composite technology is specified, combining rapid-build strategies with efficient structural systems and high performance.

C. Raymond Hunt Associates, Inc.

John H. Deknatel, President
69 Long Wharf
Boston, MA 02110
617-742-5669 Fax: 617-742-6354

For over 30 years, Hunt Associates has designed powerboats for wood construction. Designs are available for cruising boats from 22′ to 63′, and for sportfishing boats from 35′ to 55′. Most recent design is a 40′ traditional-style offshore runabout for the GarWood Boat Company.

Island Canoe

Tena Doan
3566 W. Blakely Ave. NE
Bainbridge Island, WA 98110
206-842-5997

Plans list available.

Plans for canoes and sea kayaks. Sail plans for sailing canoes.

Michael Kasten, Marine Design

Michael Kasten
P.O. Box 1512
Port Townsend, WA 98368
206-385-6401 Fax: Call first

Study plan list available.

Traditional, ocean-cruising designs in wood, plywood, and metal. Lengths from 7′ to 60′. Gaff rig a specialty; partial to schooners. Custom design service.

Kaufman Design, Inc.

Mike Kaufman, Ken Court, and
Hal Whitacre
222 Severn Ave., P.O. Box 4219
Annapolis, MD 21403
410-263-8900 Fax: 410-263-8923

Kaufman Design, Inc. has been in business for over 20 years, designing beautifully engineered sail and power vessels of sizes ranging from 12′ to 200′. Their design expertise includes engineering in all forms of wood construction, composites, steel, and aluminum.

King Boat Works

Graeme King
P.O. Box 234
Putney, VT 05346
802-387-5373

Design and construction of rowing shells and boats for racing, exercise, and pleasure.

Bruce King Yacht Design, Inc.

Bruce King
Newcastle Square, P.O. Box 599
Newcastle, ME 04553
207-563-1186 Fax: 207-563-1189

Bruce Kirby, Inc./Norwalk Islands Sharpies

Bruce Kirby
213 Rowayton Ave.
Rowayton, CT 06853
203-853-1899 Fax: 203-853-1298

Bruce Kirby, Inc. designs embrace a variety of craft, from the Laser to AMERICA's Cup contenders, IOR racers, and performance cruisers. Norwalk Islands Sharpies is a line of shallow coastal cruisers designed by Bruce Kirby, Inc. Models range from 18′ to 31′, and work is progressing on larger designs.

Wm. Daniel Knott

Wm. Daniel Knott
P.O. Box 272
Barnstable, MA 02630-0272
508-362-3159

Designer of 36′ schooner ARIES and other traditional and utilitarian craft. Inquire regarding availability of plans.

James S. Krogen & Co., Inc.

James S. Krogen, President
799 Brickell Plaza, Suite 701
Miami, FL 33131
305-577-3455 Fax: 305-577-6062

This company has been designing boats, yachts, and small ships since 1960 and is experienced in all building materials. Several stock designs available in wood from 15′ to 65′ in both sail and power. Most are cruising designs.

Louis L. Kromholz

Inquire for price and availability of plans.

Mystic Seaport Museum
Ships Plans Division
Mystic, CT 06355
203-572-5360

F. D. Lawley

Inquire for price and availability of plans.

Mystic Seaport Museum
Ships Plans Division
Mystic, CT 06355
203-572-5360

George Lawley and Son

Hart Nautical Collections, MIT Mus.
265 Massachusetts Ave.
Cambridge, MA 02139
617-253-5942 Fax: 617-258-9107

1910-1940 Lawley designs. Write for plans price and availability.

Spencer H. Lincoln–Naval Architect

Spencer H. Lincoln
P.O. Box 12
Brooklin, ME 04616
207-359-8837

Loon Kayaks

Chip Chandler
HCR 32, Box 253
Sebasco Estates, ME 04565-9519
207-389-1565

Design catalog available.

Chip designs well-tracking, touring sea kayaks for large river, lake, and ocean use. There are four strip-plank designs in plan form, for construction with wood, fiberglass, and epoxy; three singles and one family double, tested in rugged conditions. Plans package includes full-sized forms and multi-page text.

F. K. Lord

Inquire for price and availability of plans.

Mystic Seaport Museum
Ships Plans Division
Mystic, CT 06355
203-572-5360

Lucander Designs

Nils Lucander
P.O. Box 7752
Tacoma, WA 98407
206-752-6528

Design list and individual data sheets available.

"When fiberglass first appeared I had an ad picturing snow-covered trees, captioned: Out of the trees and into the water. I still believe wood is the most pleasing material. I offer 20 designs, the latest a near 100′ special dive vessel currently under construction, strip-planked in Douglas-fir."

Alan Lutz Yacht Design

Alan E. Lutz, N.A.
15 Chagnon Lane
Hudson, NH 03051
603-883-4182

Specializes in small craft design and consulting for amateur and professional builders. Stock and custom designs available. Developed-surface plywood hulls, including stitch-and-glue, are a specialty. Computer-faired offsets and patterns can be provided utilizing state-of-the-art CAD Systems.

Charles G. MacGregor

Inquire for price and availability of plans.

Peabody & Essex Museum
East India Square
Salem, MA 01970
617-745-1876

MacNaughton Associates, Inc.

Thomas A. MacNaughton
P.O. Box 190
Eastport, ME 04631
207-853-6049   Fax: same

Design catalog available.

Best known for designing in wood, MacNaughton Associates design yachts and commercial craft and, most often, serious cruising vessels. They supply scantlings rules for all-wood construction types to designers and builders worldwide. The firm designs, builds, and repairs boats all on the same premises. They also are running the Yacht Design School. Advice is free.

Marine Design Inc.

Joseph F. Hack
5418 Trade Winds Rd.
New Bern, NC 28560
919-633-2806

Designer of 36' Periwinkle sloop, featured in *WoodenBoat* No. 65. Company is primarily involved in the design of commercial towing vessels, but has designed a few wooden yachts as well.

John Marples Multihull Designs

John Marples
4530 S.E. Firmont Dr.
Port Orchard, WA 98366
206-871-5634   Fax: same

Design catalog available.

Sailing vessels to 64', USCG-certified vessels for sail and power. Marples has expertise as a builder, surveyor, and designer.

Roger Marshall, Inc.

Roger Marshall
44 Fort Wetherill Rd.
Jamestown, RI 02835
407-423-1400   Fax: 401-423-2322

Design catalog available.

Company's latest wooden boat, the 47' sloop LUCAYO, was launched in June 1993 at Brooklin Boat Yard, Brooklin, Maine. The WEST System hull is mahogany with a laid teak deck. LUCAYO's arrangement was designed to suit a couple, with a walk-in engineroom and three staterooms. Many other designs in lengths from 15' to 54' are available for wood construction.

David P. Martin–Naval Architect

David P. Martin
306-23rd St.
Brigantine, NJ 08203
609-266-8950

Design catalog available.

Custom and stock wooden boat designs for power and sail, 16' to 100'.

Middle Path Boats

André de Bardelaben
Box 8881
Pittsburgh, PA 15221
412-247-4860

Design catalog available.

Middle Path Boats specializes in high-performance human-powered cruising craft. For two decades, their extensive line of lightweight (32-125 lbs) wood-epoxy composite canoes and rowing craft have distinguished themselves on America's lakes, rivers, and bays. Write for information on their award-winning designs.

Monfort Associates

Platt Monfort
RR #2, Box 416
Wiscasset, ME 04578
207-882-5504

Brochure of 18 designs available for $2.00.

Ultralight airplanes inspired the innovation of GEODESIC AIROLITE® boats, a new dimension in lightweight cartop boating. The tough, basketlike framework is braced with Kevlar roving, then covered with heat-shrunk airplane Dacron. Interesting, simple, low-cost techniques provide enjoyment while introducing people to boatbuilding. Designs for canoes, dinghies, and a Whitehall.

C.D. Mower

Inquire for price and availability of plans.

Mystic Seaport Museum
Ships Plans Division
Mystic, CT 06355
203-572-5360

Gordon Munro

Write for price and availability of plans.

Hart Nautical Collections, MIT
   Museum
265 Massachusetts Ave.
Cambridge, MA 02139
617-253-5942   Fax: 617-258-9107

Charles Neville Associates

Charles Neville
223 Broadway
Centreville, MD 21617
410-758-1891   Fax: 410-758-3724

Design catalog available.

Charles Neville Associates design cruising yachts and commercial vessels up to 100'. Specialties include motorsailers, displacement and semi-displacement speed motoryachts, and power catamarans. Materials include wood and wood composite, metal and fiberglass. Custom design service.

Dick Newick

Dick Newick
5 Shepherds Way
Kittery Point, ME 03905
207-439-3768   Fax: 207-439-8591

Design catalog available.

Thirty-seven years' intensive experience with all types of multihulls—designing them, building them, and sailing them. Dick knows what works and how to make it work better. Emphasizing buildable, high-performance seaworthiness; but luxury accommodations can be had if budget allows. Study plans $15.00; mostly trimarans, 23' to 60', wood-epoxy, 'glass-sheathed construction.

K. Aage Nielsen

Inquire for price and availability of plans.

Peabody & Essex Museum
East India Square
Salem, MA 01970
617-745-1876

Northrup Boat Works

Bruce Northrup
224110 N.W. Gilkison
Scappoose, OR 97056
503-226-6822

Company has been designing and building traditional wooden watercraft since 1969, using materials and techniques which would not have seemed out of place one hundred years ago. Drawing on the rich historical heritage of North American and European oar- and sail-powered working craft, Northrup is committed to re-creating objects of utility and beauty, from the prosaic to the exotic.

Tracy O'Brien Marine Design

Tracy O'Brien
156 Bunker Creek Rd.
Chehalis, WA 98532
206-748-4089 Fax: 206-748-6455

Design catalog available for $3.00.

Known for his detailed and easy-to-follow construction drawings and instruction manuals, Tracy O'Brien has over 10 years of design and construction experience, and has authored more than two dozen articles on boatbuilding and design. He does stock and custom designs in taped-seam plywood for oar, power, and sail, under 30'.

Opus Custom Craft

Gary Ungarean
P.O. Box 1701
Framingham, MA 01701
508-620-9002

Design, engineering, and manufacturing of performance and classic sailing craft and accessories. Engineering and fabrication of performance foils and masts. Industry consulting.

George Owen

Write for price and availability of plans.

Hart Nautical Collections, MIT
    Museum
265 Massachusetts Ave.
Cambridge, MA 02139
617-253-5942 Fax: 617-258-9107

A.C. Paine and Associates

Art Paine
P.O. Box 33
Bernard, ME 04612
207-244-5845

Art Paine is a creative boatbuilder, who occasionally is asked to both design and build/oversee a yacht. Inventor of "Nova Keel," internal chassis, mid-seaming, and a pioneer of jettisonable ballast. Designer of TWO BITS, PAINE MONOMARAN, and wooden B.O.C. contender AIRFORCE.

C.W. Paine Yacht Design, Inc.

Chuck Paine
P.O. Box 763
Camden, ME 04843
207-236-2166 Fax: 207-236-4108

Many yachtsmen, unable to locate their ultimate yacht on the market, turn to C.W. Paine Yacht Design, Inc. to design and oversee custom construction. The firm collaborates with boatbuilders world-wide in composite, aluminum, and laminated-wood construction. With over 1,000 yachts afloat, the company's expertise is well proven, and given sufficent resources, a client's boat can become a masterpiece.

Parker Marine Enterprises

Reuel B. Parker
Box 3547
Fort Pierce, FL 34948
407-489-2191

Catalog of Cruising Sailboat Designs, $10.00; *Catalog of Sharpie Designs*, $10.00.

Parker Marine Enterprises specializes in the adaptation of traditional American working craft for modern cold-molded wood construction. Books available by Reuel Parker are *The New Cold-Molded Boatbuilding* and *The Sharpie Book*.

H.H. Payson Co.

H.H. Payson
Pleasant Beach Rd.
South Thomaston, ME 04858
207-594-7587

Design catalog available for $5.00.

Plans for 36 Instant Boats designed by Phil Bolger. Catboats, skiffs, dories, dinghies, schooners. Boat plans and "how-to" books.

Robert H. Perry Yacht Designers, Inc.

Robert H. Perry
6400 Seaview Ave. N.W.
Seattle, WA 98107
206-789-7212 Fax: 206-789-7214

A progressive naval architecture practice specializing in yachts tailored to the client's needs and personality. Past designs include the Valiant 40, the 70' ultralight MERIDIAN, and STEALTH CHICKEN, the latest IMS cruiser/racer. Firm is interested in developing performance technologies to suit cruising and racing designs.

Murray G. Peterson Associates, Inc.

William M. Peterson, N.A.
Jones Cove, HC 64, Box 700
South Bristol, ME 04568-9319
207-644-8100 Fax: same

Designers of sail and power vessels for over 60 years, specializing in custom designs in wood and steel, with emphasis on traditional quality, experienced supervision, sound engineering, and detailed drafting.

Tom Pfeffer Marine

Tom Pfeffer
3 Timberlane Dr.
Pennington, NJ 08534
609-737-1569

Study information available for $5.00.

Designs for modern sailboats to 25'. "Instant" one-off wood-epoxy construction. Recognized in *Cruising World* design competitions. Plans for 12' "Instant" sharpie; 19' soft-chined centerboarder with amazing accommodations; 24' "Instant" multi-chined monohull catketch rocket with buoyant beam keels; 24' soft-chined keel/centerboarder.

Franklin G. Post

Inquire for price and availability of plans.

Mystic Seaport Museum
Ships Plans Division
Mystic, CT 06355
203-572-5360

Tom Potter & Associates

Tom Potter
101 Mount Hope Ave.
Jamestown, RI 02835
401-423-1397
(continues)

(Tom Potter & Associates, continued)
Inquire about availability of catalog.

Custom and stock designs; displacement hulls only. Past clients include Bristol Yachts, Ryder Corporation. Over 30 years' experience in yachting industry (semi-retired).

Philip L. Rhodes

Inquire for price and availability of plans.

Mystic Seaport Museum
Ships Plans Division
Mystic, CT 06355
203-572-5360

James P. Richardson

James P. Richardson
Island Rd.
Essex, MA 01929
508-768-6429

Inventive designs for experienced yachtsmen. Specializing in simple, swift, and seaworthy shoal-draft boats including sharpies, trimarans, and proas — 6' to 60', primarily wood.

Raymond H. Richards, N.A., M.E.

Ray Richards
P.O. Box 3271
Newport Beach, CA 92663
714-642-6592 Fax: 714-642-5433

Registered Professional Engineer, with 40 years' experience. Original designs for commercial and pleasure vessels, for power and sail. Modification and restoration design and consultation. Lines-taking and delineation of classic and historic vessels.

Arthur Robb

Inquire for price and availability of plans.

Mystic Seaport Museum
Ships Plans Division
Mystic, CT 06355
203-572-5360

Bruce Roberts Ltd.

Dane Goodson
836 Ritchie Hwy. #19
P.O. Box 1086W
Severna Park, MD 21146
410-544-4311 Fax: 410-544-8228

Design catalog available.

Free catalog of boatbuilding designs for steel, including radius chine, aluminum, fiberglass and wood-epoxy. Sail and

power 20' to 70'. Huge range of designs, all with full-sized patterns and scale plans. Technical support during construction included with purchase of plans.

B.A. Rosenberg Boat Designs

Bernard A. Rosenberg
3110 Peninsula Rd. #629
Oxnard, CA 93035-4221
805-985-1408

Stock plans for a wooden rowing pram with bright finish. Intended for the first-time builder with only a few hand tools. The plumb-ended dory-type construction is strong and uses no plywood or fiberglass. A simple design for a handsome, easy-rowing wooden boat for the home builder.

J.H. Rushton

Inquire for price and availability of plans.

Adirondack Museum
Blue Mtn. Lake, NY 12812
518-352-7312

Schaffer & Associate

Dennis Schaffer
P.O. Box 568
Milton, MA 02186
617-849-1855 Fax: same

Schaffer designs in a variety of hull materials, including wood and wood composites. He works with a completely computerized system and specializes in sailboat designs for non-professional builders. Consultation is available on an hourly basis.

Henry A. Scheel

Inquire for price and availability of plans.

Mystic Seaport Museum
Ships Plans Division
Mystic, CT 06355
203-572-5360

Carl Schumacher, Naval Architects

Carl Schumacher
1815 Clement Ave.
Alameda, CA 94501
510-523-2580 Fax: 510-865-1989

This firm was begun in 1977. Since then, they have established a reputation for designing performance yachts, both racing and cruising, with style and elegance. Have proven capabilities to handle the variety from the traditional

Alerion-Express to lightweight Santa Cruz-style speedsters such as the Express Line.

Charles L. Seabury

Inquire for price and availability of plans.

Mystic Seaport Museum
Ships Plans Division
Mystic, CT 06355
203-572-5360

Sea Sled Corp.

Inquire for price and availability of plans.

Mystic Seaport Museum
Ships Plans Division
Mystic, CT 06355
203-572-5360

Shell Boats

Fred Shell
RD #2, Box 289C
St. Albans, VT 05478
802-524-9645

Design catalog available.

Plans are available for both monohulls and trimarans in lengths from 7' to 28'. All designs utilize the glued-lapstrake-plywood building method. Shell strives for simplicity of construction, light weight, durability, and low cost. Plans are suitable for amateur and professional builders.

Walt Simmons/Duck Trap Woodworking

Walter J. Simmons
P.O. Box 88
Lincolnville Beach, ME 04849
207-789-5363 Fax: 207-789-5124

Design catalog available for $2.00.

Designs for traditional small craft such as wherries and double-enders. Plans have been drawn with the needs of non-professionals in mind, and there are companion books detailing the building process.

Smaalders Yacht Designs

Mark Smaalders
P.O. Box 61493
Honolulu, HI 96839
808-941-1321

Design catalog available.

Specializing in classic designs for wooden construction—carvel, strip, and cold-molded. Stock designs include 26' cutter WYNFALL (*WoodenBoat* No. 102), as well as 29′ and 32′ versions, and 35′ schooner EIRENE. Custom designs for sensible and affordable cruising boats are also available.

Howard M. Smith, Jr.

Inquire for price and availability of plans.

Mystic Seaport Museum
Ships Plans Division
Mystic, CT 06355
203-572-5360

Eliot Spalding, N.A.

Eliot Spalding
Box 22
South Freeport, ME 04078-0022
207-865-6691

This company has been designing, building, and surveying boats for over 40 years. In that time, it has turned out plans for wooden boats ranging from an 8′ dinghy to a 95′ schooner, with just about everything in between—power and sail, pleasure and commercial.

Sparkman & Stephens, Inc.

Inquire for price and availability of plans.

Mystic Seaport Museum
Ships Plans Division
Mystic, CT 06355
203-572-5360

Sponberg Yacht Design Inc.

Eric W. Sponberg, N.A.
P.O. Box 661
Newport, RI 02840
401-849-7730 Fax: 401-849-7898

Newsletter and stock plan brochure available.

SYDI specializes in cruising sailing yachts, offshore and round-the-world racing sailboats, yachts for adventuresome voyages, power vessels, and luxury motoryachts. Their Corroboree design, a wood-epoxy, strip-plank and veneer sloop, was named one of the 100 Greatest North American sailboats by *Sail* magazine.

George H. Stadel, Jr. & Sons, Inc.

Bill Stadel
1088 Shippan Ave.
Stamford, CT 06902
203-324-2610 Fax: 203-961-0351

Design catalog available.

George H. Stadel Jr. began his design career in 1928. He designed traditional sail and power boats, both yachts and commercial vessels. His boats have navigated the waters in locations found all over the world. George H. Stadel, Jr. & Sons, Inc. continues this tradition, providing traditional and contemporary designs for all purposes.

Robert W. Stephens Wooden Boats

Bob Stephens
P.O. Box 464
Searsport, ME 04974
207-548-0129

Design catalog available.

Bob Stephens specializes in modern wood-epoxy boats under 30′ in length. His designs display traditional elegance of line, combined with clean, sensible construction. An experienced boatbuilder himself, Stephens appreciates the importance of clear, easily read plans. He offers custom work at attractive rates, and a catalog of stock plans.

W. P. Stephens

Inquire for price and availability of plans.

Mystic Seaport Museum
Ships Plans Division
Mystic, CT 06355
203-572-5360

Robert M. Steward

Robert M. Steward
4335 Lucera Rd.
Jacksonville, FL 32244
904-387-0211

In addition to custom work, Bob has stock plans for the popular 11′3″ flat-bottomed rowing skiff Susan, hundreds of which have been built; the 19′6″ arc-bottomed centerboard daysailer Triton; and the 18′7″ inboard-powered launch Barbara Anne. Descriptions available.

Stimson Marine, Inc.

David Stimson
RR #1, Box 524
Boothbay, ME 04537
207-633-7252 Fax: 207-633-6058

Design catalog available.

Stimson's education in boat design and construction was acquired through Merton Long, an old-timer from Maine who specialized in catboats. He was

also influenced by Pete Culler's work. He's especially fond of elegant but affordable small craft of traditional wood construction, and skin-on-frame boats. Favorite types are catboats, sharpies, skiffs, kayaks, double-paddle canoes, and dories.

Albert Strange

Inquire for price and availability of plans.

Mystic Seaport Museum
Ships Plans Division
Mystic, CT 06355
203-572-5360

Strayer Yacht Design

Charles M. Strayer
1744 Oak Grove Circle
Green Cove Springs, FL 32043
904-284-7964

Design catalog available for $5.00.

Strayer Yacht Design specializes in the design of sailing craft from dinghies to bluewater cruisers. Stock plans are available and include computer-lofted, full-sized patterns. Custom design service also available in hull material of your choice.

Harry V. Sucher

Smithsonian Institution
Div. of Trans./NMAH 5010/MRC 628
Washington, DC 20560

His work is included in a 250-page catalog of plans available for $10.00, ppd.

Swan Design & Swan Boats

Ken Swan
P.O. Box 267
Hubbard, OR 97032
503-982-5062

Catalog of stock designs available for $7.00.

Plans for boats from 11′ to 26′. Custom designing is limited to skiffs for the amateur and professional builder.

Tanton, Inc.

Yves-Marie de Tanton
America's Cup Ave., P.O. Box 270
Newport, RI 02840
401-847-4112 Fax: 401-849-8835

Design catalog available.

Designers for over a quarter-century of
(continues)

(Tanton, Inc., continued)
boats in all sizes, ranges, and materials, with emphasis on seaworthiness, character, personality, and special interest.

Tender Craft Boat Shop Inc.

Barbara Williams
284 Brock Ave.
Toronto, ON, M6K 2M4 Canada
416-531-2941 Fax: 416-323-0992

Design catalog available.

The Tender Craft Boat Shop Inc. is a production boat building shop specializing in small strip-planked craft to 25'. Many of these designs are available to the amateur builder and include canoes, tenders, sailing dinghies, rowing skiffs, and more recently, 12', 16', and 18' electric inboard launches.

Rollin Thurlow

Northwoods Canoe Company
336 Range Rd.
Atkinson, ME 04426
207-564-3667

Canoes designed by Thurlow are based on historic bark or canvas canoes. Because of their excellence, Thurlow has tried to preserve their style, grace, and function. Canoes worked on are generally but not limited to 10' to 20'.

Trailcraft

Ron Overstreet
405 State
El Dorado, KS 67042
316-321-9538

Design catalog available.

Complete plans, patterns, and step-by-step instructions for a 16' wood-canvas canoe or kayak. Ideal family or group project.

Tri-Star Trimarans/Catamarans

Ed Horstman, N.A.
P.O. Box 286
Venice, CA 90291
310-396-6154 Fax: same

Design catalog available for $9.00.

Ed Horstman BSAE. His 1961 Tri-Star 40 was the first trimaran to race in the 1966 multihull Transpacific Race and won 2nd place. Tri-Star 38 was the first trimaran to sail around Cape Horn, 1979. Custom designs or 55 stock trimaran/

catamaran designs, 14' to 104'. Double-diagonal sheet-plywood or cold-molded construction. Comprehensive plans, full-sized patterns, easily built by amateurs.

Tucker Yacht Design

Tom Tucker
P.O. Box 328
Port Townsend, WA 98368
206-385-7346

Design, construction, and repair of wooden boats since 1968, specializing in cruising sailboats. Most popular design is 21' gaff sloop LYRA, published in *WoodenBoat* No. 10. Most recent design is the 39' strip-planked/cold-molded ketch ALAGRIA.

Johan Valentijn Inc.

Johan Valentijn
80 Ayrault St.
Newport, RI 02840
401-849-6926 Fax: 401-849-6448

Design and engineering services for all methods of construction. Power and sailing yachts 60' and over.

Van De Stadt Design—USA

Graeme Webber
1/1200 St. Joseph St.
Carolina Beach, NC 28428
910-458-6384 Fax: 910-458-3040

Design catalog available for $10.00; study plans available for all designs.

Van De Stadt Design offers a range of stock designs for modern wood-epoxy sailboats from 15' to 50', generally cruiser/racers. Each set of plans is very comprehensive and well detailed, with full materials list. Full-sized Mylar mold patterns eliminate lofting.

Bob Wallstrom

Delta Marine Small Craft Design & Survey, Inc.
P.O. Box 828
Blue Hill, ME 04614
207-374-5404 Fax: same

Bob Wallstrom has over 30 years' experience in the design of wooden vessels. Cruising designs for sail and power, from 18' to 55', traditional in form, detailed in execution. Sorry, no catalog! Please inquire with your needs.

Winthrop L. Warner

Inquire for price and availability of plans.

Mystic Seaport Museum
Ships Plans Division
Mystic, CT 06355
203-572-5360

J. Murray Watts

Inquire for price and availability of plans.

Mystic Seaport Museum
Ships Plans Division
Mystic, CT 06355
203-572-5360

John H. Wells

Inquire for price and availability of plans.

Mystic Seaport Museum
Ships Plans Division
Mystic, CT 06355
203-572-5360

Chris White Designs

Chris White
48 Bush St.
South Dartmouth, MA 02748
508-997-0059 Fax: same

Design catalog available for $20. *The Cruising Multihull* is also available for $30.

Since 1978, Chris White has specialized in the design of high-performance cruising catamarans and trimarans. Stock plans are available for 20 different designs ranging in size from 15' to 65'. Construction is wood-epoxy or fiber-epoxy composite. Many plans are suitable for amateur construction. Several designs are USCG-approved for charter. Custom design projects always welcome.

Joel White

Brooklin Boat Yard, Inc.
P.O. Box 143
Brooklin, ME 04616
207-359-2236 Fax: 207-359-8871

While much of his design work is in small craft, Joel occasionally does larger custom designs, such as the 74' cruising ketch now under construction. He has a few stock designs, mostly cruising sailboats from 28' to 45'.

Wildfire Racing Team

Michael Sternberg
1206 S.E. Astorwood Place
Stuart, FL 34994
407-286-1925

Designers and builders of custom one-off powerboats, specializing in catamaran hulls. With extensive offshore racing experience, Wildfire designs have passed the ultimate test for efficiency and strength. The Wildfire Team draws on this background to design custom racing, pleasure, or fishing boats for cold-molded or other methods of construction.

Fenwick Williams

Inquire for price and availability of plans.

Peabody & Essex Museum
East India Square
Salem, MA 01970
617-745-1876

Windward Designs

Karl Stambaugh
794 Creek View Rd.
Severna Park, MD 21146
410-544-9553

Design catalog available.

Designs you can build for fun and adventure including skiffs, sharpies, and many other cruising designs. Sail and power 8′ to 48′. Custom designs are a speciality—inquire for further information.

Ralph E. Winslow

Inquire for price and availability of plans.

Mystic Seaport Museum
Ships Plans Division
Mystic, CT 06355
203-572-5360

Charles W. Wittholz, N.A.

Mrs. Estelle A. Wittholz
100 Williamsburg Dr.
Silver Spring, MD 20901
301-593-7711

The Catboat Design Booklet is available for $4.00, ppd; *Motor Yachts Catalog* for $6.50, ppd.

Charles Wittholz had over 50 years' experience as a naval architect, and is perhaps most well known for his trawler-yachts and plywood catboats. His designs have been built by amateur and professional builders alike. Plans are nicely detailed and available through his wife, Estelle Wittholz.

The WoodenBoat Store

P.O. Box 78
Brooklin, ME 04616
1-800-273-SHIP (7447) Fax: 207-359-8920

Catalogs available: *Fifty Wooden Boats*, $11.95; *Thirty Wooden Boats*, $10.95.

Plans by some of the best designers of this century for boats ranging in size from a 7′ pram to a 41′ schooner. Canoes, tenders, pulling boats, daysailers, powerboats, and cruising sailboats. Designs selected for their beauty, construction methods, and superior performance. Plans for both the amateur and professional builder utilizing plank-on-frame, plywood, cold-molded, strip-planked, or lapstrake-plywood construction.

Thomas Wylie Design Group

Tom Wylie
86 Ridgecrest
Canyon, CA 94516
510-376-7338 Fax: 510-376-7982

Design catalog available for $25.00.

Sailing designs for strip-plank and cold-molded veneer: 37′ cutter WILD SPIRIT, 31′ cutter LOCO, and 25′ Ultralight Displacement Boat DURANGO.

Yacht Designs

Robert Reynolds
P.O. Box 898
Solomons, MD 20688
410-326-0825

Custom small craft. Small, medium, and large power craft in wood or other materials. Full-sized lofting. References/examples available.

Nelson Zimmer, Naval Architect

Nelson Zimmer
505 Maple
Marine City, MI 48039
313-765-3376

Custom designs to 150′, sail or power, in wood, aluminum, or steel (no fiberglass commissions accepted). In continuous practice since 1936. Existing plans available.

Zurn Yacht Design

Doug Zurn
P.O. Box 110
3 Beacon St.
Marblehead, MA 01945
617-639-0868 Fax: same

The consumer looking for new product development, renovation, or repair, can rely on Zurn Yacht Design for engineering-related work in every aspect of yacht design. Complete designs, keel and rudder development, rigging calculations, exterior and interior alterations, damage analysis, and system studies for cold-molded, fiberglass, and aluminum yachts.

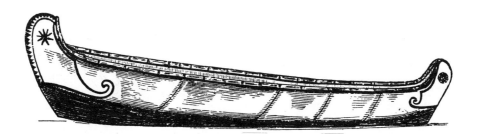

INDEX

Abrahamsson, Todd W., 11
Acadia Canoe Shop, 24
Accumar Corporation, 165
Ackland, Bob, 59
Adirondack Goodboat, 89
The Adirondack Guide Boat Shop, 89
The Adirondack Guide-Boat, 120
Ajootian, Fred, 123
Charles Akers Boatbuilding and Repair, 14
John G. Alden, Inc., 165
Alder Bay Boat Co., 142
Alder Creek Boat Works, 89
Alderette, Richard, 42
Alekna, Mike, 140
Aleut Wood & Skin Kayak, 89
Alguire, Dave, 159
Alldrin, Lance, 2
Allen, Taylor, 42
Allman, Roy, 153
Ambler Boat Works, 116
Anderson, Alan R., 70
Applegate Boatworks, 109
Apprenticeshop of Maine Maritime
    Museum, 24
Apprenticeshop of Nobleboro, 24
Apprenticeshop, Rockport (see Artisans
    School)
Arbor Vitae Canoes, 147
Arey's Pond Boatyard, 57
Argo Wood Boat Restoration, 108
Ark Works, 2
Arnotts Boat Yard, 90
Arrand, Russ, 70
The Artisans School, 24
Asay Boats, 86
Asay, Robert, 86
Aspoya Boats, 124
Atkin & Co., 165
Atkin, John, 165
Atkins, Fred, 60
Atlantic Boat Works, 57
Au Sable Riverboat Shop, 69
Avoures, Daniel, 17

Bad River Boatworks, 69
Baer, David S., 84
Baird Boat Co., Inc., 125
Baird, Ernie, 125
Baker, Brian, 70
Robert H. Baker Boats, 165
Baker's Custom Canoes & Boats, 70
Baker, W.A., 165
Bald Head Boatworks, 25
Ballentine's Boat Shop, Inc., 58
Ballentine, Stephen, 58

B & B Yacht Designs, 165
Baraboo River Canoe Co., 137
de Bardelaben, André, 112, 172
Barkdoll, Scott Ira, 75
Barker, Robert, 113
Barnes, Stephen E., 24
Barney, Morgan, 165
Baron, Walter, 65
Barrett, Tom, 103
Barrington Boat Shop, 81
Barto, Marc, 53
Bassett, Ken, 84, 165
Bates, Charles W., 8
Bates Designs Ltd., 8
Battenkill Boatworks, 90
Grant W. Bauer & Co., 165
Baxter Boat Co., 125
Baxter, David E., 125
Bayberry Creek Boatshop, Inc., 9
Bay Boats, 137
Baycrest Lodge, Marina & Yard, 154
Bayne, Mark, 117
Bay Ship and Yacht Co., 2
Beach, David D., 165
Beach Naval Architecture, 165
Beals, Barry W., 49
Beal, Willis A., 48
Bear Mountain Boat Shop, 154
Beavan, Leslie, 58
Beetle, Inc., 58
Belkov, Larry, 49
Belkov Yacht Carpentry Co., 49
Bell, Tim, 145
J.W. Beltman Woodworking, 77
Benford, Jay R., 165
Benford Design Group, 165
Benjamin, Nathaniel P., 61
Benjamin River Marine, 25
Betsie Bay Kayak, 70
Betula Canoe, 20
Bibby, Gill, 154
Biersach, Jim, 80
Bigfork Canoe Trails, 22, 78
Billings Diesel & Marine Service, Inc., 25
Billings, Harlan, 25
Bill's Business, 125
Bingham Boat Works Ltd., 70
Bingham, Joseph, 70
Biscayne Bay Boat Works, 102
Bishop, Gart, 147
Black Duck Boat Shop, 9
Black River Boats, 102
Blackwater Boatworks, 117
Blake Boatworks, 103
Blake, Bryan, 103

Blevins, Thomas, 26
Blue Streak Marine, 88
Blume, Jeffrey L., 165
Boathouse Woodworks, 90
Boat Plans International Ltd., 166
Boats, Cabinets, & Joinery, 14
The Boat Shop, 21
Boat Works, Inc., 137
The Boatwright, 125
Boessel, Ray and Christie, 78
Phil Bolger and Friends, 166
Boone, Jim, 119
Boothbay Region Boatyard, 26
Boudreau, Peter, 54
Bourquin Boats, 78
Bourquin, Jeanne, 78
Bower, Nigel, 49
Bowers, Larry B., 145
Boyd's Boats, 9
Brass Tacks Canoe Shop, 26
Bratton, Al, 113
Breen, Peter, 154
Breiby, John, 1
Breiby's Boatbuilding, 1
Brepet Holdings Inc., 154
Brewer, John S., 26
Brewer's South Freeport Marine, 26
Ted Brewer Yacht Designs Ltd., 166
Brightcraft Boats, 3
Bright Water Canoes, 10
Brightwork Boat & Leyda Lumber Co.,
    Inc., 137
Bristol Classics, 78
Bristol Services Co., 3
Brookins Boatworks Ltd., 21
Brookins, Gary W., 21
Brooklin Boat Yard, 27
Brown, Charles H., 150
Brownell Boat Yard Inc., 58
Brown, Foy W., 27
Brown, Gary, 166
Brown, Jim, 99
J.O. Brown & Son, Inc., 27
Brownstein, Carl, 134
Bryan Boatbuilding, 147
Bryan, Harold B., 147
Bryant, Paul S., 41
Budsin Wood Craft, 103
George Buehler Yacht Design, 166
Buffalo Bateaus, 119
Bullhouse Boatworks, 28
Burgess & Paine, 166
Burgess, John, 36
Burgess, Swasey and Paine, 166
Burgess, W. Starling, 166

Burke, Geoffrey, 81
Burnham, Cecil, 45
Burns, Chuck, 166
Burt's Canoes, 28
Byrnes, Graham S., 165

Cabin Boat Shop, 126
Cadillac Boat Shop, 70
Cady, Allen, 50
Calkins, George, 129, 166
Cameron, James, 90
Campbell, Hugh, 146
Camp Nominingue Inc., 163
William Cannell Boatbuilding, 28
Canoe Craft, 155
Canoes & Kayaks/Kayak Way, 126
The Canoe Shop, 14
Canoesport, 71
The Canoe Works, 28
Canonita Dories, 8
Canvasback Canoe Shop, 126
Cape Elizabeth Boat, 29
Cape Fear Community College, 103
Caretta Kayaks, 20
Carl's Canvas Canoe Care Co., 10
Carroll, Gregory C., 55
Carrying Place Canoe & Boat Works, 155
Carrying Place Boat Co., 29
Cassell, Charlie, 107
Cavanaugh, Thomas A., 66
Cayard, Stephen, 29
Cayuga Wooden Boatworks, 90
Cedar Creek Canoe, 155
Cedar Lane Boatworks, 29
Center for Wood Construction —
   S.C.C.C., 126
Center Harbor Boat, 29
Chadwick, John M., Jr., 87
Chalk, Duane J., 91
H. Chalk & Son Inc., 91
Chamcook Boat & Canoe, 147
Chance & Company, Inc., 166
Chance, Britton, Jr., 166
Chandler, Chip, 36, 171
Chapelle, Howard I., 166
Chapin, E. Barton, III, 25
Chapin, Steve, 132
Charlot, Deny, 110
Charlot Marine Works Inc., 110
Chatsick, Jim, 158
Chebeague Marine, Inc., 30
Cherubini Boat Co., Inc., 86
Cherubini, Lee, 86
Cheticamp Boatbuilders Ltd., 148
Chris-Craft Corp., 166
David Christofferson Design, 78
Clapp, Peter C., 46
Clarion Boats, 155
Clark, Bill, 3
Clark Craft, 166

Clark Custom Boats, 3
Clark, Gary, 156
Clark, John R., 167
Clark, Oliver K., 97
Classic Boat Restoration, 14
Classic Boat Works, 106
Classic Canoes, 103
Classic Marine, 106
Classic Watercraft, 71
Clear Rock Boats, 91
Clements, Gary F., 86
Clements, William, 59
Clifts Marine Sales Ltd., 156
Clipper Craft Mfg. Co. Inc., 110
Clubhouse Boatworks, 50
Clyde Craft, 4
Coastal Composites, Ltd., 50
Codega, Louis T., 166
Coe, Bob, 135
Coecles Harbor Marina & Boat-
   yard Inc., 92
Colvin, Thomas E., 167
Collins, Mike, 51
Comb, Alex, 80
Common Sense Designs, 167
CompuMarine, 167
Conanicut Marine Services, 114
Concordia Co., Inc., 59
Condon, Albert E., 167
Connecticut River Boat Works, 81
Connell, Mark, 147
Conner, Philip, 50
Consolidated Shipbuilding Corp., 167
Cook, Bill, 167
Cook, Marilyn, 99
Cook Yacht Design, 167
Coolidge, Leigh, 167
Cooper, Dexter, 120
Cooper, Douglas E., 60
Corcoran, David, 28
Cormorant Canoe and Boat Works, 149
Cornelius, Terry, 126
Correll, Thomas, 18
Cosine Boats, 167
Costa, Peter, 68
Court, Ken, 171
Covey Island Boatworks Ltd., 149
Cox & Stevens, 167
Craftworks/Electra-Ghost Canoes, 50
Cramer, Gilbert, 109
Cranberry Cove Boat, 34
Croan, Gary, 3
Crocker, Samuel Sturgis, 59
Crocker's Boat Yard, Inc., 59
Crocker, S.S., 167
Crocket, Jim, 4
Crockett Bros. Boatyard, Inc., 50
Crosby, William F., 167
Crowninshield, B.B., 167
Culler, R.D. (Pete), 167

Cunningham, Christopher, 126
Cunningham, S. Bruce, 40
Cunningham Woodworks, 126
Curtis, Don, 4
Curtis Marine, 4
Custer, Geoff, 127
Custom Canoes, 110
Custom Boat Designs, 167
Cutler, Nelson, 152
Cypress Marine Inc., 51
Cyr, Guy, 28

Dahl, Christian W., 79
Daniels, Joe, 137
Daniels, Marc, 128
Danielson, Thad, 66
Dano Canoes, 92
Dano, Donald and Pamela, 92
Dante, Bruce A., 90
Dark Ages Boatworks, 30
Darling, George, 120
Darling's Boatworks Inc., 120
Arch Davis Design, 167
Davis, Dwight, 106
Davis, Mike, 7
Davis, R.O., 168
Davis, Tony, 57
Davy, Malcolm, 5
Dawe Craft Boats, 4
Dawe, Ernie, 4
Day, Arno N., 168
Dearborn, Mike, 158
Deed, William J., 168
Delangre, Philippe, 14
Delima, Anthony, 50
Delta Marine Small Craft Design &
   Survey, 176
Denman Boat Co., 10
Denman, Ron, 10
Designautics, 168
De Silva Co., 20
De Silva, Ralph, 20
Devenny, Jay, 117
Devereaux, Henry, 168
Devlin Designing, 168
Devlin Designing Boatbuilders, 127
Devlin, Sam, 127, 168
DeVoll, Scott, 76
Diamond Boat Works Inc., 71
Antonio Dias/Marine Design &
   Construction, 92, 169
Dickes, Geoffrey, 168
Dickes Yacht Design, 168
Difede, Richard A., 119
F. J. Dion Yacht Yard, 60
Disappearing Propeller Boat Co. Ltd., 156
Dobler, Joseph C., 168
Dodington, Paul, 156
Dodson Boat Yard, 10
Doherty, Patrick, 162

Dorrer, Scott, 98
The Dory Shop, 149
Double J. Boatworks, 112
Eric Dow Boat Shop, 30
DownEast Peapods, 30
Downunder Boat Works, 5
Duck Trap Woodworking, 31, 174
Dugan Small Boat Shop, 114
Duke Marine Services Ltd., 156
Dunbar Marine Service, 127
Dunbar, Roy, 127
Dunham, Gilbert, 168
Durnford, Matt, 149
Dutch Harbor Boat Yard, 114

Eagle Harbor Boatyard, Inc., 128
East Bay Boat Works, Inc., 103
Eastport Boat Yard & Supply, 31
East/West Custom Boats, Inc., 31
Eau Galle Boat Shop, 138
Eddy, Wayne, 147
Edmonson, Mark and Nancy, 71
Ehrheart, Lee H., 129
Eldred - Cooper Boatbuilders, 60
Eldredge & Matteson Co., 168
Eldredge-McInnis, Inc., 168
ELCO — Electric Launch
   Company, Inc., 93
Elco Works, 168
Elk, Jim, 32
Elk Spar & Boat Shop, 32
Elliott, Robert, 61
Ely, Ronald R. "Ron", 104
Ely Trail Crafts, 104
Emery, George, 30
Epstein, Ed, 121
Era Past Boat, 15
Erickson, Andy, 132
Essex Boat Works, 10
European Custom Yachts Ltd., 61
Eustace, Ed, 147

Faering Design Inc., 120
Weston Farmer Associates, 168
Far North Designs, 128
Farrier, Ian, 169
Farrier Marine, 169
Farrin, Bruce A., 32
Farrin's Boatshop, 32
Feather Canoes Inc., 15
Fenger, Frederick A., 169
Fiddlehead Boatworks, 51
Five Points Inc., 93
Flagler, David, 103
Fleder, Jules, 169
Fleet Marine Inc., 128
Fleetwood Boats, 118
Fleming, Joseph W., II, 93
Fletcher Boats, 129
Fletcher, Simon, 129

Flinchum, Allen J., 51
Flyer's, 61
Flynn & Flynn Custom Boat Works, 111
Flynn, Rik, 111
Fogman, Jeffrey R., 81
Forden, Harvard, 85
Forestport Boat Co. Inc., 93
Foss, John, 39
Foster, Gregory, 145
Fournel, Jean-Pierre, 164
Fox Farm Repair Service, 72
Franklin Cedar Canoes, 32
Fraser, Aimé Ontario, 13
Fraser, Donald, 148
Frechette, Jim, 118
Freeport Skiffs, 32
Fuller, Bob, 67
Fuller, Gar. and Jean, 142
Furness, Glenn, 169

Gannon & Benjamin Marine
   Railway Inc., 61
Gannon, Ross M., 61
Gar & Wood Yacht Restorations, 142
Garden, William, 169
Gardiner Marine, Inc., 115
Gardiner, Paul D., 115
Gartside, Paul, 169
GarWood Boat Co., Inc., 94
Gaworek, Davide, 141
Geary, L.E., 169
Geiger, Frederick C., 169
Geisler, William, 118
Genchi, Bob, 20
George's Lil Shipyard, 129
G.F.C. Boats, 86
Giblin, Andy, 11
Gibson Canoe, 157
Gibson, Dan, 157
Gielow, Henry, 169
B. Giesler & Sons Limited, 157
Giles, Bill, 62
Giles Racing Hydros, 62
Gilless, Charles, 56
Gillesse, Philip, 157
Gillikin, Ricky, 103
Gillmer, Thomas C., 169
Glen-L Marine Designs, 169
Glupker, Bruce, 74
Gockel, Paul W., III, 157
Gold Coast Yachts Inc., 119
Goodall, Louis, 33
Goode, Ferdy, 138
Goudreau, Ray, 10
Gougeon Brothers, Inc., 169
Gould, Steve, 101
Grand Craft Corp., 72
Grand Mesa Boatworks, 8
Gray, Clayton, 104
Great Lakes Boat Building Co., 72

Greene Marine Inc., 33
Greene, Walter, 33
Gregory, J.F., 169
Gregory, Thomas A., 37
Greig, Eddy, 23
Griffin Boatworks, 22
Griffiths, Jim, 48
Grinnell, Gary, 62
Griswold, Mary M., 122
Grosjean, Charles, 32
Guzzwell, John, 129
Guzzwell Yachts, 129

Hack, Joseph F., 172
Hacker Craft Boat Co., 94
Hacker, John L., 169
Hadden & Stevens Boatbuilders, 33
Hafeman Boat Works, 78
Hagar, Howard, 34
Hale, Philip P., 64
Hall, Mary O., 94
Hall's Boat Corporation, 94
Hamlin, Cyrus, 169
Hammond, Jeff, 132
Hamm, William R. (Bill), 22
H & H Boatworks Inc., 34
Hand, William H., Jr., 170
Hankins, Charles, 86
Ken Hankinson Associates, 170
Hanna, Carol, 89
Hanna, Jeff, 40
John G. Hanna Designs, 170
Harbor Craft, 72
Harman, Eric, 131
Harper & Sons' Boat Sales &
   Restoration, 82
Harper, Jerry W., Sr. & Jr., 82
Hartsock, John, 167
Harvey, Robert, 155
Hatfield, Roger, 119
Hathaway Boat Shop, 94
Have Tools Will Travel, 62
Havorn Marine Services, 129
Heater, C. Ray, 111
Heisler, Cecil R., 150
Clarence R. Heisler & Son Ltd., 150
Henry, Robert G., 170
Herbert, Martin, 142
Herreshoff, N.G., 170
Herreshoff Designs, 170
Herreshoff, Halsey C., 170
Herreshoff, L. Francis, 170
Herreshoff Mfg. Co., 170
Herring Cove Marine, 150
Hesselink, Tom, 103
Lyle C. Hess Designs, 170
Heyse, Paul Jeffery, 135
Hicklin, Bill, 137
High Rock Boat Yard, 104
Don Hill River Boats, 111, 170

Hill Family Boatbuilding Co., 121, 170
Hill, Thomas J., 121, 170
Henry R. Hinckley & Co., 170
Hingham Boat Works Inc., 62
Hoban, Art, 129
Hodgdon, Timothy S., 34
Hodgdon Yachts, Inc., 34
Hogtown Bayou Boatworks, 15
Hohmann, Russell D., 170
Hollis Bros. Inc., 117
Hollis, R.B. "Bobby", 117
Holmes Boat Works, 118
Holmes, Robert C., II, 118
Holzmacher, Roger H., 95
Horn Harbor Boatworks Inc., 122
Horstman, Ed, 176
H.S. Boats/Boat & Sport Boat Plans, 170
Huckins Yacht Corp., 15
Huddlestun, Bernard P., 51
Huddlestun Cold-Molded Catboats, 51
Hughes, Cymbrid, 34
Kurt Hughes Sailing Designs, 170
Hull, Lucy W., 25
Hundley Boat Co., 118
Hundley, Byron Kibler, 118
C. Raymond Hunt Associates, Inc., 171
Hurd, Pete, 133
Hurley, Jack, 161
Huron Lagoons Marina, 106
Hvalsoe Boats, 130
Hvalsoe, Eric D., 130
Hylan, Doug, 25

Inland Yacht, 79
Int'l. Historical Watercraft Society, 51
Island Canoe, 171
Island Point Construction, 52
Island Woodworking/Cranberry
    Cove Boat, 34

Jackimovicz, Joseph, 44
James Boatworks, 52
James, Gary, 52
James, Thomas M., 100
Jechort, Dwight, 138
Jechorts' Wood Boat Works, 138
Jenkins, Roy, 38
Jenkins, Spencer R., 100
Jensen, Jim, 23
Jespersen, Bent, 143
John's Bay Boat Co., 35
Johnson, Elmer L., 73
Johnson, Marshall, 127
Johnson, Ralph F., Jr., 63
Jones Boats, 86
Jones, Debbie, 106
Jones, Emmet, 6
J.E. Jones Boat and Prop, 35
Jones, Jim, 35
Jones, Rebecca C., 123

Jones, Steve, 135
Jones, Thomas Firth, 86
Jonientz, Nadine, 128
Judson Boats, 123
Judson, David, 123
Julian, Mark, 128

Kallusch, William, 95
Kamitakahara, Harold, 141
Kass, Peter, 35
Michael Kasten, Marine Design, 171
Kaufman, Mike, 171
Kaufman Design, Inc., 171
Kaulback, Steve, 120
Kavanagh-Beltman, John, 77
Kayle, David, 143
Kearney, Brian, 96
Keele, Susan, 10
Kelley, Bill, 114
Philip A. Kendall Custom Boat-
    builders, 82
Kerns, Timothy M., 52
Ketten, Larry, 72
Keyes, Jonathan F., 29
Kiefer, Michael J., 72
The Kijik Canoe Company, 158
Kilbridge, John C., 161
Kincaid, Gary, 63
Kindervater, Eric R., 87
King Boat Works, 121, 171
Bruce King Yacht Design, Inc., 171
King, Graeme, 121, 171
Kirby, Bruce, 171
Kirkpatrick, Clyde, 4
Klondike Woodworks, 73
Knott, Wm. Daniel, 171
Knowles, Bill, 16
Knowles Boat Co., 16
Ted Knowles Shipwright Services, 143
Kohn, Seth, 68
Kolin Boat Works, 130
Kolin, Richard S., 130
Konitzky Boat Works Inc., 35
Konitzky, Gustav A., 35
Kootenay Joinery, 143
Koroknay's Marine Woodworking, 107
Koroknay, Tom, 107
Kortchmar & Willner, 95
Kortchmar, Michael, 95
Koss Klassic Boats, 73
Koss, Michael and James, 73
Krase, William, 5
Tom Krieg's Boat Shop, 96
James S. Krogen & Co., Inc., 171
Kromholz, Louis L., 171
K Squared Aeromarine Woodworks, 143
Kurz, Karl, 36

LaBelle, Lee K., 24
LaHave Marine Woodworking, 150

Lahey, Ted, 10
Lakes Region Restorations, Inc., 82
Lamar, Sam S., 14
Landing School of Boatbuilding &
    Design, 36
Langille Boat Building, 151
Langille, Ernest J., 151
LaPointe, Jack, 162
Latif, Fuat, 121
Latimer, Anthony R., 144
Latimer Marine, 144
Laughing Loon Custom Canoes &
    Kayaks, 63
Laurentian Kayaks, 79
Lavalette, Ken, 163
Lawley, F.D., 171
George Lawley and Son, 171
Lee, Doug and Linda, 39
Lee, Lance, 24
Leeman, Gary, 38
Legacy Wooden Boats, 158
Leilani Boatworks, 96
Lemon, R. Bruce, 89
Libby, Burt, 28
Liebow, M. Charles, 34
Lincoln, Spencer H., 171
Lindrooth, Dan H., 113
Lindstrom Boat Building, 144
Lindstrom, Stephen, 144
Linnell, William S., II, 29
Little, Douglas, 102
Little, John D., 37
Lockwood, John, 133
London, Peter, 144
Loon Kayaks, 171
Loon Sea Kayaks, 36
The Loon Works, 87
Lopez Marine Inc./Upright Boat
    Works, 130
Lord, F.K., 171
Lorensen, Fred, 114
Louchard, Ed, 132
Lovric's Sea Craft, 130
Lovric, Tony and Florence, 130
Lowell, Jeff, 26
Pert Lowell Co., Inc., 63
Lowell's Boat Shop, 63
Lowery, Maynard W., 53
M.W. Lowery Boat Yard, 53
Lucander, Nils, 171
Lucander Designs, 171
Ludlow Boatworks, 158
Ludlow, Philip C., 158
Lumsden, John W., 2
Alan Lutz Yacht Design, 172
Geo. Luzier Boatbuilders Inc., 16
Luzier, Homer, 16

MacAdam, Robert W., 50
MacDermott, Jerome, 170

MacGregor, Charles G., 172
Machiasport Marine Railway Co., 36
MacKenzie, Tom, 87
MacKercher, R. Scott, 73
MacKercher Antique & Classic Marine
  Specialties, 73
Mackie, Alan, 74
Mackie Boat Works, 74
Macks, Rob, 63
MacNaughton Associates, Inc., 172
MacNaughton, Thomas A., 31, 172
Maher, Kevin, 143
Mahon, Patrick J., 134
Maine Journeys Canoe, 36
Malone Boatbuilding Co., Inc., 37
Malone, Bruce, 37
Manchester Marine, 63
Marine Design & Construction, 92, 168
Marine Design Inc., 172
The Marine Exchange, 5
Marine Painting & Refinishing Co., 37
Marks, Stephen, 52
Marolina Yachts, 53
Marples, John R., 131
John Marples Multihull Designs, 172
Marshall, Roger, 172
Marshall Marine & Woodworking, 74
Marshall, Thomas F., 74
Martha's Vineyard Shipyard, Inc., 64
Martin, David P., 172
Martin, Kevin, 83
Martin, Tim, 108
Mason, Mark P., 83
Mast and Mallet, Inc., 53
Matheson, Michael M., 102
Matteson, Craig E., 168
Maynard, Gary S., 64
Mayo, James H., 98
McCaffrey, Frank, 115
McCallum, John and Laura, 109
McCallum, John H., 105
McCarthy, Henry "Mac", 15
L.A. McCarthy, Boatshop, 37
McCarthy, Lucy, 37
McClave, Philbrick & Giblin, 11
McCurdy & Reed Canoes, 151
McCurdy, J. Kip, 151
McDougall, Stewart, 135
McEvoy, Michael, 90
McFadden, David, 1
McGreivey, John, 96
McGreivey's Canoe Shop, 96
McInnis, Alan J., 168
McLachlan, Reid, 162
McLaughlin, Damian, 65
McLearn, Bill, 57
McMullen, Stephen, 48
McQueen Boatworks Ltd., 145
Meanor, Allen B., 96
Mefferd, Boyd, 9

Mehls, Katherine, 92
Meinzinger, Carl, 131
Mendocino Bay Boats, 5
Meredith Marine, Inc., 107
Meredith, W.R. "Spike", 107
Merryman Boats, 74
Mertaugh Boat Works Inc., 74
Metz, Don, Sr., 9
Middle Path Boats, 112, 172
Mierke, Bruce, 104
Mierke's Yacht Service, 104
Mile Creek Boat Shop, 37
Millar-Potter Boat Restoration, 159
Mill Cove Small Boat Works, 38
Miller Canoes, 148
Miller, William V., 148
Mills, Scott, 79
Minehart, Jack, 22, 78
Charlie Mink Custom Boats & Canoes, 16
Misty Mountain Boat Shop, 38
Mittleman, Howard, 97
Mobile Marine, 113
Monfort Associates, 172
Monfort, Platt, 172
Monterey Marine Inc., 16
Montgomery Boat Yard, 65
Montgomery, David H., 65
Mooney, Jed, 77
Moore, Dave, 75
Moores, Ted, 154
Moose Island Marine, 38
Morley Cedar Canoes, 80
Morley, Greg, 80
Morrow, Ralph, 97
Morrow's Boat Shop, 97
Mosher, Wayne D., 151
Mower, C.D., 172
Mowery, A. Wayne, 113
Mullen, Chris, 88
Mullens, David, 126
Muller, Bo and Kathy, 83
Muller Boatworks, 83
Arthur F. Mulvey Construction, 6
Munger, William, 114
Munro, Gordon, 172
Murray, Mark R., 45
Murray, Robert E., 62
Mussey, David, 36
Myers, John, 5
Rob Myhre Design/Boat Restoration, 79
Naches Boats, 131
Najjar, Steve, 6
Narragansett Shipwrights Inc., 115
Needham, John and Peter, 92
Needler, David, 147
Charles Neville Associates, 172
New Dublin Watercraft, 151
New England Boat & Motor, Inc., 83
New Era Design, 75
Newick, Dick, 172

Nexus Marine Corporation, 131
Nielsen, K. Aage, 173
Nimphius Boats Inc., 139
Nimphius, F.M., 139
Noah's Boat Shop, 107
NOA Marine, Inc., 17
North Bay Canoe Company, 159
North Boats, 6
North End Shipyard Inc., 39
Northern Bay Boats, 39
North River Boatworks, 97
Northrup Boat Works, 173
Northrup, Bruce, 173
NW Historic Watercraft, 145
Northwest School of Wooden Boat
  Building, 132
Northwood Boatworks, 75
Northwoods Canoe Co., 39, 176
Norton Boat Works, 139
Norton, Joe, 139
Norwalk Islands Sharpies, 171
Nova Scotia Community College, 152
Nungester, William G., 71
Nutt, David, 39
Nyman, Don, 126

Oat Canoe Co., 40
Tracy O'Brien Marine Design, 173
O'Connell's Wooden Boats, 53
Ocran Boat Shop, Inc., 123
Okoboji Boats, 23
Old Delta Canoeworks, 159
Old Lyme Marina, 11
Old Squaw Canoe Co., 139
Old Time Boat Co. Inc., 17
Old Town Canoe Company, 40
Old Tyme Sail and Oar, 2
Old Wharf Dory Co., 65
Oliver Canoes, 97
Onion River Boatworks, 84, 165
Opus Custom Craft, 173
Oskar, Fred, 137
Owen, George, 173
Owen, Patrick, 75
Owl Brook Boatworks, 84

Padebco Custom Boats, 40
A.C. Paine and Associates, 173
Paine, Art, 173
Paine, Chuck, 173
C.W. Paine Yacht Design, Inc., 173
Paine, William, 125
Paris, Jay E., Jr., 168
Parker, Jay, 58
Parker Marine Enterprises, 18, 173
Parker, Reuel B., 18, 173
Parsons, Jay B., 20
Patch & Co. Boat Repair Inc., 121
Patch, Nick, 121
Patrick, Bruce W., 75

Patrick's Landing, 75
Patterson, Peter, 152
Patterson's Mobile Marine Services, 152
H.H. Payson Co., 173
Pease, Capt. Dan, 29
Pelasara, R.J., 54
Penny Boatworks, 132
Peregrine Woodworks, Inc., 54
Perrine Boat Works, 87
Robert H. Perry Yacht Designers, Inc., 173
Perry, Ted, 31
Perry, Whitney, 84
Persson, Jon and Rick, 11
Seth Persson Boat Builders, 11
Petenwell Boatworks, 140
Peters, Ed, 108
Peterson Canoe & Paddle, 40
Peterson, David W., 69
Peterson, Jeffrey, 40
Murray G. Peterson Associates, Inc., 173
Peterson, William M., 173
Pfannenschmidt, Ernie, 167
Tom Pfeffer Marine, 173
Philbrick, Ben, 11
Phoenix Woodwork, 159
Pickhardt, Carl, 97
Pieklo, Mike, 141
Pike, Dean, 38
Pilots Point Marina, 12
Pleune, Mark, 72
Point Hudson Boat Shop, 132
Poole, Arthur L., 49
Port Bay Boats, 98
Port Dover Boat Works, 160
Porter, Michael, 30
Port Townsend Shipwrights Co-op, 133
Possley, Roger G., 71
Post, Franklin G., 173
Poston, Clark, 54
Potter, Jim, 159
Tom Potter & Associates, 173
Potts, Rives, 12
Powell, Jack W., 29
Powichroski, Paul, 54
Prazak, John, 140
Preservation Shipyard, 66
Price, Donald, 99
Proctor Boat Co., 133
Proctor, E. Tyler, Jr., 41
Proctor, Peter W., 133
Pulsifer, R.S. (Dick), 41
Pygmy Boat Co., 133

Ragged Ass Boat Shop, 133
Rainshadow Marine Inc., 134
Rander, Steve, 134
Ransley, Thomas and Guy, 67
Raven Boats, 79
Rawl, Allen C., 55
Ray's River Dories, 111

Reagan, Tim, 136
Redd's Pond Boatworks, 66
Reeves, Charlie, 20
Reid, Joe, 53
Resmondo Boat Works, 1
Resmondo, L.W., 1
Reynolds Marine, 12
Reynolds, Robert, 177
Reynolds, Tucker, 12
Rhodes, Philip L., 174
Rice, Brad, 125
Richard, Harold R., 14
Richardson, James P., 174
Richards, Raymond H., 174
James H. Rich Boat Yard, 41
Rights O'Man Boat Works, 134
Rivendell Marine, 66
Rivers Edge Boats, 55
Riverside Boat Company, 41
River Valley Boatworks, Inc., 42
Robb, Arthur, 174
Roberts, David, 131
Bruce Roberts Ltd., 174
Robinhood Marine Center, 42
Rock City Restorations, 98
Rock Hall Boat Shop, 123
Rockport Apprenticeshop (see Artisans
    School)
Rockport Marine, Inc., 42
Rocky Mountain Canoe Works, 145
Rogers, John, 98
Rogers, Mark A., 141
Rolland, Seth, 88
Rollins, Paul E., 43
Ronning, Larry J., 79
Rosenberg, Bernard A., 174
Ross Bros., 66
Greg Rössel Boat Carpentry, 43
Ross, Mitchell, 81
Ross, Robert P., 66
Royall Boat Works, 43
Royall, Thomas B., 43
Ruch Canoes, 160
Ruch, Will, 160
Rudy, James, 160
Rudy's Watercraft, 160
Rumery's Boat Yard, 55
Rushton, J.H., 174
Russell Boatworks, 44
Russell, Kevin D., 44
Russell, Stan, 112
Russell, Tommy, 104
Russell Yachts, 104
Rutherford, Jeffrey, 6
Rutherford's Boat Shop, 6

Sailboat Shop Inc., 98
St. Clair, Jerry, 38
Hugh Saint Inc., 18
St. Lawrence Restoration, 99

Salton, Bob, Ron, and Greg, 155
Samples Shipyard, 44
Sanstad, Gordon, 126
Santos, Francis J., 61
Sausalito Boat Builders Co-op, 7
Sawdust Boatworks, 117
Sayre, Zenna and Bud, 108
Scarano Boat Building, 99
Scarano, Richard, 99
Scarbrough, David, 123
Schaffer & Associate, 174
Schaffer, Dennis, 174
Scheel, Henry A., 174
Scherb, Gary, 17
Schofield, Robert, 18
Schofield's Boatworks, 18
Schooner Creek Boat Works, 134
Schorse, William, 159
Schumacher, Carl, 174
Scott Boatyard Inc., 105
Scott, Christopher R., 116
C.R. Scott Marine Woodworking
    Co., Inc., 116
Scott, Michael, 105
Scully, John, 22
Seabury, Charles L., 174
Sea Hoss Skiffs, 45
Seal Cove Boatyard, Inc., 45
Sea Sled Corp., 174
Seattle Shipwrights, 135
The Second Century, 100
Service Maritime Independant, 164
Shady Rill Boatworks, 121
Shaw Boats Inc., 135
Shaw's Boat Yard, Inc., 67
Shelburne Shipyard, 122
Shell Boats, 122, 174
Shell, Fred, 122, 174
Shelton, Philip, 24
Shew & Burnham, 45
Shibley, Wayne C., 152
Ship Creek Boat Works, 105
Silva, Nelson L., 105
Silver Bay Guideboat and Canoe Co., 100
Simmons, Walter J., 31, 174
Skagit Bay Boatyard, 135
Skiff Craft, 108
Skinner, Ed, 156
Skoriak, John, 5
Skywoods, 75
Slaunwhite's Boat & Joinery Shop, 152
Slaunwhite, Stephen H., 152
Sligh, Richard, 72
Smaalders, Mark, 174
Smaalders Yacht Designs, 174
Small Island Builders, 135
Smith, Charles R., III, 56
Smith, F. Jay, 124
Douglas Smith-Ginter & Associates, 7
Smith, Howard M., Jr., 175

Smith, John,   116
Smith, Kim,   149
Smith, Mason,   89
Smith, Melbourne,   51
Snaith, Skip,   126
Snapp, Geremy,   130
Snead, Parker,   93
Snyder, Philip R.,   153
Snyder, R.J.,   10
Snyder's Shipyard Ltd.,   153
Solberg, Thomas,   106
Sorensen, Darrell,   7
Sorensen Woodcraft,   7
Sosnove, Nancy,   131
South Cove Boat Shop,   113
South Shore Boatworks,   67
Spalding, Eliot,   175
Sparkman & Stephens, Inc.,   175
Speck, Ray,   136
Spencer & Hurley Canoe Co.,   161
Spencer Boatworks Inc.,   100
Spencer, Jim,   161
Spencer, Philip K.,   82
Sponberg, Eric W.,   175
Sponberg Yacht Design Inc.,   175
Sprague, Scott,   165
Spring Harbor Kayak Co.,   140
Spring, John B.,   89
George H. Stadel, Jr. & Sons, Inc.,   175
Stambaugh, Karl,   177
Stan-Craft/The Boat Shop,   21
Stango, Victor,   32
Stanley, Ralph W.,   45
Stanton, Jim,   159
Star Boat Co.,   46
Steele, James,   30
Steele, Keith D.,   111
Steele's Boats,   111
Steiss, Bill,   161
Robert W. Stephens Wooden Boats,   175
Stephens, W.P.,   175
Sterling Marine,   88
Sterling, Newton S.,   88
Sternberg, Michael,   19, 177
Steven's Boatworks,   153
Stevens, Robert,   33
Steward, Robert M.,   175
Stewart, Derald,   8
Stewart River Boatworks,   80
C. Stickney, Boatbuilders, Ltd.,   46
Stickney, Chris,   46
Stimson, David,   46, 175
Stimson Marine, Inc.,   46, 175
Story Boatbuilding,   67
Story, Brad,   67
Strange, Albert,   175
Strayer, Charles M.,   175
Strayer Yacht Design,   175
Streblow Custom Boats Inc.,   140
Streblow, Randal,   140

Stulen, Chip,   120
Sucher, Harry V.,   175
Summerfield Boat Works, Inc.,   18
Superior Kayaks, Inc.,   141
Surosky, LeRoy,   54
Sutherland Boat & Coach, Inc.,   100
Sutherland, Daniel R.,   100
Swain, John E.,   55
Swan Design & Swan Boats,   112, 175
Swan, Ken,   112, 175
Swanson Carpentry & Boatworks,   47
Swanson, Mark,   47
Sweet, David,   47
Swinamer, Steven,   153

Taber, James M.,   69
Yves-Marie de Tanton,   175
Tanton, Inc.,   175
Tassell, Dale,   15
Tassier Boat Shop,   76
Tassier, Gary,   76
Taylor & Snediker Woodworking,   12
Taylor, Bill,   12
Taylor Boat Works,   105
Temagami Canoe Company,   161
Tender Craft Boat Shop Inc.,   161, 176
Tenmile Marina Inc.,   112
Terrace Wood Works,   23
Thayer, Jim,   8
Thomas Fabrication & Boatworks,   7
Thomas, Steven,   7
Thompson, Craig K.,   74
Thompson, Joseph,   15
Thomson Canoe Works,   13
Thomson, Schuyler,   13
Thornapple River Canoes,   76
Thurlow, Rollin,   39, 176
Tiffany Yachts Inc.,   123
Tocha, Carolyn,   93
Toeffer, Bo,   53
Tolman, Renn,   2
Tolman Skiffs,   2
Tomlinson, Geoff,   162
Toombs, Cecil,   155
Traditional Boat Caulking,   136
Trailcraft,   176
Trailhead,   162
Traveling Boatworks,   13
Trayner, Jay,   84
Trayner's Boatshop,   84
Tremblay, Lin,   147
Triad Boatworks Inc.,   68
Trinh, Tao,   110
Tri-Star Trimarans/Catamarans,   176
Tri-Werx,   68
Troyan, Jim,   112
Tucker, Tom,   136, 176
Tucker Yacht Design,   136, 176
Turcotte, Thomas R. and Lawrence A.,   94
Turner, Norman,   122

Tutass, Helmut,   2
Tuxworth, Greg,   68

Ungarean, Gary,   173
Upright Boat Works,   130
Up The Creek Boatworks,   56

Vaillancourt, Henri,   85
Valentijn, Johan,   176
Van Bibber, Vordaman H.,   19
van Cleef, David,   36
Van Dam, Stephen,   76
Van Dam Wood Craft,   76
Van Den Berg, Jim,   137
Van De Stadt Design—USA,   176
Van Mar Boat Co.,   19
Van, Martin A.,   138
van Oldenborgh, Boudi,   146
Van Syckel, Steven,   26
Vantol, Gary,   68
Van Wagner, Peter,   163
Vaughn, Robert,   45
Velatura Werk,   141
Verge, Ed,   105
Victory Boat Co.,   68
Viking Boatbuilders,   101
Vintage Boat Works, Inc.,   77
Vintage Boat Works,   80
Vintage Boatworks,   108
Virgin Forest Boatworks,   142
Vlahovich, A. Michael,   136
Vlahovich Boat Corp.,   136

Wahlman, Erik,   3
Wald, Phil and Sally,   110
Wallstrom, Bob,   176
Wambach, Kevin,   150
Warner, F. Todd,   78
Warner, Winthrop L.,   176
Michael Warr Woodwork,   47
Washburn, Richard,   39
Washington County Technical College,   48
Watson Marine Ltd.,   146
Watson, Peter,   91
Watson, Tom,   146
Watts, J. Murray,   176
Weeks, Brian,   101
Frank M. Weeks Yacht Yard,   101
Welling Boat Co.,   68
Welling, Mark,   68
Wells, John H.,   176
West Coast Canoe Company,   145
West Cove Boat Yard,   48
Westport Canoe,   162
Whalen, Tom,   85
Whitacre, Hal,   171
Chris White Designs,   176
White, Joel,   176
White, Joel (see also Brooklin Boat Yard)
Robb White & Sons,   20

Whiticar Boat Works Inc., 19
Whiticar, John C., 19
Wikander, Stuart A., 56
Wikander Yacht Yard, Inc., 56
Wilcox, Elliot J., 9
Wildfire Racing Team, 19, 177
Wild Meadow Canoes, 85
Williams, Barb, 161, 176
Williams, Bill, 102
Williams, Carl H., 10
Williams, Fenwick, 177
Williams, George M., 68
Williams, Milo B., 100
Williams Wood Boat Shop, 102
Willis Boat Yard, 48
Willoughby, Gary, 69
Wilmes, Daniel, 13
Winard Wood Ltd., 146
Winder, John, 63
Windward Designs, 177
Winslow, Ralph E., 177

Winterport Marine & Boatyard, 48
Wise Marine Co., 22
Wise, Paul, 22
Witt, Glen-L (see Glen-L Marine
    Designs), 169
Witte, A. Franz, III, 134
Wittholz, Charles W., 177
Wolstenholme, Tom, 66
Wood Boatworks, 162
Wood Canvas Canoes, 146
The Wooden Boat Company, 49
The WoodenBoat Store, 177
The Wooden Boatworks, 20
The Wooden Canoe Shop Inc., 109
Wooden Tangent, 69
Wood, Jackson, 145
Woods Hole Woodworks, 141
Woodstrip Watercraft Co., 113
Woodward, Christopher, 94
Woodwind Yachts, 163
Wren, Patrick J., 158

Thomas Wylie Design Group, 177

Yacht Designs, 177
Yacht Maintenance Co. Inc., 56
Yacht Standard, 22
York, Charles F., 58
Young, Sydney H., 21

Zachorne, George W., Jr., 116
Zatek, Kaz, 61
Zebcraft, 85
Zendigo Boat Works, 49
Ziemba, Joe, 155
Zimmerman Boat Works, 109
Zimmerman, D. Matthew, 109
Zimmerman Marine Inc., 124
Zimmerman, Steve, 124
Zimmer, Nelson, 177
Zurn, Doug, 177
Zurn Yacht Design, 177

More Good Reading from WoodenBoat Books

Herreshoff of Bristol
A Photographic History of America's Greatest Yacht and Boat Builders

by Maynard Bray and Carlton Pinheiro

An in-depth look at the inner workings of America's greatest yacht construction yard, from 1898 to 1946. Herreshoff's built the fastest sail and steam yachts of its time and was responsible for many of the innovations that define the modern yachts of today. With more than 250 previously unpublished photographs, reproduced in luxurious duotone, this volume provides a history of the firm and the remarkable men, Nathanael and John, who founded it. Includes an appreciation of the revolutionary building methods employed by the firm and shows in detail their system of framing and planking, the casting of lead keels, and the launching of magnificent yachts built to unparalleled standards.

256 pp., illus., hardcover

#325-085 Ship Wt. 3 lbs **$49.95**

How to Build the Haven 12½-Footer

by Maynard Bray

Developed by Joel White for a client who loved the Herreshoff 12½, but required a shallow draft, the Haven 12½ is a keel/centerboard variation of the original. This book will show you how to construct her using the same process used to build the original Herreshoff boats in Bristol, Rhode Island. She's built upside down, with a mold for every frame. No lofting is required. Each step in this unique process is carefully explained and illustrated, which, with detailed construction plans, provides a thorough guide for advanced amateurs.

64 pp., illus., softcover

#325-077 Ship Wt. ½ lb **$15.00**

How to Build a Wooden Boat

by David C. "Bud" McIntosh
Illustrated by Samuel F. Manning

Everything you need to know to construct a cruising boat with no more than a set of plans, a pile of lumber, and determination. Written and illustrated by experienced boat-builders, *How to Build a Wooden Boat* covers the entire process, from lofting to finishing out. Setting up molds, lining off, ribbands, steaming and fitting frames, planking, pouring the keel, bulkheads and floorboards, decks, rudders, spars, the works. Written with style, humor, and, above all else, clarity.

264 pp., over 200 illus., hardcover

#325-075 Ship Wt. 2½ lbs **$36.00**

The Expectant Father's Cradle Boat Book

by Peter Spectre and Buckley Smith

A wonderful and engaging book for anyone who wants to create something special for a new baby. *The Expectant Father's Cradle Boat Book* is your guide to the design and construction of traditional cradle boats for infant children. Inspired by a series of cradle boats that have been featured in numerous issues of *WoodenBoat*, this book contains instructions and patterns for two different types of cradle boats, a gallery of photographs of a variety of completed cradles, and an appendix of sources of supply. If you can handle basic woodworking tools and follow directions, you'll find building a cradle boat both simple and satisfying.

96 pp., illus., softcover

325-095 Ship Wt. ½ lb **$14.95**

Keeping the Cutting Edge

by Harold H. Payson

A valuable manual for all woodworkers. Written by a professional boatbuilder who abhors dull saws, this book tells you how to sharpen and maintain all types—handsaws, bow and buck saws, powersaw blades, dado sets, bandsaws, chainsaws, and more. It is packed with tips, including descriptions of a variety of jigs and special tools, and never leaves you in doubt about what to do in even the most difficult sharpening situation. This heavily illustrated shop manual contains everything you need to know to keep your cutting edges sharp.

32 pp., illus., softcover

#325-015 Ship Wt. ½ lb **$7.95**

The Shipcarver's Handbook

by Jay S. Hanna

A carver for over 40 years, Jay Hanna takes you through the steps of traditional marine carving in this revised and expanded version of his *Marine Carving Handbook*. Learn how to carve sternboards, billetheads, trailboards, eagles, dolphins, rope borders, and more. Learn design and lettering, set-up and carving techniques, woods, tools and sharpening, finishing, and gold leafing. A well-illustrated, beautifully designed book that will guide and inspire both the amateur and professional.

108 pp., illus., hardcover

#325-080 Ship Wt. 1 lb **$17.95**

Plans & Kits Available from WoodenBoat

The Shellback Dinghy Plans

Drawn by Joel White, the six sheets of plans include: lines and offsets, building jig details, plank layout, sailing rig details, full-sized patterns for molds, frame, stem, stern, knees, and breast-hook. No lofting required.

#400-109 Ship Wt. 1½ lbs **$75.00**

The Shellback Dinghy Kit

The kit includes all parts pre-cut, made of the highest-quality materials, plus fastenings, hardware, plans, and instructions. Choose from the sailing or rowing version. You supply the paint and epoxy. Shipped freight-collect from Maine; please allow 2–4 weeks for delivery. (Sails sold separately.)

Sailing Kit #603-001 **$1,495**

Rowing Kit #603-002 **$1,295**

The Shellback Dinghy Model Kit

Make this model as a dry run for building the full-sized boat. This is no "snap piece A to piece B" kit—instead you will learn the actual building process, but in a table-sized scale. This is our first kit at a 3" to 1' scale, making the pieces very easy to handle. The result is a thorough understanding of glued-lapstrake plywood construction, plus a finished model measuring just over 33" long, that you can actually sail. Available Late '94.

The Nutshell Pram Scale Model Kit

Scaled from the 7' 7" Nutshell Pram, also with the purpose of helping to teach you how to build the full-sized Nutshell—from our plans or kit. We provide the wood, sail, plans, and instructions. You provide the glue, paint, and effort.

#620-001 Ship Wt. 1½ lbs **$39.95**

Nutshell Pram Kits

Full-sized boat kits available in 7' 7" or 9' 6" versions. As with the Shellback, the kit includes pre-cut wood, fastenings, hardware, plans, and instructions. Shipped freight- collect from Maine. Please allow 2–4 weeks for delivery. (Sails sold separately.)

9' 6" Sailing Kit #605-002 **$1,150**

9' 6" Rowing Kit #605-001 **$950**

7' 7" Sailing Kit #600-002 **$850**

7' 7" Rowing Kit #600-001 **$700**

How to Order

PHONE ORDERS
TOLL-FREE U.S. & Canada:
1–800–273–SHIP (7447)
Overseas: 207-359-4647
Mon.–Fri. 8am– 6pm EST
24-Hour FAX: 207-359-8920

Please fill out the order form before you call. It is your record of the order. Use the info below to figure shipping costs. We will ask for your catalog code, which is located after your phone # on the right side of your order form.

VISA, MASTERCARD & DISCOVER ARE WELCOME

OR WRITE:
The WoodenBoat Store
P.O. Box 78
Brooklin, Maine 04616-0078

Payment must be made in U.S. dollars payable on a U.S. bank.

CUSTOMER SERVICE
If you have any questions about a product or an order, please call customer service toll-free, 1–800–273–SHIP (7447).

RETURN POLICY
We want you to be pleased with every item you receive. If you are not, just return it for a courteous replacement, refund or credit.

OUR GUARANTEE
Our products are guaranteed to be 100% satisfactory. Return anything that proves otherwise. We will replace it or refund your money.

SHIPPING
Please select the appropriate area shipping charge according to destination & delivery method & include that charge in the corresponding box on your order form. We ship most orders in 2 working days. **For our Canadian customers;** we will make an extra effort to see that your order is shipped in <u>one</u> package.

U.S. Shipping Charges				
	Zip Code up to 49999	50000+	Two Day Delivery	Next Day Delivery
Minimum	$1.75	$1.75	$5.50	$12.00
1/2 to 1 lb.	3.00	3.00	6.00	13.00
up to 2 lbs.	3.00	3.00	8.00	14.50
up to 5 lbs.	3.50	5.00	9.50	18.50
up to 10 lbs	4.50	7.00	14.50	26.00
up to 15 lbs	5.50	9.00	19.50	31.00
ADD for each additional 5lbs.	$1.00	$2.00	$5.00	$5.00

Alaska & Hawaii Priority Add $5.00 to Two Day and Next Day Charges

Canadian Charges	Overseas–Surface	Overseas–Priority/Air
Up to 1/2 lb.$3.00	Up to 1/2 lb.$4.00	Up to 1/2 lb.$7.00
Up to 2 lbs. 5.00	Up to 2 lbs. 7.00	Up to 1 lbs. 13.00
Up to 3 lbs. 6.50	Up to 3 lbs. 9.00	Up to 2 lbs. 22.00
Up to 4 lbs. 8.00	Up to 4 lbs. 11.00	Up to 3 lbs. 28.00
		Up to 4 lbs. 34.00
ADD $1.50 for each additional lb. Priority: ADD $2.00 to Total	ADD $2.00 for each additional lb. (Allow 2-4 months for delivery)	ADD $6.00 for each additional lb.

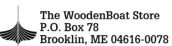

The WoodenBoat Store
P.O. Box 78
Brooklin, ME 04616-0078

The WoodenBoat Store

Toll-Free U.S. & Canada: 1–800–273–SHIP (7447)
Overseas: 207–359–4647
Hours: 8am–6pm EST, Mon. thru Fri.
24-Hour FAX: 207–359–8920
(Please Fax completed order form including VISA, MasterCard, or Discover card information)
Or write us: The WoodenBoat Store, P.O. Box 78, Brooklin, Maine 04616-0078

NAME _____

ADDRESS _____

CITY/STATE/ZIP _____

SHIP TO (if different than above)_____

ADDRESS _____

CITY/STATE/ZIP _____

YOUR DAY TEL# _____   Catalog Code **WBP**

Pre-payment is required. Payment MUST be in U.S. funds payable on a U.S. bank, VISA   MasterCard   Discover   Check, or Money Orders.

CARD NUMBER												EXPIRES Month/Year
SIGNATURE OF CARDHOLDER												

QTY	PRODUCT #	SIZE	COLOR	ITEM	SHIP WT.	PRICE EACH	TOTAL

TOTAL LBS.	
SUB TOTAL	
Maine Residents Add Tax	
Regular Shipping	
Priority Shipping (from Chart at Left)	
TOTAL	

WoodenBoat's Guarantee. . .
Satisfaction or Your Money Back!

Free Catalogs from WoodenBoat

Send us your name or the name of anyone who might enjoy either or both of our FREE catalogs. Please check box(es).

☐ **Merchandise Catalog.** Tools for Learning—books, boatbuilding plans, model kits, clothing, hard-to-find tools, and more.

☐ **School Brochure.** General information on sailing and boatbuilding courses offered throughout the year.

NAME _____

ADDRESS _____

CITY/STATE/ZIP _____

NAME _____

ADDRESS _____

CITY/STATE/ZIP _____